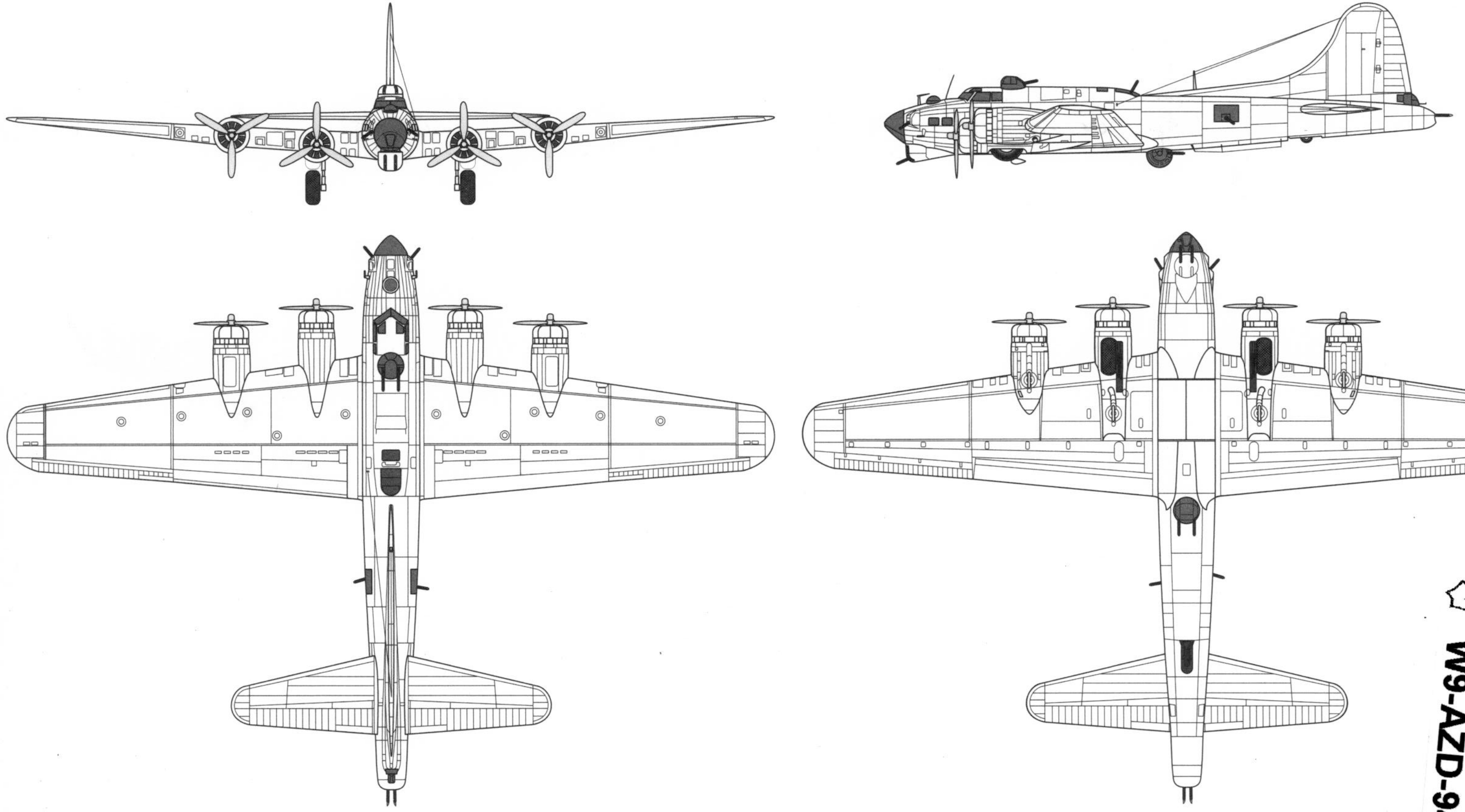

B-17G

Mission to Berlin

Mission to Berlin

The American Airmen Who Struck the Heart of Hitler's Reich

Robert F. Dorr

Zenith Press

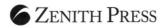

First published in 2011 by Zenith Press, an imprint of MBI Publishing Company, 400 First Avenue North, Suite 300, Minneapolis, MN 55401 USA

Zenith Press titles are also available at discounts in bulk quantity for industrial or sales-promotional use. For details write to Special Sales Manager at MBI Publishing Company, 400 First Avenue North, Suite 300, Minneapolis, MN 55401 USA.

To find out more about our books, join us online at www.zenithpress.com.

Library of Congress Cataloging-in-Publication Data

Dorr, Robert F.
Mission to Berlin : the American airmen who struck the heart of Hitler's Reich / Robert F. Dorr.
p. cm.
Includes bibliographical references and index.
ISBN 978-0-7603-3898-8 (hb w/ jkt)
1. Berlin (Germany)—History—Bombardment, 1943-1944. 2. World War, 1939-1945—Aerial operations, American. 3. Airmen—United States—Biography. I. Title.
D757.9.B4D67 2011
940.54'213155—dc22
2010045976

Credits

On page 10: Original by permission of Edward Sion; recreated by Barbara Drewlo

On page 161: Original by USAAF, recreated by Barbara Drewlo

All photographs are from the author's collection unless noted otherwise.

On the cover: Main: Boeing B-17G Flying Fortress crew after a mission. *Norman Taylor*

Background: B-17F formation over Schweinfurt, Germany. *USAF photo*

On the endpapers: B-17F and B-17G schematics by Onno Van Braam

On the back cover: Very young at age twenty-three, and very well liked among Flying Fortress crewmembers, Lt. Col. Marvin D. Lord was on his second combat tour as operations officer of the 91st Bombardment Group. He lost his life flying lead over Berlin on February 3, 1945. *Stan Piet*

Printed in the United States of America

Fifteen thousand Americans took part in the
air assault on Hitler's Third Reich on February 3, 1945.
This book is dedicated to four of them:

Frank T. Chrastka, tail gunner of the B-17 *Blue Grass Girl*
Robert Des Lauriers, copilot of the B-17 *Purty Chili*
Ray Fredette, toggleer-gunner on the B-17 *Fancy Nancy*
Marvin D. Lord, mission leader on an unnamed B-17

Of the four, two survived.

—Robert F. Dorr
Oakton, Virginia

Contents

CHAPTER ONE

Wake-Up

Mission to Berlin
February 3, 1945—3:00 a.m. to 6:00 a.m.

IT WAS ALWAYS COLD.

It was always cold at high altitude and Staff Sgt. Frank T. Chrastka compensated, even when on the ground.

He slept in flannel underwear. He was sleeping in flannel underwear, in his bunk, when the floorboards of his barracks creaked. A silhouette loomed above him. The flashlight burned. A bright sickly yellow illuminated his face.

"Up."

It was just one word. It was said just once. Even the voice sounded cold.

It was 3:00 a.m. British Summer Time—the standard used in Britain in winter by American bomber crews. The date was Saturday, February 3, 1945.

The first question that came to Chrastka's mind upon awakening was usually, "What's the target today?" The CQ, the charge of quarters—checking bunks, aiming the flashlight, shaking awake semisomnolent bomber crewmembers—didn't know the target, didn't have a clue. The CQ worked in the squadron orderly room and might well be the last person in the squadron to learn where the bombers were going today. The target to be attacked was usually decided only the day before, because planning a long-range bombing mission depended on the weather forecast.

Without a word, the CQ handed over his clipboard with a pencil attached on a string. In the flashlight's glare, Frank Chrastka ran a fingertip down a list of names until he found his own and scratched out his signature next to it. If any question arose later, this was the evidence that he had been awakened. "Okay," the CQ said, and moved on.

Chrastka, nineteen, blond, a bit larger than his buddies at 180 pounds—a lady's man, they said—was fully awake and very cold. His size was a disadvantage, his buddies said, because he was a tail gunner, which meant that he spent much of his time in the air in a bent, kneeling position, facing to the rear of the aircraft as if in prayer, his knees supporting his weight. Chrastka, of Polish origin, from Forest Park, Illinois, looked exactly like the lifeguard he'd been in civilian life and his buddies knew that he'd recently saved a member of his own bomber crew from drowning during a mishap at a lake. Chrastka was something of a prankster, too, his buddies said. If he ever played a serious prank on anyone he didn't speak of it, but later on this day others would wonder about that trait.

At American bomber bases clustered around the easterly rim of the British aisles known as East Anglia, American bomber crews had spent the last two days being briefed for the same target only to have the mission cancelled before takeoff. Chrastka was one of those. So he had a nearly certain idea of what today's target might be, but could not be completely sure. Almost none of the men knew for certain that on this day, the Eighth Air Force planned to dispatch 1,437 heavy bombers and 948 fighters with the principal purpose of attacking the capital of the Third Reich.

Chrastka belonged to the 832nd Bombardment Squadron, 486th Bombardment Group, at Sudbury, England, a location that was—what else?—cold and wet. Out on the hardstand in the darkness, a mile from the plywood hut clad with tarred paper where Chrastka slept with twenty-six other men, the members of the ordnance company had a clear idea what the target might be. Throughout the night, they were loading a specific type, size, and number of bombs into the fuselage bay of each B-17 Flying Fortress. The bombload differed from one bomber base to another. Still, the bombload was all but a giveaway of what the target would be.

It never bothered Chrastka, but other members of his B-17 crew often said they felt their stomachs churning as they wondered whether a particular day would bring a milk run or a maximum effort. One radioman-gunner would put his head between his knees, apparently struggling not to vomit while uttering, "Don't let it be the Big B, please." Every crewmember feared learning that the target was Berlin.

Chrastka and his fellow airmen were near the end of the third winter of the American bombing offensive. Few had been here a year ago, so this was a new experience—the bone-chilling weather that brought colds and flu; frostbitten body parts at high altitude; electrically heated flying suits that had been redesigned several times and still malfunctioned; snow, sleet, freezing rain, pea soup fog, and howling winds; ice-coated roads, runways, wings, and windshields. By these standards, based on last night's weather forecast, this particular morning held the promise of being less remarkable than most.

In the semidarkness of his Quonset hut, Chrastka's first task was to reach for the fresh set of long flannel underwear he'd laid out the night before. It went over his standard undershorts and shirt.

Chrastka shaved in dim light and lukewarm water. He'd remembered to fill his helmet and leave it on the barracks "space heater"—a kind of potbelly stove—before going to sleep. When he was finished, in the slow and methodical way that was part of his nature, Chrastka pretended he'd done nothing, started from the beginning, and shaved again. Without a super-clean shave, an oxygen mask could chafe and scratch, causing annoyance or real injury, while facial hairs could be an irritant at high altitude, where temperatures varied from minus ten to minus seventy degrees Fahrenheit.

COPING WITH FEAR

Even after every precaution, Chrastka knew that on this day—February 3, 1945—there were no guarantees against the rigors of flight at low temperatures and high altitudes. Today, he would wear an oxygen mask for hours. The moisture in his breath, perspiration, and blood from facial wounds and nosebleeds could cause the mask to freeze to the skin, and occasionally the ice buildup could cause the mask to malfunction. As he worked through his ablutions, Chrastka told himself he had no guarantees about anything on this day.

Hot water was an intermittent luxury, rarely available at wake-up, but Chrastka had been able to take a hot shower before going to bed. Now, he dressed using the attire laid out the night before: his standard khaki trousers and long-sleeved shirt, his black socks, and his low-quarter brown GI shoes. Said an airman who flew with Chrastka: "If you bailed out in enemy territory, those shoes immediately identified you as an American. We were given a pair of European-type shoes that stayed with our flying suit, helmet, and goggles and were tied to our parachute harness, all located in the personnel equipment building."

While still in the barracks, still groggy, still coming awake in the cold, Frank Chrastka's last step was to put on the crewmember's standard B10 jacket. He kept the jacket near his bed to wriggle into—always cold.

Ahead lay chapel, breakfast, briefing, and donning equipment, followed by the ride in a four-by-four weapons carrier, the square truck-of-all-trades, to the B-17. After wake-up, about two hours were to elapse before Chrastka and his fellow bomber crewmembers learned their target. Today, many thought they knew it already because of preparations during the two previous days. Still, for many, the target would be the only thing on their minds.

Today would be the end of Chrastka's war, if not in the way he expected. Like all of the airmen thrown together in the crew of a bomber called *Blue Grass Girl*, Chrastka was about to fly his thirty-fifth combat mission. That was the magic number. It meant your tour was over. It meant a ticket home.

Chrastka was not the first American bomber crewmember to be awake on this cold Saturday morning. Colonel Lewis E. Lyle of the 379th Bombardment Group at Kimbolton in East Anglia was the leader of what would become a 2,400-plane Eighth Air Force mission, and Lyle had little patience for those who argued that bomber crewmembers needed sleep.

"For this mission, we received Field Order 620 via tickertape at about midnight," Lyle said in an interview for this book. "The order included a call for a certain number of people. I found the lead crews for the squadrons of our group—pilots, bombardiers, and navigators who had trained for this mission. Each lead crewmember had an area of responsibility, and we had some who had studied nothing but today's target.

"My rule was, as soon as we knew about the mission, we dragged the lead crews out of their bunks. At other bombardment groups in East

Anglia, they didn't do that. They said the lead crews needed their sleep. In my view, that was untrue. These young men didn't need sleep. They needed several hours to study every aspect of the mission and the target." After the lead crews did their homework, Lyle pulled them together in a small dining area over breakfast. Similar preparations were taking place all over East Anglia, but only Lyle was in charge of the entire mission.

At one bomber base, otherwise called a combat station, the early-morning situation was different from all the others. There was no wake-up for many members of the 91st Bombardment Group at Bassingbourn. Many had never gotten to sleep. According to Theodore M. "Mike" Banta, who was then a first lieutenant and a B-17 Flying Fortress pilot, the men had been told there would be no mission today and were holding a party that lasted into the morning. It is unclear how this miscommunication occurred. Some crewmembers got sleep. Some didn't. Some, like Maj. Immanuel L. "Manny" Klette, who was at this juncture the most experienced combat pilot in the Eighth Air Force, had been given a pass to travel to London and would not be able to return to Bassingbourn in time to fly.

While bomber crews elsewhere in East Anglia were being shaken out of slumber, many of the 91st crews were already wide awake, fully dressed, and—with one exception—grumpy. For the past two consecutive days, they had diligently prepared for a mission that had been canceled at the last minute. Today, they'd been told there would be no mission. And then they'd been told there would be.

The exception was Lt. Col. Marvin D. Lord, operations officer of the 91st group, another very experienced pilot now on his second tour of duty flying combat in B-17s. "He was a red-faced, chubby-cheeked twenty-three-year-old lieutenant colonel," said one pilot. "I never saw a more cheerful man when we were preparing for a mission. We were to lead the group and I believe the wing that day. Manny Klette, who flew just about every time we went up and never missed a lead mission, was delayed in London that morning, so Lord pulled rank and asked to take Klette's place flying with Klette's crew. I was amazed by Lord's happy disposition. I need hardly say it was not shared by too many of us in the squadron."

BECOMING AIR COMMANDER

According to a different account of how Lord was chosen to lead his group, Klette, who customarily handled group lead, had been told there would be no mission today and had traveled to London. Lord caught Klette on the telephone and pleaded with Klette to relinquish group lead. Unable to get back to Bassingbourn in time, Klette—"begrudgingly," according to this account—agreed that Lord should take the lead. There are other versions of the story as well, some of which were recounted by eyewitnesses after the war, but the likeliest explanation is simply that Klette wasn't available and Lord, who was of higher rank with comparable experience, stepped in. It is unlikely that Lord's assignment to be one of the battle commanders was made as a result of a telephone conversation with the lower-ranking Klette.

Because he is a key figure in this narrative, it is important to "see" Marvin Lord. Born March 21, 1921, and now just five weeks shy of a twenty-fourth birthday, he was bright, gifted, and musical: He graduated from high school in Bay View, Wisconsin, at age sixteen, enlisted in the Wisconsin National Guard, and was a cavalry soldier before he joined the Army Air Corps in 1938 and entered pilot training. Lord's sister Phyllis Carpenter said he was a great dancer and a cheerful soul. As he prepared to lead his group on this cold English morning, we know little about whom Lord spoke to, or what he said. We know only that Lord, so youthful, so boyish, was happy to be handed the job of leading men in battle.

When a military photo publicity team had visited Bassingbourn to take rare color photographs of a handful of bomber crewmembers, Lord was dragooned into posing in full flight gear in a portrait that would appear, one day in the far future, in *National Geographic* magazine. "He didn't want to take the picture," said a crewmember who knew Lord. "It wasn't him." The image of quiet, stern nobility, captured on Kodachrome, belied Lord's loud, loose, jovial manner.

While other bomber crewmembers were just beginning to find their way out of sleep, Lord was talking up the mission. He slapped one bomber crewmember on the shoulder and uttered words of encouragement. His personality was a bright light among men who were accustomed to being wet, cold, and—especially today—downtrodden.

At other bomber bases across East Anglia, more Eighth Air Force bomber crewmembers were being awakened. In some squadrons, the

CQ flipped on the ceiling lights and blew a whistle. In some, the men traveled from barracks to breakfast by bicycle. At a few of the B-17 and B-24 Liberator bases, just about everyone owned a bicycle.

During breakfast, Staff Sgt. Frank T. Chrastka and his buddies attempted to pick up gossip about the fuel and bomb loads in order to divine their destination. "I hope they don't have a really good breakfast set up with fresh eggs and lots of bacon," thought Tech. Sgt. Daniel "Clint" Pentz, who was Chrastka's best friend, had flown ten missions with him, but would be aboard a different plane today. Except for the mess hall of an American heavy bombardment group, there was no place in England where you could find fresh eggs. When they heaped fresh eggs on the men's metal trays, that was a strong clue that today's target would be very tough.

Eating, making eye contact with the others but saying little, Chrastka wondered if he could find someone who knew today's fuel load. Maximum fuel capacity for a B-17 was 2,780 U.S. gallons—the aviation world had not yet begun the practice of measuring fuel in pounds—barely enough gas for the farthest-reaching missions to the most distant targets, like the Big B. Powdered eggs and 2,000 gallons meant an easy trip with less exposure to German defenses. Real eggs, cooked to request, over easy in Chrastka's case, plus 2,780 gallons were harbingers of a maximum effort with prolonged exposure to the Reich's flak and fighters.

THINKING AHEAD

At some airfields in East Anglia, crewmembers detected another clue about what lay ahead for them. All night, they heard trucks hauling bombs out to the flight line. It was a distinctive rumble, one that couldn't be confused with anything else. When it reached a certain decibel level, it meant the morning's mission would be a deep penetration.

It probably meant Berlin.

It was 4:00 a.m., British Summer Time. They were still waking up bomber crewmembers all over East Anglia. At Mendlesham, Suffolk, home to the 391st Bombardment Squadron, 34th Bombardment Group, someone was waking up 1st Lt. Robert Des Lauriers, a B-17G Flying Fortress copilot. The CQ had a flashlight and a clipboard but sought no signature. Enlisted men like Chrastka often lived in Quonset huts, slept in double bunks, rendered a signature to confirm they'd been awakened, and walked to chapel and chow. Officers like Des Lauriers lived in larger, peaked Nissen huts, slept in single beds, nodded when they woke up, and pedaled their bicycles to chapel and food.

Des Lauriers was always surprised at himself for being calm in those initial moments of the day of a big mission. "What we all confronted was the cold, the fog, the mist. We especially felt the cold. Asleep, awake, on the ground, in the air, we were always cold.

"They divided us up among Protestants, Catholics, and Jewish crewmembers," said Des Lauriers. "In my bomber, the four officers who sat up front were all Catholics, and we often went together to receive encouragement from a chaplain who was a priest. In the wet English darkness before a mission, I think just about everybody went to chapel whether he was devout or not." Des Lauriers *was* devout. He was also artistically inclined, a trumpet player in the bomb group's band with a nascent interest in architecture.

Another B-17 crewmember, Staff Sgt. Joseph D. Pace, said that some men prayed B-24 Liberators accompany them on today's mission. "German fighters would go after the B-24s first because they were an easier target, being larger and flying in a looser formation," Pace wrote in a memoir. He belonged to the 96th Bombardment Group at Snetterton-Heath, England, and he was wrong on several counts. First, the B-24s would be going to a different destination today. And after the war, German pilots denied singling out B-24s for attention. In fact, they had no reason to: A B-24 was faster than a B-17. The notion of the Luftwaffe preferring to pick on the Liberator was a myth. These prayers, if they were prayers, were for naught.

At Bassingbourn, home of the 91st Bombardment Group, some Fortress crewmembers were surprised to see the ebullient Lt. Col. Marvin D. Lord, today's mission lead for the group, attending a Roman Catholic service and taking communion. "I'm pretty sure he's not a Catholic," said one. "I think he goes to all of them, to show that he cares about us," said another. Lord was too cheerful not to be well liked. Few bomber crewmembers knew or cared whether he actually had a deep-rooted faith. In fact, Lord's letters home to his family reveal a man with deep religious faith but equally willing to attend Catholic or Protestant services.

All over East Anglia, men of faith and men with none began to emerge from chapel and start thinking about chow. *It was 4:30 a.m., British Summer Time.*

Emerging into the outdoors again, the men were, again, cold. "It was always miserably cold," Des Lauriers said. Today his crew would operate a Flying Fortress named *Purty Chili*. Some thought the bomber was named for Chili Williams, the iconic "Polka Dot Girl" of pinups, but Des Lauriers said the bomber got its name because he and his crewmates were always chilly.

At some of the stations, crewmembers rising in the morning chill could see the flight line and the Flying Fortresses being readied. Some, undoubtedly, thought of what lay ahead. They thought about the ugly black bursts of smoke that accompanied a blast of flak—*Flieger Abwehr Kanonen*—when the German antiaircraft shells, including those from the infamous 88 cannon, got too close. Although German fighters were no longer as formidable a threat as they once had been, the men pictured a Fortress, surrounded by Messerschmitts and Focke-Wulfs, taking hits, burning, stumbling drunkenly through the air: It's an enduring image that was repeated frequently in a war fought at high altitude over Europe, fought ultimately over Berlin itself, at speeds, heights, and temperatures where no one had ever fought before, in battles like nothing that happened ever before or would happen ever again.

Chrastka, Des Lauriers, Pace, Lord, and their fellow Americans in heavy bomber crews, with help from American fighters, routinely waged war at altitudes three times higher than men had ever been in combat before, in a place where it was always cold, where the temperature could stay far below freezing for hours, and where the air outside the metal skin of their unpressurized aircraft was too thin for humans to breathe. Lose your oxygen and you could die. Lose the electrical connection to your light-blue ("blue bunny") F-2 four-piece heated flying suit and you could die. Simply do your job while everyone in the Third Reich seemed to be throwing metal at you and you could die. How cold was it up there? One crewman had to tear his penis loose after it stuck fast to the frost-covered relief tube.

How cold was it, really? After a request by Eighth Air Force commander Maj. Gen. (later, Gen.) Carl A. "Tooey" Spaatz and endorsement from Army Air Forces (AAF) chief Gen. Henry H. "Hap" Arnold, the War

NORTH SEA

The Wash

Ludham
Great Yarmouth
Norwich
Lowestoft

EAST
ANGLIA

Cambridge

"Pinetree"
High Wycombe

London
Bushy
Park

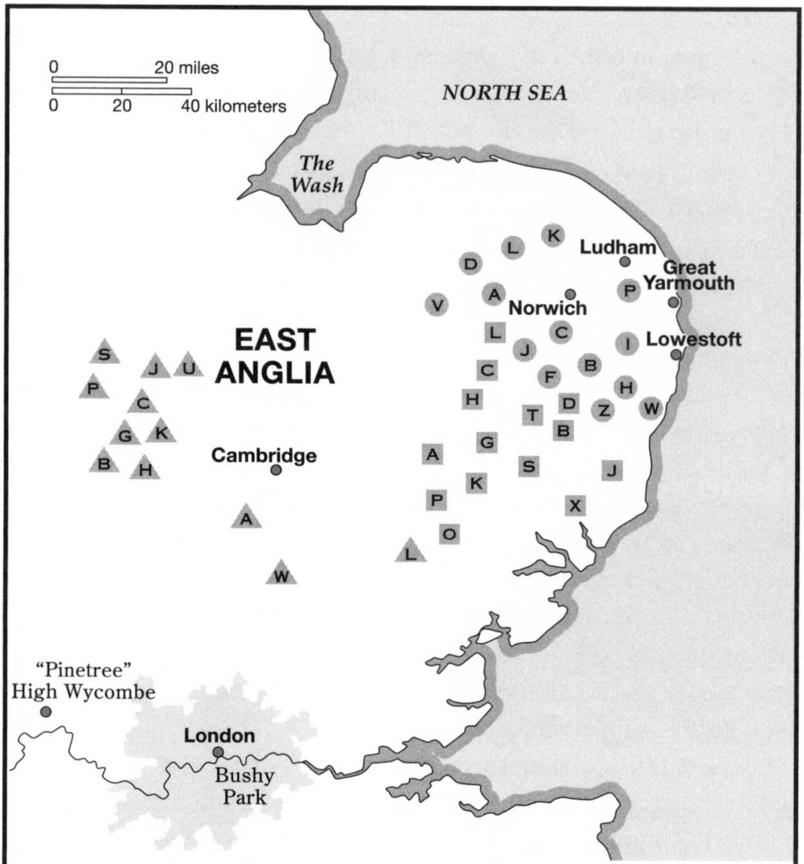

1ST AIR DIVISION		B 17s
LETTER IN → △		

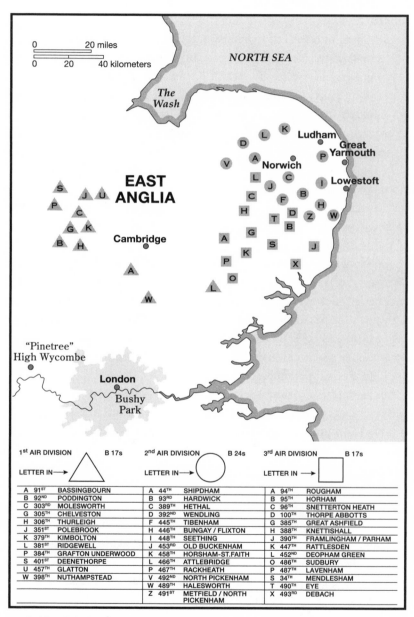

2ND AIR DIVISION		B 24s
LETTER IN → ◯		

3RD AIR DIVISION		B 17s
LETTER IN → ☐		

A	91ST	BASSINGBOURN
B	92ND	PODDINGTON
C	303RD	MOLESWORTH
G	305TH	CHELVESTON
H	306TH	THURLEIGH
J	351ST	POLEBROOK
K	379TH	KIMBOLTON
L	381ST	RIDGEWELL
P	384TH	GRAFTON UNDERWOOD
S	401ST	DEENETHORPE
U	457TH	GLATTON
W	398TH	NUTHAMPSTEAD

A	44TH	SHIPDHAM
B	93RD	HARDWICK
C	389TH	HETHAL
D	392ND	WENDLING
F	445TH	TIBENHAM
H	446TH	BUNGAY / FLIXTON
I	448TH	SEETHING
J	453RD	OLD BUCKENHAM
K	458TH	HORSHAM-ST.FAITH
L	466TH	ATTLEBRIDGE
P	467TH	RACKHEATH
V	492ND	NORTH PICKENHAM
W	489TH	HALESWORTH
Z	491ST	METFIELD / NORTH PICKENHAM

A	94TH	ROUGHAM
B	95TH	HORHAM
C	96TH	SNETTERTON HEATH
D	100TH	THORPE ABBOTTS
G	385TH	GREAT ASHFIELD
H	388TH	KNETTISHALL
J	390TH	FRAMLINGHAM / PARHAM
K	447TH	RATTLESDEN
L	452ND	DEOPHAM GREEN
O	486TH	SUDBURY
P	487TH	LAVENHAM
S	34TH	MENDLESHAM
T	490TH	EYE
X	493RD	DEBACH

Airfields of the Eighth Air Force.

Department changed its regulations in September 1943 to define those wounds eligible for the award of the Purple Heart to include any "injury to any part of the body from an outside force, element, or agent sustained as the result of a hostile act of the enemy or while in action in the face of the enemy." It was the only time in history that the Purple Heart was awarded for frostbite.

Curtis E. LeMay, a great bomber general who was still a colonel when he pioneered B-17 missions over the Third Reich, bristled with anger when his bomber missions were characterized as "raids." The word was inadequate, LeMay insisted. They were "full-scale battles, fought in the thin air, miles above the land."

Chrastka, Des Lauriers, Pace, Lord, and their fellow airmen flew warplanes that looked robust, performed well, and sometimes were tough enough to save a crew that got into trouble, but the four-engined heavies could also be fragile and vulnerable, and if the wrong combination of events converged, a B-17 could become a flying coffin.

EVOLVING WAR

The air war in Europe began on a modest scale and escalated until tens of thousands of bombers and hundreds of thousands of men hurtled into battles high in the sky by the Eighth Air Force in England and the Fifteenth Air Force in Italy. The airmen battled frostbite, oxygen deprivation, mechanical glitches, and German flak and fighters all at once while ensconced inside a narrow steel tube, tripping over each other's oxygen lines, intercom wires, and ammunition belts. Replacing the bulky metal ammunition boxes in early B-17s wasn't easy; the ever-present, clunky, jam-prone belts of copper-jacketed cartridges were twenty-seven feet long and may have inspired the term "the whole nine yards."

They were flying very large aircraft in very large numbers that would never again be matched: Today's mission—again, it was the largest ever against a single target and the second largest in the history of warfare—would see 1,437 bombers taxiing out of their parking places at thirty-five combat stations concentrated in Norfolk, Suffolk, and Cambridgeshire. Almost every Fortress carried nine men—by this juncture in the war, eliminating one of two waist gunners had reduced the size of most crews from ten. When a Fortress came under attack, it could burn and break up suddenly, which might be merciful, or it could be riddled by flying metal that severed hydraulic lines, shattered oxygen tasks, disabled engines, and ripped through human flesh. Hit by enemy fire, a Fortress could go down in an instant. Or it could veer out of control, its floorboards sloshing with blood, crewmembers fighting frantically to administer aid and to keep their ship in the air.

Decades later, when there was no going back to change any part of what happened, a U.S. national survey showed that the B-17 Flying Fortress was the most-recognized aircraft in aviation, more readily identified by the citizen on the street than the Wright Flyer, the Douglas DC-3, the Supermarine Spitfire, or the Boeing 747. This narrative about the American daylight bombing offensive over Germany, with its emphasis on the aerial siege of Berlin, tells of other aircraft like the B-24 Liberator, P-38 Lightning, P-47 Thunderbolt, and P-51 Mustang, but no other aircraft touched hearts and minds the way the Fortress did. If the Fortress appears to dominate these pages, remember that it was the most numerous aircraft in the Eighth Air Force.

The B-24 was manufactured in greater numbers and was in most ways the better performer. It was faster, farther reaching, and could carry more bombs. A B-24 flying on three engines could overtake and pass a B-17 flying on four. But the B-24 was difficult to pilot, almost impossible to ditch safely in the English Channel (where so many bombers lie submerged today), and more vulnerable to gunfire. If there was one crowning difference that set apart the B-17 and the B-24, it was that the internal systems aboard the B-17 were nearly all electrical and therefore less vulnerable to damage, while those of the B-24 were nearly all hydraulic. "The only hydraulic system on the whole airplane [the B-17] was the brakes and the cowl flaps," said Sam Hill, a B-17 mechanic.

B-24 crews would forever swear that theirs was the overlooked and better of the two bombers that took Americans to targets like Berlin, but the B-17 was, always and forever, the plane they loved.

American factories built 12,731 Boeing B-17 Flying Fortresses during the war, coming in second to the 18,000-strong B-24. Flying Fortresses initially fought in every theater, beginning when a flight of them cruised straight into the Japanese attack on Pearl Harbor, but they were eventually concentrated in Europe.

The majestic B-17 is remembered for its heroism with the Eighth Air Force—setting an unsurpassed combat record in terms of the sheer courage and staying power of its crews. Day after day, month after month, huge formations of these great warplanes thundered through the skies of Europe, risking all to press home history's greatest bombing campaign. They were always cold inside that seventy-five-foot fuselage, terribly cold in an aerial campaign that ranged up to 33,000 feet, but B-17 formations pressed on in spite of frigid temperatures and furious defenses.

BOEING'S BOMBER

When Boeing unveiled its silvery Model 299 prototype in 1935, critics argued that the world was not ready for such a big bomber. The best American bomber then was an inadequate, twin-engined adaptation of the DC-3 transport. When Boeing's behemoth first flew on July 28, 1935, no other bombing plane offered its size or range. In a stroke of genius, *Seattle Times* reporter Dick Williams dubbed it the Flying Fortress. Boeing happily trademarked the name. Ten-cent pulp magazines of the late 1930s added parapets and cannons to help the Fortress live up to the appellation.

Despite the lofty name, however, the early B-17 was not ready for modern warfare. B-17B, B-17C, and B-17D models, easily recognized by their unbroken smooth lines and small vertical fin, did not even have a tail gun position. On the eve of U.S. entry into hostilities, the Army Air Forces, the AAF, began receiving the B-17E, which introduced a much broader fin and a much-needed tail gun position. Seen at first as a guardian of the ocean approaches to an isolated North America, the B-17 was placed into production. Americans sensed that their isolation was coming to an end and had a plan to place four bomber groups in the Philippines by April 1942 to deter Japanese aggression. Unfortunately, the plan was four months out of kilter: A dozen B-17s intended for this purpose departed California for a transit stop in Hawaii on the night of December 6, 1941—and arrived twelve hours later, in the midst of the Japanese attack on Pearl Harbor.

Now more than four years later, B-17s were battle-tested veterans, and bomber crewmember L. W. "Mac" McFarland was facing his next mission on February 3, 1945.

"On our way to breakfast the half-haze, half-fog morning mist practically concealed the men just ahead of us. The mess hall looked cheerful and warm after the cold of the early English morning. Faces equally as tired as my own looked up from the tables," he wrote in a memoir to his family. "We gulped down our breakfast and coffee, and then we rushed to the trucks waiting outside to take us to the briefing room." *It was 4:45 a.m., British Summer Time.*

McFarland continued: "Little red glowing coals all around told us we were not alone. The cigarettes were the only lights in the trucks. The bumps on the way to the briefing room woke even the sleepiest of us.

"Benches were lined in two rows on either side of a huge Nissen hut that was the briefing room. There was an aisle between the two rows for the projection machine. A screen was hanging before the map. Concealed behind the screen was our target for the day. We were all seated when the group commanding officer came in.

"Someone yelled, 'Attention!' and we stood until he reached the front of the room. 'Please be seated. Let's get this target today, and we won't have to go back.' He took his chair, and the briefing got under way.

"Before they peeled back the curtain to reveal where you would be flying, you looked at the briefing room board for the letters DP, meaning deep penetration. If the letters were there, that was a bad sign."

Ask any of them. Ask Chrastka, Des Lauriers, Pace, or any of the 350,000 Americans of the Eighth Air Force: Which was the worst target?

When the moment of truth came at the briefing, when the intelligence officer pulled back the map-curtain on the briefing room wall and airmen finally looked at the long, colored yarn stretching from England, which was the German city they least wanted to see at the end of their route? Des Lauriers led his crew to Berlin three times but believed the worst target was Merseburg. It was near the Romanian border, twelve miles west of Leipzig, home to a synthetic oil refinery. It was last remaining producer of significant amounts of fuel for the German war machine. One memoir called it "dreaded Merseburg," recalling a ring of four hundred antiaircraft guns, "twice the number protecting Berlin." Some crewmembers called it "Mercilessburg." Many agreed with Des Lauriers, but no one discounted Berlin, ever, and others said it was the destination they least wanted. John Pesch, who was a first lieutenant and B-17 pilot long before the February 3, 1945, mission to the German capital, said it this way: "The most difficult target was the one that was the most heavily defended and that was Berlin."

Bombardiers, who peered through their vaunted Norden bombsights at marshalling yards, ball bearing plants, aircraft assembly plants, and other targets used the term MPI to refer to the toughest targets. Eighth Air Force Bomber Command at High Wycombe, England, assigned these "main point of impact" targets as frequently as it could after analyzing many factors, including the risk to bomber crews. "The MPI least popular to me was an airplane factory on the outskirts of Berlin," said bombardier James Hensley, who, like Pesch, was a first lieutenant.

Whether it was going to be a good day or a bad day depended on the temperature, the prevailing winds, the timeliness of the fighter escort, and dozens of challenges to airmanship that related to takeoff, forming up, and formation flying. To a man, bomber crews most dreaded the first fifteen minutes of a mission, before the bomber stream had been assembled in its prescribed formation, when the chances of a midair collision in the wet, murky English sky were unjustly high. Next to that, however, they dreaded Berlin.

McFarland's description of the crew conveys the suspense of learning the destination: "Altogether too slowly the screen was raised, and the map was exposed. Colored pieces of yarn charted our courses in and out of Germany. The red yarn showed our course in; it went up over Holland and then to Berlin—the 'Big B.'

"The blue yarn indicated our course out through northern France. There were pieces of transparent plastic outlined in red covering sections of the map. They represented flak gun positions. The large areas were for many flak guns, the smaller ones for fewer guns. There was a noticeably large piece over Berlin. It indicated a concentration of antiaircraft guns in and around that city."

"FAT BOY" READY TO FIGHT

Ray Fredette, another airman who awoke early for the mission on February 3, was a tech sergeant and gunner with Des Lauriers's 34th Bombardment Group at Mendlesham, Suffolk, and was one of thousands of American who harbored certain doubts. Only months earlier, Fredette, a washed-out bombardier candidate, had been one of the few buck privates on any B-17 but "rank was fast in those days," he said. Fredette thought of himself as an unremarkable twenty-year-old kid from Massachusetts who drew good-natured razzing for being five-nine and two hundred pounds. "Everybody on our crew had a nickname and I was Fat Boy," said Fredette.

"Usually, a military target, such as a bridge, a marshalling yard or a tank plant, was shown at the site of the target. We looked at Berlin and saw no such target, just a big black dot," Fredette wrote in the diary he kept, against regulations, at the end of the day of this mission. "Someone asked, 'What's the target?' We all asked: 'What are we aiming at here? What are we supposed to hit?' He says, 'You want a target? I'll give you one. The target is every subway station and every telephone pole in the city of Berlin. . . . We're going after every block, every building, and every street.' With the Russian Army now forty miles away, the whole thing for the Eighth Air Force was to go after Berlin."

First Lieutenant Robert Fitzgerald, a bombardier with the 100th Bombardment Group, remembers being told at the February 3, 1945, briefing that the target was the Friedrichstrasse railroad station in Berlin "where a Panzer division is moving toward the eastern front." It is unclear whether U.S. intelligence believed the German Sixth Panzer Army—a formation considerably larger than a division—was moving through Berlin by train on its way to the Eastern Front.

It wasn't. Possibly the 100th Bombardment Group airmen, and crew-members in some other groups, were deliberately lied to. As Fredette of the 34th group fully understood, "We knew Americans for the first time would be bombing a city and its population."

McFarland's account continues: "The screen was lowered after the navigation officer briefed us on the courses. We were warned not to leave the course being flown except in emergencies. Next, the weather officer took over. His was the most complete data in any theater of operations. Aircraft sent over Germany during the night called in the weather reports. 'Low clouds are at 5,000 feet—topped at 7,000. Another layer is at 10,000 feet—tops unreported. Contrails will form at 15,000, if you're in the clear. The high clouds at 30,000 feet probably won't bother you. Temperature at flight altitude will be 35° below zero.'

"The navigators were given wind velocities at all altitudes by the navigation officer, and then he synchronized our watches. 'Coming up on 0147 in 30 seconds—20 seconds—10 seconds—5—4—3—2—1, hack!' Now all our watches told the same time."

Chrastka always wore flannel underwear. On top of that he wore the standard olive drab uniform and a heated suit. In the beginning, the men had white silk gloves that went up to their elbows, but they gave too many of those to English women. After Chrastka's third or fourth mission, they got brown ones instead. They had leather helmets with flaps on the ears. Enlisted men were issued a harness to clip the parachute on, while officers wore their chutes on their backs, remembered Chrastka's best friend, Pentz. But the practice varied. Robert Des Lauriers, a pilot, said he wore a chest chute.

The distance from London to Berlin is 578 miles. From the Eighth Air Force bomber bases clustered in East Anglia, the distance averaged about 540 miles. The combat radius of a B-17G Flying Fortress was about 800 miles when carrying a bombload weighing 6,000 pounds. The combat radius of the longer-legged B-24 Liberator was about 1,000 miles with a 6,000-pound bombload. The reach of the P-51D Mustang with external fuel tanks was an extraordinary 955 miles, for the P-47D Thunderbolt less than 800 miles with tanks. All of the figures for aircraft are from dry tables and specifications: They make no allowance for wind, temperature, altitude, time spent loitering over a target, or time spent in combat. To put it another way, Berlin was within reach of the B-17 with difficulty, the B-24 with ease, the P-51 with little difficulty, and the P-47 only when all conditions were ideal. Given the weather over Europe, all conditions were almost never ideal.

HITLER'S SPRAWLING CAPITAL

Berlin was Germany's largest city. No other came close. Indeed, it was the largest and richest metropolitan center on the European continent.

It was a legitimate military target. It boasted the headquarters not just of the Third Reich but of every component of the German armed forces. It had dozens of square miles of bombed-out rubble but a functioning opera house. It also had a dozen aircraft assembly plants and a similar number of factories for military vehicles. It was a vital rail and transportation hub.

Its prewar population of three million bloated by slave laborers and refugees from the advancing Red Army, its infrastructure in chaos, its people demoralized as much by Nazi leaders' rhetoric as by the approach of defeat, much of the city of Berlin was in ruins. Antony Beevor, author of *Berlin: The Downfall 1945* wrote:

"In streets where the facade of a house had collapsed, pictures could still be seen hanging on the walls of what had been a sitting room or bedroom. The actress Hildegard Knef gazed at a piano left exposed on the remnants of a floor. Nobody could get to it, and she wondered how long it would be before it rumbled down to join the rubble below."

Even at this late juncture in the war, though, there was still almost no damage to Gestapo headquarters on Berlin's Prinz-Albrechtstrasse. The army supreme command, or OKH, headed by tank hero Gen. Heinz Guderian and responsible for the Eastern Front, continued to function uninterrupted in an underground bunker in Zossen, just south of Berlin. The high command of the Wehrmacht—armed forces—or OKW, headed by Hitler lackey Field Marshal Wilhelm Keitel, also continued to operate unfazed inside its underground offices in Zossen. Also untouched by Allied bombs was the People's Court, where Berlin's infamous "hanging judge," Roland Freisler, was preparing to conduct that day's trial of anti-Hitler conspirators. "Raving Roland," as they called him, was a man so noxious that even Adolf Hitler, who had narrowly escaped assassination at the hands of defendants in the judge's courtroom, despised him. When Freisler awoke that morning, he must have thought it would be another day of business as usual.

With an area of 1,600 square miles and its human density up from three to four million or more, Berlin was four times the size of the port of Hamburg and ranked as the sixth largest city in the world. Its antiaircraft defenses stretched across more than forty miles of searchlights, flak batteries, decoy fires, decoy marker flares and target indicators, and airfields brimming with German air force, Luftwaffe, fighters. Even under siege, the German aircraft industry continued to turn out new Messerschmitt Bf 109, Focke-Wulf Fw 190, and other fighters, and to develop the formidable Messerschmitt Me 262 jet. The Allies were gradually whittling away the finest of the Reich's pilots, but once the Germans readjusted their production priorities to focus on fighters, they never lacked sufficient aircraft. By one estimate, the Luftwaffe had more than 1,600 combat-capable warplanes available to defend the city.

Long before the first American bomber crew ever awoke in a chilled darkness to begin a journey that would culminate over Berlin in daylight, British, Canadian, and Australian Lancaster crews attacked the city during the nocturnal hours. The Royal Air Force's Bomber Command chief, Air Marshal Arthur "Bomber" Harris, eager to weaken the Third Reich at its core, declared the "Battle of Berlin" beginning in August 1943. Harris's bombers carried out the longest, most sustained effort against a German city during the war. In darkness, they battered Berlin repeatedly while their American counterparts continued to argue for daylight bombing. The British went after cities at night while the Americans went after installations by day. Sometimes, a formation of Fortresses or Liberators, flying into a sunrise in the east, would pass alongside Lancasters and Stirlings—their British equivalent, flown singly in bomber streams, never in formation—emerging from Germany and from the night.

In a February 13, 1944, article in *Das Reich*, Germany's propaganda virtuoso Joseph Goebbels attempted to portray Allied bombing of Berlin as a "series of terror attacks," never mentioning the city's industrial or political clout. He also portrayed Berliners as stoic and heroic, enduring frequent attacks. He was premature in that the only Allied bombers over his capital so far had been British. The Americans would not arrive until March 1944.

"In Berlin as in all the other German cities affected by enemy air terror we have learned to simplify our lives, returning to a primitive war style that has taken from us many of the pleasures of everyday life," wrote Goebbels. "We are now marching with a lighter pack. Along with the other populations of other German districts affected by heavy enemy air terror, we have learned to do without some things that are still taken for granted in those parts of the Reich that have been spared. It would be an exaggeration to say that has been easy for us. It deeply hurts a city to see significant parts of its housing, its artistic and cultural monuments, its churches, theaters and museums, reduced to soot and ashes."

The western Allies carried out 314 bombing missions to Berlin between 1940 and 1945. The American portion, conducted by the Eighth Air Force, began with the tentative mission of March 4, 1944, continued with the first all-out assault two days later and, after a brief hiatus in summer and fall, continued from late 1944 until war's end.

The Berlin mission of February 3, 1945—the one for which gunner Frank Chrastka shook himself awake in his cold barracks, toward which pilot Bob Des Lauriers felt surprisingly calm—was to become the next-to-last major Eighth Air Force effort against the German capital. It was also to be the largest bombing mission undertaken against a single target. There had been a larger formation attacking Germany the previous Christmas Eve, but it had struck dozens of widely scattered targets.

Ray Fredette walked out of the briefing surrounded by other crewmembers feeling a chill and not just from the cold. *It was 5:00 a.m., British Summer Time.* "We were bombing one of the largest cities in Europe, already crowded with refugees because of the Soviet advance," Fredette said. "If the enemy had not been so ruthless or so merciless in their occupation of lands they conquered, if they had not committed so many atrocities, I might have refused to go on this mission. I wrote in my diary that, 'This is mass murder, nothing else.' "

Fredette did not know that the commander of the Eighth Air Force, Lt. Gen. James H. "Jimmy" Doolittle, was hopping mad about what he saw as a shift in U.S. policy, from pinpoint bombing of military targets to less discriminate bombing of a city. Ordered by his boss Gen. Carl Spaatz to undertake today's mission, Doolittle felt he would "violate the basic American principle of precision bombing of targets of strictly military significance." When Doolittle protested to Spaatz, the reply was: "hit Berlin—center of [the city]."

But although Fredette recalled being "repulsed" that his plane's bombs might fall on innocents, he did not fully embrace the misgiving that leaped from a page of his diary. At 5:00 a.m. on February 3, 1945, in his heart if not in his diary, Fredette believed the war was just. He believed American B-17 Flying Fortress crews could help to shorten the war. But mostly he believed that it was cold. It was so cold. And he was surrounded, amid the first shimmering of sunrise, by men like himself who were cold and afraid and who were preparing to climb aboard their bombers.

Copilot Robert Des Lauriers was cold, too, but if he was afraid, he kept it from view. As he finished the briefing and mixed with his crewmates, all came to the same thought at the same time, but Des Lauriers does not remember who said the words aloud:

"I hope we get Hitler today."

CHAPTER TWO

Starting

The B-17 Flying Fortress in the American Air Campaign
December 7, 1941 to March 18, 1943

AMERICANS INVENTED this new kind of warfare at high altitude. Americans pioneered aviation medicine. They cobbled together the first working oxygen masks. They designed protective garments and helmets worn at heights and at subzero temperatures where no human would be able to survive, let alone function, without them. Americans conducted one of the first exhaustive studies of how extreme cold temperatures at high altitude affected a crewmember's ability to fly and fight.

Most importantly because it changed everything about the heights at which men could do battle, Americans pioneered the four-engined heavy bomber. After early missteps, the B-17 Flying Fortress and B-24 Liberator were pouring from production lines on the eve of conflict.

The attire, the equipment, and the bombers were entering widespread service when the December 7, 1941, Japanese attack on Pearl Harbor brought the United States into World War II. One of the most experienced B-17 pilots at that juncture was Curtis E. LeMay, who pioneered bomber tactics before the war and later commanded a bomb group, and then a wing, and then an air division, during early stages of the air campaign in Europe.

Less than a month after Germany broke diplomatic relations and declared war on the United States on December 11, 1941—with the United States responding in kind later in the day—Americans faced the unprecedented challenge of using these new heavy bombers to create a new kind of fighting force for operations at high altitude, in extreme cold.

On January 19, 1942, an initial contingent of just seven men established VIII Bomber Command at Daws Hill, England. They had no troops and no bombers, but they brought with them a body of knowledge about strategic bombing that didn't exist anywhere else. Leading the seven was newly promoted Brig. Gen. Ira C. Eaker. Within months, VIII Bomber Command became a component of the Eighth Air Force, which set up headquarters at High Wycombe. In the early spring of 1942, the first three heavy bombardment groups were activated, the 97th, 301st, and 303rd. The planes were beginning to arrive at new bases being built for them on British soil but owned by the Americans. Aware that his newly arriving bomber crews were untested, Eaker famously told his British hosts: "We won't do much talking until we've done more fighting. After we've gone, we hope you'll be glad we came."

The men who accompanied Eaker were all future luminaries. They included a junior officer, Capt. Beirne Lay Jr., who would later command the 487th Bombardment Group. A key figure was Brig. Gen. Frank Armstrong, eventual commander of the 97th Bombardment Group and a pioneer in bombing tactics. Armstrong was brave, gruff, and irritating, an unforgettable character who never asked anyone to take a risk he wouldn't take.

On May 5, 1942, Lt. Gen. Carl "Tooey" Spaatz assumed command of the Eighth Air Force. Eaker retained responsibility for VIII Bomber Command, while Brig. Gen. Frank O. "Monk" Hunter ran the newly forming VIII Fighter Command, initially with American-crewed Spitfires and newly arrived P-47 Thunderbolts.

Also in the group was Capt. Frederick W. Castle, the son of a 1907 West Point classmate of Army Air Forces' boss Gen. Henry "Hap" Arnold. The younger Castle graduated from the U.S. Military Academy in 1930. To historian Roger Freeman, Fred Castle "seemed to many to be a strange man because he did not conform to the general pattern of social behavior amongst fighting men. He was the antithesis of the tough, hard talking leader that tended to dominate the combat commands in the Eighth Air Force." To historian Barrett Tillman, Castle was "quiet and reserved [and] told his garrulous, combat-blooded officers that he expected proper dress and gentlemanly behavior."

Castle was destined to rise through the ranks and to become one of a handful of men who distinguished themselves on big missions. He will reappear in this narrative four ranks and 28,000 feet higher and in mortal peril (chapter ten). Like Lay, 1st Lt. Harris Hull, and others on Eaker's fledgling staff, Castle was a civilian in uniform rather than a career military officer, reflecting Eaker's distance from the professionals with whom he'd pioneered military flying over the past two decades. The men gathered around Eaker were sometimes dismissed as "Eaker's Amateurs," but the term was unfair: They were working hard to accomplish something that had never been done before. No one had experience with what lay ahead.

With this handful of men laying the foundation for what would become history's greatest air armada, the Eighth Air Force (standard usage was to spell the word, not render it as 8th) evolved into a growing military formation with four principal components—Air Service Command, Ground-Air Support Command, Fighter Command, and Bomber Command. A Roman numeral eight (VIII) before the title was the usage when referring to these components. Eaker's VIII Bomber Command would itself evolve and would in due course have two B-17 Flying Fortress units for every B-24 Liberator outfit. And under this headquarters in a year's time three air divisions would be formed, the 1st and 3rd with B-17 groups (with a few exceptions) and the 2nd Air Division having responsibility for most B-24 combat wings, groups, and squadrons—but in 1942 that command structure was still in the future.

Fully six months after Eaker's arrival in July 1942, B-17 Flying Fortresses and other warplanes traversed the Atlantic in Operation Bolero and positioned in Britain.

STARTING TO GROW

Americans amazed their British hosts with the speed and ingenuity with which they pressed ahead with a military buildup that had never been undertaken before. A farm boy in an English pasture could look across the grass and see row after row of heavy bombers, occupying airfields in East

Anglia that faced German-occupied Western Europe. In English villages, they could hear the clanking of Cyclone engines being run up by crew chiefs during the night and the clattering of .30- and .50-caliber machine guns being test-fired into shooting pits. You could walk in the English countryside and observe the majestic sight of a Flying Fortress taking off as crews prepared for something that would become very big, indeed bigger than almost anyone could imagine.

But the bombing of Europe began on a small scale, and it began with both the brass and the bomber men pinning their prospects on a firm belief that the bomber would always get through. Hardly anyone was thinking about fighter escorts. It was, Eaker told an aide, nice to have fighters around, it was always good to have them, but the bomber would always get through. With more than a little justification, Eaker was more concerned about how men would fight at altitudes where war had never before been waged, in temperatures where some lubricants could freeze. Eaker was also looking ahead to creating a fighting force in numbers for which no precedent existed.

The flight path that took American bomber crews to Berlin began with an August 17, 1942, effort that was almost laughably modest. Author Martin Bowman quoted a crewmember as saying that in the dark, cold, early hours of that day, "the lights of the briefing room might have been glowing from the electricity in the air." He must have had his days confused. This first, preliminary mission took place not near dawn, as later missions did, but late in the day.

Just eighteen B-17E Flying Fortresses of the 97th Bombardment Group took off from Polebrook, England. Led by Armstrong, this first American bombing mission in Europe was a short-range trip to railroad marshalling yards at Rouen-Sotteville in France. On the flight line, crewmembers saw a handwritten sign that implored: "Ruin Rouen."

The bomber will always get through, the crews were told.

Major Paul W. Tibbets Jr. led the August 17 formation in the Fortress named *Butcher Shop*. This was neither Tibbets's regularly assigned plane nor his crew, but *Butcher Shop* would eventually become the longest-serving Fortress in Europe, surviving the war in Europe only to be scrapped long after the end of the war in Europe—on the very day Tibbets bombed Hiroshima.

(The name of an aircraft often came from its pilot, but not always. Often, the crew chief exercised naming rights, although pilot Tibbets himself would later christen a bomber *Enola Gay*, his mother's name. For the remainder of this narrative, aircraft are identified by their names or as being "unnamed." Crewmembers, who knew little about designations, block numbers, or serial numbers, were most likely to refer to a plane by its name. In the literature of aviation, one common error is to call these "nicknames" when they are, in fact, names. Other identifying information of key aircraft, such as serial numbers, appears in appendix 1 and appendix 2).

Eaker went along in the copilot's seat of *Yankee Doodle*, piloted by 1st Lt. John Dowswell. The German air force, the Luftwaffe, did not challenge the bombers.

Tibbets wrote: "It was just mid-afternoon when we lifted off into sunny skies. All the planes were in the air by 15:39 hours. We started our climb for altitude immediately and had reached 23,000 feet, in attack formation by the time we left the coast of England and headed south across the Channel. I wondered whether all aircraft would make it or whether there would be aborts. However, it was a banner day with no aborts.

"As we departed the English coast, the [Royal Air Force] escort of Spitfire Vs joined us. Group Captain Harry Broadhurst was leading the RAF escort fighters and it was an emotional, spine-tingling event—we were off to do battle for real and fighters were there to give us protection and comfort." Having Spitfires was convenient for such a short trip and they were probably the best-looking fighters of the war, but they would become useless on future, deeper penetrations of the Reich.

German high-frequency radio traffic between ground defense stations warned that a formation of "twelve Lancasters" was approaching. But these were not the familiar British Lancaster, Halifax, or Stirling bombers that traditionally operated at night.

There was some German fighter resistance, but not much. Aboard a B-17E named *Birmingham Blitzkrieg*, ball turret gunner Sgt. Kent R. West squeezed off a burst of fire, and then another, at a German fighter. West became the first Fortress gunner to fire upon, and the first to be credited with shooting down, a German fighter. The Germans also lost a second fighter and claimed two Spitfires. First Lieutenant Thomas H. Border was the pilot of West's aircraft.

The dozen Fortresses unleashed 36,900 pounds of bombs. All were British bombs because the Americans did not yet have their own. Said Tibbets: "We caught the Germans by surprise. They hadn't expected a daylight attack, so we had clear sailing to the target. Visibility was unlimited, and all twelve planes dropped their bomb loads." Tibbets also said, "Our aim was reasonably good," but that the results didn't match the claims of the American top brass that they were conducting "pinpoint bombing." He added, "We had a lot to learn."

EVOLVING AIRPOWER

The fledgling VIII Bomber Command of the Eighth Air Force flew another ten missions without serious fighter escort or opposition. Then many B-17s were diverted to the North African front in late 1942. Others remained in East Anglia. And at Eaker's headquarters, officers debated using their growing bomber force to attack German U-boat pens. It was a decision born of necessity: Allied supply convoys were being slaughtered in the Atlantic.

On September 6, 1942, Fortresses attacked the Avions Potez factory at Meaulte, France. Crews flew part of the mission without fighter escort, after the fighters and bombers failed to meet up on time. This time, the bomber did not always get through. Two B-17Es were lost.

The B-17E was the first version to be used in Europe. This model was slightly longer than earlier Fortress versions and was the first with twin .50-caliber machine guns in a manned position in the tail, but it really was an interim while American industry geared up to build the B-17F and, later, the B-17G. By the fall of 1942, the number of bases in East Anglia was growing exponentially and B-17F models were populating most. Army Air Forces planners were taking the first steps to build up a second force equipped with B-24s.

The B-17F was equipped with newly designed self-sealing oil tanks, more efficient paddle-bladed propellers, and more armor. Its bomb bay could accommodate a dozen 500-pound bombs or half a dozen 1,000-pounders, but only a single 2,000-pound bomb.

Hunter wanted to send his fighters ranging over Europe far from bomber formations, conducting offensive operations that were separate from the bombing missions. Eaker was at least ambivalent and probably was convinced that bombers could defend themselves without help. Spaatz, on the other hand, favored fighter escort from the start and lobbied his boss in Washington, Army Air Forces commander-in-chief General Arnold, for more fighters. By late 1942, the 4th, 56th, and 78th Fighter Groups were in operation with Spitfires and P-47s but were operating mostly independently of the bombers.

The B-17 was not alone for long as the heavy of the Eighth Air Force. The 93rd Bombardment Group introduced the B-24 Liberator.

"Ted's Traveling Circus," they called this outfit, after commander Col. Edward J. "Ted" Timberlake Jr. At the beginning, at the group's first base at Alconbury, Hunts, also known as Station 102, these first Liberator crews arrived in dark olive drab and neutral gray B-24D models (lacking the nose turret on all subsequent variants of the Consolidated heavy bomber).

October 9, 1942, witnessed the debut of the Liberator on the continent. It was also the American bomber force's first true, full-scale mission. The Eighth Air Force dispatched 108 bombers, including twenty-four B-24s of the 93rd group in a five-group assault against the French city of Lille. Principal targets were the steel and engineering works of the Compagnie de Fives and the locomotive and freight car works of Ateliers d'Hellemmes.

Timberlake took off at 7:47 a.m. to lead the Liberator force at the controls of *Teggie Ann*, named for his wife. P-38 Lightnings and Spitfires went along. It was a milestone in the early growing pangs of the fledgling Eighth Air Force—the first time more than a hundred heavy bombers were dispatched. The Luftwaffe was ready with an aggressive mix of Messerschmitt Bf 109s and Focke-Wulf Fw 190s, which made seventy passes at the bombers in a running, thirty-minute duel.

Sergeant Arthur Crandall, a gunner, was credited with shooting down an Fw 190 near Lille that day. He was a gunner on the Liberator *Ball of Fire*. Captain Joseph Tate was his pilot. While over the target, three Focke-Wulfs made an attack and fired a shell through *Ball of Fire*'s right vertical stabilizer. Crandall's appears to be the first aerial victory for an Eighth Air Force B-24 crewmember. Alas, "Ted's Traveling Circus" lost a B-24 on this first mission.

Even on this short-distance mission, so modest compared to the marathon journeys to Berlin and beyond that would come later in the war, only 69 of the 108 aircraft reached the target. German fighters were waiting for them, ignored their fighter escort, and shot down a B-17 in addition to the B-24.

The Fives-Lille assault began a trend that has been prevalent in all wars and would continue throughout this one. Men caught up in the heat of battle thought they were seeing successes that never happened: American gunners claimed an incredible fifty-six Luftwaffe aircraft destroyed, more than the actual number that were in the air that day. German records for the day show the Americans shot down one Luftwaffe fighter. Most of the American fighters never engaged the foe at all.

One officer who flew that first mission was 1st Lt. Ramsay Potts, a future squadron commander who would rack up an impressive list of achievements as a Liberator pilot and leader. On one of his early missions, five fighters attacked Potts's lone Liberator over the Bay of Biscay while flying an antisubmarine mission. His crew shot down two Junkers Ju 88s, and Potts dived into the clouds, shaking off the others.

The fixation with German submarine pens was becoming a painful and costly diversion. An October 21, 1942, mission to the U-boat pens at Lorient produced unremarkable results.

TWELVE O'CLOCK HIGH

Noteworthy was the fact that Luftwaffe began making head-on attacks from ten degrees above the centerline flight path of each bomber, the position the Americans called twelve o'clock, high. Beirne Lay, who was a writer as well as a bomber leader, and Sy Bartlett now had a title for their novel with its hardheaded group commander, Gen. Frank Savage, a clone of the real-life Armstrong. They called their book *Twelve O'Clock High.* It was later an influential movie.

A frontal attack required nerves of steel and unparalleled skill on the part of a Luftwaffe pilot. Later in the war, maintaining skill levels would become the greatest challenge facing Adolf Hitler's air force. But if a Messerschmitt or Focke-Wulf pilot could ignore all the instincts that were shouting at him to peel off, and if he could stay on course for a closeup shot from the front, he had a strong chance of killing both of a bomber's pilots. Even if the pilots survived, a frontal attack could confuse and break up a bomber formation. The B-17E had no real defense against a head-on firing pass, while B-17Fs carried two cheek guns that were ineffective until their position in the nose was changed.

On December 1, 1942, Eaker replaced Spaatz as commander of the Eighth Air Force and pinned on a second star. On December 20, 1942, 101 bombers attacked a Luftwaffe support installation at Romilly-sur-Seine. No fighters reached the target with them. Six B-17s were lost. Thirty-one were damaged. The Americans claimed they shot down three German fighters, although more were written off while landing. It was a day filled with mediocrity for a target barely a hundred miles inside enemy territory.

The first real test of this new plan to attack U-boat pens came on January 3, 1943, during an attack on St. Nazaire. Of 107 bombers dispatched, 7 were lost. Nineteen forty-three promised to be a very expensive year.

U-BOAT PEN ATTACK

Even today, they don't like to talk about the St. Nazaire raid.

Compared to the thousand-plane raids that went deep into Germany to Berlin and beyond later in the war, the January 3, 1943, bomber mission from England to the coast of German-occupied France was small and spanned only a modest distance. It introduced new tactics from a leader who later made his mark by innovating aerial warfare. Yet Col. Curtis E. LeMay's attack on St. Nazaire ended up being mostly a debacle. Airmen paid a high price for achieving little.

The purpose was to bomb the German submarine pens at St. Nazaire, which were dispatching the U-boats that were wreaking havoc in the Atlantic. The Germans had U-boat pens at Lorient, La Rochelle, and Toulon in France and Trondheim in Norway, and they were all difficult, heavily shielded targets for the new technique of mass daylight bombing, but none was more a challenge than the mammoth bunker base at St. Nazaire.

The Royal Air Force (RAF) attacked St. Nazaire in February and March 1942 with Halifax and Whitley bombers. Construction was only being finished then, and the pens might have been more vulnerable than they were later. Still, the RAF achieved mixed results, lost several aircraft to mishaps rather than German fire, and apparently did little to the savagery being inflicted on Allied shipping in the Atlantic by Adm. Karl Donitz's U-boat *rudeltaktik* or wolf pack strategy. Squadron Leader Michael Curphey, an RAF intelligence analyst, said that his bosses concluded the

U-boat pens were too heavily reinforced by concrete to be neutralized by bombing. Allied leaders believed, however, that they could hamper the U-boat campaign by bombing torpedo and optics facilities that were above ground.

"There was some disagreement between the British and the Americans on this," said Curphey. "Frankly, the Americans went into the war overconfident in their daylight bombing capabilities. We had plenty of experience with bombing by then and had chosen to do most of ours by night. The Americans eventually made daylight bombing work, but it's debatable whether it ever worked against U-boat bunkers."

"We learned a lot that day," said former Sgt. Arnold Burton, referring to the first St. Nazaire raid. A newly minted aerial gunner—who would return for a second tour and fly the Berlin mission at the core of this narrative—Burton was manning a .30-caliber air-cooled machine gun in the waist position of the B-17F *Heavy Weight Annihilators* of the 322nd Bombardment Squadron, 91st Bombardment Group. Burton was in a formation of eighty-five bombers that included seventy-two B-17s from the 91st, 303rd, 305th, and 306th groups and thirteen B-24 Liberators from the 44th group.

"Our aim point was a torpedo shed near the U-boat pens," Burton wrote in a diary. He was among thousands who ignored a rule, apparently unwritten, against keeping a diary. "Our bombload was five 1,000-lb. general purpose bombs. We took off at 9:12 a.m. and were scheduled to return at 2:10 p.m." Burton's 91st group, nicknamed "The Ragged Irregulars," was based Bassingbourn in Cambridgeshire, about a dozen miles from Cambridge. Later in the war, one of the group's leaders would be a young, cheerful Lt. Col. Marvin D. Lord (chapter eleven).

LeMay had experimented with various ways to stagger three- and four-plane elements so their defensive gunfire would have the most effect against fighters. He believed that the survival of a bomber crew battling winds, weather, and German fighters depended in large measure on the performance of aerial gunners like Burton.

Burton was struggling with the faulty equipment and bad ideas that came part and parcel with the early days of the American daylight-bombing offensive over Europe. The problems resulted from flying higher and being colder than ever before in a combat aircraft. "The early, bladder-style oxygen mask didn't work," said Burton. "Your saliva would freeze up if you didn't do something; you would pass out. So you had to jerk off the whole bladder and mask, pull the hose out of the mask, and stick the oxygen hose directly into your mouth and suck on it." Later in the war, bomber crews received demand-type oxygen masks that were less troublesome but still far from perfect.

Burton was even more irritated at the electrical suit designed to protect him from the terrible cold at high altitude. "Remember, the waist-gun position on the B-17F was just an open rectangle in the side of the fuselage," said Burton. "Only much later, with the B-17G, did we have a window to keep the air from rushing in."

"Heated boots and suits were constantly burning your ankles," he said. "It was a terrible design. The suit was blue with wires all through it. The shoes that went into the boots were blue with an electric plug-in; the gloves that went inside your gloves were blue. You got cold, so you turned the rheostat up, and when you did that you'd start to burn at the wrist and the ankles. The suit literally burned you, and sometimes it caught fire."

Burton and the 91st Bombardment Group also had a lot of aborts from guns freezing up. "You would chamber one round in your gun and be ready. When you were airborne, you were supposed to test-fire a couple of rounds. You'd shoot off one round and the gun would freeze." Later in the war, there was a type of gun oil that didn't freeze, no matter how low the temperature.

BECOMING A GUNNER

Burton was a product of the Midwest, born in 1921 in Pella, Iowa. He took business classes in high school. He was doing office work, "not anything great, just menial office work," when he learned of the attack on Pearl Harbor. Like many Americans, Burton did not at first recognize the term "Pearl Harbor" or know what place it referred to.

Burton enlisted and went through gunnery training at Lowry Field, Colorado, in 1942. "They had a P-37 fighter mounted on a rack with guns that fired two .30 calibers through the propeller," Burton said. "We had to learn how to maintain and synchronize those guns. We had a class where we assembled and disassembled various kinds of machine guns, rifles, and pistols." Initially a member of the 91st group's ground cadre (and only later a member of a flight crew), he went to war aboard the ocean liner *Queen Mary* and set up shop with the rest of his group at Bassingbourn. He was shifted to flight status. St. Nazaire was his third combat mission.

LeMay was nothing if not an innovator. He wanted his bombers to maintain a steady course during their bomb run, which began at an imaginary spot in the sky called the initial point and continued to the aiming point, a torpedo storage shed astride the St. Nazaire submarine pens. In *Flying Fortress*, author Edward Jablonski, without naming LeMay, described what LeMay wanted: "A new bombing technique was introduced on this mission which was to have an important effect upon future operations. Instead of each plane dropping bombs individually, all bombardiers released when they saw the bombs leave the bomb bay of the lead plane. This technique resulted in greater accuracy (for the most skilled bombardier and pilot were in the lead aircraft) and a massive concentration of strikes in the target area."

Still, even though studies showed that the odds of getting hit by flak went down if the bomber remained straight and level, crews didn't like the new tactic. Burton's pilot, 2nd Lt. Don C. Bader, didn't like it. Burton's bombardier, 2nd Lt. James W. Hensley, didn't like it. Burton didn't like it either.

"The weatherman said we would have ninety-mile-per-hour tailwinds," said Burton. "He got it exactly wrong. We had ninety-mile-per-hour headwinds." An official record indicates that the bomber force was flying into an unprecedented, 115-mile-per-hour gale. Whatever the exact speed of the headwinds, they had the effect of slowing the bombers to a near-standstill in midair, meaning that the bomb run—the period when the crews went straight and level into German flak—lasted for an eternity.

Moreover, wrote Jablonski: "Instead of attempting to follow the formations as was the usual practice, the flak gunners introduced their own innovation. They predicted the area through which the B-17s would have to pass on the bomb run and filled that area with flak bursts. Three Fortresses were shot down over St. Nazaire [by flak] on that mission and dozens returned in various stages of damage."

Burton said he did not feel the impact but "saw it happen" when a flak shell exploded near his B-17 and battered its number one, or right outboard, engine. "I saw the propeller get feathered and the smoke trailing back," Burton said.

With LeMay in the lead, just 76 of the intended 101 Flying Fortresses actually found the target. LeMay's tactic called for a straight and level bomb run, flak or no flak, and the result was that 7 bombers were shot down and 47 damaged.

German fighters made a belated attack on the B-17F of Staff Sgt. Alan Magee and shot off a section of the right wing, causing the aircraft to enter a deadly spin. Wounded ball turret gunner Magee leapt from the plane without a parachute. He rapidly lost consciousness due to the altitude.

Magee fell four miles and crashed through the glass roof of the St. Nazaire railway station, which softened the impact of his plummeting body. German troops discovered Magee alive inside the station, took him prisoner, and administered medical treatment. He had twenty-eight shrapnel wounds, several broken bones, severe damage to his nose and eye, and lung and kidney damage; his right arm was nearly severed. Magee was liberated in May 1945 and received the Air Medal and Purple Heart.

ATTACK AND AFTERMATH

The bombers completed their runs, but German flak and fighters shot down three B-17s (of the seven lost altogether) as they emerged from the target. Burton said his bomber was swarmed over by Messerschmitt Bf 109 and Focke-Wulf Fw 190 fighters. He fired at them when he could, but by the time they crossed his gunsight, their work was done.

The Germans were building on and exploiting their new tactic of intercepting the bombers from above and head-on—striking from the position crews called "twelve o'clock, high."

Coming off target, the aircraft was hit by flak, and one engine and wing caught fire. It lost speed and fell behind the group. Pilot Bader called the group leader over the command set, but got no response. According to the after-action report, Capt. Campbell, the leader of B flight, whose first name is not recorded, heard *Heavy Weight Annihilators* in trouble and made a 360-degree turn to pick the crew up. According to the report, Campbell's gunners shot down two German fighters and the remainder ceased swarming over Bader's bomber.

Crewmembers remember the situation differently. They got away from the target, all right. But as Bader struggled to nurse the damaged bomber over the English Channel, German fighter pilots saw the B-17 lagging and attacked it again. Gunfire wounded Bader and bombardier Hensley. In the air-to-air battle that ensued, two of the gunners aboard *Heavy Weight Annihilators*—though not Burton—were credited with shooting down German fighters. In an after-action report, one wrote of "a Focke-Wulf hit by our slugs, pinwheeling and tearing itself apart with just a little fire and smoke."

"With our wounded pilot struggling to keep us out of the water, we eluded the fighters and made a very rough landing at a British base in the south of England," said Burton. "Our B-17 never flew again."

Counting other bombers that made it home but were too damaged to fly again, total losses on the St. Nazaire raid were seven, according to official records. German records indicate that the Luftwaffe claimed fifteen bombers were destroyed by fighters, although fighters were actually responsible for just four of the seven.

Historians disagree whether this attack on concrete-reinforced submarine pens, or any other, had much impact on the Battle of the Atlantic, where German U-boats wreaked havoc on Allies convoys. Early in the aerial campaign against Germany's submarine bases, Allied air commanders decided they would not be able to penetrate the concrete bunkers that protected the U-boats, but believed they could achieve the same purpose by targeting the adjacent torpedo depots that were above ground.

That first mission to St. Nazaire was ultimate confirmation of the flaw in the idea that the "bomber will always get through"—at the core of Army Air Forces doctrine. At great cost, and all too slowly, it was being learned that bombers needed fighter escort to get through. Two years later, as the end of fighting in Europe approached, the long-range P-51 Mustang commanded the sky all the way from takeoff to target. By then, Luftwaffe fighters were no longer a serious threat to B-17s or B-24s. The cohort of aerial gunners that followed Burton by a year or two often flew thirty missions without ever firing their machine guns at a German aircraft.

Consultations between the British and the Americans were becoming more frequent and more formalized as both tried to carve out a joint policy for using heavy bombers against the Third Reich. For almost a year, Britain's Royal Air Force had been operating under an air ministry order directing RAF Bomber Command " . . . that the primary objective of your operations should be focused on the morale of the enemy civil population and in particular the industrial workers." This was the highly controversial policy of "area bombing," or bombing which made no allowance for sparing civilians, and it was a striking contrast to the American doctrine of daylight precision bombing of military and industrial targets. Already, bomber crewmembers were caught up in a controversy that would remain with them forever: Were they carrying out a legitimate mission against an enemy's military under the law of war or were they (as the British were often all too ready to admit) engaged in terror bombing aimed at breaking the will of the German people?

This was one of many issues debated at the January 14 to 24 Casablanca Conference in French Morocco attended by the United States' President Franklin D. Roosevelt, Britain's Prime Minister Winston Churchill, and France's Gen. Charles de Gaulle. Large military staffs accompanied the leaders. Notably absent was the Soviet Union's Premier Josef Stalin, who was preoccupied with the fighting at Stalingrad. It was at this conference that the Allies issued a declaration demanding the unconditional surrender of the Axis powers. This would become a controversy all its own. Was it really necessary? Could the war have been ended some other way, perhaps with lesser loss of life?

At Casablanca was Army Air Forces' chief Gen. Henry H. "Hap" Arnold, who was on an extended journey to several war fronts even though he was already weakened from the first of the four heart attacks he would suffer during the war. Arnold was concerned about reducing loss of life, but it was among his bomber crews, not among people on the ground, where he wanted this saving to take place. He was an administrator, a leader who delegated authority. At Casablanca, where he could have stood beside the likes of Air Chief Marshal Arthur "Bomber" Harris or Air Chief Marshal Norman Bottomley (a key architect of area bombing policy), Arnold chose instead to exert influence in the background but to allow Brigadier General Eaker (the most important advocate of precision bombing) to convene meetings and conduct briefings. The British and the Americans clearly had very different ideas about how to use four-engined airplanes to deposit bombs within the Third Reich. Eaker proved an excellent spokesman with his mix of modesty, knowledge, and persuasiveness.

On January 21, 1943, the British "area bombing directive" was replaced by the "Casablanca directive," which was approved by the combined chiefs of staff and was a key part of the British-American combined bomber offensive (CBO). The critical language in the Casablanca edict established the following as the CBO's prime objective: " . . . the progressive destruction and dislocation of the German military, industrial, and economic systems and the undermining of the morale of the German people to a point where their capacity for armed resistance is fatally weakened. Every opportunity to be taken to attack Germany by day to destroy objectives that are unsuitable for night attack, to sustain continuous pressure on German morale, to impose heavy losses on German day fighter force, and to [divert] German fighter strength away from the Russian and Mediterranean theaters of war." Short version: the British would conduct area bombing at night, the Americans precision bombing by day.

As the Eighth Air Force grew and the number of bomber bases in East Anglia increased, bomber crewmembers began journeying deeper into the Reich. The first large attack on a target on German soil took place on January 27, 1943, when ninety-one B-17s and B-24s were launched and fifty-five reached the Wilhelmshaven U-boat base and port just after 11:00 a.m. and dropped 120 tons of bombs. The two B-24 groups assigned to the mission were unable to locate their targets due to poor visibility and poor navigation and had to return to their bases with their bombs. Two B-17s that could not find the target dropped their bombs on Emden. Luftwaffe fighters damaged thirty-two B-17s and nine B-24s, forcing thirty crewmen to bail out.

On March 18, 1943, high over Vegesack, Germany, bombardier 1st Lt. Jack Warren Mathis was bent over his Norden bombsight, the target approaching, when a flak shell detonated a few feet away from him on the side of the nose of his B-17F *The Duchess* of the 359th Bombardment Squadron, 303rd Bombardment Group. Mathis, a Texas boy who'd trained alongside his brother, Mark, was gravely injured, although the other crewmembers did not immediately know it. As historian Barrett Tillman wrote: "Metal shards blasted the Plexiglas with such force that Mathis was hurled to the rear of the compartment, mortally wounded. Incredibly, the young Texan found the strength to ignore his nearly severed right arm and severe wounds in his body, crawl back to his sight, and drop his bombs." Mathis collapsed when reaching to close the bomb bay doors.

Mathis perished aboard *The Duchess*, an aircraft that survived the war. Posthumously, Mathis became the first recipient of the Medal of Honor of the European air campaign. His brother Mark, also a bombardier, also in the 359th squadron, was killed on a mission to Kiel a few weeks later.

The Americans were struggling. Bomber crews were still using tactics that were pressed upon them by a paucity of escort fighters. The few but growing number of fighter pilots were improvising. Capt. Robert Johnson of the P-47 Thunderbolt-equipped 56th Fighter Group devised a tactic that was counter-intuitive: When attempting to turn against the supremely maneuverable Bf 109 and Fw 190, Johnson threw his aircraft into a barrel roll opposite the turn. Handled properly, this could put the American on the tail of the German. This kind of thinking, guts, courage, and initiative enabled Johnson to shoot down twenty-seven German aircraft.

But the victories were coming at a time when German defenses were succeeding. A Flying Fortress or Liberator crewmember had a less than even chance of completing twenty-five combat missions in the face of German flak and fighters. The fledgling Eighth Air Force was still barely getting started. Nowhere in sight, so far, was a turning point where the Americans might decide they could no longer lose or the Germans might decide they could no longer win. In May 1943, with their first visit to Berlin still almost a year away, the Americans were just beginning to find their way in the war and already many felt they were being defeated.

Boeing B-17F Flying Fortress

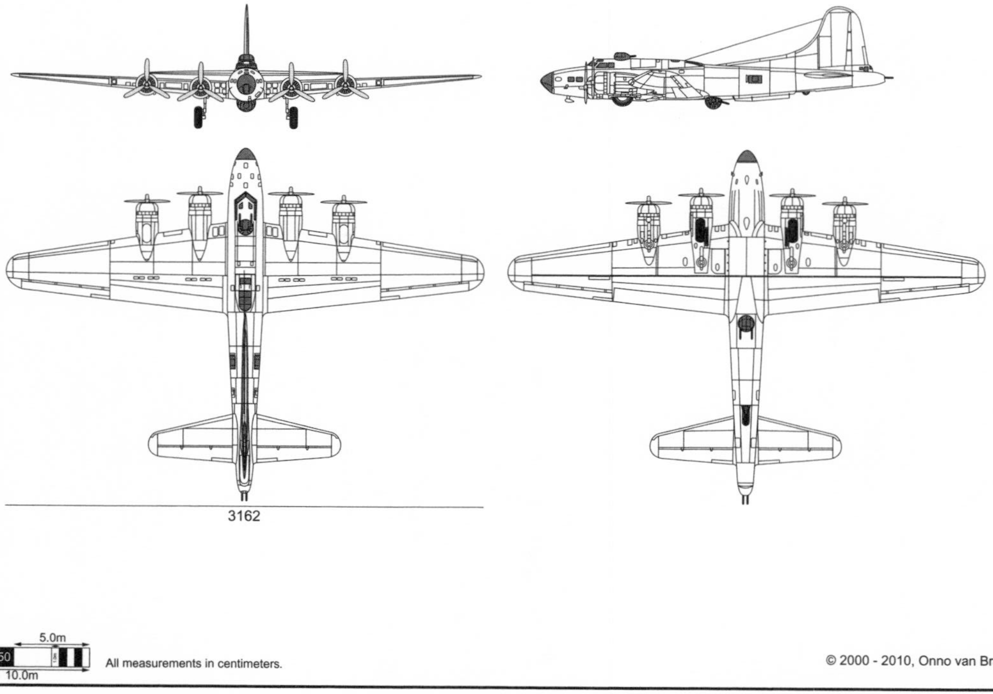

All measurements in centimeters.

CHAPTER THREE

Warm-Up

Mission to Berlin
February 3, 1945—6:00 a.m. to 8:30 a.m.

NEAR THE END OF THE BRIEFING at a combat station in East Anglia, an intelligence officer said: "There are five hundred heavy guns and plenty of mediums in Berlin. We've routed you so you won't be under fire longer than necessary. Mostly, you'll meet barrage flak.

"You may see fighters. There are three airfields near Berlin. Tell your gunners to be alert. Focke-Wulf Fw 190s and Junkers Ju 88s are the fighters you're most likely to see, and the Ju 88s may be carrying rockets.

"You'll be over water for some time. Keep your eyes open for ship movements. If there are convoys on the Autobahns, let us know that too. Keep your eyes open, especially for traffic on the Dutch canals." The intelligence officer, who would not be climbing into a cold bomber and launching into the cold sky, finished with: "See you when you get back. Good luck!"

At Sudbury, three crewmembers who knew each other well talked about the significance of the target. Staff Sgt. Frank Chrastka seemed upbeat and positive when he reminded Tech. Sgt. Daniel "Clint" Pentz that he, Chrastka, was on his thirty-fifth and last mission. "What a way to end your tour, going to Berlin," he said smiling. But ball turret gunner Staff Sgt. Johnnie L. Jones looked somber. "I don't feel good about it," he said.

It was 6:00 a.m. British Summer Time, Saturday, February 3, 1945.

At bomber bases all over East Anglia, in wet and numbing cold, a pink hue shone through the fog, signaling impending sunrise on a day that would be recorded by many as CAVU ("ceiling and visibility unlimited"). That term applied only over the continent, only over Berlin, and only for part of the day. Three hours after wake-up, officially daylight in just a few minutes, the combat stations in East Anglia were still cold, still shrouded in wet murk, still lacking the sharp open visibility crewmembers wanted when it was time to take off and form up.

The men on the ground could not detect it, but another weather phenomenon was brewing—an extremely powerful tailwind. For the first time in aviation history, pilots and crews were discovering what would later be called the jet streams—meandering, west-to-east, sustained currents of air, blasts really, above 23,000 feet. Today, these natural forces would increase to as much as 250 miles per hour at elevations where the Fortresses would be bombing, between 25,000 and 28,000 feet. At some of the morning briefings, pilots were being told that if they were hit over the target it would make no sense to turn around and try to get home while fighting against these winds. Instead, they should attempt to continue eastward and allow the airstream behind them to push them across Soviet lines, where Soviet troops could offer rescue and refuge.

Today, the Eighth Air Force was dispatching 1,003 B-17 Flying Fortresses to Berlin and 434 B-24 Liberators to Magdeburg, escorted by 904 P-51 Mustangs and 44 P-47 Thunderbolts.

Some fourteen thousand–plus American bomber crewmembers came to the end of their briefings. The Eighth Air Force was almost ready to go to Berlin. The force would include twenty-six bombardment groups in two of the Eighth's three air divisions.

Although procedures varied from one combat station to another, most crewmembers shuffled out of the briefing to proceed to the equipment room. Most were waging a battle between the drowsiness that clung to them on this cold, wet dawn and the adrenaline that churned in their bodies, prompted by the knowledge that today's flight would be long and difficult and would include a prolonged period inside German defenses. The smells of oil, smoke, and sweat clung around them in the damp morning. As they prepared to man their planes, some experienced odd moments that seemed not to fit. *It was 6:50 a.m., British Summer Time.*

Was it really true that one bomb group commander became obsessed with the common cold? Lieutenant General James H. "Jimmy" Doolittle had replaced Lt. Gen. Ira C. Eaker as commander of the Eighth Air Force fully a year ago and yet an Eaker memorandum about respiratory disease was still making the rounds, warning: "A survey of one combat group disclosed that 35% of the flying personnel are suffering from upper respiratory infections while only 9% of the ground crews are. During this survey, it was noted that some flying personnel were wearing short underwear while, with few exceptions, ground crews were wearing long woolen underwear. Also, ground crews tended to wear heavier outer clothing than flying personnel."

Decades later, it proved impossible to find a copy of this memorandum, which appeared to make little sense. After all, no one needed to tell Fortress crewmembers that temperatures were cold. Still, the legend persists that at one combat station after the briefing on February 3, 1945, a group commander wandered among flight crewmembers pulling up their pants legs and peeking to see if they were wearing their long johns. According to lore, this group commander did not enjoy much respect from his men. A tug on the pants from the boss was not what a crewmember needed.

Emerging from the equipment room, the men carried chute packs, leather helmets, gloves, oxygen masks, and flak helmets.

SUITED-UP TO FLY

On most crews, the copilot checked out the K-rations that would be the only nourishment on the aircraft crewmembers could ingest.

There were no drinks. Bomber crews carried no liquids. The temperature in a bomber was so far below freezing that no way could be found to use liquids, even drinking water. The risk of dehydration was another of the many dangers bomber crews faced.

For many, the initial preparations were now too familiar: At Mendlesham, Tech. Sgt. Ray Fredette completed the premission routine: ablutions, often in cold water; breakfast; chapel, where Fredette took holy communion; the main briefing; a second briefing for bombardiers and toggleers—enlisted gunners like Fredette who toggled the bombs on command from a lead aircraft—the equipment room where Fredette picked up his flying gear and lugged it to the aircraft; and finally the return trip from the B-17 Flying Fortress to the armament shack, where Fredette checked out and cleaned his guns.

Fredette's aircraft was a Fortress named *Fancy Nancy.*

It wasn't a smooth beginning for Fredette, who would complete thirty-three missions, including three to Berlin on December 26, 1944; February 3, 1945 (the current mission); and February 26. When checking out his personal equipment, "Fat Boy" from Massachusetts ran into a snag. To his consternation, he discovered that someone had stolen one of his flight boots. ("What would a guy do with one boot?") When he should have been thinking about Berlin, about toggling, about gunnery, Fredette was locked in a head-to-head debate with squadron equipment officer 1st Lt. Howard Sugarman, who only reluctantly grasped that this crewmember wouldn't go to Berlin or anywhere else without a fresh set of footwear. With the reluctance ingrained in supply officers, Sugarman provided a new pair, which seemed ill fitting to Fredette at first. "I got over that, stowed my gear in the plane, and had plenty of time at the armament shack," Fredette remembered.

He picked up two Browning M2 .50-caliber machine guns, spread them out on a table, and oiled them. "You would shove something down the barrel to clean it," he said. In the back of Fredette's mind gnawed the words from the briefing about how the target would be every telephone pole, every subway station, in Berlin. "I was the oldest man on my crew and maybe I reacted differently from the others. I had to keep telling myself that we needed to do this." He would have been surprised to learn that Doolittle, the Eighth Air Force commander, had similar misgivings about using aiming points in the center of a civilian population.

Most of the bombers departing for Adolf Hitler's Fortress Europe this morning carried toggleers (or toggliers), enlisted crewmembers that trained to drop their bombs on cue from a lead aircraft. Others carried bombardiers. The bombardiers left the briefing and headed not for the equipment room but for their own special and private briefing, which took place at about the same time at all combat stations. *It was 6:55 a.m. British Summer Time.*

First Lieutenant Lee Sackerman, bombardier on the Dean Hansen crew of the Flying Fortress named *Purty Chili*—where the copilot was

Robert Des Lauriers—kept telling his crewmates in the 34th Bombardment Group that the top secret aura surrounding the vaunted Norden bombsight was a thing of the past. Sackerman didn't know the half of it. The Germans had been studying captured Nordens almost from the start of fighting and now knew the device as well as any American.

At another bomber base, Thorpe Abbotts, another bombardier, and 1st Lt. Richard R. "Dick" Ayesh of the 349th Bombardment Squadron of the 100th Bombardment Group, the "Bloody 100th," attended the second briefing held for bombardiers and toggleers. At five-feet-seven and 135 pounds, the Kansas-bred Ayesh was smaller than the pilot and copilot of his Flying Fortress, which hadn't been given a name.

Photos of Ayesh show a ready grin and a cheerful disposition, which may have been subdued amid the grimness of this morning. "We went over targets and maps," he said. "We discussed what the lead plane would be doing." He and the bombardiers and toggleers around him had been briefed for Berlin the day before and had gone nowhere. Ayesh's diary, prepared a short time later, noted that the target was "a building in the center of" Berlin and that bombing altitude would be 26,000 feet. He would be flying in the low flight, low squadron lead position, beneath his group's air commander for the day, Maj. Robert "Rosie" Rosenthal. His Flying Fortress, Ayesh wrote, was loaded with ten 500-pound general-purpose RDX bombs. These were bombs that used plastic explosives and were deemed highly efficient. Ayesh remembers no one being concerned about the nature of the bombing. "This was war," he said.

Rosenthal was the air commander not just for the 100th group but for the entire 3rd Air Division. Rosenthal was by this time well known as an accomplished pilot and leader, but even some who flew with him didn't know that he was also an attorney recently out of Brooklyn Law School who enlisted the day after the Japanese attacked Pearl Harbor even though he'd been offered a coveted position with a Manhattan law firm.

Rosenthal's aircraft was an unnamed Fortress of the 418th Bombardment Squadron of the 100th group, piloted by Capt. John Ernst. Today, it would be one of the key command aircraft of the all-out effort against Berlin, together with other bombers carrying overall mission commander Lewis Lyle and group air commanders, such as Harris E. Rogner, James A. Smyrl, and Marvin D. Lord. When manning their planes, every one of these men bore a heavy responsibility: Dozens of other Fortress crews would be following them into the air, following them to the target, and bombing on their cue. Rosenthal bore an extra burden, in a sense: He was Jewish, and rumors abounded among crewmembers that he had relatives who'd been murdered by Adolf Hitler's thugs or who were held in concentration camps. All his life, Rosenthal attempted to debunk these rumors and to argue that he was fighting as an American, not as a Jew. He consistently denied having family members inside the Third Reich. "I don't even have any idea how that got started," Rosenthal said.

TO THE AIRCRAFT

The final event in the busy, choreographed morning was the trip to the aircraft. "Everybody was in the right frame of mind," said copilot 1st Lt. Robert Des Lauriers—"Mister Calm," they called him, the artist, trumpeter, would-be architect. Near the briefing hut, exhaust fumes rose from the dozens of Jeeps and trucks, many of them 4x4 weapons carriers. Nobody had to worry about which truck to get into: The trucks shuttled back and forth.

It was 7:00 a.m. British Summer Time. Takeoff times were slightly different for each group, but for Des Lauriers's crewmates it was a half hour before takeoff. They snubbed out and field stripped their cigarettes, threw their gear into the trucks, brushed against one another, and talked in hushed syllables about the mission ahead. No B-17 was parked more than half a mile from the briefing hut, so the ride was short. Every man knew that takeoff might be delayed, that they might have to lounge around their aircraft in the grass, or that it might scrubbed entirely. Today, none of those things happened. They piled out of their trucks and started toward their planes.

This was the time when doubts and fears dissipated. "You did not have time for those things once you began doing the job," said copilot Des Lauriers. He climbed down from his truck in front of *Purty Chili*, just a couple of rows of planes away from Fredette at Mendlesham.

Des Lauriers saw himself, now, as part of a team, with responsibilities and obligations to the others in his nine-man crew. It was cold and murky at Mendlesham's parking area, but *Purty Chili* appeared ready.

"You feel pretty good about yourself after the chapel, breakfast, and briefing, and you feel up to the job you have to do—which is to bomb the enemy," Des Lauriers said. "Before you climb into the plane, you want to make certain you're going to contribute your part as a member of a team because you know that nine men are depending on one another.

"My job was to do a complete visual check of the airplane. I inspected everything on the exterior of the plane to make sure the ground crew hadn't missed anything, remembering that they did all their work in the dark. I kept in mind that another crew used the aircraft the previous day when we didn't fly, and there was no telling how they'd treated her.

"I walked around the B-17 slowly and deliberately. I checked ailerons, vertical stabilizer, and flaps, by placing my gloved hands on them and making sure they moved properly. I made sure gas caps had been screwed back on. I made sure the tires were inflated properly. Once you climb aboard, you can't see most of your own aircraft from inside, so if you're going to spot a mechanical issue, you have to find it while you're on the ground and that means a really tough, all-around inspection."

With help from the ground crew, Des Lauriers pulled each propeller through three revolutions to clear the combustion chambers of the engines. The checklist called for ground crews to perform this task after the pilots were aboard, but Des Lauriers wanted to do it himself.

It was exactly 7:00 a.m. when Des Lauriers climbed aboard his B-17. Of the nine men climbing aboard *Purty Chili*, five of them (two pilots, a bombardier, a navigator, and an engineer/gunner) threw their gear into the plane through a small, square hatch in the nose and then pulled themselves physically up through the hatch—grabbing the bottom of the lip of the entrance as if about to chin themselves and pulling themselves awkwardly aboard. The last was bombardier 1st Lt. Lee Sackerman. Into the gaping nose hatch, Sackerman pitched his chest parachute, bombardier's case, and two gun barrels. When he swung up into the aircraft, the Fortress seemed to creak slightly from the addition of his weight.

Four more crewmembers (a radioman, a waist gunner, a ball turret gunner, and a tail gunner) stepped up far more easily through an automobile-style side door in the rear fuselage behind the bomb bay. At other bases, or among other crews, the men in the forward section of the Flying

Fortress chose the easier path of stepping up to the rear door and squeezing their way through the bomb bay to get to the nose.

On this damp and cool—but brightening—morning, the smell inside the Flying Fortress was like that of a vault being opened to early morning fresh air. Groans and whispers, plus an occasional slight trembling of the airframe, meant crewmembers were getting into place and performing preflight duties.

AIR COMMANDERS ALOFT

The records of the 457th Bombardment Group at Glatton in East Anglia are precise: *It was 7:00 a.m. British Summer Time*, fully a half hour ahead of most other bomb groups when the group's Fortresses began straining into the sky. As part of the complex plan for assembling the formation, the 457th group was one of the first off the ground but would be the seventh of twenty-six bomb groups over Berlin.

The 457th assembled on the Glatton Buncher, both a familiar landmark and a beacon, at 8,000 feet with Col. Harris E. Rogner in the lead. Rogner was the air commander for his group and would be up front when the group's Fortresses entered harm's way. An air commander for a different group was rosy-cheeked, cheerful Lt. Col. Marvin D. Lord, leader of the 91st. Lord was checking procedures, talking up the mission, exuding eagerness. His would be the eleventh group over Berlin.

If anyone doubted Lord was made of the right stuff, or found his cheerfulness and good humor to be out of place as bomber crews manned their planes, it would have been useful to remember that Lord already held the Silver Star for gallantry, a serious award for an earlier mission over Europe that the good-natured Lord seemed not to take very seriously. In a letter home, Lord mentioned a lieutenant who was providing haircuts for bomber crewmembers—"he 'cut' his way through college," Lord wrote—before mentioning the medal, which he did not name. "It really is a nice looking medal," Lord wrote. "I haven't decided whether to send it home or keep it with me until I come home. I don't know exactly how long that will be but it won't be too long, I reckon."

He was wrong.

Major James A. Smyrl, who was scheduled for promotion to lieutenant colonel within a couple of weeks, was another battle commander that day. Smyrl led the 92nd Bombardment Group on the day's air assault. He was a tall, handsome, active figure who sometimes seemed to display the "thousand-yard stare"—the expression often mistaken for a blank look that signifies prolonged exposure to the trauma of battle. Smyrl was "one of the greatest men I've ever known," said 1st Lt. James W. "Bill" Good, who was his navigator for the Berlin mission. Yet we know almost nothing about Smyrl today. One crewmember who accompanied him into the high cold said that Smyrl was never observed wearing a hat.

PURTY CHILI CREW

In the murky cold at Mendlesham, the five men who performed veritable gymnastics to swing themselves up into the front of *Purty Chili* were pilot 1st Lt. Dean Hansen, copilot Des Lauriers, bombardier Sackerman, navigator 1st Lt. Ralph Wathey, and flight engineer/gunner Staff Sgt. John Green.

Was Sackerman a prankster? The record isn't clear. But we know that the bombardier was married and that his wife mailed whiskey for the troops concealed in hair-tonic bottles. Every officer aboard *Purty Chili* had taken a sip or more from time to time, Green a lot more than just a sip. We know also that Sackerman was a perfectionist when signing out, inspecting, and readying his Norden bombsight and the twin .50-caliber guns in *Purty Chili*'s chin turret. He installed the gun barrels and then made his way back to the bomb bay, where, with doors open, he checked bomb fuses, armature wires, and the fuse cotter keys to be sure they were straight so he could pull them once in the air.

Separately, the four rear-fuselage crewmembers of *Purty Chili* who stepped up through the hinged, car-style entrance door in the right rear were radio operator Sgt. Gerald Shoaf, ball turret gunner Sgt. Darryl Young, waist gunner Sgt. Val McClellan, and tail gunner Sgt. Harold Griffin.

"We didn't carry any liquid on board," Des Lauriers said. "It would freeze. It could short-circuit a flight suit. We were always miserably cold, and we couldn't risk a short in the electrical wiring of our flight attire. And the last thing you want on an airplane is a fire."

"In the cockpit we had laid out our maps and charts," Des Lauriers added. "We made sure the windshield and side windows were clean because we would be flying a four-engined plane at high altitude, and we didn't want a problem that could be solved before we started engines. I checked to make sure the oxygen was functioning properly. I made sure the bottles were full, the main tank was in good condition, and the oxygen was flowing properly."

The Flying Fortress checklist required Des Lauriers to check that upper turret switches were "off" and the guns in aft position, to confirm that maps, the radio facility chart, instrument let-down procedures, and direction finding charts were on board and up-to-date. He also confirmed that first-aid packets were on board. Finally, he checked the number, condition, and location of fire extinguishers on board.

"Just before the scheduled taxi-out time, we were ready to go. But fog rolled in. For a time, we sat. We waited. This was our thirteenth mission and we knew the drill. On our previous mission, we'd had to wait so long, we'd climbed out of the airplane and sat around under the nose." That time, the whole "hurry up and wait" drill, was a miscue. The men had barely climbed out of the Fortress when the signal came to climb back in. *It was 7:15 a.m. British Summer Time.*

At airbases across East Anglia for the bomber groups that would make up the bulk of today's formation—at the one shared by Robert Des Lauriers and Ray Fredette, at Frank Chrastka's, at Marvin Lord's—it was time to start engines.

No one used radios. It had been the practice earlier in the bombing campaign for group operations to order engine startup over the radio, but the brass now knew that German intelligence aggressively monitored Eighth Air Force transmission frequencies. A flare from the operations building, arching in a curve through a sky now beginning to clear, signaled each squadron to start engines in turn.

On a four-engined Fortress, the Wright Cyclone engines were identified by engine numbers. The engine-start process began with number one, outboard on the pilot's side, the left side of the bomber (the side opposite the car-style door for crew entry in the rear fuselage); continued with two, also on the left; and then three and four on the right side. The engine numbers were also written on the corresponding thrust levers in the cockpit's center console, sitting between Hansen and Des Lauriers on *Purty Chili*.

CRANKING UP ENGINES

While an enlisted man looked up from the ground where he was standing fireguard—a job performed by a crewmember in some units—the two pilots went through quick checks and switch settings. Hansen gave Des Lauriers the order, "Start number one"—meaning the left outboard engine. Des Lauriers pushed the number one start switch down to energize the engine while simultaneously pumping air from the primer. He heard the Bendix starter come to life and start to gain revolutions per minute as it gave off a high-pitched whine. Hansen then instructed him, "Mesh number one." He toggled the number one mesh switch down with the start switch while pumping fuel into the cylinders with the primer pump located against the wall to his right. He heard the solenoid slam the dogs (heavy metal gears) against the crankshaft of the engine. A shriek resounded and then a cylinder fired, and smoke came rushing past the trailing edge of the wing. It was easy to see: There was full daylight now, and despite the wet and murky beginning, it was going to be a sunlit day.

As each engine fired up and gained speed, the smoke dissipated, the risk of fire declined, the fireguard stepped away, and small blue flames stabbed back from the engine exhausts. Four Wright R-1820-97 Cyclone radial engines now came to life and ran at full power, making the fully braked *Purty Chili* tremble in its hardstand. Hansen nodded and gestured and Des Lauriers cut power on engines four and one, so the Flying Fortress would be able to taxi out on two engines.

Ever after, Des Lauriers could remember the growing sound that grew to a roar, not just on his own flight line but across the narrow spaces that separated tightly packed combat stations in East Anglia. "When you start those engines up, that's a lot of engines," Des Lauriers said. "Each squadron had twelve planes, each group four squadrons. And we were only a couple of miles from the base. This is when the adrenaline starts to flow a little because now you're ready to go. You have a positive feeling, not a negative feeling, knowing that you are part of a team and have a job that must be done."

During takeoff, the five gunners in the rear fuselage gathered in the radio room (close to the trailing edge of the wing), the safest location in the event of a crash or ditching. At each combat station, directed by flares and ground lights and hand signals, Flying Fortresses pulled out of their parking spaces, turned onto the taxiway, turned again at runway's end, and began their takeoff rolls.

"The pilot's main thing is to get that bombload, gas load, and crew off the ground," Des Lauriers said. "The copilot monitors, watches, and helps." Des Lauriers looked to his left as his pilot, Hansen, turned into the wind and called for an engine runup check. "Brakes set," Des Lauriers responded. Together, the pilots took the throttles over 1,000 revolutions per minute. Des Lauriers set the trim tab for takeoff. He double-checked to make sure all three tabs were at the zero setting. Hansen signaled that he had the airplane and advanced throttles to 1,500 rpm. Both men checked propeller performance, looked warily for a drop in rpm—none came—and put turbo controls in "off" position. Hansen was now grasping all four throttles with his right hand, palm upward thus maintaining a grip with palm and fingers.

More checks, mostly by Des Lauriers—tailwheel, gyros, and generator. Now Hansen advanced the throttles of the four Wright Cyclone engines until they were roaring at thirty-seven inches manifold pressure and 2,500 revolutions per minute. Eyeing the Fortress in front of him, Hansen released the brakes and began the takeoff roll. *Purty Chili* gained speed, Des Lauriers looking warily in all directions, John Green monitoring gauges.

The tailwheel lifted off. *It was 7:25 a.m., British summer time.*

Accelerating in two-point position on its main wheels, the Fortress reached 115 miles per hour and began to leave the ground. Hansen looked at the aircraft in front of him, mindful that this could be the moment of a collision. Des Lauriers watched the engine instruments, particularly manifold pressure, rpm, pressure gauges, and temperature gauges. As instructed by the flight manual for the B-17, Des Lauriers divided his attention between the engine instruments and the actual progress of the takeoff.

Des Lauriers applied the brakes very gently to halt the rotation of the wheels, which no longer had a runway to rotate against. He then raised the gear and, as required, the flight-deck crew performed a visual check.

Hansen: "Landing gear up, left."

Des Lauriers: "Landing gear up, right.

Green: "Tailwheel up." Des Lauriers placed the landing gear switch in the neutral position.

Purty Chili, all twenty-five tons of her, was now a missile with men in it, being propelled upward in the East Anglia morning.

"After takeoff, the first danger was getting into formation," said Edward Hinrichs, a flight engineer in the 452nd Bombardment Group. "The weather was a big concern. We took off in bad weather and climbed to a predetermined altitude for forming. It sure gives you a scare to suddenly see a plane materialize out of the clouds, heading for you. Climbing into the soup, everyone kept their eyes open for other planes. Everyone feared a midair collision. When they happened, your chance of survival was about one in eight.

"Another danger that caused planes to go down was prop wash. If a plane got caught in prop wash at the right time, it could cause the pilot to lose control. I believe the worst time to hit prop wash was when the plane was in a turn. If the pilot couldn't regain control, the plane would break up due to the heavy stress put on it."

Regarding vertigo: "At times, the contrails were as thick as clouds," said Des Lauriers. "Fortunately, we'd had 'under the hood' training in flying blind. Still, it was easy to become disoriented and not understand where you were. When we were forming over England and were crossing the Channel, one squadron in front of us hadn't completed the process of establishing its formation. One plane flew into a wingman. Both planes exploded and parachutes came out. I watched a propeller spin down and cut through the parachute of a crewmember as he descended." He was referring to an incident unrelated from this day's Berlin mission, but a midair collision during the forming-up process was among the men's greatest fears.

BLUE GRASS BEGINNINGS

Takeoffs were routine at other East Anglia bomber bases, such as Sudbury where the 486th Bombardment Group dispatched thirty-nine Fortresses. Ever after, members of the group would remember the mixed emotions of the crew led by 1st Lt. Lewis K. Cloud in the Fortress called *Blue Grass Girl*.

Cloud reshuffled his crew, dropping two men who owed an extra mission and picking up two others from another crew, in order to bring together nine men who shared a common benchmark: Today would be the thirty-fifth and final trip over the Third Reich for every crewmember aboard *Blue Grass Girl*. One of the men added to *Blue Grass Girl*'s loading list was Staff Sgt. Frank T. Chrastka, the tail gunner who initially had expected to fly with a different crew. It was Chrastka who seemed cheerful about wrapping up his war with a trip to the German capital. The Cloud crew's other "add on" crewmember, ball turret gunner Staff Sgt. Johnnie L. Jones, was making it clear to anyone who would listen that he had a bad feeling about Berlin.

Fully awake, huddled beneath his bundle of protection from the cold, Chrastka picked up his guns at the armament shack, just as another bomber crewmember, Fredette, had done at a different base.

"The night before, you removed your guns from the plane and stacked them up in the armament shack," said an airman who flew with Chrastka. "You cleaned them with oil. Now, preparing for the mission, you took the guns down from the rack, wiped the oil off of them, and carried them out to the plane." Before becoming a Fortress crewmember, Chrastka had never been in an aircraft. Now, like the others in today's Cloud crew, Chrastka had reached the magic number thirty-five. After today's mission, there would be no more. It was a milestone to celebrate. Chrastka may have been thinking that men who'd completed their full schedule of missions were handed a certificate marking them as members of the "Lucky Bastards' Club." He may have been thinking about what he would do with the certificate, although he wasn't much for trinkets, baubles, or written symbols of recognition.

On the hardstand before takeoff, others remember pilot Cloud uttering reassurances that the Luftwaffe wouldn't be able to oppose the Americans today in any significant numbers. Cloud assured his crew, including Chrastka and Jones, that the flak wouldn't be too difficult and that all of them would live through the day. He was right about the Luftwaffe and wrong about everything else.

Also at Sudbury was 1st Lt. Arthur H. Ogle, a Minnesotan who was an "old man" of a pilot at age twenty-eight. He was piloting a Fortress named *Lady V II* and carrying his squadron's air commander, Maj. John L. "Junior" Rex Jr., twenty-five, in the right seat. At Sudbury, with daybreak behind them, the sky was clearing and visibility was excellent as Cloud, Ogle, and the others rammed their throttles forward, hurtled down the runway, tucked in their wheels, and vaulted into the air. *It was 7:30 a.m., British Summer Time.*

Several of the groups in the day's mission were now in the air, jockeying into position to occupy their place in the formation and head toward the continent.

TAKEOFF MISHAP

Not everyone in the aerial armada made a successful start. At Ridgewell, home of the 381st Bombardment Group, 1st Lt. John Kuhns of the group's 535th Bombardment Squadron was taking off in the left seat of his Fortress named *Male Call* when he lost three of his four engines. The Fortress had a very limited capability to remain in the air with just one engine turning, so it was no way to begin a mission. Moreover, the critical period before climbing to cruising altitude was the worst possible time to find an aircraft in an asymmetrical condition—difficult to control and trying to veer off course. Other bombers were all over the sky, climbing to assemble in formation, and this was no time to be in their midst.

Kuhns turned out over the English Channel, stayed at an altitude well below the assembling bomber stream, and jettisoned his bombs in the water. This eased his burden somewhat, but he was still trying to cope with keeping *Male Call* in the air with just one powerplant. Kuhns broke radio silence to declare an emergency, turned back to landfall, and reached Ridgewell with just one propeller in motion.

In what began as a smooth-looking letdown, the Fortress began to veer sideways and pull out of control. Its wheels hit the ground and *Male Call* plowed straight into the crew chief's hut belonging to the 533rd Bombardment Squadron, setting the building on fire while the crew evacuated the aircraft. No one in the Fortress or on the ground suffered serious injury, although crewmembers were hospitalized for observation, but *Male Call* became a "Category E"—an aircraft wrecked beyond repair.

Ignoring this mishap and the damage and embarrassment it caused, the aerial armada continued skyward, assembled into formation, and proceeded toward the all-important objective of the day. A mighty force was being unleashed, and the fate of one crew, or one crew chief's hut, was too unimportant to change anything.

UNIQUE VIEWPOINT

Because air battles like the one over Berlin on February 3, 1945, never occurred again, those who witnessed the mission being launched had a unique eye on history. One such eye belonged to a youngster.

"It was the spectacle provided by the aircraft that made the greatest impression," said Roger Freeman, who was a teenager tending his farm near a bomber base. On the morning of February 3, 1945, said Freeman, "As a sixteen-year-old farmhand I was shoveling mangolds [root fodder] off a cart for cattle in a meadow to eat. There was not a cloud in the sky and visibility was excellent, as it often is on cold frosty mornings. The meadow was at the top of a hill, a valley hill, for there is no high ground in this part of East Anglia. Bombers were passing high overhead, a common enough occurrence that by this date warranted only a casual glance, but as a break from my labors I rested on the fork and turned my head skywards."

"Directly overhead at around 20,000 feet a group of forty B-17s was headed out towards the coast," Freeman continued. "Ahead of the group I could see more contrailing groups and behind it others approaching. In all, there were twelve formations between the west and east horizons, obviously making for the departure landmark on the coast, probably Clacton or Harwich. Then I looked to the north and could see many more distant formations, not individual aircraft but the massed contrails that indicated a bomber group. I counted another sixteen, some no more than a white smudge in the distant blue, for such was the exceptional visibility that morning my vista must have taken in fifty miles or more. In total, I saw twenty-eight contrailing formations.

"It was several years later before it finally dawned on this addled brain just what I had seen that morning. Twenty-eight groups preparing to go to war at a date when a group formation was thirty-six bombers or more. I had probably been looking at a thousand bombers, with nearly ten thousand young men about to do battle—a sight that can compare with having been on the White Cliffs of Dover as the Spanish Armada sailed by."

CHAPTER FOUR

Struggling

P-47 Thunderbolt and the American Air Campaign
January 28, 1943 to January 1, 1944

"THE JUG WAS SEVEN TONS of scrap iron," said Chester Van Etten, using the pilots' universal nickname for the P-47 Thunderbolt. As a young lieutenant, Van Etten was dashing—a tall, handsome, patrician figure, an active skeet shooter, and one-time football collegian who, when in his flight suit, often flouted regulations to make a point. He once piloted a P-47 upside down for fifteen minutes to show it could be done. More to the point, Van Etten wanted to demonstrate to younger pilots his unwavering confidence in their aircraft.

"The P-47 was robust, heavy, and heavily armed," said Van Etten. "Those eight .50-caliber machine guns in the wings could rip apart anything they hit. It was a great fighter, but it wasn't ideal for escorting bombers. You could only thin out your fuel mixture so much, and even then you just didn't have the range.

"The only time I escorted bombers we strapped a 108 U.S.-gallon fuel tank under the belly. Even then we couldn't go all the way to the target, but we could escort the bombers beyond the border inside Germany. We were coming back from that mission when a single, lone Messerschmitt 109 jumped us. My number three was closer to him than I was, so I said,

'Go get him.' My number three used those powerful guns to saw a wing off the Messerschmitt, and he exploded and rolled away in flaming pieces. We didn't see a parachute." Van Etten, a major at the time and later a colonel, always wondered if the P-47 Thunderbolt could have somehow been given greater range, enabling the Jug to play a larger role in supporting the American daylight bombing campaign.

On the mission to Berlin at the core of this narrative, the Eighth Air Force launched 2,385 combat aircraft, but only 44 of them were P-47s (the remainder being 1,003 B-17 Flying Fortresses, 434 B-24 Liberators, and 904 P-51 Mustangs). That was cameo appearance in the grander scheme of things, but it was the first time the Jug made it to Berlin after years of trying, thanks to a new version of the external fuel tanks that were constantly being tried.

In earlier days when the American air campaign was struggling, when no one even knew whether it would work, the Jug began with a bigger role, including a bigger role during earlier missions to Berlin—although without traveling all the way to the German capital.

Whatever its demerits, nothing prevented Thunderbolt pilots and maintainers from loving their aircraft unconditionally.

Not for nothing, the Farmingdale, Long Island, manufacturer of the Thunderbolt was called the Republic Iron Works and had a reputation for building fighters that were big, roomy, and survivable. One P-47 returned to its English base with body parts from a German fighter pilot embedded in its engine cowling. Another landed safely riddled with 183 holes from bullets and shrapnel.

P-47s rolled out of American factories in greater numbers than any other U.S. fighter, ever. There were 15,683 Thunderbolts, a total that compares to 15,486 P-51 Mustangs and 10,037 P-38 Lightnings. In the Jug, pilots and ground crews had a rugged, reliable fighter, perfect for the wet, corrosive English weather and the mud that sometimes clogged taxiways.

The P-47 was designed as a high-altitude interceptor and was already flying when the United States entered the war. Around the two thousand–horsepower Pratt and Whitney R-2800 Double Wasp eighteen-cylinder radial engine and the ducting for its turbo-supercharger, the brutish P-47 fuselage was wedded to a graceful pair of elliptical wings, mounting eight heavy .50-caliber machine guns. With full tanks, ammunition, and two

1,000-pound bombs, later models of the milk bottle–shaped Thunderbolt (hence the "Jug" nickname) weighed in at an astonishing 16,475 pounds, more than Van Etten's "seven tons" and the heaviest single-engine fighter of World War II. Yet its massive engine could push it to a speed of 420 miles per hour at 30,000 feet, and the new Thunderbolt had a two hundred–mile combat radius, about fifty miles greater than the British Spitfire. Delayed by technical glitches after reaching England months earlier, the Jug entered combat in March 1943. The combat mission took place on March 10 and was simply a fighter sweep over France. The mission was plagued by radio malfunctions and achieved little.

"The 47s haven't any combat yet, but should soon," 2nd Lt. Grant Turley wrote in his diary at Dale Mabry Field in Tallahassee, Florida, on April 11, 1943. In fact, they had just begun, but Turley didn't know it.

Turley was twenty-one years old, a former high school athlete who'd made a watercolor painting of Lindbergh's 1927 transatlantic flight while in the fourth grade in Aripine, Arizona. The newly married, eager Turley was quite tall but otherwise was an exact double of a Hollywood actor who had not yet been born and whose life would not overlap with his own—Bill Murray. Turley had a slightly mischievous streak that sharpened his resemblance to the future actor.

PILOTS AND WAR

But Turley could be shy and inner-directed. He had many facets, like all of the young citizen-soldiers from modest upbringing who squeezed into cockpits and went to war near the edge of the stratosphere. He was more withdrawn, more rural in his roots, than the happy-tempered, impish B-17 Flying Fortress air commander Marvin D. Lord, who took the same pilot training class exactly a year earlier, and the decidedly urban, erudite B-17 copilot Robert Des Lauriers, who took the pilot training course exactly a year later.

Lord was in Army Flying Class 42-D, was married to his wife Evelyn (known as Evey), was the father of a baby, and graduated on October 9, 1942; he wrote about his first solo flight in a letter home and later pinned on his wings at Foster Field, Texas, but the boyish, cheery Lord included little else about flying in his letters. In fact, despite an outgoing nature and an ebullient manner, Lord's letters contained almost no information about anything. One was devoted entirely to a description of the process of writing it. In his wedding photo, Lord is grinning like a Cheshire cat, overjoyed at being matched up with a pretty and charming young woman.

Turley was in class 43-D, graduated March 25, 1943, was married to his wife, Kitty (whose name would later be painted on his Thunderbolt), and wrote effusively of his experiences in the cockpit.

Des Lauriers was in class 44-D, graduated April 15, 1944, and has no surviving letters, although one suspects they revealed the neat and careful hand of a future architect. Des Lauriers would remain single until the final day of the war.

An often-overlooked fact is that nearly twenty thousand military pilots were killed in the United States during training. Lord, Turley, and Des Lauriers weren't among them—several hundred thousand survived to press on—but all three observed fatal flying accidents while in training.

While these young pilots were in training, American bomber crews were going through their most difficult period of the war. The fighters and flak defending the Third Reich were taking a terrible toll. Eighth Air Force commander Lt. Gen. Ira C. Eaker, VIII Bomber Command boss Maj. Gen. Frederick L. Anderson, and 3rd Air Division commander Brig. Gen. Curtis E. LeMay were among leaders who were forging new tactics for a new kind of warfare. Initially, however, they were placing too much trust in the combat box formation that concentrated the defensive fire of a bomber's guns and not enough in the protection that could be provided by escort fighters. Bomber crews were fighting under unspeakably horrible conditions and sustaining almost unbearable numbers of killed, wounded, and captured. Yet Eaker, Anderson, and LeMay believed, correctly, that the bombing campaign was inflicting serious hurt on Adolf Hitler's war machine. The risks to crewmembers would decline, and the size of the hurt to Germany would increase, once escort fighters could form a buffer between the Luftwaffe and the bombers.

While the Thunderbolt was the best escort available, bomber crewmembers were already referring to escort fighters—any kind of escort fighters—as "little friends." But all too often, the "big friends" were still fending for themselves. That was the situation on May 1, 1943, when Sgt. Maynard "Snuffy" Smith flew his first mission, one of several misguided and largely ineffectual visits to the U-boat pens at St. Nazaire, France. Smith was a gunner aboard a B-17F Flying Fortress of the 423rd Bombardment Squadron, 306th Bombardment Group. The Fortress may have been too new to be given a name by its crew.

If Thunderbolt pilot Turley could be laid back and shy, "Snuffy" Smith—there was a newspaper cartoon character of that name—was an argumentative, rebellious, in-your-face character who at age thirty was very old to be flying missions and who was not well liked within his bomb group. "A moderately pompous little fellow with the belligerent attitude of a man trying to make up with attitude what his five-foot-four, 130-pound body left him wanting," wrote another Fortress crewmember, the future television commentator Andy Rooney.

"We were hit by Fw 190s prior to the target," wrote Smith in the Air Force Sergeants Association magazine, *Sergeants*. "Eighty-eight-mm flak hit our left wing. It cut the wing tank off. Gasoline poured into the airplane and caught fire. I was in the ball turret. At this point I had lost my electrical controls and I knew something was wrong. I manually cranked the thing around, opened the armored hatch and got back in the airplane when I saw it was on fire. The radioman became excited and jumped out the window without a parachute. At this point we dropped our bombs. It was minus 50 degrees outside.

"After we made the drop, the pilot took the plane down real fast. They shot down probably eight or nine of our planes on their first attack. We lost our formation.

"We got down to 2,000 feet when one of the waist gunners panicked and tried to bail out but got caught on a .50-caliber gun. He jumped high, the stabilizer hit him and he must have broke into a dozen pieces."

"I took my oxygen mask off as the system was knocked out," Smith continued. "All the radio equipment was on fire, wires were burning everywhere. I proceeded to put out the fire with fire extinguishers and water bottles. I did the best I could while being shot at. They were coming in at us from both sides. While not fighting fire, I manned the workable waist guns. Every time they would make a swoop, one or two more planes would go down. Eventually the fighters ran out of gas. In those days pursuit planes were limited to something like 25 minutes. We wound up with four B-17s out of the original thirty-six."

STRUGGLE FOR SURVIVAL

"The tail gunner came crawling out of the back," Smith continued. "He was all shot up real bad. Blood was coming out of his mouth. He had been shot on the left side of the back. I remembered very distinctly from my classes on how to handle a situation like this. I laid him down, gave him a couple of shots of morphine, which put him to sleep immediately. By doing this, he lived; I am very thankful for that.

"In the meantime, the plane started to go down and up. I went forward to find the pilot and copilot pretty well shot up. I put some tourniquets on them so they could maintain control of the plane. I then went back to put the control cables together as we had no tail control. I remember I repaired the six wires. I then threw all the ammunition out. I didn't receive burns during all this time because I had wrapped a scarf around my face and hands for protection.

"Somehow we got the plane back. The plane was riddled with about 3,500 bullet holes. It was all burned out in the center. There was nothing but the four main beams holding it together. Ten minutes after we landed, the plane collapsed." The Fortress never flew again. Secretary of War Henry Stimson, while crossing the Atlantic from Washington for a routine inspection, carried with him a Medal of Honor that he presented to Smith—after the trouble-prone sergeant was summoned from disciplinary kitchen police duty.

In those early days, it was always grim and gory in the cold high reaches where Americans were fighting a new kind of war. Captain Robert L. Campbell had already survived one shoot-down of a Flying Fortress when, on a mission to Hanover on July 28, 1943, Focke-Wulf Fw 190s swarmed down from twelve o'clock, high and blasted the nose of his bomber. Campbell was struck in the head and thrown forward, exerting a steel grip on the control yoke. His aircraft was the B-17F *Ruthie II*, of the 326th Bombardment Squadron, 92nd Bombardment Group. Campbell's engineer-gunner, Staff Sgt. Tyre C. Weaver, was hit by the same fusillade, which ripped off Weaver's left arm at the shoulder and sent him sprawling into the navigator's compartment, blood spouting from his open injury.

Ruthie II was now in the hands of copilot Flight Officer John C. "Red" Morgan, at age twenty-eight an oldster from Vernon, Texas, who had worked in the Fiji Islands in the 1930s and had been in the Royal Canadian

Air Force before joining the Army Air Forces. Unknown to Morgan—who initially had no intercom contact with *Ruthie II*'s crew—1st Lt. Keith J. Koske found that his morphine syringe didn't work and that not enough remained of Weaver's arm to permit a tourniquet. Koske placed Weaver's right fingers around the D-ring of his parachute and shoved him out of the lower-fuselage door in the nose. Weaver's parachute opened.

Morgan, with enormous difficulty, was able to loosen the dying pilot's grip on the yoke but not to dislodge Campbell from his seat. Morgan's own, right-side windshield was smashed, so he was flying partially blind. Morgan realized that the B-17 was still in formation and now on its bomb run. One hand on the yoke, the other on Campbell's pulse, Morgan used sheer physical strength to keep the bomber straight and level.

Ruthie II headed for home, four men in the rear fuselage unconscious because of damage to the oxygen system. Koske eventually pulled the pilot free, and Morgan shifted to the left seat, where his vision was better but still imperfect. At every point during this crisis—believing that the crewmen out back had jumped—Morgan had the option of saving himself by bailing out. Instead, he stayed at the controls and kept a hand on Campbell. To this day no one quite knows how he reached England or landed *Ruthie II*. As the bomber sputtered to a halt, the four men in back were stricken with frostbite, Campbell was dead, and Weaver was a prisoner in a German hospital. At his base in England, Morgan was awarded the Medal of Honor. He later was commissioned as a second lieutenant, but even receiving the nation's highest award for valor didn't mean that he'd finished fighting. No Flying Fortress crewmember had yet been to Berlin. Morgan didn't know it, but fate had decreed that he not finish his war without seeing the German capital.

THUNDERBOLT TRAINEE

Still in training, student pilot Grant Turley wrote that he'd "turned in the questionnaire on the P-47," had done a blindfolded cockpit check, and faced a demanding ground instructor who "asked me for everything—from gun switch to the oxygen flow indicator."

The next day, Turley wrote: "Checked out in a P-47 today. Gee, it was a thrill to open up 2,000 horses on a 13,000-pound crate. This is the day I have been dreaming about. The plane flies very smoothly. It is quite heavy but very responsive. I'm going to love it. It's a fairly simple plane to fly." Turley also wrote: "Landing a P-47 is easier than any of the trainers I have flown. It is just like climbing out of a Model T into a Cadillac."

While the young pilot was being introduced to his mount, the Eighth Air Force's VIII Fighter Command in England was struggling to give the P-47 enough range to accompany bombers to their targets. A couple of months earlier, this would have been easy because the bombers were not traveling far. But now the Flying Fortresses and Liberators of the Mighty Eighth were beginning to range farther into Hitler's Festung Europa, or Fortress Europe. As Roger A. Freeman wrote: "During 1943, much attention was paid to increasing the Thunderbolt's radius of action. While the under fuselage drop tank proved most successful, there was a limit to the size and thereby capacity due to limited ground clearance; P-47s operating from rough grass airfields could not use 108 gallon tanks for this reason."

In April 1943, VIII Fighter Command began flying P-47s with big, bulbous two hundred U.S.-gallon ferry tanks dangling from the fuselage centerline. The tanks were unpressurized, so they proved to be effective only at low altitudes. However, they could be carried half full, used during the long climb over the English Channel, and then dropped, adding 75 miles of radius. This method was awkward and apparently used only briefly. Moreover, carrying this type of center point drop tank on the outbound leg of an escort mission increased the reach of the P-47 only to 325 miles, which was nowhere near enough. The Luftwaffe readily understood when Jug escorts would have to turn back because of fuel restrictions and waited to intercept bombers just a few miles beyond the Thunderbolt's radius of action. The number of miles kept changing with the addition of larger tanks, but bombers kept traveling deeper into the Reich and no change to the Thunderbolt would enable it to keep up.

Eventually, underwing shackles brought to England from the United States permitted several options for external fuel tanks for the Jug. By February 1944, the Thunderbolt could carry a single 150-gallon belly tank or, to travel even farther, two 108-gallon underwing tanks, increasing the P-47's radius of action to between four hundred and five hundred miles. Thunderbolts could now reach Frankfurt or Hamburg (with difficulty) but not more distant targets, such as Munich, Prague, and Berlin. By mid-1944, a P-51D Mustang with two 108-gallon tanks could travel anywhere American bombers might go, not merely to Berlin but as far as Prague. The Mustang's range was the key as bombers kept going deeper and deeper into Nazi-occupied Europe.

Before the P-47 belatedly began accompanying them, bomber crews relied heavily on the twin-engined Lockheed P-38 Lightning. P-38s covered all or part of about a dozen missions before the Jugs appeared. "The P-38 pilots were very much aware that their primary duty was to protect the bombers," said B-17 pilot 1st Lt. David Shelhamer, while the notion of fighter escort was still being developed. Interviewed by Brian D. O'Neill, Shelhamer revealed a common prejudice in late 1942 and early 1943: "I'm prejudiced but I always thought that the P-47 pilots just loved to make pretty contrails about 5,000 feet above us while the Germans were shooting the living hell out of our formations. The P-38s came in quite close to us, and the moment they were aware of enemy activity, they were right on the Germans."

This was an enormous misperception to overcome. Many P-47 pilots believe they never did. But Maj. Gen. William E. Kepner, who replaced the unctuous Brig. Gen. Frank "Monk" Hunter as head of VIII Fighter Command on August 29, 1943, didn't share the prejudice. Kepner wrote: "If it can be said that the P-38s struck the Luftwaffe in its vitals and the P-51s gave the coup de grace, it was the Thunderbolt that broke its back."

Lying in wait for the growing American air armada in East Anglia was a German fighter force that in 1942 and 1943 was experienced, robust, and aggressive—German officers constantly refreshing their tactics to defeat Allied fighters and attack four-engined bombers. In large measure, the air campaign was aimed at neutralizing the Luftwaffe fighter force. Early in the campaign, the Germans had the top hand. As the war progressed, the Allies overcame their air defenses not by shooting down their aircraft or bombing their production plants—although both actions inflicted horrendous harm—but by killing their pilots. As the air campaign in Europe progressed, the Luftwaffe would continue to have plenty of fighter planes, but its leadership, talent, and experience would become casualties of war.

WAR MACHINES OF THE AIR

Confronting the Americans were twin-engined, rocket-armed Messerschmitt Bf 110 and Me 210 fighters, joined later in the war by the Me 410 Hornisse, or Hornet—all of which would ultimately be defeated by single-engined Allied fighters. Later in the war, the jet-propelled

Messerschmitt Me 262 joined the mix. But in the early months of the campaign, the same months when only the P-38 Lightning and P-47 Thunderbolt were available as escorts, the German fighter force relied most heavily on its two iconic, single-engine fighters.

The Messerschmitt Bf 109 was a nimble, versatile, numerous, and reliable high-altitude fighter of light construction that crumpled easily when sustaining battle damage. It was already out of date, eclipsed by newer and better fighters in all air forces, including Germany's, but it remained the mount of most Luftwaffe aces, remained in production, and was a potent adversary until the final day of the war. The Bf 109G, or "Gustav" version, confronting the Eighth Air Force in 1943 was powered by a 1,475-horsepower DB 605A inverted V-12 liquid-cooled inline engine and armed with four nose- and wing-mounted machine guns and a hub-mounted cannon. A German pilot's manual listed a top speed of 579 kilometers per hour (360 miles per hour), although the speeds of all fighters varied according to weight, temperature, payload, and other factors.

The Focke-Wulf Fw 190 Wurger (Butcher Bird) was powered by a 1,700-horsepower BMW 801D fourteen-cylinder radial engine that initially caused overheating problems, high cockpit temperatures, and leaking gasses in the cockpit. The Focke Wulf had the fastest rate of roll of any fighter and featured an automatic system that operated the manifold pressure, revolutions per minute, and fuel mixture, relieving the pilot of these duties. The Butcher Bird lacked the leading edge automatic slats, which sometimes caused gun-laying accuracy in the Bf 109, but it had better visibility and had an unusually wide track main landing gear for easier takeoffs, landings, and ground handling. It was the only World War II fighter that had electrically operated flaps and landing gear. The Fw 190 had only a mediocre rate of climb and sometimes could not get to altitude quickly enough to be effective against American bombers.

The other escort fighter, the twin engine P-38H Lightning, was fast and maneuverable and had substantial reach with internal fuel and two external tanks—about 450 miles, or enough to cover many targets inside Germany. But most P-38s were diverted to North Africa early in the daylight bombing campaign. Although it performed brilliantly in the Mediterranean and Pacific, the Lightning never established superiority over German single-engine fighters.

In freezing-cold European skies, the P-38's two 1,600-horsepower Allison V-1710-111/113 inline piston engines proved unreliable at high altitudes, due to limitations of the leading-edge intercoolers, which raised the temperature of the compressed air from the supercharger entering the carburetor. This meant that when the P-38s were cruising and then had to rapidly apply full combat power, the power surge could cause seizures, thrown connecting rods, and even explosions. On one of their first deep penetration missions, fully a quarter of P-38s escorting a formation of bombers had to turn back with engine problems.

Though the problem was hardly unique to the P-38, the Lightning's cockpit heater performed so poorly that pilots could become incapacitated from the cold. The theme is a recurrent one in every part of the war in Europe: The cold was always an enemy.

By April 1943, three VIII Fighter Command combat groups were flying P-47 Thunderbolts to support Eighth Air Force bombers. The 56th Fighter Group, led by Col. Hubert "Hub" Zemke, flew the Jug along with the 4th and 78th Fighter Groups. The first Thunderbolt air-to-air engagement took place on April 15, 1943, when Maj. Don Blakeslee of the 4th Fighter Group was credited with downing a German aircraft.

It was not until August 17, 1943, that P-47s performed their first large-scale escort mission, providing B-17s with penetration and withdrawal support of the Schweinfurt-Regensburg mission and claiming nineteen kills against three losses. Soon, the P-47 would foster a generation of storied aces, such as Robert Johnson and Francis Gabreski, plus some air aces—including Turley—who never became so famous. Yet while the sight of a P-47 comforted most bomber crewmembers, the crewmembers were not seeing the Thunderbolt when they went deep.

The P-47-equipped 78th Fighter Group, the least known of the three P-47 Thunderbolt outfits in England, went into battle with high morale but lost two commanders in short order—Col. Arman D. Peterson, shot down and killed in a furious battle with Focke-Wulf Fw 190s, and Lt. Col. Melvin McNickle, shot down and captured.

P-47 PROGRESS

P-47s began carrying early, unpressurized drop tanks that—even though jettisoned before reaching the enemy coast—enabled them to fly right into

Germany. That day, the group was escorting bombers returning from Kassel and flew most of the way to the bombers' target. P-47 pilots of the 78th group scored several aerial victories. Captain Charles P. London toted up his fourth and fifth kills, a Messerschmitt Bf 109 and a Focke-Wulf Fw 190, to become the first American ace in the European theater of war. After the loss of McNickle, Lt. Col. James J. Stone became the 78th commander. He was a superb leader but never became a legend like Zemke of the 56th group or Blakeslee of the 4th.

For bomber crews, the August 17, 1943, Schweinfurt-Regensburg mission—on the first anniversary of the first, puny bombing mission dispatched by the Eighth Air Force—was a horror. Two hundred thirty bombers launched against Schweinfurt and another 146 against aircraft factories in Regensburg. Fully 60 were lost before returning to base, and another 87 had to be scrapped due to irreparable damage.

It was over Regensburg that supremely experienced German pilots attacked, slashed through the bomber formations from the front, and shot down twenty-four Flying Fortresses. German fighters intercepted many of the bombers using the infamous head-on firing pass from twelve o'clock, high, aiming to kill the B-17 pilots and, too often, succeeding. Gun camera film from the German side portrays the majesty of a Flying Fortress under attack, but it also depicts B-17s catching fire, breaking up, sometimes tumbling end-over-end, the crewmembers inside often pinned by gravity forces and sometimes burned by flash fires. In addition to the shootdowns, the Luftwaffe defenders damaged fifty more bombers during the first stage of the day's fight over Regensburg. At this stage of the war, Germany had plenty of battle-seasoned pilots, the Americans were still feeling their way, and the battle was one-sided. Despite all the years the Americans had spent forging their daylight, precision-bombing doctrine, the Germans were winning a mighty battle high in the freezing sky and seemed closer to winning the campaign. Small wonder that some Luftwaffe pilots talked of halting the American bomber offensive in its tracks. Having begun their air campaign so recently with such spirit and optimism, the Americans were being defeated.

Schweinfurt-Regensburg was viewed as a disaster, even a debacle, but unknown to the Americans, the Regensburg portion of the air attack destroyed most of the manufacturing jigs for a new German aircraft, the

Messerschmitt Me 262 jet fighter. Anything that delayed the German jets was a huge plus for the Allies. The results at Regensburg were better than just anything: The Luftwaffe was forced to disperse Me 262 production into small, crude factories hidden in deep forests. This imposed a requirement to transport assembled components for final assembly, and chaos in the German transportation network brought on by Allied bombing significantly delayed completion of the first jets.

In the second phase of Schweinfurt-Regensburg, 183 Flying Fortresses attacked Schweinfurt's ball-bearing plants. The idea was a good one—unlike submarine pens, ball-bearing factories were vulnerable and losing them would cramp the Reich's war effort. But the execution was flawed. Again, Messerschmitts and Focke-Wulfs ripped into the bomber formations. The Luftwaffe extracted a horrendous toll—36 Flying Fortresses shot down, including two that ditched in the frigid North Sea. Total B-17 losses at Schweinfurt-Regensburg were 60 aircraft lost, 4 damaged beyond repair and 168 damaged.

U.S. planners rated Schweinfurt-Regensburg a disaster. There can be no other interpretation. It was a sign that the entire plan for bombing Germany might be a prescription for failure. This first of two disastrous missions to Schweinfurt removed any doubt that bombers needed help protecting themselves and that some way would have to be found to extend fighter cover all the way to the target. Schweinfurt-Regensburg was the best evidence that the Americans were struggling.

Still, the Americans were inflicting damage to a vital sector of Reich industry and their next step must have surprised the Germans.

They backed off.

RETHINKING THE AIR CAMPAIGN

Having attacked the center of the ball-bearing industry in force, they hesitated to return. LeMay biographer Warren Kozak wrote:

> [T]he Allies did not understand the impact of the mission on the other side, as ball bearing production dropped by 38 percent after the raid. Albert Speer said that Germany 'barely escaped a catastrophic blow' and that the Allies were right to take aim at the ball bearing plants. But their crucial mistake was in spreading out their forces and not concentrating

> on Schweinfurt. It was not just the Allies who did not understand the impact of these attacks. When Speer spoke to Hitler after the attack on Schweinfurt, the German leader was in great spirits because 'the countryside was strewn with downed American bombers.' Although true, every plant in Schweinfurt had been hit and was on fire. 'But what really saved us was the fact that from this time on, the enemy, to our astonishment, once again ceased his attacks on the ball bearing industry,' Speer later revealed.

Schweinfurt-Regensburg was a staggering blow to the Eighth Air Force. Bomber crews flew only six missions in the nineteen days that followed. The next mission to Germany on September 6, 1944, was a catastrophic foray to Stuttgart, in which forty-five heavy bombers were shot down and ten more were written off.

The persisting problem was that the P-47 Thunderbolt remained the best escort fighter the Americans had, and for all its qualities it wasn't good enough. During the Schweinfurt-Regensburg disaster, amid fierce battles over Germany, Belgium, and the Netherlands, the three Thunderbolt groups claimed nineteen German aircraft shot down, including sixteen by Zemke's 56th Fighter Group. It was a good showing, but it was a poor tradeoff for the loss of so many bombers. The Thunderbolts didn't have the reach to get anywhere near Stuttgart three weeks later.

On September 13, 1943, pilot Turley arrived at Duxford, England, to become part of the 82nd Fighter Squadron, 78th Fighter Group. Turley now had about 140 flying hours in the P-47. He flew his first routine mission on October 9.

The following day, a bomber pilot who would later distinguish himself over Berlin earned the first of two Silver Star awards that preceded his moment of destiny over the German capital. First Lieutenant Robert "Rosie" Rosenthal was credited with "conspicuous gallantry in action against the enemy" as pilot of a B-17 Flying Fortress of the 418th Bombardment, 100th Bombardment Group, the unit to which he would be inextricably linked until war's end. On a bombing mission over Germany, Rosenthal was short of the target when one engine of his aircraft was knocked out and the bomber sustained other serious damage sustained "during vicious assaults by enemy fighters." Although subjected to constant attack and intense antiaircraft fire, Rosenthal continued on to the target and bombed it. When unable to remain with the formation on leaving the target area, his aircraft became the object of concentrated attacks by German fighters. Another engine was knocked out, the oxygen system almost completely destroyed, the wing badly damaged, and two gunners seriously wounded. "Maneuvering his crippled aircraft with great skill," read the citation for his award, Rosenthal fought his way back to England and landed. It was one of several times Rosenthal would face high risk and emerge intact.

Thunderbolt pilot Grant Turley was among thousands of Americans for whom the target on October 14 was one of the most dreaded of the war—Schweinfurt. Members of Turley's family believe he was unaware that a plant at Schweinfurt manufactured half the ball bearings for the German war machine.

Still unable to accompany the bombers all the way to their target, Turley wrote: "Had a long 'Fort' raid today, clear across Germany. Our group of 47s was supposed to give withdrawal support—meeting the bombers about 70 miles on the other side of Paris." But the 78th Fighter Group's portion of the mission was cancelled after Turley and his fellow pilots had warmed up and taxied out. "Orders came through to cut off the engines but remain in our planes," Turley wrote. "We waited for 45 minutes this way and then were told to taxi back to the dispersal area and get out of our planes." Though his part of the mission was "scrubbed due to bad weather," Turley wrote that Messerschmitt Bf 110Gs and Me 210s intercepted the unescorted bombers firing air-to-air rockets and "the Flying Fortress crews suffered terribly."

Turley may not have known the details, but the German twin-engined fighters each had four underwing tubes firing spin-stabilized 248-pound Wurfgranate 210mm mortar rockets. This standoff method of air defense was decimating U.S. bomber formations. Twin-engined Messerschmitts could fire the rockets from almost a mile away, far beyond the reach of the bombers' machine guns. If a rocket detonated within fifty feet of a bomber, it was likely to go down. In a tight formation, a bomber thrown out of control by a rocket blast could plow through several more bombers before falling from the sky. The Achilles' heel of the rocket-launching scheme was the launch platform. If the right fighter could be found to go up against them while far from home in hostile sky, the twin-engined Messerschmitts would be unable to continue using their rockets to pick off bombers like ducks in a shooting gallery.

Turley was describing a mortar rocket attack introduced on a large scale during the second big mission to Schweinfurt, the war's most infamous target and a center for Germany's ball-bearing industry. On the second mission on October 14, "Black Thursday," 196 Thunderbolts from other fighter groups, although not Turley's, got into the air—but most were unable to find the bombers they were supposed to escort partway. The entire 4th Fighter Group, still equipped with P-47s then, had to be recalled after going astray in heavy clouds. The 352nd Fighter Group attached itself to a segment of the bomber stream that eventually abandoned the mission. Of the 291 bombers sent on the mission, 77 were lost. Despite the availability of P-38s and P-47s in vast numbers, despite the firepower of the bombers' own guns when they clung together in tight, combat-box formations, and despite the growing size and reach of the bomber force, German defenses were still more formidable than the American attackers.

It was a time of bad news and great danger for bomber crews. A study showed that a typical bomber crew stood only a fifty-fifty chance of completing the required combat tour of twenty-five missions. While the ink was still wet on the study, the required total was raised to thirty. It was a time of heavy casualties and—for some—low morale.

But there was good news. The bombing campaign against the Third Reich was becoming serious. An October 20, 1943, mission to attack aircraft-industry targets at Duren became a fiasco when 212 bombers were dispatched but only 86 reached the target, dropping 209 tons of bombs over the city. Still, even the ability to launch a couple of hundred bombers was a giant step forward. And by October, a second front was opened in the great air war when the Fifteenth Air Force in Italy began dispatching B-17s and B-24s in significant numbers against Reich targets.

NEW BOMBER

On June 26, 1943, at Seattle, Boeing had completed the first flight of a new bomber, the B-29 Superfortress. A four-engine, midwing, "very heavy" bomber with a crew of ten, the B-29 was powered by proven 2,200-horsepower Pratt & Whitney R-3350 Duplex Cyclone eighteen-cylinder radial pistol engines. Its size was demonstrated with a 141 foot, 3 inch wingspan and a maximum takeoff weight of 135,000 pounds, although crews would later fly it at 140,000. Crewmembers traversing the fuselage from nose to tail in the B-29 used a "personnel tunnel" above the bomb bay. The B-29 was pressurized and used remote-controlled guns to defend itself. It could carry about half again as many bombs as a B-17 Flying Fortress and travel about twenty percent farther. In short, it was the new bomber the Eighth Air Force needed to press the war against the Third Reich.

It never happened. Deliveries to stateside units began before some of the new bomber's internal systems were fully integrated. The B-29 would, however, serve in the Far East in the last year and a half of the war, culminationg with the dropping of the atomic bmbs that ended the war with Japan.

GROWING BOMBER FORCE

After "Black Thursday," the Eighth Air Force temporarily halted deep penetrations of German airspace and began agonizing over, and analyzing, the role of the escort fighter. Daylight missions into Germany were, for the time being, called off. But everyone knew it was temporary. Everyone knew the bombers would eventually be traveling in vast numbers across the German border.

Turley wrote in his diary that he flew his first escort mission on October 24, 1943, briefly glimpsing a gaggle of Bf 109s and logging 4.0 eventless flight hours. In fact, no bombers were launched that day; Thunderbolts flew a fighter sweep. VIII Fighter Command had changed leaders, Hunter sent packing to a meaningless assignment in the United States and replaced by Kepner. Hunter's policy of conducting fighter sweeps served little purpose, but Kepner and his bosses were only slowly beginning to change things. The Eighth Air Force was still developing tactics, and for now Hunter's fighter sweeps were still going on.

"It was not Hunter's fault that he had been equipped with short-range [P-47s]," wrote Eric Hammel, exaggerating the limit of the Thunderbolt's reach. "The fault he exhibited was a lack of imagination and some native inability to surround himself with men who could imagine a way out of the tactical stalemate in which VIII Fighter Command remained when it [had] three P-47 groups in hand." Hammel wrote that acquisition of jettisonable auxiliary fuel tanks remained "fairly low on VIII Fighter Command's to-do list."

None of that could be blamed on Kepner, born in 1893 and now approaching fifty, an extraordinary figure who had been a Marine, cavalryman, infantryman, and balloonist before flying fighters on the eve of war. Kepner's moustache was less impressive than Hunter's gilded-age version, but he was, as Hammel described him, sanguinary—eager for bloodshed. Kepner apparently lacked the right chemistry with Eighth Air Force boss Eaker, but that would change within a couple of short months when Eaker, too, would be gone.

October and November 1943 marked a time of optimism for the Americans and their unprecedented air campaign. Cracks were beginning to show in Third Reich defenses, and more bombers were getting through—just as the brass had said, all along, they would. The Luftwaffe could mount a formidable defense against combat boxes of Flying Fortresses and Liberators, but it could no longer counter both the Eighth and Fifteenth Air Forces, which were hitting from two directions. It was not unusual, now, for as many as five hundred heavy bombers to arrive over the Third Reich at once, and the Germans had to pick and choose where and when to mount a defense. The Eighth Air Force and its subordinate VIII Bomber Command and VIII Fighter Command were continuing to grow. On November 4, 1943, the ground echelon of the 354th Fighter Group arrived in England, not yet accompanied by its aircraft but soon to be the first fighter group in Europe to operate the new, long-range P-51B Mustangs. The 354th was assigned to IX Fighter Command but was tapped to fly escort. More P-47 and P-51 fighter groups arrived before the end of November.

The bomber war continued. A bloody mission to Bremen on December 20, 1943, was traumatic for radio operator Tech. Sgt. Forrest Lee "Woody" Vosler of the 385th Bombardment Squadron, 303rd Bombardment Group, and for one of the principal figures in this narrative, then-Capt. Marvin D. Lord of the 532nd Bombardment Squadron, 381st Bombardment Group. The impish, happy-go-lucky, and visibly youthful Lord had written home just weeks earlier that he was "acting as squadron commander for about 10 days as [the regular squadron commander] has been in the hospital and at the rest home. It sure is a job to keep a man busy."

On that day, according to historian Roger Freeman, the Eighth Air Force dispatched 546 bombers—419 B-17s and 127 B-24s—and 491 fighters—26 P-38 Lightnings, 418 P-47s, and 47 of the newly arrived P-51

Mustangs—against Bremen. It was a tragic day for many, including the crew of a B-17 that collided with a German fighter and the crew of a B-24 that collided with a P-47.

The German response was ferocious. As historian Barrett Tillman wrote: "The Luftwaffe was up in strength. Heavy bombers bound for Bremen were intercepted by German single- and twin-engine fighters, which barged through escorting P-38s and P-51s to fire cannon shells and aerial rockets into the Fortresses and Liberators. The defenders knocked down twenty-seven bombers, but nearly all were victims of Messerschmitts and Focke-Wulfs since the Eighth Air Force had chosen this mission to introduce 'window,' aluminum strips cut to match enemy fire-control radars. It was good timing as the Jagflieger [German fighters] were trouble enough."

Aboard a Fortress called the *Jersey Bounce Jr.*, "Woody" Vosler was seriously injured in both legs when gunfire from a German fighter exploded in his radio compartment. Bleeding and in danger of losing consciousness, Vosler remained at his machine gun and continued firing as new waves of German fighters kept swarming in. When a second shell from a German fighter exploded, smashing Vosler's radio and spraying him with metal fragments, he refused to quit fighting. Ting fragments of metal penetrated his eyes and blood poured down his face. When a crewmate offered medical aid, Vosler pushed him off and kept shooting.

During a brief respite from fighter attacks, when he should have been tending to his wounds, Vosler worked almost entirely by feel and reconstructed his radio. He was able to transmit *Jersey Bounce Jr.*'s position to the rest of the bomber force. Vosler—all but totally blind—transmitted an emergency message and went to the aid of another wounded crewmember. Vosler was barely alive when rescued and spent months recovering, and regaining his eyesight, before receiving the Medal of Honor personally from President Franklin D. Roosevelt.

That same battle, that same day, was critical for one of the key bomber pilots in this narrative. Captain Marvin D. Lord had been a year ahead of P-47 Thunderbolt pilot Grant Turley in his military career, having had been in the cavalry before the war. Now, Lord had big-time responsibilities. A future group leader himself, today Lord was pilot for the group leader of his mission when he approached his bomb run on Bremen.

It was the first tour of duty in B-17s for Lord, who would become a lieutenant colonel before journeying to Berlin more than a year later. His ride to

Bremen was a Fort named *Big Time Operator II*. Gathering experience that would help him later when it became his time to lead a bomb group, Lord was flying as pilot for Lt. Col Conway S. Hall of the 381st Bombardment Group. Lord would become group leader on a mission one day, but today that was Hall's job.

The formation of twenty-seven Forts of the 381st encountered a large amount of flak. "As a result of a most unusual event that took place en route to the target," read an official document—without further explanation—"his group, alone and unsupported, continued on to the assigned target . . . Lord maintained a tight defensive formation and fought his way through viciously attacking enemy fighters. In spite of intense concentrations of antiaircraft fire, he made an exceptionally long bombing run and thus insured accurate hits upon an installation of great importance to the enemy." Lord's task was complicated by the fact that bombardier 2nd Lt. Tom Hester was severely wounded. This quote is from the citation for which Lord was awarded the Silver Star, the third highest U.S. award for valor. All these years later, the wording of the document raises a question. Every other record of this very difficult Bremen mission says that no German fighters attacked the 381st group that day. Did the awards committee mean to write that Lord fought his way through vicious flak rather than vicious fighters? All these years later, it is impossible to know.

Lord was now officially a hero. And all recognized Bremen as a difficult target. But Lord's destiny lay ahead—over Berlin.

Thunderbolt pilot Grant Turley's family sent him a clipping from *Life* magazine that reported: "P-47s can protect Flying Fortress bombers even on round-trip raids of 800 miles into German territory" but not mentioning that Berlin would require a 1,150-mile round trip. Accumulating combat hours without having yet fired his guns in anger, Turley wrote home on December 21, 1943: "Our main job is escorting B-17s and B-24s. We go in at about 30,000 feet zigzagging over the bombers and keeping enemy fighters away. My main job right now is to fly formation and keep my eyes open." Turley wrote that he expected to be promoted to first lieutenant in three months' time.

He was right but not in the way he thought. Within three months Turley would be a part of something that hadn't happened yet—a mission to Berlin, but he would never pin on a set of silver first lieutenant's bars.

CHAPTER FIVE

Way Up

Mission to Berlin
February 3, 1945— 8:30 a.m. to 9:40 a.m.

ONCE THEIR WHEELS left the ground and their bomber began to climb into the cold English morning, the first challenge for a Flying Fortress crew was the hardest.

In fact, this was the moment many crewmembers considered the most dangerous, involving even greater peril than confronting flak and fighters over the Third Reich: The bombers would have to climb through low-hanging fog and cloud cover and assemble into formation. If it was done correctly, each of the twenty-six bombardment groups heading for Berlin would be lined up in its designated order, each with a lead aircraft and a group air commander up front.

A few days earlier, on a mission expected to be far easier than Berlin, two Flying Fortresses collided after one had just left the runway and the second had followed it a few seconds too soon. Metal fragments, fiery debris, and pieces of human beings were hurled in all directions as two B-17s were destroyed and eighteen men died, all in an instant, far from enemy territory.

"We took off one at a time, a minute or two apart," remembered 1st Lt. Don Maier. "Once in the air, we headed for a radio beacon that was located on the British coast.

"The purpose of aiming for a radio beacon was in case there were clouds"—as there were, in East Anglia, on this day—"and we couldn't see the other aircraft. We would put the radio beacon to our left and begin circling and climbing at the same time. The aircraft in front of us was two miles ahead of us and above us, so we weren't in danger of colliding with him. The first beacon is the tool that led us to where we created our formation."

In some bombardment groups, tail gunners carried a red strobe light that could be adjusted to blink and to be seen from a considerable distance. Aboard *Blue Grass Girl* of the 486th Bombardment Group, tail gunner Staff Sgt. Frank T. Chrastka had such a light and held it close to the glass plate in his gun position. "This was an extra measure for safety," said Chrastka's best friend, Tech. Sgt. Daniel C. "Clint" Pentz, who was flying with a different crew today. "The fear of a midair collision while forming for a mission was a very real thing and we needed any tool that would help prevent it. A blinking light from a tail gunner may have prevented a midair disaster more than once during those perilous initial moments."

Said Maier: "The second navigation beacon let us go out over the Channel two to three minutes apart. At that point, we were above the clouds and could see the formations ahead of us. After we made the turn out over the Channel, we could see all the formations behind us."

Today, it was a spectacle.

In formation, en route, crossing the North Sea and approaching the enemy coast, thousands of American bomber crewmembers completed final preparations and looked in awe at the aerial armada around them. *It was 8:30 a.m. British Summer Time on February 3, 1945.*

In each of the three air divisions, the twenty-six bomb groups, the dozens of squadrons, the experience was similar.

"We in the 490th Bombardment Group were somewhere in that massive bomber stream," said Staff Sgt. Frank McKinley. "The advantage of my top turret position was the ability to observe 360 degrees of sky. On this day, as far as I could see were our bombers and fighters in front of us and to the rear. It was an excellent example of the 'Mighty' Eighth."

Colonel Lewis E. Lyle, commander of the 379th Bombardment Group, was the Eighth Air Force's overall air commander for the mission aboard an unnamed Fortress. Lyle had completed twenty-five combat missions in an earlier tour two years ago and need not have volunteered to return to a combat cockpit. He would eventually complete seventy-six missions and become one of the legends of the Flying Fortress saga, along with other air commanders including Curtis E. LeMay, Robert "Rosie" Rosenthal, Harris E. Rogner, James A. Smyrl, Immanuel L. "Manny" Klette, and Marvin D. Lord. For now, however, Lyle paid scrupulous attention to the formation keeping of the B-17 pilots around him, studied the European expanse ahead, and wondered how soon the shooting would start.

One of the few people to talk on the radio in a mostly radio-silent bomber stream, Lyle sought an updated weather report. "The weather was 10/10ths cloud cover from a point just after the continental coast until approximately at the IP [the initial point]," Lyle wrote later. "I contacted the scouting force" which consisted of Mosquito aircraft ahead of the bomber stream. After initially reporting otherwise, they said the target was open "and would stay open until we got there."

In his unnamed Fortress, 91st Bombardment Group air commander Lt. Col. Marvin D. Lord was comfortable, even seemingly happy, occupying the copilot's seat beside 1st Lt. Frank L. Adams. If Lord's behavior was typical, he was probably chatting up the mission, saying positive things, reassuring himself and those around them that they would see the sunset on this day. Lord was also paying rigorous attention to the location of every bomber in his group's formation. He was expected make certain everyone was in the right place.

Lord wrote in a letter home: "There is just so much work to be done over here and the sooner we get it done the better it will be."

"And," Lord wrote, "I sort of like these raids"—there it was, the word Curtis LeMay despised for giant air battles. "'Course, I get scared lots of times but it gives you a feeling of confidence to look out and see all those other Forts plowing along. And Germany is such a beautiful country—from five miles up! You'd never think the people there are such big fools as they are.

"They fight like heck," Lord added, "but that hasn't stopped us yet. Some of the Jerries have come whizzing by so close we could see them in their cockpits and I'll bet they could read the name on our ship. I'd like to meet some of those German boys after the war 'cause some of them are good pilots . . . "

BALL TURRET GUNNER

Not every man in the formation was concerned with the strategic big picture. Aboard *Blue Grass Girl* piloted by 1st Lt. Louis K. Cloud, the dour and diminutive ball turret gunner, Staff Sgt. Johnnie Jones, bid a temporary "so long" to tail gunner Chrastka and set forth to position himself in the loneliest spot on the airplane. Jones had plenty of experience with this—today was his thirty-fifth mission, remember—but there was always something unnatural about squeezing into an inverted dome on the bottom of a bomber.

"Inside the ball there was something like a curved chair in which you sat in a normal position when the guns were pointed downward," said another ball turret gunner who sometimes flew with Jones and Chrastka. "But you would lie on your back when the guns were pointed horizontally. Most of the time the guns were more or less horizontal, and I have stayed in the ball for as long as nine hours at a time. One day my back was almost frozen, and it has hurt ever since.

"The Sperry ball was electrically operated and moved by a hydraulic system through controls located overhead, somewhat like joysticks. You looked through the gunsight and round window located on the front of the ball. The gunsight had cross hairs—one horizontal and two vertical. As a fighter flew toward you, it would appear larger in your gunsight, and to feed this information to your so-called computer, you would let up or raise your left foot and attempt to keep the vertical cross hairs at the wingtips of the approaching fighter.

"Yes," said the ball turret gunner, "this was difficult to do correctly while moving the hand controls to follow the Jerry, especially when you saw his guns fire as red flashed across the leading edge of his wing. The tip of your right toe was used to control the mike switch, and when all hell broke loose you were expected to identify the fighter. Was it a Bf 109 or a P-51? An Fw 190 or a P-47? Set its wingspan, call out, 'Fighters at nine o'clock, low!' after pushing your mike button, keep the bastard centered on the cross hairs by moving your left foot and hand controls and firing the twin fifties with your thumb!"

For the time being, in a bomber formation approaching German defenses, Jones could only wait and worry. "When there was nothing else to do, you checked our oxygen supply, set the thermostat for the electrically heated suit, pointed your guns down, and opened your hatch. It was very cold and humidity went up because of sweat. Ice formed within the oxygen mask, requiring you to squeeze the mask to crack the ice," he said.

"LITTLE FRIENDS"

Major Paul A. Conger, commander of the group's 63rd Fighter Squadron and today leading the 56th Fighter Group, kept his eyes on the fuel mixture and temperature of the round, fat R-2800 engine pulling his P-47 Thunderbolt through the sky. Of 948 fighters launched by the Eighth Air Force, just 44 of them were Thunderbolts, and today, with new drop tanks and fuel-saving airmanship techniques, they fully expected to see the rooftops of Berlin—the first time Thunderbolts had done so. Among the pilots was 1st Lt. David M. Magel. It is questionable whether crewmembers in the bomber stream ever got more than a quick glance at Conger, Magel, and the other Thunderbolt pilots. They were out in front, a kind of bumper guard for the trundling bomber stream. They were going to be the first American fighters to encounter German aircraft today, but it would happen far out of sight of the bomber crews.

Ahead of, above, and around the bomber formation, slicing neatly through the air, were the "little friends"—the P-51 Mustang escort fighters that had entered the fight the previous year, taking the job over from P-38 Lightnings and from all but one combat group of P-47 Thunderbolts. A few miles inside the Dutch coast, Mustang pilots saw no sign of the Messerschmitt Bf 109s and Focke-Wulf Fw 190s they'd expected to rise in defense of the Reich. There were not yet any dogfights, guns rattling, and fighters tumbling in pieces from the sky. Lt. Col. Elwyn Guido Righetti—"Eager El," they called him—of the 55th Fighter Group, using the call sign Tudor Leader, led one of the Mustang formations. Righetti strung his Mustangs out in front of the Fortresses, stayed within eyesight of the bomber stream for a short time, and then banked and headed away. Just as the Eighth Air Force wanted them to do, the "little friends" were going off on their own, roaming ahead of, and to the side of, the bomber stream. Barely inside Holland after making landfall from the sea, one of Righetti's pilots had a brief encounter with a pair of Messerschmitts. It lasted only seconds. No threat to the bombers and not ready to fight 904 Mustangs and 44 P-47 Thunderbolts, the Messerschmitts simply disappeared as their inexperienced pilots made tracks. There was going to be a fight, an odd one of sorts, but it was not ready to happen yet.

THE FLIGHT DECK

Aboard *Purty Chili* of the 34th Bombardment Group, 1st Lts. Dean Hansen and Robert Des Lauriers piloted the aircraft. "Formation flying in four-engine airplanes presents greater problems than formation flying in smaller aircraft," the pilot training manual told them. "The problems increase in almost direct proportion to the airplane's size and weight. In the B-17, relatively slower response to power and control changes requires a much higher degree of anticipation on the part of the pilot." With help from engineer-gunner Staff Sgt. John Green, the two pilots monitored engine performance, eyed the other Fortresses around them, peered ahead for the unexpected in terms of weather, flak, fighters, or the terrifying prospect that one of their squadron mates might become disoriented or suffer a mechanical glitch, lose control, and come careening in front of them. A Fortress was a very large and very heavy object moving at a considerable speed, and only one could occupy a particular spot in the sky.

Purty Chili's four 1,200-horsepower Wright R-1820-97 Cyclone nine-cylinder, air-cooled radial engines were in cruise mode, each turning a three-bladed Hamilton Standard propeller 11 feet, 7 inches in diameter. The aircraft had a wingspan of 103 feet, 9 3/8 inches, which was about 25 percent greater than its length. Like the other Fortresses in the bomber stream, Hansen's Fortress was gradually burning off its 2,780 U.S. gallon fuel capacity while traversing the North Sea at about 25,000 feet.

Hansen and Des Lauriers sat side-by-side, with Green looking over their shoulders much of the time. The pilot and copilot were the same rank, spoke amenably to each other, and were even similar in appearance—although Hansen, at twenty-six fully five years older than Des Lauriers, was to a significant degree the shorter of the two. Hansen had slightly more chiseled features; Des Lauriers was a little more round-faced. "He was from Minnesota," Des Lauriers said later. "He was very quiet, very calm." They got along well, in and out of the flight deck of *Purty Chili*, but there was nothing buddy-buddy about the two men. Hansen, pleasant yet authoritative, was in charge. Hansen was in charge not merely of the flight deck but of all nine men aboard this heavy bomber trundling relentlessly eastward. "I respected his authority," Des Lauriers said.

The pilots had to pay constant attention to cylinder head temperatures, the position of cowl flaps, oil temperatures, carburetor air temperature, and a range of other things. When a Fortress was performing smoothly, it was like a well-oiled machine, but if anything went wrong, it could become a thirty-ton missile in motion, propelled by enormous inertia and capable of creating more trouble than a crew could handle. Hansen took a cautious approach to keeping the Fortress where it was supposed to be. "His formation was looser," Des Lauriers said. "I was friskier in flying formation. I tucked it in tighter."

For the pilots to get where they were, they'd had to prove themselves better than a lot of men who didn't make it. Many would-be pilots flunked out in flight school. Some simply couldn't grasp the basics of handling a flying object in a three-dimensional arena. Those who graduated pilot training and began as flight officers or second lieutenants went from flight school to a formal training course for their aircraft. Most Fortress pilots underwent a ten-week transition course before being assigned to a bombardment group. After that, it was on-the-job training with the more experienced taking the lead. Once airmanship skills were adequate, the next challenge in a pilot's life was to be prepared to fight.

The men knew that if they came under frontal attack from fighters, their armored seats would not protect them from cannon shells pouring through the windshield. Hansen and Des Lauriers had flak vests and helmets at the ready but knew basically that because they faced forward, unarmed, they were vulnerable.

The crew of *Purty Chili* was fortunate: The men liked and admired Hansen. They liked each other, for the most part. They performed well as a team. It usually worked that way on a Fortress crew because men were forced to cooperate, but there was the occasional dysfunctional crew where leadership was lacking, coordination was a little off-key, and morale wasn't where it should have been. A pilot like the fictional character Capt. Buzz Rickson of John Hersey's novel *The War Lover*—Steve McQueen, in the film version—sometimes made it through the personnel system to take undue risks, act too much as the lone wolf, and revel in the fighting and destruction. But those who loved war were usually weeded out early, and there was no one aboard Hansen's *Purty Chili* who had any such proclivities.

If Hansen was indisputably, although quietly, in charge of *Purty Chili*'s crew, copilot Des Lauriers was in every way just as essential in keeping the bomber boring toward its target. "No one has ever doubted the need for a copilot in the B-17," said one of Des Lauriers's fellow right-seaters. "The strength of one man is not enough to control a Fortress during difficult formation flying, let alone in combat."

In the book *B-17 Combat Missions*, Martin Bowman quotes 2nd Lt. Robert "Bob" McCallum on the function of the copilot. "A pilot and co-pilot pal around together a lot," said McCallum—although this was less true of Hansen and Des Lauriers than of many. "They're usually closer than anybody else in the crew. They split up the flying time, about every fifteen minutes, switching generally every time the big hand on the clock hits 12, 3, 6, and 9. The big difference between the two jobs is the pilot has to decide what to do when you get in trouble."

On *Purty Chili*'s flight deck, engineer-gunner Green was the old man among the men on the flight deck, now thirty-three. "Our engineer loved to have a drink at night so we sometimes had to sober him up," said Des Lauriers. "[Green] was an Irishman and Oklahoma boy whose birthplace was Boggy Depot, Oklahoma."

Said a family member: "He was about five-eight, very stocky, with black wavy hair and green eyes. He had a wife and a daughter. He was an Irishman to whom St. Patrick's Day was important. He was an alcoholic. He once fell asleep in his turret and fired his gun by mistake. He had narcolepsy. He was 'Pops' and was the oldest. They teased him unmercifully. Still, he was very laid back. He told his children to put work in its proper place and to enjoy life. One of his favorite memories was going into London and dancing at a big ballroom."

Said Des Lauriers: "He was right behind the pilot, and he also manned the top gun. He was the guy who kept track of the fuel, anything that was critical in the handling of the ship that was not in the control element, one small example being the relief tube, the urine tube in the bomb bay. He and I and the waist gunners had conversations about checking to see that things worked. The engineer observed visually, checked the flight surfaces from his turret. His penchant for a drink wasn't a problem as long as we watched him. That was easy. We did it with oxygen."

It would be impossible to exaggerate Green's role in helping the Fortress fly, Des Lauriers said. "He was the man responsible for airplane hygiene," said Des Lauriers. "He had been trained thoroughly on the B-17: He knew every rib, every inch, of that airplane. There wasn't a question he couldn't answer about what was keeping us going and what was working and what wasn't."

THE BOMBARDIER

The bombardier of a Fortress—aboard *Purty Chili* it was 1st Lt. Lee Sackerman—sat in a small, office-like chair facing the nose bubble of the aircraft. He had the broadest panoramic view of anyone in the crew, although his vision was impeded by his Norden bombsight and, above it, the Sperry optical gunsight for the Bendix electrically powered, remotely operated chin turret with its two .50-caliber Browning M2 air-cooled machine guns. A graduate of a twenty-week bombardier training course—often given to someone who'd begun in pilot training and been shifted to bombardier duty because of an eyesight issue, aptitude, or personnel requirements—the bombardier had to know how to shoot and how to drop bombs. Perhaps he needed nerves of steel as well: Even more than the two pilots above and behind him, or the navigator behind and beside him, the bombardier was out there in the open, exposed to frontal attack.

As the February 3, 1945, bomber stream continued its relentless progress through the sky, *Purty Chili*'s bombardier, 1st Lt. Lee Sackerman, was doing a lot of the work—in fact, a lot more than usual. Normally, the bombardier armed the bombs while the Flying Fortress was still at sea approaching landfall on the continent. Each bomb had an eight-inch propeller or vane on the nose fuse, which was kept motionless by an installed cotter pin, to which a warning label was tied. Throughout the bomber formation over the North Sea, most bombardiers were now arming each bomb by removing a cotter pin and inserting a wire attached to the bomb bay through the cotter pin hole. Procedure was to do this after climbing above 5,000 feet. When the bombs were dropped over target, the wire disconnected and the propeller began to turn. After falling about 500 feet, the propeller wound itself off the fuse and the bomb was then armed and ready to detonate.

Today, however, Sackerman was doing something different. The crew of *Purty Chili* was one of six Fortress crews in the 34th group tapped to carry chaff only. Packed in paper-wrapped bundles, the chaff consisted of thousands of small, thin strips of aluminum that, when dropped and scattered, would form a cloud designed to confound German radar. On every mission, when carrying a full bombload, the radio operator dispensed chaff through a tube in the floor positioned to the left and behind his seat. But today, the amount of chaff was much greater. It filled *Purty Chili*'s bomb bay. It was *Purty Chili*'s only cargo.

Now Sackerman, sometimes a prankster, always intent on the job, left his position in the nose of the B-17G, passed the flight deck, and worked his way back to the flight deck. The enemy coast lay ahead. *It was 9:00 a.m., British Summer Time.* While hundreds of other bombardiers and toggleers armed their bombs, Sackerman ran his hands over the bundles of chaff, checking each fold, assuring himself that once dropped, the bundles would break open, scattering chaff all over the sky.

NAVIGATOR UP FRONT

In the nose of *Purty Chili*, navigator 1st Lt. Ralph Wathey was stubbornly telling himself that he wasn't likely to have bad luck again and that he wouldn't be tested to the limit today—and that if he was, he could handle it. He was doing this while plotting the route, monitoring to make sure the lead navigator was in the right.

More than any other man aboard the Flying Fortress, Wathey was a creature of codes, maps, charts, aircraft recognition guides, a protractor, a slide rule, and, above all, pencils. "You can always tell a navigator by his pencils, maps, and such," crewmembers joked. "You can always tell a pilot, but you cannot tell him much." In the case of navigator Wathey, there was no need to tell him much. His navigator table—located below and in front of the pilot, in the nose on the left side of the aircraft and placing him back-to-back with bombardier Sackerman—was neat, his tools carefully stowed. Wathey, of course, was also qualified as a gunner, and he had his own pair of .50-caliber Browning M2 cheek guns, each in a ball-joint mounting at a side window along the contours of the nose. These guns were of limited value and were unlikely to keep any Luftwaffe pilot awake at night: Their field of fire was restricted to a very small circle of space in the sky beside the Fortress.

The only Protestant aboard his B-17's otherwise all-Catholic crew, Wathey tended to believe partly in his faith but mostly in himself. "He was always laughing," Des Lauriers remembered, but "on a mission his happy-go-luck personality was zipped up." As he looked out at the other bombers droning high over the North Sea, Wathey remembered the mission back on November 30 when the target was "merciless Merseberg," when he'd involuntarily earned a Purple Heart.

Wathey sustained a major wound, a sizable piece of shrapnel piercing his leg from the rear and lodged in his left testicle. As stubborn as he always was, Wathey refused when another crewmember—Des Lauriers sent engineer John Green down to do the job—attempted to inject him with morphine. Wathey's uncle and grandfather had issues with addiction to morphine, so Wathey never took meds for pain. Wathey had even had teeth drilled by a dentist without any novocain.

Suffering great pain from his wound, Wathey focused, that day, on seeking a safe return by his plane and crew. That day, *Purty Chili* wound up becoming the lead plane on the return flight to England because the others ahead of it had been shot down or otherwise removed from the mission by this time. Wathey's plane had also taken heavy damage, including his navigational devices. Wathey was forced to navigate his crew and the remaining planes back to England by peering through a crack in the bottom of the fuselage of the aircraft. He was cold. Like so many these men, so much of the time, he was always cold. He was cold and in almost unspeakable pain, but he brought his Flying Fortress home. Because of the location of his wound—"The piece of shrapnel entered about where the ischium [the lower rear portion of the hip bone] is and was stopped from going out the front side by his parachute harness," an official report said—others aboard *Purty Chili* gave him the nickname "Iron Balls Wathey."

Described by a family member as "a man's man" and "stern at times with just the right tone and sense of correction," Wathey was—well, stubborn. He was also busy. Paradoxically, every bomber carried a navigator, and even though the formation proceeded through the air by following wing, group, and squadron lead aircraft, every aircraft had a man just as busy as

Wathey. His slide-rule device, known as an E6B computer or "whiz wheel," helped him with the math as he calculated air speed, ground speed, wind velocity, and other forces influencing *Purty Chili*'s pathway through the sky. Today, high over the North Sea, Wathey worked with engineer-gunner Green and radio operator Sgt. Gerald Shoaf to triangulate the bomber's course, satisfied himself that the formation was in the right place, and looked out at the other bombers.

Wathey remembered the wound he'd suffered and said to himself: "This won't happen today." He was right. The enemy coast lay ahead. *It was 9:10 a.m., British Summer Time.*

THE RADIO OPERATOR

Located just behind the bomb bay in a compartment that actually had a heater, a token response to the ever-oppressive cold, the radio operator might have seemed among the most comfortable of Fortress crewmembers. But with *Purty Chili* arriving at the enemy coast, Shoaf was too busy to be comfortable. Together with the officers in the front of the aircraft, Shoaf kept watch on a piece of paper called a flimsy that provided identification codes, call signs, code words, and radio frequency assignments. Shoaf wasn't transmitting anything on his BC-348 radio because the bomber stream was maintaining radio silence except for urgent messages about navigation—or, later in the day, distress calls—but he was monitoring frequencies while staying on the intercom with the crew.

Even during radio silence when bomber crews were not using voice communication, a radio operator like Shoaf still sent and received messages via Morse code. It was his job to stay alert for prearranged signals that would tell of a recall of the entire mission, or of a diversion to another target. He was expected to block out all of the commotion occurring around him, to receive any Morse message that related to his group or aircraft, and to keep succinct records in a written radio log. Not everyone had the aptitude to process dot-dash signals, separate the meaningless from the meaningful, make sense of it all, and keep a pilot like Hansen informed when appropriate. A radio operator in another crew, Staff Sgt. Harold M. Mauldin, said: "Each mission was different with most being filled with hours of mainly dealing with the cold and listening to music, which often turned into short periods of intense message traffic and the associated sounds and feel of battle all around it. It was like that on most missions, going from near boredom to fighting for your life in a matter of seconds."

Radio operator Shoaf was one of six men aboard the Fortress—along with bombardier Sackerman, navigator Wathey, engineer-gunner Green, ball turret gunner Sgt. Darryl Young, waist gunner Sgt. Val McClellan, and tail gunner Sgt. Harold Griffin—who'd been trained to operate the machine guns that bristled from the Fortress, including the open hatch gun just a few feet from Shoaf's fingertips. By this late juncture in the war, the Army Air Forces had decided that it had too many pilots and not enough gunners, so many of those manning the machine guns aboard the Fortresses had started out hoping to become aviators. In practice, there was not a huge prospect of the radio operator actually hitting anything. Still, like all of the enlisted members of the crew, he'd been to aerial gunnery school and knew how to shoot. Shoaf, Green, Young, McClellan, and Griffin were among three hundred thousand men trained in aerial gunnery schools during the war. With the exception of mechanics, theirs was the largest number of individuals trained for a specific duty.

Up front, when he wasn't preoccupied being in effect a kind of third pilot, engineer-gunner Green operated the Sperry top turret above and behind the flight deck. The turret could traverse a full 360 degrees, carried 375 rounds of ammunition, and could be reloaded in flight. Green's top turret also afforded him very good visibility to the front and to the rear of the Fortress. If under attack, he was in an ideal position to shoot and to call out shots to the other gunners.

Waist gunner McClellan had guns available on either side of the aircraft (until recently a Fortress crew had been ten men, not nine, with waist gunners on both sides), firing through mountings set in the glass of square windows that gave him a wide-angle view of just about everything. McClellan's guns were fed from a plywood crate that could accommodate 500 to 750 rounds of ammunition, but his prospects for shooting were limited. Any German aircraft passing by the waist gun position would remain in sight only long enough to attract a quick burst.

Copilot Des Lauriers regarded McClellan as typical of *Purty Chili*'s crew and of the teamwork and camaraderie among them: "Val was a quiet young man from Roosevelt, Utah," said Des Lauriers. "He was a dedicated good gunner, always ready, shy but always willing to try anything. He handled the two waist guns well and aided the ball turret gunner [Young] like a brother."

Tail gunner Griffin, like every "tail end Charlie" in a Fortress formation, sat in a cramped compartment in the centerline of the fuselage behind the rudder. Like all late-model Fortresses (meaning production lines B-17G-90-BO, B-17G-50-DL, and B-17G-55-VE onward from Boeing, Douglas, and Vega, respectively), *Purty Chili* was equipped with the Cheyenne or "pumpkin" tail turret, a late-in-the war innovation from United Airlines' modification facility in Cheyenne, Wyoming. With bigger windows and a tail gunner's seat located farther back than on earlier Fortresses, the Cheyenne offered a greater field of fire and improved gunsighting. The Cheyenne also offered an improved reflector sight and an emergency escape door below the horizontal stabilizer that could be used by the tail gunner if he needed to bail out. The Cheyenne tail actually reduced the fuselage length of a Fortress by about 4 inches (to 74 feet, 3.9 inches). Griffin's tail stinger was equipped with two Browning M2s, each with two hundred rounds of .50-caliber ammunition.

By February 3, 1945, many of the newer Fortress gunners in the Eighth Air Force had never fired a shot at a German aircraft. What remained of the Luftwaffe was too busy contending with Mustangs and Thunderbolts to have much opportunity to challenge a heavy bomber directly. But each day was a new day and no one could be sure about today or tomorrow.

At the enemy coast, *Purty Chili* was functioning at the top of its game. "We were a pretty solid crew, dependent on each other, and spent time together on leaves." Des Lauriers said everyone on Purty Chili's crew trusted everyone else. That was what it was all about.

ENEMY COAST AHEAD

Most of the bomber stream was still approaching the coast of Western Europe, much of which was still occupied by the Germans. There was not supposed to be any serious shooting yet. It was too early.

Still . . .

The pathfinder B-17 leading the 92nd Bombardment Group crossed the Dutch coast and found itself almost immediately under fire. Major James A. Smyrl, the group's air commander, exchanged glances with pilot 1st Lt. Russell Bundesen. Both began talking on the intercom with navigator 1st Lt. James W. "Bill" Good. Smyrl said something to the effect that the Germans were not supposed to be shooting at them so early and not in this location.

"We were issued 'flak maps' that showed us the whereabouts of known German antiaircraft gun concentrations," said Good. "There were not supposed to be any German guns here. But the stuff was exploding near us."

There was a crumpling sound as a shell went off within feet of the Fortress. Fragments of metal tore through the bomber's thin skin just behind Good.

The Flying Fortress had two, redundant oxygen systems. Good's oxygen mask was connected to the system that was knocked out by the hit, and he scrambled to reach a "walk-around bottle"—a temporary measure that would enable him to breathe while he found a way to connect to the functional system. Half of the crewmembers of the Fortress did the same thing, causing some confusion on the intercom while all tried to learn how badly they'd been battered.

Smyrl and Bundesen looked at each other again. All four engines were turning over. The flak hit hadn't damaged a fuel tank. The loss of one oxygen system heightened danger to the crew, but could prove manageable. With Smyrl nodding quietly, the 92nd group's lead B-17 continued on its way across Holland and toward Germany, retaining the lead position at the front of both the group and the 40th wing. "I don't know everything that was said," recalled Good, "but I'm pretty sure Smyrl never considered turning around." The bomber would be hit again, but no one knew that yet. *It was 9:15 a.m., British Summer Time.*

Aboard *Fancy Nancy*, toggleer and gunner Ray Fredette later wrote: "The bombers of the Eighth Air Force crossed the North Sea—an endless procession of planes neatly arranged in battle formation. The number of bombers was something beyond the imagination. And though I have seen such a sight many times now, I am always impressed by the hugeness and striking power of our air forces.

"We hit the Dutch coast at Bergen aan Zee just north of Altmark, carefully flying the plotted course to avoid flak defenses in the immediate vicinity. The weather was clear now and the Zuider Zee [sic] was visible as we crossed it. As our formation reached eastern Holland, I observed two contrails from V-2 rockets, distinctly visible against the blue sky. The contrails formed an arch, which extended to a very great height where they ended."

Near the front of the bomber stream, in the 457th Bombardment Group, nicknamed "The Fireball Outfit," Col. Harris E. "Rog" Rogner was scrutinizing the way his crews held formation and nodding with satisfaction at the way they were boxed in as tightly as Flying Fortresses could fly. Rogner was now one of the most experienced bomber pilots in the Eighth Air Force. Taking over the 457th, he'd introduced himself to the troops in writing: "Combat operations prohibit my taking your time to call you together. I hope, in the near future, to become acquainted personally with each of you. I am extremely proud to be permitted to serve with the 457th Bomb Group, just as you are proud to be a member of it. Let's continue as the best group in the European Theatre of Operations."

Rogner, just thirty years of age, a looming six feet, three inches in height, was an alumnus of the West Point class of 1938. During one of his breaks in prolonged combat service in Europe, he supervised training at Goodfellow Field in San Angelo, Texas, where he was in charge of Army Flying Class 43-D—the class that produced P-47 Thunderbolt pilot Grant Turley. Ruffled black hair adorned Rogner's head in seemingly untended ripples. He had a handsome, boyish look so typical of the fliers of the era, but his face could turn quickly into a stern expression. His fighting spirit had been reported first in the 1937 edition of *Howitzer*, the West Point yearbook:

> Harris Rogner, captain of next year's team, played good basketball all season, always consistent, always fighting. Rog played center, and being a semi-runt in "M" Company, he was usually topped by the six feet plus centers used by most of our opponents. Rog could be found most of the time fighting during games under either basket, and many are the times that he's ended up on the floor—wearing out his pants by lengthy slides over the court. Rog is a very likeable fellow as well as a natural-born fighter, and after being formally inundated in the Mess Hall into his job of captain, he scraped off the mashed potatoes and laughed it off with the rest of the squad.

◆ ◆ ◆

He hated the name Harris, which he considered unmanly. But few addressed him as Rog any longer, now that he was a group commander. Some called him a ramrod. Some called him aloof. At least one fellow pilot, Wayne Eveland, accused Rogner of taking unnecessary risks and being difficult to get along with. But that accusation took place a full tour of duty ago, and now, high over the Netherlands, boring toward Berlin—admired by those with whom he flew and fought—Rogner believed he'd attained the goal he'd challenged his men to meet. He believed his group was the best. Now, Rogner's 457th group finished its traverse of Holland near Emmen and reached the German border.

It was 9:40 a.m. British Summer Time.

CHAPTER SIX

Mission to Berlin

B-17s, B-24s, P-47s, P-51s, and the American Air Campaign
January 1, 1944 to March 6, 1944

AFTER MORE THAN A YEAR of heavy fighting in the high, cold expanses above the Third Reich, American bomber crewmembers and fighter pilots were still striving to establish their place and begin to push back against a formidable Germany with strong defenses. Few of the Americans had much confidence, as yet, that they were gaining an edge over the flak and fighters that defended Hitler's Reich and that claimed the lives of so many of their comrades.

What the Americans did know was that their air armada was growing and their organization becoming more complex. The size of the effort became evident with the establishment on January 1, 1944, of United States Strategic Air Forces (USSTAF). The new headquarters at Bushy Park, England, was created to provide operational control over the East Anglia–based Eighth Air Force and the Italy-based Fifteenth Air Force. Both were striving to overcome growing pains and to solidify their roles in the American portion of the Combined Bomber Offensive, now called Operation Pointblank.

FIGHTER TACTICS

On January 6, 1944, Lt. Gen. James H. Doolittle replaced Lt. Gen. Ira C. Eaker as Eighth Air Force commander. Eaker, who wanted to stay, was shunted off to the Mediterranean theater. That day, because Gen. Dwight D. Eisenhower wanted him as his principal air commander, Lt. Gen. Carl A. "Tooey" Spaatz returned to England and became Doolittle's boss as head of the new USSTAF, which occupied what had until then been Eighth Air Force headquarters at Bushy Park. Included in Spaatz's responsibilities, the Fifteenth Air Force in the Mediterranean theater was now dispatching B-17s and B-24s to many targets in Austria, Romania, and Germany—but remained out of reach of Berlin.

The change was a blow to Eaker who had been an aviation pioneer in prewar years and who was deserving, many felt, of a fourth star. In an "eyes only" message to Spaatz, written in telegraphic shorthand, Eaker wrote: "Believe war interest best served by my retention command Eighth Air Force. Otherwise experience this theater for nearly two years wasted. If I am to be allowed, my personal preference having started with the Eighth and seen it organized for major tasks in this theater, it would be heartbreaking to leave just before climax. If my service satisfactory to seniors, request I be allowed to retain command Eighth Air Force." If not, argued Eaker, command should go to Maj. Gen. Idwal H. Edwards, Eaker's chief of staff, while, as Eaker saw it, Doolittle should head up Fifteenth. Not one of Eaker's arguments was accepted.

To the end of their days, Doolittle and Eaker, who knew each other well for decades, addressed each other as "General" and not by first name. Doolittle welcomed his new assignment but had no role in denying Eaker an opportunity to continue in the slot. Though Eisenhower was not particularly fond of Doolittle, the British General Sir Harold Alexander was, and he recommended that the same staff that had been in charge of the North African campaign should be brought back to England to run the war for the invasion of the continent. Eaker was relegated to the Mediterranean as the senior air officer. Edwards went with him.

As part of the reorganization, VIII Bomber Command went out of existence and assumed the identity of the Eighth Air Force. This meant that Eighth Air Force headquarters was now located at High Wycombe, England. Doolittle, famous as a former air racer and already a Medal of Honor recipient as the "Tokyo Raider," issued an edict: "Win the air war and isolate the battlefield." In time, this approach would be called gaining air superiority, or air supremacy, but at this juncture it lacked a name and was merely a goal Americans could strive for.

One of Doolittle's first steps was to give VIII Fighter Command's audacious Maj. Gen. William E. Kepner orders for a significant policy change. Doolittle and Kepner had chemistry. It showed.

Doolittle felt fighters should be used to destroy the Luftwaffe rather than exclusive close bomber escort. He visited Kepner's VIII Fighter Command. On the wall of the office was the sign "THE FIRST DUTY OF EIGHTH AIR FORCE FIGHTERS IS TO BRING THE BOMBERS BACK ALIVE." When asked the origins of the sign, Doolittle was told it was there when Kepner arrived. Doolittle ordered another sign put up, reading: "THE FIRST DUTY OF THE EIGHTH AIR FORCE FIGHTERS IS TO DESTROY GERMAN FIGHTERS."

Until then, escort fighters were supposed to stay close to the bombers when actually escorting them and not fly useless sweeps. Now, Doolittle and Kepner freed many fighters to go "down on the deck" and become far more aggressive, seeking out the Luftwaffe and attacking German airfields. Immediately, Luftwaffe losses began to increase and, correspondingly, U.S. bomber losses began to decline—though U.S. fighter losses went up.

This happened as the North American P-51 Mustang became available in significant numbers.

No one was more enthusiastic about the North American P-51 Mustang than Maj. James H. Howard.

Thirty years old, Howard was stately in appearance, even patrician—more settled and more mature than those around him. Nothing about Howard would suggest that he'd been born in Canton, China, the son of a surgeon, or that he was a naval aviator before he became an army pilot. He was "uncommonly reticent for a fighter pilot," said historian Barrett Tillman. "His personality was low-key, pleasant, and focused." A fellow airman who later became a broadcast personality, Andy Rooney, called Howard "the greatest fighter pilot of World War II."

Howard had more flying experience than most at his level. He'd flown biplane fighters off carrier decks before the war. He was already an air ace, having first tasted battle with the legendary Flying Tigers in the China Burma India theater. Now, the courtly Howard commanded a squadron in the 354th Fighter Group, the first to introduce the P-51B to combat.

For all of his achievements, like others in the "Pioneer Group," as the first Mustang outfit labeled itself, Howard had less than a hundred hours of cockpit time in the "Fifty-one."

On January 11, 1944, Howard was leading P-51s providing support for a bomber formation on a long-range mission to the Brunswick area to attack the Oschersleben Focke-Wulf Fw 190 factory. As Howard's group met the bombers near the target, numerous German fighters struck. Howard led his group in engaging the foe. Split off from his wingmen and surrounded by German fighters, he shot down a twin-engine Messerschmitt Bf 110. Alone, out of contact now with his group, Howard returned to the level of the bomber formation. He saw that the bombers were being heavily attacked and that no other friendly fighters were at hand. While Howard could have waited to attempt to assemble his group, he chose instead to attack single-handedly a formation of more than thirty German fighters. For his utter disregard for his own safety, for pressing home determined attacks for some thirty minutes, and for destroying three more German fighters—with three of his guns out of action and his fuel supply dangerously low—Howard survived to become the only fighter pilot in the European theater awarded the Medal of Honor. He drew even more satisfaction from the accolades of bomber crewmembers, some of whom spotted the AJ-X code on his Mustang (not the plane assigned to him and, to this day, not further identified) and praised his performance. Asked about it later, Howard, who had a refined deftness with the English language, jokingly responded in a patois that wasn't natural to him: "I seen my duty and I done it."

After more weeks with little meaningful action and too many fighter sweeps, P-47 Thunderbolt jock 2nd Lt. Grant Turley shot down two Bf 109s on February 10, 1944. "We were bounced at 26,000 feet by those jokers," he wrote. "Well, yours truly and his wingman got on their tails and followed them down. I shot short bursts on the way down, then when the leader leveled off on the deck got a second burst from dead astern. He blew up and went into the deck from 300 feet. Looked like one big splash of flames when he hit the ground."

Turley continued: "I then got on the tail of the second and he crash-landed in flames. My wingman followed me to the deck where he lost me. There was another 47 around. I would like to meet the pilot of that 47, who covered my tail." Turley noted that two of his buddies were shot down that day. It was learned later than they'd been killed.

MORALS AND MESSERSCHMITTS

As the air war in Europe grew, the men of the Eighth Air Force were on a collision course with a human dilemma. Eventually—by the time of the mission to Berlin that makes up the core of this narrative—they confronted moral questions about dropping bombs on cities. Doolittle would lose his temper when ordered to drop bombs in a way that was certain to kill many civilians, even though the British had been doing it from the start. For now, however, two-kill fighter pilot Turley wrote in his diary of a simpler dilemma: "Right now it worries me that I have caused the death of one man and possibly two. War is hell. I guess I'll get callused." He wrote that it was more convenient to speak of aircraft destroyed "and not think of the pilots."

Probably unaware that a major bombing effort against the Luftwaffe was being planned, Turley went up the next day, February 11, 1944, and shot down two—yes, an extraordinary four aerial victories in just two days.

"Forts raided Frankfurt," Turley wrote. "We escorted them out [of Germany] from north central France. Just after rendezvousing with bombers we ran into 15 or 20 ME-109s." Americans used this term for BF 109s throughout the war.

"I was No. 3 in 1st Lt. John J. Hockery's flight and we went right into the middle of them. My wingman lost me (a bad habit my wingmen have had lately), but I bounced a 109, followed him through a cloud, and got off a good burst. Saw strikes all over the cockpit and wing roots and a lot of smoke. He went straight down out of control. I am sure that the pilot had had it."

While Turley was drawing blood as a fighter pilot, the Eighth Air Force—commanded by Doolittle and under Spaatz at USSTAF—was building up to a sustained aerial assault on the German aircraft industry that would be dubbed Operation Argument or, simply, "Big Week."

With far-ranging P-51 Mustangs in his quiver alongside Turley's shorter-legged P-47s, Kepner could now route fighters to maximize their endurance in a relay system, or "phased escort," with P-47s and P-38s accompanying the bombers the first part of the way to the target. On a given mission, when the P-51s arrived to take over deep escort, the P-38s and P-47s dropped down and attacked German fighters as they took off and landed, then strafed German fighter airfields. The Germans no longer had the option of holding their fighters back until the escorts turned for home, so they began to attack all along the approach route, giving P-47s an opportunity to engage they would have lacked had there been no P-51s.

And what about those lethal but vulnerable, twin-engined Messerschmitt Bf 110s and Me 210s with their air-to-air rockets? As Marshall L. Michel wrote in *Air Power History*: "On a mission to Augsburg, the P-51s marked the end of the greatest German threat, the rocket armed twin engine fighter, when they shot down 23 of the 77 that were airborne. One [German] unit was disbanded after this mission and the two engine rocket fighters were only used in the future against rare unescorted bomber formations." Under a more aggressive Doolittle, a downright bloodthirsty Kepner, and a mix of P-38s and P-47s now being augmented by Mustangs, American fighter pilots were changing the air war—reducing bomber losses, pounding the Luftwaffe, and taking over the enemy's home skies.

In early 1944, P-51s were just ten percent of the available escort fighters but racked up 30 percent of the kills.

The Eighth Air Force wanted to lure the Luftwaffe into a decisive battle by launching massive bombings of the German aircraft industry. Clearing the skies, if it could be done, would set the stage for bombers to travel to Hitler's capital and for the Allied invasion of Nazi-held Europe.

Battling the Luftwaffe closer and closer to the heart of the Reich, American fighter pilots, including Thunderbolt ace Turley, were still struggling to establish a position of strength in the skies over Europe, but they were closer, now, to the time when many would see the rooftops of Berlin.

The proportion of air-to-air victories scored by Mustang pilots continued to rise. The Mustang was a sleek thoroughbred compared to the portly, clunky P-47 Thunderbolt, and it quickly began the process of picking off German warplanes and killing pilots whom the Third Reich had no realistic ability to replace. As an example of how the Mustang influenced air-to-air scores, Col. Donald Blakeslee's 4th Fighter Group had just fifty kills while employing Thunderbolts through February 1944 when the group converted to P-51s. Yet a month later, the group scored its four hundredth victory.

BIG WEEK

In what became known as Big Week, February 20 to 25, 1944, the Eighth Air Force was the main participant in a furious campaign against Nazi Germany's aircraft industry. Hitler viewed that Germany would continue to produce aircraft "no matter how many bombs are dropped on us," and the Allies, who called the effort Operation Argument, did not disagree. Their goal was to lure the Luftwaffe into a decisive battle and to defeat the Germans in the air—opening the way for an Allied invasion of German-occupied Europe.

Big Week saw some of the hardest fighting ever waged in the air. It was a full-scale effort in every way. "No bomber will do us any good if it is sitting on the ground this week," one crewmember recalls an officer saying. "We're striving to get everything into the air and to cover Germany with the shadows of our bombers."

The casualties to B-17 Flying Fortress and B-24 Liberator crews were horrendous. Big Week did little to slow down the pace of German aircraft assembly and, while experts disagree, many view the prolonged battle as an overall setback for the American side.

The Germans placed great faith in their twin-engine fighter force and expanded it during the winter of 1943 and 1944. During the period leading up to Big Week, the Luftwaffe expanded its bag of tricks. Some German fighters dropped bomblets on the Fortresses and Liberators from above. Some dragged a bomb with an impact fuse that dangled from a cable behind the fighter. Some single-engine Bf 109s and twin-engine Bf 110s carried mortars that lobbed projectiles into American bomber formations. A Bf 110G-2 could carry four Rüstsatz M5 underwing mortars and could strike from well outside the reach of gunners aboard the B-17s and B-24s. American crewmembers also claimed to see unmanned Bf 110s and Me 210s being used as radio-controlled missiles. Arnold Burton, a gunner who pulled two tours in B-17s and flew forty-six missions, said he saw a Bf 110 pass beneath his Fortress: "Both seats in the cockpit were empty and the aircraft was stuffed full of explosives." Historians have found no confirmation that the Germans really used remotely piloted Bf 110s.

The Germans already knew that their twin-engine fighters—the Bf 110, Me 210, and Me 410 Hornisse (Hornet) collectively called Zerstörers (destroyer) fighters—had little chance of survival in an eyeball-to-eyeball duel with a single-engine fighter opponent. As long as bombers arrived over their targets unescorted, that didn't matter. Big Week changed everything. For the first time, it became routine for P-51 Mustangs to reach out in force and cut into the aerial armada defending the Reich.

Suddenly, the Fortresses and Liberators attacking Leipzig, Gotha, Regensburg, Schweinfurt, Augsburg, and Stuttgart had "little friends"—Mustangs—along for the ride. In six days, Eighth Air Force bombers flew three thousand sorties while the recently formed Fifteenth Air Force based in Italy contributed five hundred. Bomber losses were heavy—almost a hundred B-17s and forty B-24s for the Eighth Air Force—but the Luftwaffe no longer enjoyed easy pickings. The Luftwaffe losses were high in Zerstörer units and the German fighter force also lost significant numbers of single-engine Bf 109s and Fw 190s. Even worse, and a portent of what lay ahead for the Jagdwaffe—the fighter force—the Americans killed almost a hundred of the best-trained and most experienced German pilots. Aircraft could be replaced. Replacing pilots was a greater challenge.

The Americans were striving, exactly as an officer had said, and some felt they were finally showing clear results—but at a price. During the Big Week's February 20, 1944, Leipzig mission, two Bf 109s attacked from twelve o'clock, high, and sent cannon shells tearing into the flight deck of a Fortress called *Ten Horsepower*, piloted by 2nd Lt. Clarence R. "Dick" Nelson. The copilot was decapitated. His head rolled around in a blood-soaked aisle between the seats.

The Luftwaffe tactic of shooting down a B-17 by killing its pilots appeared to have worked, as it did far too often. Pilot Nelson appeared to be dead, slumped over the control yoke with a portion of his face blown away. It was a terrible denouement for a very junior and relatively inexperienced bomber crew. The thirty-ton Fortress was now plunging from the sky. Of those aboard who could function, none had been trained as a pilot.

Staff Sgt. Archibald Mathies and 1st Lt. Walter E. Truemper, each of whom had had a few hours' preflight training, reached around the casualties, ignored the blood and spatter, and fought to pull the Fortress out of its dive. Removing the copilot from his seat took time and effort by several men, during which time Mathies and Truemper handled the control yoke but could not reach the rudder pedals. With a howling wind tearing through openings in the windshield and the remainder of their vision hindered by blood and debris, they somehow got *Ten Horsepower* level. The bombardier bailed out, but the remainder of the crew, seeing that all four engines were functioning, wanted to try to get home to the 351st Bombardment Group's combat station at Polebrook.

STRUGGLE FOR SURVIVAL

Fighting windblast and centrifugal forces, finally able to seat themselves, Mathies and Truemper struggled with the controls. It was so cold that the two men alternated handling the controls—the first time either had touched a Fortress yoke, throttle, and rudder pedals. At some point they discovered that the pilot, now sprawled on the bloody floorboards and unconscious, was still alive. That ended a heated discussion about bailing out.

It was nothing short of a miracle that brought *Ten Horsepower* all the way to Polebrook. Neither man on the flight deck had any idea how to land a plane. Truemper radioed: "The copilot is dead. The pilot we think is dead. The bombardier has jumped. I am the navigator, the only commissioned officer on board. What should we do?" Mathies thought he had a chance to bring the plane down on Polebrook's runway. Colonel Eugene A. Romig, 351st group commander, authorized the men to attempt to land and another bomber drew close to try to assist. But Mathies was frigid from the cold and battered with exhaustion. His first landing attempt was a weaving, wobbly effort that gave Romig second thoughts. Mathies made a second try nevertheless. Romig told Truemper to turn toward the English Channel, set the automatic pilot, and have the crew parachute to safety. Truemper and Mathies replied that they now knew the unconscious pilot to be alive and they could not abandon him.

The last crewmember to see Truemper and Mathies shook hands with them, maintained eye contact for what seemed an eternity amid the howling noise, gave them a thumbs-up, and dropped through a door on the floor of the fuselage.

There was to be no happy ending. Making a third attempt to land at a different airstrip, the bomber stalled, fell off on a wing, and smashed into a field. Truemper and Mathies were killed instantly. Nelson, the pilot they'd given their lives for, was pulled from the wreckage but died soon afterward. Truemper, who had wanted nothing more than to be an accountant at a business firm, and Mathies, a feisty Pennsylvania-born Scotsman who'd been in the enlisted ranks since 1940, were posthumously awarded the Medal of Honor for "conspicuous gallantry and intrepidity at risk of life above and beyond the call of duty."

On the same day, a heroic effort by 1st Lt. William Robert Lawley Jr. saved the lives of another Flying Fortress crew, nursing his plane home while staring into a shattered, bloody windshield. This resulted in another award of the Medal of Honor, which Lawley was able to receive in person.

AZON BOMB

Among other achievements during Big Week was introduction of the Azon bomb. The term was short for "Azimuth Only." It was a finned unit bolted to a 1,000-pound general-purpose warhead. This transformed the Azon into a missile that could be guided by the bombardier using a toggle switch that operated the fins.

The debut of the Azon was handled not by the sleek, graceful B-17 Flying Fortress (which, if Doolittle could have his way would be the only bomber in the Eighth Air Force) but by the ungainly B-24 Liberator (which Doolittle despised). The ability of the B-24 to carry a heavier payload was the key factor in the choice. Lt. Col. Robert W. Vincent of the 458th Bombardment Group led the Azon effort.

Ten Liberators were assigned to Azon duties and were fitted with radio antennas beneath the lower rear fuselage. The bomb was dropped from about 15,000 feet but only in clear weather, which was a rarity for Europe. More often than not, as George A. Reynolds, a historian on the 458th, remembered later, "Crews were subjected to many alerts only to have a last-minute scrub because of weather."

Although the Azon bomb succeeded in the China Burma India theater—to which 458th group crews had been en route when Eighth Air Force sought them for bridge and dock missions as D-Day approached—Reynolds saw it as "a limited achievement" for the 458th because only seven Azon sorties out of the total of thirteen were deemed to be successful. On one of these missions, not long after Big Week, a Liberator named *Lorelei* used four Azon bombs to collapse the spans of four bridges, although no mention of the achievement ever reached official Army Air Forces records. No fewer than seven of the ten Liberators assigned to Azon missions were eventually lost, most in landing mishaps. Azon crews designed, but never had time to manufacture or wear, an unofficial patch that identified them as the "Buck Rogers Boys," named for the movie-serial outer space adventurer of the previous decade.

What were the designers of the Azon thinking? There is no evidence they sought anything more than a large bomb. They probably did not have the concept of a weapon to be used against "leadership targets," which came along at a late time in air war doctrine. But given that many Nazi leaders spent a lot of time in heavily reinforced bunkers in Berlin—more so than Adolf Hitler himself, who was usually at his retreat far from the capital—it cannot have escaped the minds of Eighth Air Force crewmembers that the bomb could be used to decapitate the leadership of the Third Reich. It was never successful enough for that. Other efforts to develop a guided bomb or an outsized "bunker buster" never produced an item of ordnance more effective than the standard 500-pound and 1,000-pound projectiles that were entrusted to gravity in such extraordinary numbers.

Big Week unquestionably inflicted monumental damage to the Third Reich. But as official historians Wesley Frank Craven and James Lea Cate wrote, it was also the time of heaviest casualties for bomber crews. "Losses, though heavy, were less than had generally been anticipated," the historians wrote. "USSTAF planners were prepared to accept losses of as many as 200 heavy bombers on a single day's operation. The Eighth actually lost some 137 heavy bombers in the entire six days' campaign, the Fifteenth [Air Force] 89—an overall average of about 6 percent. Fighter sorties in support of the heavy bomber missions amounted to approximately 2,548 for the Eighth Air Force, 712 for the Ninth, and 413 for the Fifteenth. Total fighter losses were 28. A rough estimate of crewman lost, including those killed in action, missing, and seriously wounded, would be 2,600."

MISSION TO BERLIN

On March 6, 1944, American heavy bombers mounted the first-ever, full-scale daylight attack on Berlin.

It came after days of trying. "We tried twice to get to Berlin, the third and the fourth of March, and were recalled," said former Capt. Charles R. Bennett, a bombardier in the 390th Bombardment Group.

The first, full-scale assault on the German capital did not come easily, nor was it a sign that the American daylight precision bombing campaign had matured—not yet. Reaching Berlin was a symbolic milestone in the relentless building up of the Eighth Air Force and its bombing capabilities, and it would have been impossible without escort fighters to accompany the B-17 Flying Fortresses and B-24 Liberators. But striking Berlin remained a difficult task that meant terrible loss of life on the American side—the highest number of aircraft lost in any mission mounted by the Eighth Air Force—as crewmembers fought every inch of the way to their objective. "As we went toward Berlin, you could just about navigate by the planes that had gone down ahead of us," said Bennett. "Every hundred miles or so, you'd see a burning plane on the ground." Many airmen on both sides saw the first Berlin mission not as an achievement for the Americans but a debacle, and indeed as a victory for the Germans.

The mission included 262 B-17 Flying Fortresses of the First Air Division, 226 B-24 Liberators of the Second, and 242 B-17s of the Third, a total of 730 bombers launched against the capital of Adolf Hitler's Third Reich. The escort force included 86 P-38 Lightnings, 615 P-47 Thunderbolts, and 100 of the magnificent new P-51D Mustangs that were the only fighters with the range to go all the way. The mission happened after weather and other factors aborted all-out efforts on March 4 and 5. It was known as Eighth Air Force Mission No. 250.

One participant was B-17 pilot Capt. James A. Smyrl of the 92nd Bombardment Group, today merely another bomber pilot but destined to become a group mission leader upon his return to Berlin the following year. A radio operator in Smyrl's group, Staff Sgt. Alfred L. Carll, was possibly the only other member of the group on the March 6, 1944, Berlin mission who would find himself over the German capital again during the later air assault that makes up the bulk of this narrative. Carll fired at German fighters on that first visit but would not have a target for his guns on the later mission.

One of the escort pilots, P-47 Thunderbolt airman 2nd Lt. Grant Turley, said to a buddy as they rode to the flight line: "This is the big one."

The same thought had to be on the minds of P-51D Mustang pilots like Col. Donald Blakeslee and Lt. Col. Tommy L. Hayes, who'd been chafing to go all the way to the city that symbolized the foe. Perhaps unaware that the Führer spent little time in the capital, Hayes thought it wouldn't be a bad idea to bring the war personally to Adolf Hitler. For bomber crewmembers, it was a day that would see both courage and carnage.

The thousands of airmen heading into a massive sky battle on March 6, 1944, belonged to a different generation, in terms of their combat experience, than those who would fly to Berlin 334 days later on February 3, 1945. Almost no bomber crewmember or fighter pilot would pull a tour of duty that encompassed both missions. The March mission was taking place while the Luftwaffe was still a formidable air-to-air threat and while a crewmember's prospects for survival were far less than they would be later. Today's American bomber pilots faced the certainty of the now-familiar head-on attacks by German fighters from twelve o'clock, high—for the specific purpose of killing the bomber pilots. Today's American fighter pilots would duel with the Luftwaffe all the way in and all the way out.

Berlin was the first large-scale mission for the final wartime model of the Flying Fortress, the B-17G, which boasted a chin-nose turret with two .50-caliber guns. Turbo-supercharged Pratt & Whitney R-1820-97 Cyclone engines powered the G model, which raised the service ceiling to 35,000 feet.

B-17 crews that assaulted the German capital came from the Eighth Air Force's First and Third Bombardment (later, Air) Divisions. Also in the raid were Liberator crews of the Second Bomb Division. The B-17 groups were mostly equipped with a mixture of B-17F and B-17G models, an exception being the 401st Bombardment Group, which had Gs only. Although the Army Air Forces had just made the decision to dispense with camouflage, and B-17s were beginning to emerge from factories in natural metal, it appears that every bomber on that first Berlin raid was adorned in olive drab. At this juncture in the war, each bomb group wore its own letter of the alphabet on the bomber's fin.

The running air-ground battle raged along hundreds of miles of invisible highway in the sky. The bomber stream stretched ninety-four miles from the very first Pathfinder to the final "tail end Charlie."

For bomber crews, the mission began with a wakeup shortly after midnight. Briefing, warmup, takeoff, formup, and ingress all entailed work and risks. The fighting began around 11:00 a.m., when the first Focke-Wulf Fw 190s engaged Flying Fortresses over Holland. The first casualty may have been the unnamed Fortress piloted by 2nd Lt. Brent Evertson of the 322nd Bombardment Squadron, 91st Bombardment Group, which was riddled by gunfire from fighters near Magdeburg. Evertson's crew bailed out, and the Flying Fortress smashed to the ground at Wilmersdorf near Bernau, northeast of Berlin. Evertson's ten-man crew became prisoner, but others were not so lucky. At least three bombers were rammed by German fighters, one by a twin-engined Messerschmitt Me 410. Although the combat box formation of the bombers enabled them to concentrate defensive gunfire, more bombers took hits and fell away. Sometimes there was no smoke. Sometimes there were no parachutes.

Some Liberators fell short of the German capital. *Balls of Fire* of the 445th Bombardment Group, piloted by 1st Lt. Norman Serklund, suffered an electrical failure in its number two engine and had to drop away from the main bomber stream and turn for home. Pounced upon by a fighter, it went down ten miles northeast of Furstenau. Three of the crew were killed, the remainder taken prisoner. *De-icer* of the 93rd Bombardment Group with 1st Lt. James Harris at the controls was hit by heavy bursts of flak and went down in Spandau district, Feldstrasse, with seven killed, three taken prisoner.

GUNNER'S PERSPECTIVE

Dale VanBlair, a B-24 Liberator gunner with the 448th Bombardment Group, remembered how it felt to have "the big B" his destination that day. "I participated in the first mass daylight raid on Berlin," said VanBlair. "A few of those 'other planes' [B-17s] had briefly hit the outskirts of the city on March 3 and 4 after ignoring a recall, but this was the first true mission to the capital. Although I normally flew in the tail turret, I was drafted to occupy the nose turret with another crew for this one. I knew the enlisted men of this crew but not the officers; and when I looked ahead at the flak barrage we were approaching, my main concern was whether the navigator or bombardier on this crew would take the time to let a stranger out of the nose turret if we had to bail out.

I always left the doors of my tail turret open, thus didn't have to depend on anyone to let me out. I couldn't do that, of course, in the nose turret. Fortunately, we made it through without any major damage. After that, I was ready to go back to my tail turret where I didn't have to worry about the flak that I saw, since by the time I saw it, we were leaving it: 'Out of sight, out of mind.' "

Blakeslee's 4th Fighter Group had worked hard to integrate the P-51 Mustang into air operations. Still, the Mustang that traveled to Berlin on that first mission was a work in progress. The P-51B model of March 6, 1944, was not fully developed and was plagued by reliability issues. The Mustang's four (later, six) Browning M2 .50-caliber machine guns were mounted in the wing at an acute angle, which made them susceptible to jamming during high-G maneuvers. Sometimes, a pilot was reduced to only one gun within moments of opening fire. Moreover, the extreme cold at high altitude froze the oil in the guns. The U.S.-produced Packard V-1650 version of the famous Merlin engine had problems operating with the poor-quality British aviation gasoline until U.S. airmen scrounged up British spark plugs. The big, four-bladed Hamilton Standard paddle propeller was flexible and reliable but could run hot, bleeding off some of the "push" that was supposed to propel the Mustang through the air. As late as two months after that first journey to Berlin, more Mustangs were being lost to mechanical failure than to enemy action.

Bomber crews called them "little friends" anyway. The sight of a friendly fighter was sometimes grounds for cheering.

The P-47 Thunderbolt lacked the Mustang's teething problems but still could not travel all the way to Berlin, a city whose rooftops 2nd Lt. Grant Turley never saw.

Over Germany, but still many miles from the capital, apparently near the point where they would have to turn back, Turley's 78th Fighter Group was intercepted by Focke-Wulf Fw 190s."We were escorting American bombers in Germany when suddenly some Germans appeared," group commander Col. James Stone later wrote. "They were going to attack the bombers, but before they could, Grant and a few other pilots intercepted them and a dogfight started. In the general confusion of the dogfight, everyone became separated and Grant was last seen chasing a German fighter that was headed for the ground."

"This all took place at a very high altitude," continued Stone, "so that Grant disappeared below before anyone could go after him to help. Grant probably chased this German and shot him down. Then he was probably all alone, and may have been attacked by a superior number of German fighters while close to the ground.

"We will never know what happened," the Thunderbolt fighter group commander concluded. "Grant, by his will to do all he could for his fellow flyers and his country, was responsible for saving the lives of many of the bombers and their crews."

Major Richard Hewitt, commander of the group's 82nd Fighter Squadron, wrote that after Grant Turley chased an Fw 190 toward the ground, "three other 190s were seen to bounce Grant's flight. Grant's wingman fought with one of them and Grant got on the tail of one of the others and shot him down. The third 190 positioned himself behind Grant and several hits were seen on his ship. It is believed that he crashed. This story was told by Grant's wingman and he is the only one who saw the fight."

Turley became a first lieutenant, just as he'd predicted in a letter he'd sent home—but the promotion was posthumous.

THUNDERBOLTS IN BATTLE

The Thunderbolt-equipped 56th Fighter Group led by Lt. Col. Hubert "Hub" Zemke got within eyesight of the flak clouds over Berlin. Over the Dummer Lake area, Zemke shot down an Fw 190 and a Bf 109. It was not enough to prevent other German fighters from swarming over the bomber stream.

Of the three air divisions arrayed in a continuous stream en route to Berlin, two made a minor navigation error and swung farther south than planned en route to Berlin. This confused both friend and foe, and some Luftwaffe fighters didn't engage because of the confusion.

"BLOODY 100TH" AT BERLIN

The worst place to be, that day, was with Third Air Division, especially the division's 13th Combat Wing that included the 95th, 100th, and 390th Bombardment Groups. Maj. Bucky Elton of the "Bloody 100th" watched fighters transform six Flying Fortresses into blazing torches that plummeted from the sky in front of him. Elsewhere in the formation, aggressive Luftwaffe pilots racked up additional kills while one Fw 190 collided with the B-17 piloted by Capt. Jack R. Swartout. After the impact, only a spar secured what was left of the rudder, which began flapping from side to side, causing the aircraft to lurch violently. With this unstable and dangerous situation continuing, Swartout coaxed his bomber and its crew back to England.

The Luftwaffe made its most intense thrust against roughly three pairs of combat wings between Osnabruck and Hanover. Following an initial twenty to forty stabbing attacks by single-engined fighters, more than one hundred Bf 109s and Fw 190s descended like a tidal wave on the center pair, which was far from friendly fighter escort.

In forty-five minutes, Luftwaffe pilots shot down twenty Flying Fortresses, twelve from the 100th Bombardment Group. After that, the bombers flew through intense flak at the Berlin outskirts and, after releasing bombs, were struck by fighters again. The 3rd division alone lost thirty-five bombers that day.

While still approaching the target, the Berlin-bound bomber stream came under assault from a second wave of "destroyer" Messerschmitt Bf 110s and Me 410s. Escorting P-51 Mustangs proved a deterrent to some, but Bf 110s were able to close on the formation and fire air-to-air rocket projectiles from one thousand meters behind the bomber stream. At least eight Fortresses were claimed by this twin-engined Messerschmitt attack.

Far back in the bomber stream, the 388th Bombardment Group battled Fw 190s for twenty minutes and then flew into a new swarm of Bf 109s and Fw 190s. The concentrated defensive fire of the Flying Fortresses was extremely effective, but many fighters broke through. Like many B-17 crews, those in the 388th released bombs over Berlin only to face a new onslaught by the Luftwaffe after turning for home. Second Lieutenant Augustine V. Christiani's Douglas-built B-17G-30-DL (42-38177) *Shack Rabbits* was one of the last shot down by a fighter around 2:45 p.m. The Flying Fortress went down near Zwolle on the German-Dutch border. Half the crew died and half, including pilot Christiani, were taken prisoner.

Flying as copilot in an H2X radar-equipped lead PFF, or pathfinder Fortress, of the 813th Bombardment Squadron, 482nd Bombardment Group, was 1st Lt. John C. "Red" Morgan, who had been awarded the Medal of Honor for a B-17 mission to Hanover months earlier. That day, Morgan's pilot had been fatally injured and would not release his death-hold on the control yoke, but Morgan wrenched it free. This time, Morgan's pilot was Maj. Frederick A. Rabo. Also aboard was Brig. Gen. Russell Wilson, air executive of the mission.

Wilson had been standing quietly between the pilots but asked to change places with Morgan when the outskirts of Berlin appeared below.

Abruptly, both engines on the right wing burst into flame and a fire ignited in the navigator's compartment. But the bomb-drop point was approaching, and dozens of Fortresses were going to aim their own drops on Rabo's. Rabo calmly held the bomber on course until bombs were dropped. After the bombardier announced, "Bombs away!" the B-17 dropped—then exploded.

Morgan had been holding his chute loosely in his hand. Now, he was falling through space. His only thought was to get the parachute attached to his harness, and he did. Morgan yanked his D-ring ripcord at the last possible instant, was captured by belligerent German civilians, and ultimately became a prisoner (although some B-17 crewmen, that day, were simply bludgeoned or pitchforked to death by Germans who found them). His B-17 apparently "split open like a walnut," an unusual happening for a bomber another crewman dubbed "tough as a tin can."

TOMMY HAYES OVER BERLIN

One of the "little friends" escorting Fortresses and Liberators over Berlin was a P-51 Mustang piloted by Maj. Tommy Hayes of the 357th Fighter Group, later to become an ace. Like the more refined James Howard, P-51 pilot Hayes had begun combat flying in the China Burma India theater, where, at the controls of an old and inferior fighter, he'd outfought and shot down one of Japan's vaunted Mitsubishi A6M Zeros. If Howard was a patrician gentleman, Hayes was a hard-fisted, blunt-spoken leader closer to the public image of the macho fighter pilot.

Hayes toted up his second aerial victory during the attack on the German capital. He said in an interview with the author: "I was latched onto an ME-109 [the term Americans used for the Bf 109] but lost him when distracted by a flash in my peripheral vision, then another. These were falling bombs.

"I looked up. All I could see was bombers. I split-S'ed for the deck, paralleling the bombs, pulled out on the rooftops of Berlin, and headed for the closest open area. I should have gotten that 109.

"Later, after four of my mates rejoined, I spotted an ME-109 at low altitude. Very quickly, I closed on him—closing fast. I fired as he dropped his gear. 'Hey! He's landing,' I thought. 'There's an airfield ahead.' Instead, he crashed and burned. Poor fellow, shot down on final. I carry no guilt. He was coming in to reservice and go back up against our bombers.

"Going over the Luftwaffe airfield we all got hits on twin-engine Heinkels, Ju 88s, and even some Ju 52 transports. Returning to base we shot up several locomotives and a truck convoy." Hayes's fighter was a bubble-canopy, all-khaki P-51D Mustang called *Frenesi* after a popular song—fine-tuned into perfect flying condition by crew chief Sgt. Bob Krull.

Hayes was asked how it felt to make the first appearance over the capital of the Reich that Hitler said would last a thousand years. How, especially, did it feel to be fighting down at low altitude—thanks to the Mustang's copious fuel capacity—where streets and people were readily visible? "I did not think much about Adolf Hitler," said Hayes. "I was an American officer. I was an officer first and a pilot second. My job that day was to lead my squadron and to fight." In a subsequent conversation, much later, Hayes avowed: "Well, okay, it would have been nice to put some fifty-caliber rounds into the Führer's moustache."

Surviving Fortresses and Liberators staggered home from Berlin, many wallowing through the sky trailing smoke. More than one crewmember kissed the ground in England, the same cold, wet, miserable ground that often made flying conditions abominable.

Had they accomplished much? None of the three targets around Berlin was hit effectively. The VKF ball-bearing works at Erkner and the Robert Bosch electrical works at Kleinmachnow escaped damage altogether, while the Daimler-Benz Aero Engine works at Genshagen received only a light dusting.

More than a dozen Fortresses and Liberators ditched in the English Channel coming home from the German capital. Luftwaffe pilots claimed 108 bombers and 20 fighters, in contrast to the actual losses of 69 and 11. Bomber crews claimed 97 German fighters and escorting fighters a further

82, although we know today that the Luftwaffe actually lost 66 aircraft. As a symbol of the horror in that prolonged battle over Europe, at Thorpe Abbots, home of the 100th Bombardment Group, the total number of Flying Fortresses to return safely to home base was . . . one. Only three more landed at other bases in England.

Two hundred twenty-nine Americans were killed, and 411 taken prisoner. Forty diverted to Sweden and were interned. The number of Americans killed in the air that day was almost identical to the number of Germans killed by falling bombs.

So was the first mission to Berlin a debacle? After all, sixty-nine four-engined bombers and eleven escort fighters failed to return. Authors Jeffrey L. Ethell and Alfred Price summed up the mission as follows:

> Although the German fighter and flak units destroyed more American bombers on 6 March 1944 than they had ever before, or would ever again, and the raiders inflicted only minimal damage on Berlin, the defenders had gained no more than a Pyrrhic victory. The loss of 46 fighter pilots killed and wounded in a single day was a severe blow to the dwindling Luftwaffe fighter force; at this stage of the war, the overstretched, understaffed, and underprovided German training schools were quite unable to turn out sufficient new pilots to replace those being lost. The Eighth Air Force, on the other hand, had lost fifteen times that number of trained crewmen but was able to fill the gaps in its ranks without difficulty. Similarly, the bustling U.S. aircraft factories could furnish 69 new heavy bombers and 11 escort fighters far quicker than the bomb-scarred German plants could turn out 42 single-engined and 25 twin-engined fighters. Such were the resources allocated to the Eighth Air Force, not only could it replace losses but also continue its planned program of expansion. Against this background, a lengthy campaign of attrition could have only one ending.

The Eighth Air Force had plenty of struggling and striving ahead, but now the Americans were entitled to believe that for the first time they were winning.

CHAPTER SEVEN

The Way In, Part I

Mission to Berlin
February 3, 1945—9:40 a.m. to 10:45 a.m.

BEFORE THE FIRST FORTRESSES could begin their bomb runs on Berlin, the first missions near, and over, the capital and along the route to the capital were conducted during the nocturnal hours by reconnaissance aircraft. Weather reconnaissance duties were assigned to thirty-five P-51 Mustangs, five De Havilland Mosquitos, and four B-17 Flying Fortresses. Some of this work involved scouting the region in and around East Anglia, where bombers would be jockeying into formation. An official report indicates that one Mustang was lost to unknown causes during these missions.

Photo-reconnaissance missions over Berlin and along the route to Berlin, including the assembly area near East Anglia, were assigned to nine F-5 Lightnings (reconnaissance versions of the P-38 fighter), seven Spitfires, and three Mosquitos. Before and during the mission, fifteen P-47 Thunderbolts were assigned for air-sea rescue patrol duties over the English Channel and the North Sea. They eventually had roles in four incidents that involved the rescues of seventeen men. All of these Thunderbolts returned safely.

All of this happened before the first Fortress dropped a bomb. All this and more: While the mission was still shaping up, a handful of twin-engined warplanes made of wood flew at unprecedented speed into harm's way. The Mosquito was demonstrating its versatility, not for the first time in the day.

A twin-engine, British-built, two-man bomber with no defensive armament pulled by Merlin engines, the Mosquito was used only in very small numbers by the Americans, but its purpose was critical: The 653rd Bombardment Squadron, part of the 25th Bombardment Group and stationed at Watton in East Anglia, used Mossies for weather reconnaissance, scouting routes and targets, and conveying weather conditions back to Eighth Air Force.

On February 3, 1945, some of the weather information available to VIII Bomber Command came from 653rd Mosquitos performing weather reconnaissance flights identified by the code name Blue Stocking. And while fog and murk shrouded bases in East Anglia until sunrise, several Blue Stocking Mosquitos, flown by a pilot and a navigator trained in meteorology, reported correctly that the day was going to be largely clear. Their work on this morning was part of 1,131 meteorological flights over the continent that reached every target in the Reich.

While a vast aerial army of bombers and escort fighters bored toward Berlin, Mosquitos followed up in the weather mission with another task, one that was even more critical and was code-named Green Pea: dropping chaff to foul German air defense radars. Three Mosquitos began a high-speed approach to Berlin well ahead of the bombers. *It was 9:40 a.m. British Summer Time, Saturday, February 3, 1945.*

First Lieutenant Charles F. Gleswein and other Mossie pilots opened their bomb bays and dropped packs of chaff sequentially to form a screen for the approaching bombers. Gleswein and the other pilots and navigators in the 653rd squadrons were unique: They'd already completed thirty-five combat missions with other bomb groups. Not one of them was required to sign up for another sortie. All volunteered to fly Mosquitos rather than return to the United States and the comforts of home. The Mosquito's fuselage was made of plywood, not metal, and Gleswein and his fellow pilots hoped it was true, what they'd been told, that German radar couldn't home in on their aircraft. It appeared to be happening: Bursts of flak from radar-directed guns appeared to be hitting the chaff.

While the Mossies softened things up, the bomber formation approached the Dutch coast. The men aboard the Fortresses had survived the terribly fearful act of assembling a formation and had been able to relax just a little as the bombers crossed the water. Now, the men were becoming alert again.

FORTRESS CREWMEMBER

Among the unsung heroes in the bomber formation were tail gunners like Staff Sgt. Frank T. Chrastka of *Blue Grass Girl.* With the exception of the ball turret position, occupied by Staff Sgt. Johnnie Jones aboard *Girl,* no place aboard a Flying Fortress was lonelier or more cramped than the tail gunner slot—Chrastka's perch. Moreover, it was a myth that Jones occupied the most dangerous place aboard the Fortress. A wartime study demonstrated the contrary: The ball turret was the safest place aboard the aircraft.

Tail gunner Chrastka occupied a modified bicycle-type seat in an awkward kneeling position that had to be bad for the back, in tight and drafty confines where the windows around him could easily frost over and claustrophobia might close in. At times in the turbulent high cold, the seventy-four-foot, four-inch fuselage of his bomber acted as a lever on a fulcrum, shaking up and down along its horizontal axis—pitching, in aviation-speak—and since Chrastka was at one extreme end, the motion had greater impact on him than on crewmembers near the center of the aircraft. The record does not show whether Chrastka ever became sick in an aircraft, but some tail gunners, on occasion, heaved their guts out.

Aboard the B-17G model, the two .50-caliber Browning M2 tail guns were secured to a pivot mount in a hole and covered with a canvas bag in the rear of the fuselage. Cables connected the guns to the crude, cross-haired gunsight Chrastka and other tail gunners aimed with. Most B-17G models arrived in the combat zone with the powered Cheyenne tail turret, which freed the gunner from having to muscle the guns about and gave him a greater field of fire.

As tail gunner, Chrastka was expected to spot enemy aircraft, warn the pilot about any that were closing to attack, and shoot them down. As the only crewmember always facing to the rear, he also had to be a spotter for all kinds of situations. When other bombers fell in battle, the tail gunner was often the one who counted parachutes and tried to estimate the fate of a stricken crew.

MIDAIR COLLISION

As the bomber formation pressed ahead high over the Dutch coast and bored relentlessly toward Berlin, something happened.

The sheer momentum behind a Fortress in flight, let alone a formation of Fortresses rushing ahead together in the high cold, is almost more than the mind can grasp. Consider: Although the bomber stream was at 27,000 feet when it passed over Holland, a young Dutch girl watched her mother remove dishes from a shelf and line them up on the floor so they wouldn't be damaged as their house trembled. Higher up, the sheer force of a Fortress formation was incomprehensibly powerful. If you factored in airspeed, velocity, mass, and temperature, two Fortresses colliding in midair would strike each other with approximately the same kinetic energy as two railroad locomotives colliding head-on.

It happened to the 398th Bombardment Group out of Glatton about eighty percent of the way to the target. By the best estimate, *it was 9:50 a.m., British Summer Time.* The Germans had nothing to do with it.

Battered by the prop wash and turbulence that was a constant threat in bomber formations, 1st Lt. Perry E. Powell's unnamed Fortress slewed out of control. Once veering off its flight path, for reasons that no one ever understood—the B-17, after all, was extremely flexible—Powell's aircraft broke in half. The two halves of the bomber slammed into different portions of another Fortress named *Maude an' Maria*, piloted by 1st Lt. John McCormick.

As if ripped open by a can opener, the left front side of *Maude an' Maria*'s fuselage was suddenly missing a twenty foot-long slice of metal skin.

The innards of the plane were readily visible. Crewmembers of other Fortresses stared helplessly as McCormick's navigator, 1st Lt. Ray R. Woltman, was catapulted into the high, cold emptiness and actually went up in an arc for a couple of hundred feet before starting down. As Woltman careened through the air, crewmembers watching from other planes realized that he was not wearing a parachute. Either he hadn't donned a chute or the collision had stripped the chute from his body. To others, it seemed a very long time that they looked on, watching Woltman fall.

On the flight deck of *Maude an' Maria*, with a large part of his aircraft torn away behind him, McCormick tried to help copilot 1st Lt. William

Feinstein to dislodge the entry hatch. The parachute belonging to engineer-gunner Tech. Sgt. Marvin Gooden had opened inside the Fortress and was impeding movement on the floor and billowing around the men as they struggled to bail out with winds howling around them and debris flying. Once the hatch was gone, McCormick watched Feinstein nearly thrown from the plane and then saw Feinstein halt himself momentarily in the hatch. The thirty-ton bomber careened abruptly to the left, throwing Feinstein upward and out. The number-two propeller slashed into his flailing body and threw him into the wing, tearing off the arm. Possibly already dead from the series of impacts, Feinstein plummeted away. His chute never opened.

McCormick was reaching to help engineer-gunner Gooden when he (McCormick) was heaved out of the open hatch. In the nose, toggleer Staff Sgt. William G. Logan went out of the aircraft. Eventually, McCormick and Logan got good parachute canopies and descended toward their fate as Kriegies, or German prisoners of war. In his memoir *Hell from Heaven*, 1st Lt. Leonard Streitfeld, a bombardier on a B-17 nearby in the formation, wrote of what happened to Sgt. Joseph D. "Dave" Bancroft, the third man—out of eighteen aboard the two Fortresses—who survived the collision:

> Dave Bancroft, tail gunner on the Perry Powell plane, was alone in the tail section at the time of the collision and when the plane broke in half and was still fused to the front half, he saw a pair of hands, probably the waist gunner, reaching through the opening. Although Bancroft tried to pull him through, the opening was too small. Then the front part of the plane broke away and the hands disappeared. He found himself floating down, alone, in the tail section. He struggled to open the tail hatch door, but it was jammed. He kicked, wrested, pushed and, after almost giving up, the door suddenly fell off and he bailed out.

Bancroft was not just among the lucky three out of eighteen: He was the sole survivor of the Powell B-17. The 398th Bombardment Group had not dropped a single bomb and two of its Fortresses and fifteen men were gone.

CHARLES ALLING CREW

The route followed by the bomber stream was designed to keep the Fortresses offshore for as long as possible. They flew in a succession of straight lines that inscribed a kind of "big dipper" on a flat map, with the right-hand bottom of the dipper marking the spot where they crossed the Dutch coast, turned east, and began traveling more or less directly toward Berlin very far to the east of Germany. One of the bomber pilots was 1st Lt. Charles B. "Chuck" Alling Jr., at the controls of a Fortress named *Miss Prudy* of the 4th Bombardment Squadron, 34th Bombardment Group, the Mendlesham-based outfit that included copilot 1st Lt. Robert Des Lauriers and toggleer Tech. Sgt. Ray Fredette. *Miss Prudy* was a pathfinder, flying squadron lead.

In an interview later, Alling said that the pilot's job was demanding because he could never stop monitoring the progress of the aircraft, never pause, and never rest. The hardest part was staying alert, watching instruments, keeping air speed at a steady 155 miles per hour and holding formation while there was nothing in particular going on. "There is an old adage about how military life consists of, 'Hurry up and wait,' " Alling recalled. "That's difficult when you're staring at round dials, keeping watch outside, and maintaining a vigil over every little aspect of your plane's performance."

In his diary, toggleer Fredette wrote something similar about *Fancy Nancy*'s pilot, 1st Lt. Gordon F. Barbaras, who was very much admired by his crew:

> Flying a four-engine bomber in a close tight formation is no easy task. The numerous instruments on the instrument panel [are] sufficient testimony to the constant close attention a pilot must pay. With the throttle in one hand and the control yoke in the other, it is a grueling task for a pilot, from the time engines are started to the time the bomber returns and is safely parked on the hardstand. There is no moment of rest or relaxation for the pilot. True enough, the copilot is there to assist him and relieve him at the controls but the responsibility is his every second of a flight.

Fredette thought that being a timekeeper in civilian life helped Barbaras as a Fortress pilot in wartime. "To know Barbaras is to know why he became a bomber pilot. His very appearance is typical of one. His height and stature slated him for the heavies. However, I suspect that in his heart Barbaras always wanted to be a fighter pilot. The dash, speed, and individuality of the fighter pilot no doubt must have had greater appeal to him than the responsible task of flying in a comparatively slow bomber," Fredette said.

Miss Prudy pilot Alling may have been a little less imposing. In a photo, he appears average size, perhaps five foot, ten inches tall. He exudes the look of calm and competence that was de rigueur for Fortress pilots who were not only superb airmen but leaders of men.

Once over the continent, accompanying his group about two-thirds of the way back in the bomber stream, Alling observed something that no other crewmember, that day, seems to recall. In his memoir *A Mighty Fortress*, Alling wrote: "Just before reaching the target, a German fighter flew directly through our squadron from the rear, and in front of us to the left whereupon his plane did a pirouette on its tail, like a ballet dancer, and then exploded. We flew right through the mass of exploding metal, a piece of which tore into our left wing. Somehow, all the planes in our squadron survived as they flew through the remains of the German plane."

Once groups of Fortresses began to appear over Berlin, each was preceded by a small vanguard of aircraft carrying chaff to foil German radar. "It was a clear day," said *Purty Chili* copilot 1st Lt. Robert Des Lauriers. "We, in our dive on Berlin, created a masking shield for our group to block or confuse the 417 flak guns on the ground. The last reading they had of us was at 24,000 feet. The bomb group was at 26,000. The bombardiers had a clear shot undisturbed by flak.

"My friend, you don't forget diving a Fly Fortress at three hundred miles per hour, knowing the enemy is continuously shooting at you. The sound alone of the engines and the vibration of the whole plane is beyond imagination. But none of our six planes were hit; we survived with adrenalin flowing and prayers loud and clear." The chaff, if it worked, would open a pathway for the bomber stream.

Boeing B-17G Flying Fortress

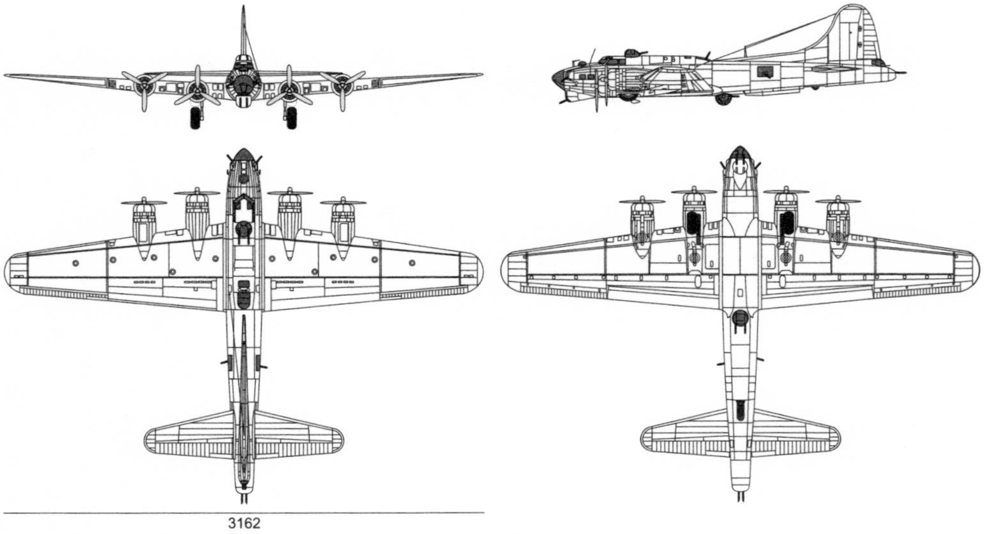

Scale: 1:250 5.0m 10.0m

All measurements in centimeters.

CHAPTER EIGHT

Striving

The B-17 Flying Fortress in the American Air Campaign
March 7, 1944 to June 5, 1944

BOMBS AWAY."

From the pilot's seat in the left front of his B-17G Flying Fortress, Capt. John Pesch heard the two words uttered by bombardier 2nd Lt. Arthur J. Rubenstein. On the intercom, the crewmember's voice had a shrill, metallic resonance.

The American air campaign was now beginning to take command of the skies over the Third Reich, but the Americans were still striving.

Eighteen thousand feet above the German city that sprawled beneath haze on this late morning of March 23, 1944, Pesch felt his Flying Fortress lighten up as its ten 500-pound general-purpose bombs fell away. Pesch hit the electrical switch that would close the bomb bay doors. Shutting the doors would clean up the thirty-ton, four-engined heavy bomber and enable Pesch to turn rapidly toward the rallying point for the journey home to England. But it didn't happen: The doors stayed open.

Free of his bombload, flying a little faster, and being pointed in the direction of home ordinarily would have enabled Pesch and his ten-man crew to heave sighs of relief into their tight-fitting oxygen masks. This was ordinarily the time to begin to ease off from the tension that had gripped them during the run-in to the target. This was ordinarily the time to feel the worst was over. Being part of a strike force of 765 bombers dispatched to hit several targets, including Brunswick, with 1,755 tons of bombs deep inside the Third Reich meant rushing straight ahead into the strongest defenses the Germans could muster. Pesch and his men had done it. They ordinarily would be able to think, now, about getting home, maybe about eating a big steak and sleeping between clean sheets.

But Pesch and his fellow bomber pilots in the high element of the 731st Bombardment Squadron were getting no free ride home today. Tenacious and persistent fighter pilots of the German air force, the Luftwaffe, were swarming with killer intent all around the Americans. Already, their bursts of gunfire had punched holes in the thin metal skin of the B-17G and had damaged the electrical system. At the start of the engagement, the Germans had attacked from straight ahead, from the position the Americans called "twelve o'clock high." Raking the bomber formation with bursts of gunfire that flickered in the cold air, they'd inflicted damage to several Fortresses, including Pesch's.

Today, the target was Brunswick, but Pesch and his crew had already been to Berlin. "You hoped they wouldn't send you to the most heavily defended target and for me that was always Berlin," said Pesch. But in a larger sense, the formidable defenses that encircled the German capital were symbolic of all the difficult targets American bomber crews went to, not just Berlin but Merseburg, Hamburg, and, for the moment, Brunswick. Pulling off the target and leaving Brunswick behind was supposed to be one of the very best things a bomber crew could do.

Just when it should have been time to escape all this, Messerschmitt Bf 109 and Focke-Wulf Fw 190 pilots were focusing their lethal intentions on Pesch's Fortress, named *Four Freedoms*. The Luftwaffe pilots had detected the scent of blood.

Pesch came under a coordinated, persistent attack. He may have been pointed in the direction of home, but his Fortress was starting to come apart as cannon shells ripped into engines, wing, and fuselage. It should have been time to begin to relax a little, but instead Pesch felt the adrenaline churning as an unintelligible cry boomed in his earphones and an Fw 190 filled the sky in front of his windscreen, its guns blazing.

John Pesch was now well into the biggest battle of his life.

BATTLE FOR SURVIVAL

There must have been pandemonium aboard John Pesch's *Four Freedoms* as the aircraft commander fought his way through a sky of Messerschmitts and Focke-Wulfs, including one that flew straight at him and peeled off at the final instant, avoiding a collision by a few feet.

"They shot out both of our left engines," Pesch said. "The ailerons, elevators, and parts of the fuselage were heavily damaged. The communications system was so heavily damaged that it was useless. One crewmember, Staff Sgt. James Rouse, was severely wounded."

Rouse, the right waist gunner of the B-17, had been struck in the head by a cannon shell or by a metal fragment from the bomber's torn fuselage. His helmet had been damaged and his oxygen mask ripped from his face. Like all bomber crewmembers who fought in this new mode of war high above the earth, Rouse could not breathe at this altitude without a mask. He was bleeding from his head, face, and shoulder, and blood sloshed on the floorboards in the rear fuselage where he was struggling to keep from being tossed around by the sudden turn Pesch was making. The seatbelt was a new invention Rouse had been wearing, but it may have been damaged.

We do not know, today, exactly what happened in the radio room behind the bomb bay—where Tech. Sgt. Cole Sage saw his equipment explode all around him—or in the rear fuselage where left waist gunner Staff Sgt. William G. Jamison rammed a morphine syringe into Rouse's neck. Incredibly, despite the damage and the coughing, sputtering left-side engines, the intercom was still functioning, but some crewmembers did not have their earphones on and others could not understand who was saying what.

There were two ways the pilot could order the crew to bail out. He could voice the order over the intercom or he could push the knob on his instrument panel that activated the bailout bell. It operated from a switch in the left-hand pilot's seat and emitted a high frequency sound over the bass of the engines. Ever after, several of John Pesch's crewmembers would say he did both. Pesch said he did neither.

If there was confusion in the back of the aircraft, there was confusion up front, too. "Webb, my navigator, thought that both I and the copilot, Amley, were dead and that the plane was going into a spiral," Pesch said, referring to 2nd Lt. Orrin F. Webb and 2nd Lt. J. C. Amley. "So Webb opened the nose hatch, and he and the bombardier [2nd Lt. Arthur J. Rubenstein] bailed out. The engineer, Tech. Sgt. Edwin M. Edwards, observed all this. He opened the bomb bay door and jumped."

Pesch was alive and uninjured but was doing the nearly impossible, piloting a Fortress that had both engines out on the left side—the number one and two engines both inoperative. A four-engined aircraft can often continue flying with one or more engines damaged or even destroyed, but losing both engines on the same side produces an asymmetrical condition that makes control nearly impossible, especially when the pilot is also struggling with electrical and other damage.

CHAOS IN THE AIR

"Years later, Webb told me that when the aircraft passed through 11,000 feet almost upside down and at an airspeed of 325 miles per hour, he knew in his heart that we [the two pilots] were dead and that, in less than ninety seconds, he and the rest of the crew would be dead too," said Pesch. "He did what he felt was reasonable at the time. I believe that when the German fighter pilots saw eight parachutes filling the sky and an airplane apparently heading for certain destruction, they assumed that they had shot down *Four Freedoms*."

Careening out of control, in a dangerously asymmetrical flight attitude, the thirty-ton Flying Fortress was indeed in danger of falling abruptly to its doom. But just as the crew hadn't realized that no bailout order was given, Pesch apparently didn't know the crew had jumped. At least he didn't know that the wounded Rouse had been helped out of the bomber and had gotten his parachute open. As far as Pesch knew, he still had an incapacitated crewmember in the aft fuselage behind the bomb bay.

Pesch probably should have ordered copilot Amley to jump and followed him out. But he didn't think that way. His response to a tough situation was to search for a solution. His response to a crisis was to act. In the Eighth Air Force, there were thousands of pilots like John Pesch—on February 3, 1945, they would lead fifteen thousand men against the Reich—and Pesch liked to think of himself as no different from any of the others. But people who know Pesch say he simply didn't know how to give up.

When John Pesch finished his World War II combat duty in August 1944, a military document summarized his contribution as a B-17 Flying Fortress pilot.

Pesch had flown "thirty-one missions," the document said, "the majority of which were deep penetrations in which he was flying as lead pilot. On several occasions his plane was shot up badly, and on one occasion he brought the ship back with two motors out and with all crewmembers except his copilot having bailed out. His crew traveled to some of the most difficult targets, including the German capital."

He frequently flew as pathfinder for entire bomber formations, on raids to Berlin, Munich, and Schweinfurt—all heavily defended by antiaircraft batteries and fighters.

Born in 1921 in Queens, New York, Pesch worked for an aircraft company before enlisting in 1942. After pilot training in flying class 43-C, he flew A-24 Dauntless dive-bombers and A-20 Havoc attack planes at stateside bases before being becoming a founding member of the 452nd Bombardment Group. He went to England to as a pilot in the group's 731st Bombardment Squadron.

MAN FOR THE JOB

Pesch was a captain on March 23, 1944, when German fighters shot out two engines on the left side of his B-17. Amid the hectic struggle for survival that followed, in the front of the aircraft, possibly unnoticed by the very busy Pesch, navigator Webb opened the nose hatch and bailed out. Engineer Edwards observed this and opened the bomb bay doors. The rest of the crew jumped. The eight crewmembers became prisoners of war and all survived to be repatriated after V-E Day.

"The copilot and I had difficulty regaining control of *Four Freedoms* since major portions of her control surfaces were no longer effective," Pesch said. "By bracing our knees against the control column, we were able to regain straight and level flight.

"We headed in a westerly direction, taking maximum advantage of the cloud cover. Much to our dismay, the solid cloud cover became broken and then scattered. We were continuing to trade altitude for airspeed and were once again under attack," he said. Pesch remembers an Fw 190 pilot passing close to his windshield, the last German fighter he would see that day although his problems were far from over. The German pilot was apparently out of ammunition.

"Ground fire, I believe would have eventually destroyed our aircraft except for the appearance of a lone P-51," said Pesch. "The pilot of that P-51 came alongside, flew our left wing, and gave us a thumbs-up. He proceeded to strafe the sites of the ground fire and effectively escorted us to the English Channel.

"Amley and I owe our lives to that P-51 pilot. We tried to locate the pilot later but were not successful. Whoever he is, he is our hero."

Pesch and his sole remaining crewmember were away from the Germans now, but they still had an extraordinary challenge of airmanship ahead. Much of the war over Europe was about airmanship, coping with wind, temperature, cloud cover, shattered instruments, severed electrical lines, and broken hydraulics.

"Once we were safely over the channel, we discussed the landing. We realized that we still faced grave danger since not only were the bomb bay doors open, but we lacked full control of our elevators. We were using our knees to keep the aircraft from stalling, but once our knees were removed, the aircraft would assume full nose up and stall. We agreed that when I determined that we could safely reach the runway, J. C. would handle the flaps and landing gear at my command. I would control the elevators with my knees and he would remove his. I then would take control of the throttle.

"When we made landfall, we searched for the first available airfield. The British fighter bases were close to the coast, and with clear weather we had little difficulty sighting one. We established a straight in approach and I called for landing flaps and the gear.

"As we crossed the runway, I throttled back on numbers three and four engines and very carefully released the pressure on my knee. The badly damaged *Four Freedoms* came to a halt and never flew again." The aircraft halted with its left wing almost totally destroyed, the left landing gear collapsed, and a part of the plane's big fin apparently missing.

ON THE GROUND

"Emerging from *Four Freedoms*, J. C. and I had our freedom," said Pesch. "After we came to a halt, J. C. and I, not knowing if any of the crew remained on the aircraft with us, quickly inspected the fuselage and the tail section.

We found the plane empty and were greatly relieved that there had been no fatalities aboard.

"Our unexpected crash landing soon drew a crowd. Both the Royal Air Force officers and airmen exhibited sincere concern for our welfare. We assured them that we were uninjured but more than a little unnerved by the ordeal that we somehow had survived. It wasn't until the next day that we returned to our base at Deopham Green and debriefed our commanding officer and our operations officer that we felt both emotions, gladness at our return but sadness at the combat loss of eight great airmen."

According to a legend told repeatedly in J. C. Amley's family in later years, the copilot's grip as he attempted to evade the fighters was so strong that his wedding ring cracked under the sheer human force he used on the control yoke. Pesch said Amley never told him about the ring breaking.

"Before returning to our base at Deopham Green," said Pesch, "we decided we would explain the crew's departure by lying and saying that we'd ordered them to bail out. We were a crew that trained together in the states, flew ten missions prior to this one, and deserved each other's loyalty. We did not want to stigmatize our eight other crew members by having them accused of abandoning the plane. It wasn't until twenty-five years later that Orrin Webb, my navigator, informed me of the real reason. The other crewmembers had been as certain as they could be that both pilots were dead. As for J. C., no pilot could have had a better copilot. J. C. had opportunities to be given his own crew but always maintained we would live or die together."

Pesch received a new crew, retaining Amley as copilot, and flew twenty-one more missions, including fifteen missions in pathfinder aircraft. "As a lead pilot flying radar-capable aircraft, a majority of our missions were deep penetrations," said Pesch. "They proved to be a very capable crew, some of whom were wounded when our new Fortress, named *Big Time Operator*, sustained battle damage."

ANOTHER BOMBER, ELSEWHERE

Following a period of almost unspeakable technical delays and difficulties, by April 1944 the Army Air Forces were finally putting a new bomber into service, but it no longer appeared that any of the new planes would reach the Eighth Air Force in Europe.

On April 4, 1944, Army Air Forces commanding general Henry H. "Hap" Arnold created the Twentieth Air Force. It was the only numbered air force ever led from Washington. It was also the only time a numbered air force was created to use a single aircraft, the silvery B-29 Superfortress.

The 58th Bombardment Wing was already on its way from Kansas to India. Soon, the 58th wing entered combat with its four India-based groups. Maj. Gen. Kenneth B. Wolfe established XX Bomber Command headquarters near the town of Kharagpur, west of Calcutta. Wolfe's Superfortresses underwent their baptism of fire June 5, 1944, attacking Makasan, near Bangkok. Maj. Gen. Curtis E. LeMay replaced Wolfe and flew a few combat missions before, because of his inside knowledge of a secret new weapon being developed by the United States, Arnold grounded him.

Some Eighth Air Force crewmembers in England began to wonder when they would receive some of the big, pressurized, heavily armed, comfortable B-29s. After all, some asked, hadn't the United States made a policy decision to give the war in Europe first priority? Soon to be flying from northwestern Pacific island bases at Saipan and Tinian, the B-29 would always be a player in discussions about bombing tactics and strategy. But although the Eighth Air Force was increasing in size by leaps and bounds, it never received a single Superfortress.

BERTIE LEE IN BATTLE

There were several followup trips to Berlin as the Eighth Air Force continued to grow in 1944 and Pesch was on one of them. A mission to Kassel was even tougher, Pesch said. And often, however, the action was in other places.

On April 11, 1944, 1st Lt. Edward Stanley Michael of the 364th Bombardment Squadron, 305th Bombardment Group, was the pilot of a Fortress named *Bertie Lee*. The target was a ball-bearing plant at Stettin, eighty miles northeast of Berlin. German fighters singled out *Bertie Lee* and attacked the bomber relentlessly, even recklessly, disregarding the Allied fighter escort and their own intense flak.

Michael's bomber was riddled from nose to tail with exploding shells. The Germans knocked the Fortress out of formation. A "very large" number of fighters followed it down, an official document later said. Seeking as usual to kill the pilots of the Flying Fortress, the Germans poured cannon shells into the B-17. A shell exploded in the cockpit; wounded Michael's copilot, 1st Lt. Franklin Westberg; wrecked the instruments; and blew out the side window. Michael was seriously and painfully wounded in the right thigh. Hydraulic fluid filmed over the windshield, making visibility impossible. Smoke filled the cockpit.

Michael found the controls unresponsive and lost 3,000 feet before he succeeded in bringing the bomber level.

The radio operator told Michael that the whole bomb bay was in flames. Three cannon shells had ignited the Fortress's cargo of incendiary bombs. With a full load of incendiaries in the bomb bay and a considerable gas load in the tanks, Michael realized he faced immediate danger of fire enveloping the plane and the tanks exploding. When the emergency release lever failed to jettison the bombs, Michael saw no choice and gave the order to bail out. Initially, six of the crew left the plane.

Historian Barrett Tillman wrote : "Both pilots were startled when the top turret gunner, Staff Sgt. Jewel Phillips, appeared on the flight deck. His head and shoulders ran crimson with blood and one eye was gouged out. He was unable to attach his parachute to his harness, so Michael assisted him forward and watched him leap from the nose hatch."

Seeing bombardier 1st Lt. John Lieber firing the navigator's gun at the enemy planes, Michael ordered him to bail out, too, expecting that he and Westberg would follow. Lieber looked for his parachute but found that it had been riddled with cannon-shell fragments and was useless. Michael realized that if the plane was abandoned the bombardier would perish. He decided that the only chance would be a crash landing. Disregarding his painful and profusely bleeding wounds, he struggled to evade the German fighters and managed to stabilize *Bertie Lee.*

After the bomber had been under sustained enemy attack for forty-five minutes, Michael finally lost the persistent fighters in a cloudbank. Upon emerging, an accurate barrage of flak caused him to come down to treetop level, where flak towers poured a continuous rain of fire on the plane. He continued into France. A crash landing might be unavoidable at any moment, but Michael hoped to travel as far westward as possible to increase possibility of escaping capture if he could find a way to land. He flew the plane until he became exhausted from the loss of blood, which had formed on the floor in pools, and he lost consciousness. The copilot succeeded in reaching England and sighted a Royal Air Force field near the coast.

Michael regained consciousness. He insisted upon taking over the controls. The undercarriage was useless; the bomb bay doors were jammed open; the hydraulic system and altimeter were shot out. In addition, there was no airspeed indicator, the ball turret was jammed with the guns pointing downward, and the flaps would not respond. Despite these apparently insurmountable obstacles, Michael landed the B-17. With wheels and flaps inoperable, Michael still had enough strength left to land the bomber on its belly. Michael survived and was awarded the Medal of Honor.

On May 19, 1944, the Eighth Air Force returned to Berlin with 495 Fortresses, while 272 Liberators attacked Kiel. It was a day of mixed signals, bad weather, and a persistent Luftwaffe. Sixteen B-17s and twelve B-24s were lost. One bomber that survived intact was *Princess Elizabeth* of the 306th Bombardment Group, which was flying her first combat mission.

The plane had originally been named, simply, *Princess*, but crew chief Master Sgt. Ed Gregory had added the name of the fresh-faced, girlish, eighteen-year-old heir apparent to the throne of the United Kingdom. As the plane's first radio operator, Staff Sgt. George Roberts recalled: "The mayor of Bedford contacted the mayor of London to see if Princess Elizabeth would christen the plane. The reply was: 'It would be a bad omen if the plane got shot down,' and suggested a different name. I am not sure whether it was the mayor of London or Bedford that suggested *Rose of York*. After the royal family gave its okay to the new name, the family also agreed to a christening."

Princess Elizabeth christened the plane in a poignant ceremony at the bomb group's base at Thurleig with King George VI, Lt. Gen. James Doolittle, and others looking on. The white rose of York is the symbol of the House of York and of Yorkshire—in historical terms, pitted against the red rose of the House of Lancaster in Britain's war of the roses. Britain's future queen was said to have been personally interested in news about this Flying Fortress and its crew—although she could hardly know that the bomber would overfly Berlin not merely on its first mission but, at a later date, on its last.

An increasing tempo of bombing missions in May and early June 1944 was a sign of what was coming: Shortly, Allied armies would be walking ashore at five invasion beaches on the French coast at Normandy.

CHAPTER NINE

The Way In, Part II

Mission to Berlin
February 3, 1945—10:45 a.m. to 10:51 a.m.

WE DO NOT KNOW what 1st Lt. David M. Magel (rhymes with bagel) was thinking when he dropped into the cockpit of his P-47D Thunderbolt and gave a thumb-up to the ground crew to prepare for engine start. Magel belonged to the 63rd Fighter Squadron, 56th Fighter Group, "Wolfpack" at Boxsted, England, and was piloting an unnamed P-47D Thunderbolt. Today, he would be doing something that had been considered impossible even a few months ago—taking his Thunderbolt to the outskirts of Berlin.

The February 3, 1945, mission to Berlin was a first for the Thunderbolt and a more familiar event for the P-51 Mustang. American pilots in both fighters were highly motivated to test themselves against the best the Luftwaffe had to offer, but today the Germans were capable of little more than a series of scattered, air-to-air skirmishes that were almost a sidelight to the bombing of the capital. It would hardly comfort Magel's family, but for most Americans in fighter cockpits, today the foe was throwing in the second team.

Originally, there had been two Magels—the Magel brothers, Robert and David, in the same squadron, flying the same aircraft, but not precisely at the same time. Flight Officer Robert W. Magel had been credited with shooting down a Messerschmitt Bf 109 half a year ago, on the anniversary of American independence but had been shot down by flak a month later on August 7, 1944. David arrived for duty the following day and reported to his new base to be told that his brother had been killed in action twenty-four hours earlier. Everyone in the "Wolfpack," including David, had been told that Robert was killed in action. We do not know whether David's thoughts included revenge, but he insisted on flying. In effect, he was a replacement for his brother.

Most of the 948 American fighters being launched on Saturday, February 3, 1945, (904 P-51 Mustangs and 44 P-47 Thunderbolts) were ordered to remain close to the Fortresses attacking Berlin and the Liberators bound for Magdeburg. Only the 56th Fighter Group—now the sole remaining group of P-47s in the Eighth Air Force—was assigned to the task of ranging ahead of the bombers to strike the Luftwaffe where it lived. It was the first time the P-47 Thunderbolt flew a planned mission all the way to Berlin, and, in fact, even farther: When the P-47 pilots got into a fight, they were actually east of the German capital.

Its best-known leader Col. Hubert A. Zemke commanded the 56th group no longer, nor did the brash and dashing Col. David C. Schilling. For only the past six days the boss at the 56th had been Lt. Col. Lucian A. "Pete" Dade Jr., who remains largely an unknown among the most experienced leaders of the war.

Dade had been one of the founding members of the 56th back in the states but at this later stage in the war was neither well known nor universally liked by the more junior pilots who flew with him. Zemke had forbidden him from flying during a period when he served as operations officer, so he was still on his first tour of duty after two years in theater, a situation that caused some pilots to ask whether he was the right figure to command them.

The group was beginning a difficult transition to P-47M Thunderbolts, which were identical in appearance to the P-47D but had new engines and brought with them a new world of engine problems. Dade was assigned a P-47M, but it appears no M models traveled into the Reich on this date; in any event Dade wasn't in the air with his group today. The need for attention to maintenance problems at Boxsted may have influenced Dade's schedule: Three weeks later, all 67 M models at the group's base in Boxsted (of just 108 built), were grounded because of the engine gremlins and would remain mostly useless in the final weeks of the war in Europe. Dade spent much of his time as commander resisting an involuntary conversion to the P-51B Mustang and preserving the 56th group's status as the only Eighth Air Force combat group to operate the Thunderbolt all the way through to the end of the war.

Major Paul A. Conger, commander of the group's (and Magel's) 63rd Fighter Squadron and an ace with ten aerial victories so far, took the 56th Fighter Group into battle today.

Conger was "an extremely aggressive individual and a great pilot," said a fellow 5th Fighter Group pilot who asked not to be named. "He was between five-ten and six feet tall, weighed about one hundred eighty five pounds and looked like a prizefighter, but he wasn't a handsome man by any means. I had a lot of respect for him. Other pilots also had a lot of respect for him."

Conger was leading the longest-duration mission ever undertaken by the group—almost six hours in the cockpit—carrying out a sweep of the Friedersdorf airfield that lay southeast of Berlin and was now barely within range of Thunderbolts carrying two 150 U.S.-gallon external drop tanks. It was a spot from which Messerschmitt Bf 109s and Focke-Wulf Fw 190s had risen to defend the Reich on other days.

Conger, too, was flustered by the P-47M. By today, he'd relinquished his P-47M and was at the controls of a P-47D. To conserve fuel and oxygen, Conger led the group in a gradual climb over the liberated areas of the continent.

FIGHTING THE FOCKE-WULFS

Conger led his Thunderbolts over a wooded area, apparently northwest of the bomber stream now arriving over Berlin, when they spotted a formation of Luftwaffe fighters below. Conger led the Thunderbolts down on top of the foe and counted fifteen Fw 190s. The Focke-Wulfs were at 3,000 feet. Unknown to Conger and his wingmen, this was just one of three gaggles of fighters that had taken off from Friedersdorf intending to engage the American bombers.

The Focke-Wulfs went into a mass-formation Lufbery circle. Conger jockeyed his Thunderbolt into position behind an Fw 190, centered it in his gunsight, and fired his eight .50-caliber Browning M2 machine guns.

While his bullets arched out toward the German aircraft, the German fired on the P-47 piloted by 1st Lt. David M. Magel. Magel's Thunderbolt was abruptly consumed by flames and went out of control. Certain that Magel's brother Robert, a pilot in the same squadron, had been killed in action a few months earlier, members of the 56th group now lamented the loss of two brothers within a few months. David Magel was the only Thunderbolt pilot to lose his life on February 3, 1945.

Conger fired a protracted burst that sawed the wing off the Fw 190. The Focke-Wulf jerked to the left and, with its remaining wing, began turning over and over as it fell.

The aerial melee moved directly over Friedersdorf and a formation of Messerschmitt Bf 109s wallowed into the middle of it. Now, low-level flak began exploding around the fighters piloted by friend and foe. Conger latched on behind a Bf 109, fired, and sent it crashing into treetops—his second kill the day and his twelfth altogether.

Captain Cameron M. Hart of Conger's 63rd Fighter Squadron was nearby. Hart stalked two German fighters. Hart later wrote: "The 190s were a dirty white color and I singled one out and closed in on him. He saw me and took very violent evasive action, ending in a split-S. I followed around and started firing at about four hundred yards, observing strikes on his canopy, wings, and fuselage. I closed and the Fw 190 tightened the turn, getting under my cowling, where I couldn't observe the strikes. I slid to the outside and saw the 190 going straight into the ground where he exploded and burned."

These were Hart's fifth and sixth (and last) aerial victories, so he now joined the ranks of American air aces.

Captain Felix D. "Willy" Williamson of the 63rd squadron, who'd distinguished himself in an earlier battle by shooting down five German planes in a single engagement and would eventually become a fourteen-kill ace, shot down two German fighters. Captain John Fahringer, 2nd Lt. Philip G. Kuhn, and 1st Lt. Frank M. Odgen of the 63rd squadron were each credited with one aerial victory.

The stage was set for Thunderbolts and, right behind them, Mustangs, to protect the bomber stream churning relentlessly toward Berlin. Their brief encounters with German fighters had been small in number and with little real military significance. But the entire American escort fighters were still in the region where the bomber stream was pouring ahead and all still had enough gas in their tanks. As far as more than nine hundred American fighter pilots were concerned, the stage was set for a battle royal.

EMPTY SKIES AHEAD

It wasn't going to happen.

The Luftwaffe was not coming.

Yes, Mustang and Thunderbolt fighters were encountering small numbers of German fighters, but within the bomber stream as it continued ahead, bomber crewmembers saw no sign of hostile aircraft.

Aboard one of the Flying Fortresses, a man who was just five feet two inches tall and weighed just 130 pounds looked ahead and saw nothing. He looked to the right. He looked to the left.

Bantamweight ball turret gunner Staff Sgt. John T. "Jack" Durkin of the 390th Bombardment Group twisted and turned inside the inverted dome that held him high over vast emptiness. Durkin peered toward the far reaches of the sky ahead. He had great confidence in his eyesight, and he'd convinced himself that he would spot swarms of Messerschmitts and Focke-Wulfs long before they would be able to tear into the bombers. He peered ahead into the sky and it was empty.

"I looked as far ahead as the eye could see," Durkin said. "We were inside Germany now. They should have hit us by now. I looked ahead and I saw our own bombers, but otherwise the sky was empty. I wondered if the Germans were waiting to pounce on us on the way out."

Durkin claimed, contrary to all intuition, that his exposed perch in the belly of the bomber was the safest place aboard a Fortress. In fact, it was and more than one ball turret gunner survived when other crewmembers did not. To Durkin, the biggest frustration about military life was one uttered all too often—that the job consisted of "hurry up and wait." Asked about the German fighter that *Miss Prudy* pilot 1st Lt. Charles Alling observed as the bombers entered Reich airspace, Durkin was certain that the ail of the fighter appearing, standing on its tail, and then exploding had to be wrong. "I was itching to turn my guns toward a Messerschmitt and blast away," said Durkin, who otherwise spent most of his time fighting cold, airsickness, and boredom. "If a Messerschmitt had been out there, I would have taken a shot at him. There was no Messerschmitt."

It was 10:45 a.m., British Summer Time.

So what were the bosses of the German air defense network thinking? This narrative does not cover the German side, but we know the condition of the Luftwaffe. Many of its best fighter pilots had been killed. The Jagdwaffe, the fighter arm of the Luftwaffe, was not one force but two, coexisting side by side. The first consisted of supremely experienced pilots who had survived years of fighting with few breaks in service. The second was made up of very young, very inexperienced fliers who received little training—fuel was a precious commodity—and who were barely able to take off and land in their Messerschmitts and Focke-Wulfs. These youngsters suffered horrendous loses in mishaps without inflicting much damage on the Allies.

German industry was still manufacturing aircraft, among them jet- and rocket-propelled fighters, but experience on the part of German pilots was at all-time low. Flak batteries—manned by Luftwaffe personnel—required less experience, had suffered less attrition, and were still functioning near their lethal best.

According to Robert Forsyth, an authority on the German air arm, by February 3, 1945, air boss Reichsmarschall Herman Göring could actually hear the guns of the approaching Red Army from his country residence on the Schorfheide.

For the Jagdwaffe, said Forsyth, losses amongst the four Jagdgeschwader (fighter groups) left for Reich defense following a massive transfer of units to the East were rising to nearly 30 percent of sorties flown, while victories gained amounted to less than 0.2 percent of Allied strength. The existing resources were simply not enough, as is illustrated in a situation report issued by the OKL Operations Staff for February 3, 1945:

> During today's heavy air raid on Berlin, the Reichsmarschall asked the Chief of the Operations Staff why no German fighters were sent up. Owing to the difficulties on the Oder, OKL had ordered that all fighter formations, including those of Luftflotte Reich [the air fleet for the defense of the Reich], be employed on the Eastern Front. These formations were engaged on bombing operations. When the enemy attack

> on Berlin commenced, [fighter group] JG 301 had already carried out one operation on the Oder Front and JG 300 was bombed-up and ready for a sortie.

Such were the odds against the Luftwaffe by this stage, said Forsyth, that in reviewing German fighter performance against Allied heavy bombers in early February, only sixty-seven single-engine fighters were deployed. This prompted the chief of the Luftwaffe operations staff to say " . . . that the employment of such a small number of aircraft is purposeless and must be regarded as a mistake."

So ball turret gunner Durkin and thousands of other American gunners peered into space and saw no German fighters.

WEATHER WATCH

Aboard *Fancy Nancy*, 34th Bombardment Group toggleer and gunner Ray Fredette later wrote that as the formation entered German air space, "a complete cloud cover slipped in below us. This 10/10 cover persisted until we reached the target.

"So none of Germany was visible to us on our course in. We continued eastward until we were some distance due north of Osnabruck where the bomber stream pivoted, heading southeast until it was south of Dummer Lake.

"A cloud cover like this, I believe, is welcomed by most who are flying. The fact that you are unseen by the enemy gives a man a feeling of security. And though the Germans are fully aware of our exact position all along the route, enemy anti-aircraft gunners must depend entirely on instruments to fire at us if we should come within range of their guns."

Fredette continued: "South of Dummer Lake our course changed again and this time the bombers headed northeast until we were again on our original course, which was practically due east. The formation flew north of the German cities of Hanover and Magdeburg, penetrating ever deeper into Germany.

"If one should gaze at a map with the plotted course for such a mission on it, it would appear absurd to him and surely he would think that we are taking the long and roundabout way to the target. He might well reasonably ask—why not fly a straight course to the target? It is true that such a course, as we fly it, adds many long and weary hours to the length of a mission, but it is not without good reason that we do this. All the areas in Germany defended by anti-aircraft [guns] are plotted. Our route in and out to any specific target is plotted so that we avoid all such defenses until we reach our particular target. Occasionally we encounter some flak due to a navigational error or from some batteries that have been up to now undiscovered. But I think it is indeed a testimony to our lead navigator's ability that a bomber formation can fly for hundreds of miles over enemy territory without encountering flak.

"Also, our course does not assume a straight line to our assigned target so that the enemy will not be able to predict with any certainty just where we will hit." Fredette may have been wrong on this point. It is likely that the Germans, with all kinds of intelligence available to them, knew where the Eighth Air Force was going today.

"As we reached a point approximately north of Magdeburg, we changed our course again and headed southeast. When the bomber stream was below Brandenburg, it pivoted and assumed a northeasterly direction for the bomb run on Berlin."

Sgt. Val McClellan, waist gunner on *Purty Chili*, remembered: "We were near the middle of the bomber stream and looking ahead some fifty miles we could see the thick black smoke."

Copilot Robert Des Lauriers in *Purty Chili*, tail gunner Frank Chrastka in *Blue Grass Girl*, toggleer Ray Fredette in *Fancy Nancy*, and 91st group air commander Lt. Col. Marvin D. Lord in an unnamed Fortress all paid careful attention to conditions around them as Holland fell behind and the bomber stream began flying due west across Germany about fifty miles north of Dusseldorf. Each saw a slightly different version of the weather. Most bomber crewmembers reported some cloud cover all the way to the target; some described the target itself as clear. Each Fortress crewmember also formed his own impression of the flak ahead. Reports filed later describe the flak variously as "moderate" and "severe."

They were, of course, watching for more than weather. Some bomber crewmembers ate a lot of carrots because they claimed it would improve their eyesight and enable them to spot the tiny silhouette of an enemy fighter approaching from miles away. Some crewmembers second-guessed their very able maintainers by polishing and repolishing the Plexiglas that surrounded them not wanting to confuse a blemish on the glass with an approaching fighter. At least one asked himself the question for which there was no answer: "I wondered when the enemy bullets came flying through the glass and into me, would it hurt very much or would it be very sudden?" Fifteen thousand American bomber crewmembers kept looking alertly to the front, to the side, even to the rear. Tail gunners like Frank Chrastka of *Blue Grass Girl* bore the full brunt of "clearing" the sky behind their onrushing Fortresses and alerting the pilot to any sign that the Luftwaffe was plotting to pick them off from behind.

Today, it was the threat that didn't materialize.

None saw a single German fighter.

MUSTANG MISHAP

One fighter pilot who never got close to Berlin was 1st Lt. Frederick Powell of the 486th Fighter Squadron, 352nd Fighter Group, the "Blue Nosers." Powell did not know he was a first lieutenant. The paperwork for his promotion from second lieutenant, effective today, arrived at his East Anglia airfield of Bodney after he took off.

Powell had grown up on a dairy farm in Rockford, Illinois, founded by his grandfather in 1900. He'd now been a member of the "Blue Nosers" group for fully five months, making him a supremely experienced fighter pilot, especially when compared to some of the inept novices the Luftwaffe was being forced to put into the air. Powell had twenty combat missions to his credit. He had tangled with Messerschmitt Bf 109s in furious, high-G maneuvers and watched as his element leader blasted several out of the sky. But, remarkably, Powell had not had an occasion to fire his Mustang's six .50-caliber Browning M2 machine guns in combat.

"The control stick handle on most World War II fighters was like gripping a big umbrella handle," said another 352nd veteran who flew with Powell. "It was about four to five inches in length and probably one inch-plus in diameter. Near the top of the grip was a trigger for firing the guns. Your forefinger wrapped around this trigger. You also had selector switches, not on the stick, which usually had three settings, i.e. 'Guns,' 'Camera,' and 'Guns and Camera.'

"If on a mission you saw something that needed to be filmed for the S-2 Intelligence guys, you could turn on the camera and film it, but you had to aim the airplane at it as you had no control over the camera or guns as far as aiming was concerned. The plane was a gun platform. You aimed the plane.

"In combat, we turned on the switch which activated 'Guns and Camera' and, when you pulled the trigger, the camera, set at infinity, was filming what you were shooting at. However, the cameras were not too dependable. If you were shooting into the sun, you often just got flashes of the sun, and if you were under heavy clouds where the light was not the best optimum for the camera, the film was often too dark. And, since we fired in short bursts (with only about thirty seconds of ammo anyway), the developed film was usually only a few seconds."

As he had done several times previously in the sky over Europe, Powell switched on "Guns and Camera" and wondered if today would be the day he'd actually pull the trigger.

As his fighter formation entered Germany, he became the latest of many U.S. airmen who searched alertly for German fighters and who saw none. But Powell did not get very far into Germany.

At 19,000 feet over Dusseldorf—at the opposite end of Germany from Berlin, and south of the bomber stream—Powell was tooling along when the Merlin engine of his Mustang quit for no apparent reason.

"I didn't know why it happened and still don't," Powell later told researcher John R. Doughty Jr. "I tried repeatedly to restart the engine, but to no avail. I turned and headed west, hoping to glide the plane past Allied lines. I figured it was better to stay with the plane than bail out." *It was 10:51 a.m., British Summer Time.*

Powell continued: "Unfortunately, the P-51 wasn't the world's best glider, and I ended up about twelve kilometers east of Allied lines. I belly landed the plane into a field and ended up in a pond, about a foot deep in water. The Germans in the area came running towards me, so I put my hands up, climbed out of the cockpit, and walked out on to the wing. I slipped on the wing and fell face first into the water. The Germans thought it was comical and laughed so hard, they didn't shoot me. That, plus they wanted me to help them pump out the gasoline in the P-51." Powell was the latest Eighth Air Force airman to become a Kriegie, or prisoner of war. He survived the war.

CHAPTER TEN

B-17 Stories, B-24 Stories

The B-17 Flying Fortress in the American Air Campaign
June 5, 1944 to January 1, 1945

IN POSTWAR YEARS, tens of thousands of U.S. airmen won their silver pilot wings—the same "rating badge" worn by bomber pilots in World War II—at Vance Air Force Base near Enid, Oklahoma. The airfield is named after the only B-24 Liberator crewman to be awarded the Medal of Honor for action in Europe.

The 489th Bombardment Group flew the B-24 against Germany from Halesworth in East Anglia. The group's deputy commander, Lt. Col. Leon R. "Bob" Vance Jr., a West Pointer, was a superbly experienced military pilot with plenty of flying hours but no combat time in his logbook.

Bob Vance was deputy commander of the 489th Bombardment Group and an accomplished B-24 Liberator pilot in May 1944. He'd studied at Oklahoma University but had transferred to the U.S. Military Academy and graduated from West Point (1939). He was expected to prepare Liberator crews for the looming Allied invasion of German-occupied Europe.

Comfortable with himself, Vance saw no need to throw his weight around. On his second combat mission, he was tapped to lead the group to its target, a German coastal defense complex near Wimereaux, France.

It was customary for the group air commander to occupy the copilot's seat of a B-24, displacing a copilot who would be unhappily shunted to another location in the aircraft and given little to do. In the cold, dark English morning on June 5, 1944—the morning before the D-Day landings at Normandy—Vance introduced himself to pilot Capt. Louis A. Mazure and copilot 1st Lt. Earl L. "Rocket" Carper. The men and their B-24, called the *Missouri Belle*, were on loan from the more experienced 44th Bombardment Group. Carper looked at the ramrod-straight West Pointer and waited for the bad news.

"You'll fly in your normal position," Vance told the astonished Carper. "I'll stand behind to observe." With no hint of an Oklahoma drawl, Vance was saying that he was in charge—but that he was willing to learn.

With ten 500-pound high-explosive bombs in its bay and twelve men crammed into its fuselage, the *Missouri Belle* roared into the English morning and climbed to take its position leading the formation. As group lead—the plane upon whose bomb drop other Liberators would unload their own bombloads—*Missouri Belle* carried a lead radar navigator, 2nd Lt. Bernard W. Bail; a pilotage navigator, 1st Lt. Nathaniel Glickman; and navigator 2nd Lt. John R. Kilgore. The bombardier was 1st Lt. Milton Segal. Also in the front of the Liberator, forward of the bomb bay, was engineer/top turret gunner Tech. Sgt. L. Earl Hoppie.

In the rear fuselage of the *Missouri Belle*, behind its lethal bombload, were radio operator Tech. Sgt. Quentin F. Skufca, waist gunners Staff Sgts. Davis J. Evans Jr. and Harry E. Secrist, and tail gunner Staff Sgt. Wiley A. Sallis.

Vance's regularly assigned B-24 Liberator was the *Sharon D.*, named for his two-year-old daughter (today known as Sharon Vance Kiernan). On the mission that would make him a legend, Vance had shifted to pilot Mazure's *Missouri Belle*, although some documents refer to the aircraft as *Missouri Sue*.

Using hand signals to communicate with the sergeant standing fire watch, Mazure started *Missouri Belle*'s engines. In the cold, soupy English morning, Mazure took off, climbed to 10,000 feet, and took up the assigned position over the airfield. Borrowing a Very pistol from engineer Hoppie's compartment, Vance slid open the right cockpit window and fired a flare to assemble the formation. Mazure turned eastward for the brief journey across the English Channel, climbing to 22,500 feet. "Looks like everybody's lined up with us," navigator Kilgore said. *Missouri Belle* rushed toward the looming French coast and Nazi-occupied Europe.

What followed was the closest thing to a routine time-over-target that a bomber crew could experience. After a turn to approach Wimereaux from the south, the crew of *Missouri Belle* began its bomb run and Segal announced: "Bombs away." With Vance still leading and observing, the B-24's two pilots turned for home.

The men may have noticed that they didn't experience the sudden sensation of change when two and a half tons of bombs depart an aircraft. As Hoppie quickly confirmed on the intercom, one or more bombs were still jammed in the bomb bay and had gone nowhere. Because the following Liberators were supposed to drop their own bombs on cue from the leader, none released their own lethal warloads. The B-24 formation, now turning for home, prepared to dump their bombs into the English Channel—sparing the target.

This would be the waste of a mission and Vance wasn't going to have it. Still wedged behind the pilots, Vance ordered Mazure: "Take her around. We're making another pass." The *Missouri Belle* pointed its nose toward the target again after completing a wide, sweeping turn. Without a word over the radio, the rest of the B-24s followed.

At this juncture of the war, when German defenses were exceedingly formidable, it was considered near-suicide to make a second pass at a target from the same direction. Mazure apparently supported the maneuver, but Kilgore later called the decision to go around "a mystery to me." Exploding black clouds and a rainstorm of flying metal signaled that the German flak gunners had found their mark. A "near miss" sent shrapnel slashing through Skufca's radio compartment, ripping off the radioman's oxygen mask and riddling his legs, which were suddenly crimson with pouring blood. Stunned, on the verge of losing consciousness, Skufca fought his way to the waist gunners' positions, with Secrist helping to shore him up. He found an emergency oxygen mask.

More flak explosions sent metal flying through the flight deck and rear fuselage. Up front, as airmen often did, fearing the loss of the family jewels as they put it, Hoppie was stooped over his flak jacket. When shrapnel tore into the bomber from beneath, this saved his life. In the nose turret, the Plexiglas shattered, Glickman suffered a bloody head wound, and he ignored his wounds trying to keep the B-24 on course to drop its bombs this time. Another blast sent blood pouring into Glickman's eyes, obscuring his view.

About to complete its bomb run, the B-24 took a near-direct hit from a flak explosion that was closer than any of the others. The bomber shook violently. A torrent of hot steel killed pilot Mazure and wounded copilot Carper. The flight deck was spattered with blood and human detritus. Three of the Liberator's engines halted. The *Missouri Belle* came to a near standstill in midair, on the verge of a fatal stall, with just one engine turning over. The bomber was out of control.

No one was at the controls.

It was the moment of truth for Lt. Col. Leon R. "Bob" Vance.

OKLAHOMA GRIT

Born in Enid, Oklahoma, in 1916, Vance had a degree of sophistication that set him apart from the stereotype of the "good old Oklahoma boy"—and his voice was devoid of any regional twang. Vance was a high achiever—an A student in high school and a promising athlete. He was a student at the University of Oklahoma, enrolled in a reserve officer training corps, when an opportunity arose to complete a competitive examination and transfer to the U. S. Military Academy at West Point, New York.

At The Point, other plebes nicknamed him Philo, after crime-solving detective Philo Vance who appeared in twelve novels by S. S. Van Dine, the pen name of Willard Huntington Wright. In contrast to some popular images of an Oklahoma native, detective Vance reeked of style and culture, and future pilot Vance had a lot of those attributes as well. As a cadet, Vance continued to excel in sports. At the academy, he met his soon-to-be wife, Georgette Drury Brown. Her middle name accounts for the initial in the *Sharon D.*, the bomber assigned to Vance, and her hometown, Garden City, New York—not Enid, where his roots were deep—became Vance's hometown in his army personnel record, known as a 201 file.

Bob Vance was commissioned a second lieutenant from West Point in 1939, married Georgette, and volunteered for flight training. Deemed a high achiever in the Army Air Forces, he advanced to lieutenant colonel and won command-pilot wings in less than five years. After a series of stateside flying assignments, he went to Gowen Field in Boise, Idaho, for advanced B-24 training and assignment as deputy commander of the 489th Bombardment Group, under Col. (later, Brig. Gen.) Ezekiel W. Napier. The 489th BG was stationed at Halesworth, England, beginning in April 1944. Vance was explicitly charged with preparing B-24 crews to support the big event everyone knew was coming—the Allied invasion of German-occupied Europe. His second combat mission was the one he flew on June 5, the day before the Normandy invasion.

When the flak hit tore into the *Missouri Belle* and decimated its flight crew, Bob Vance started to move forward to help. He discovered that his right foot was essentially severed, attached to his leg only by tendons, and was jammed inextricably behind the seat of the wounded copilot, Carper.

Navigator Bail used brute strength to dislodge the nearly severed limb, heightening Vance's pain enormously, and applied a tourniquet to staunch the hemorrhage from Vance's right leg. Copilot Carper, in extreme pain, was somehow able to turn west over the English Channel and, virtually without power, to glide the thirty-five-ton bomber in the direction of Great Britain.

Because a bomb was hung in the bomb bay, a crash landing was risky. Vance wanted everybody aboard the plane, including himself, to bail out.

But amid confusing exchanges on the intercom, someone told Vance that one crewmember was too badly injured to jump.

All but paralyzed with pain, Vance hobbled back to the flight deck and relieved Carper. Vance switched off the three damaged engines and feathered the fourth. Unable to use any of the shattered instruments, Vance then forced a side-window down a few inches. His B-24 Liberator was now falling like a rock and, although the aircraft had crossed the British coast, there was no likely spot where an emergency landing seemed possible.

"We dropped 5,000 feet in what seemed a second," Carper later wrote. "A B-24 isn't much of a glider but when we got back over England the colonel ordered the crew to bail out."

Accounts from survivors differ on how Vance took the controls. Carper remembered that the badly injured Vance gestured for him to leave the pilot's seat and then slid in after he left. But a post-action report said that, unable to sit down because of his injury, "Vance prepared to ditch the Liberator while lying on the floor using only aileron and elevators for control and the side window of the cockpit for visual reference."

Everyone got out of the stricken aircraft, but Vance didn't know that. Carper parachuted into the English Channel. The others came down on British soil, including Kilgore who broke both legs on impact and was unable to walk out of the minefield in which he landed.

Sitting beside Mazure's body on the flight deck, Vance still believed there was a wounded man somewhere in the plane behind him. He maneuvered out over the Channel and set up the B-24 to ditch.

In the never-ending argument over whether the B-17 or the B-24 was the better bomber, no one ever disagreed on one point. With its low wing and ability to glide at low speed, the B-17 offered a chance if you had to go down in the water. In contrast, crews agreed universally that the B-24 was a death trap when it had to be ditched at sea. The B-24 Liberator had a high wing, so there was no cushion.

Still certain he had a man aboard who could not jump from the aircraft, Vance saw no choice but to attempt to set down on the water. The Liberator hit the surface of the English Channel with enormous force. There would have been a horrendous rush of noise followed by a weird creaking sound as the battered aircraft began to settle—and sink.

In fact, the B-24 commenced to sink rapidly. Now, Vance was pinned in the cockpit by the upper turret, which had fallen to the flight deck right behind him. The surface of the water was disappearing above him and aircraft was filling with bitterly cold water. Vance could not move.

Exactly what caused the explosion that came next is unknown. Maybe it was a cluster of oxygen bottles going off. Whatever it was, a tremendous blast tore the bomber apart and sent Vance bobbing to the surface, saving his life. Vance clung to a piece of floating wreckage until he could muster enough strength to inflate his life vest. He began searching for the crewmember he believed to be aboard. He found Mazure's body, but there was no other crewmember.

The excruciating pain actually helped prevent Vance from succumbing to the cold and losing consciousness. He swam for what he later called "nearly an eternity," but it was actually about an hour. A British rescue boat reached the scene and pulled him aboard. To the first British sailor he saw, Vance joked, "Don't forget to bring my foot in." It was still attached by a few tendons.

Vance made it safely back to his bomber base. They told him he would be sent stateside to recover from his wounds. He was working on a written request to return to combat flying when he climbed aboard a C-54 Skymaster transport carrying wounded service members back to the United States. It was July 26, 1944, and soon after takeoff the C-54 vanished. No trace of the transport or its occupants has ever been found.

The day after Vance's heroic mission, on June 6, 1944, otherwise called D-Day, some 176,000 Allied troops came ashore on five invasion beaches in Normandy. Bomber and fighter crews of the Eighth Air Force supported the invasion. Two days later, however, Gen. Carl "Tooey" Spaatz of United States Strategic Air Forces (USSTAF) directed that Axis oil targets be restored at the top of the priorities list. Covered by P-51 Mustangs in and out, Fortresses and Liberators began spending more time over Schweinfurt, Ludwigshafen, Merseberg, and other petroleum targets.

The dubious distinction of being the first four-engined heavy bomber on liberated soil after D-Day went not to a Fortress but to a Liberator. First Lieutenant Charles Grace was a pilot in the 467th Bombardment Group, the "Rackheath Aggies," commanded by the fabled Col. Albert Shower (chapter fourteen). Riddled with shrapnel from German ground fire, Grace landed his bomber on a fighter strip in Normandy on June 12, 1944. Grace lived to fight another day and his Liberator continued flying with a newly assigned name, *Normandy Queen*.

On July 1, 1944, a youthful but experienced Maj. Marvin D. Lord took command of the 401st Bombardment Squadron of the 91st Bombardment Group at Bassingbourn, transferring from the 381st Bombardment Group. Lord replaced Maj. James H. McPartlin, who was very much admired in the squadron and realized it would be a challenge to fill McPartlin's flight boots. He needn't have worried. Lord's infectious grin, cheerful manner, and steady competence went over well in his new outfit. Already selected for promotion to lieutenant colonel (base pay: $3,500 per year), Lord was immediately accepted and appreciated.

The Eighth Air Force intensified its efforts throughout the summer, especially against oil and synthetic oil targets. Bomber crewmembers were busier than ever, but no squadron flew every day. On August 8, 1944, Lord presided over a meeting at the base theater at Bassingbourn to introduce himself and to praise the ground crews of the 401st squadron newly under his command. The next day, August 9, 1944, the Eighth Air Force dispatched 824 Fortresses and Liberators to a variety of targets that included fuel depots and airfields. Engineer-gunner Tech. Sgt. George A. Parrish of the 91st Bombardment Group flew with Lord for the first time. They were supposed to go to Munich, diverted to an alternate target in Belgium, and dodged heavy flak coming away from the target area. By now, Parrish had flown plenty of missions in a command ship, but today he was seeing something new.

"I had flown with McPartlin and would not have believed anyone could do a better job," said Parrish. "This mission, with 1st Lt. W. D. Thissell in the pilot's seat and Lord in the copilot's position, introduced me to a new kind of officer who could be 'all business' and still have incredible charm. He was just a person that you fell in love with. It made me feel real good to be around him because he was so nice. He was a real gentleman. But that didn't mean Lord wasn't also a first-class individual and a very good pilot." Parrish finished his thirty-five missions before the journey to Berlin at the heart of this narrative, but otherwise he would have gone to the German capital with Lord. "I would have been glad to fly with him anywhere," Parrish said. When Parrish needed a letter of recommendation for some purpose that he no longer recalls, Lord wrote it without hesitation.

On August 14, 1944, Fortresses and Liberators attacked Metz airfield in France, which would soon fall to advancing Allied armies. Parrish was again in the engineer-gunner slot with Lord flying in the copilot's seat as air commander. They flew a third mission together on August 25, when 1,116 Fortresses and Liberators attacked a wide range of targets deep inside Germany. It was a very busy day: The Eighth Air Force was continuing to do its far-reaching strategic job while the newly emerging Ninth Air Force was flying tactical missions on the continent. A Ninth Air Force P-38 Lightning pilot, Capt. Laurence E. Blumer, interjected himself in the middle of the heavy bombing by both strategic and tactical warplanes, and mixed it up with the Luftwaffe. Blumer shot down five Focke-Wulf Fw 190s to make himself an ace in a single day.

On September 11, 1944, the Eighth Air Force sent 1,016 heavy bombers to attack synthetic oil facilities at eight locations. It appears to have been the last mission Lord flew for a period of time.

MARVIN LORD AT HOME

Marlyn Lord was just ten months old when her father came home to Milwaukee to see her. Her first name was derived from the first names of her parents, Marvin and Evelyn (usually called Evey) Lord. Members of his family reported that Lt. Col. Marvin D. Lord was inexperienced—about babies.

Having a new baby was a very big thing to Lord and he talked about it constantly. He was a proud young father. He was well liked in his hometown community. When he wasn't holding Marlyn in his arms, he was visiting neighbors and friends. He had a special kinship with Miss Grimes, his German teacher at Bay View High School, even though her first name was never known to anyone in the Lord family. Lord visited Miss Grimes and told her he hoped he would not have a chance to practice the small amount of conversational German he'd picked up.

Months earlier, Lord finished his first tour in the war zone, changed bomb groups, and stayed in the fight. His hometown newspaper reported (probably in an exaggeration) that Lord and one other pilot were the only ones in his squadron not shot down. Wrote Journal reporter Robert J. Doyle:

"Now he is trying to decide whether to put in for a thirty-day leave. Men taking such leaves usually are away from their bases about three months and he doesn't want to miss anything."

Doyle wrote of the pilot with "blond hair and a ruddy complexion" as someone afraid to go home because it might mean missing the "best part of the war." He quoted Lord:

"I want to see the sacrifices those boys made last summer pay off. The Jerries made us pay for every raid last summer but without those raids we wouldn't have made the raids this year that paved the way for the invasion."

Family members believe his commanders ordered Lord to take time off from the war. That may be questionable: Unlike another very experienced Fortress pilot and leader Maj. Emmanuel "Manny" Klette, Lord displayed no rough edges, no sign of being frayed, no evidence of being anything but calm and happy. On October 20, 1944, just three months after the Doyle newspaper story, Lord dropped into Milwaukee unexpectedly on a thirty-day leave. Referring to his fellow crewmembers back in England, Lord said: "There are more boys over there who would rather come home to see their babies than for any other reason you can name. When it's about time for the baby to be born, they start sweating it out, and they keep it up until the telegram comes telling them that everybody is okay. Then they wait for the pictures. Just about everybody carries his baby's pictures. Whenever the fellows get together, they pull out their pictures and pass them around and compare their babies' heights and weights."

Looking boyish, almost impish, and a little toothy in a clipping from a newspaper that is no longer being published, Marvin D. Lord spoke to friends and neighbors about how much he'd missed Evey and how overjoyed he was to meet Marlyn. He said that he was the only twenty-three-year-old lieutenant colonel that he had ever known personally, but that he had heard there were others. "I'm told there's a twenty-four-year-old colonel," he said. Asked how he had gone from aviation cadet to lieutenant colonel in just two years, Lord explained that he'd completed twenty-five combat missions, pulled headquarters duty for a time, and flown seven more missions before, during, and after D-Day. Friends in Milwaukee remembered that Lord had graduated from Bay View High School and had worked as a laboratory technician at the Kearney & Trecker Corporation before becoming a cavalryman in the National Guard and later joining the Army Air Forces. The company, a maker of industrial machine tools, survived in business for another half-century before being absorbed by another firm.

The images that shine forth from Lord's brief visit to his midwestern roots—and the absence of any doubt that he would be returning to war and to the fuselage of a Flying Fortress in the cold, high blue over Europe—form just one portrait, but the picture is typical of so many. In generations to follow, Americans would forget how very young men like Lord were, how boyish their expressions often seemed, and how serious was their duty ahead. So far as can be learned today, Lord said almost nothing about the war while at home in Milwaukee, nothing about the Silver Star he had already been awarded, nothing about returning to vast aerial battles fought at sub-zero temperatures in the frigid high reaches where uncommon valor was a common virtue.

FEMOYER OVER MERSEBERG

"Merciless Merseberg," they called it. On November 2, 1944, on a day not dramatically different from others during this period in the war, the Eighth Air Force sent 1,174 bombers and 968 fighters to various targets—most to the petroleum facility at Merseberg that may have been the most-heavily defended target of the war. It was a difficult day for everyone in the air but especially difficult for the 711th Bombardment Squadron of the 447th Bombardment Group, flying out of Rattlesden in East Anglia.

A quick succession of aircraft shootdowns was followed by a heinous collision that wiped away a pair of Fortress crews in an instant. Second Lieutenant Jerome Rosenblum's bomber fell from the formation, badly riddled from flak explosions. The plane was a Fortress named *Hotshot Green*. Its navigator, 2nd Lt. Robert E. Femoyer, twenty-three, was gravely wounded but asked crewmates to prop him upright so he could see outside and check his maps.

Femoyer would later be cited, in the words that bring a chill to anyone familiar with the only context in which they are ever used, for "conspicuous gallantry and intrepidity at the risk of his life above and beyond the call of duty." With just a handful of words omitted for clarity, the citation continues:

> The bomber was struck by three enemy antiaircraft shells. The plane suffered serious damage and Femoyer was severely wounded in the side and back by shell fragments that penetrated his body. In spite of extreme pain and great loss of blood he refused an offered injection of morphine. He was determined to keep his mental faculties clear in order that he might direct his plane out of danger and so save his comrades. Not being able to arise from the floor, he asked to be propped up in order to enable him to see his charts and instruments. He successfully directed the navigation of his lone bomber for 2 1/2 hours so well it avoided enemy flak and returned to the field without further damage. Only when the plane had arrived in the safe area over the English Channel did he feel that he had accomplished his objective; then, and only then, he permitted an injection of a sedative. He died shortly after being removed from the plane.

Femoyer's Medal of Honor was awarded posthumously.

MISSION TO SAARBRUCKEN

As heavy bombers escorted by fighters continued to fly deep into the Third Reich, Eighth Air Force strategists also sought to use the B-17s and B-24s for tactical missions closer to the front lines. It rarely worked well. On November 9, 1944, the American side lost eight bombers and three fighters in takeoff or landing mishaps on a mission intended to assist Gen. George S. Patton's crossing of the Moselle River near Metz, France. As always, the weather was grim, the temperature was cold, and the men were cold. Diverted by gloomy clouds, rainfall, and frigid winds, crewmembers who'd anticipated a milk run found themselves up against formidable flak defenses at the secondary target, Saarbrucken, Germany.

First Lieutenant Donald Joseph Gott, 21, was pilot of a Fortress named *Lady Jeanette* of the 729th Bombardment Squadron, 452nd Bombardment Group, and was flying his twenty-seventh mission. Second Lieutenant William Edward Metzger Jr., twenty-two, was the copilot and was making only his second combat sortie. The Flying Fortress took heavy hits from flak while on its bomb run and fell from the formation. Crewmembers aboard other Fortresses lost sight of *Lady Jeanette* entirely.

Three of the aircraft's engines were damaged beyond control and on fire; dangerous flames from the number four engine were leaping back as far as the tail assembly. Flares in the cockpit were ignited. A fire raged inside *Lady Jeanette*, fueled by free-flowing fluid from damaged hydraulic lines. The interphone system failed. In addition to these serious mechanical difficulties, engineer Staff Sgt. Russell W. Gustafson was wounded in the leg while radio operator Tech. Sgt. Robert A. Dunlap's arm was severed below the elbow. No one could find any morphine to administer to Gustafson.

Suffering from intense pain, even after copilot Metzger fought his way to the radio compartment and helped administer a tourniquet, Dunlap fell unconscious. Faced with the imminent explosion of his aircraft, and the death of his entire crew, mere seconds before "bombs away," Gott conferred with Metzger . Something had to be dome immediately to save the life of the wounded radio operator. The lack of a static line and the thought that his unconscious body striking the ground in unknown territory would not bring immediate medical attention forced a quick decision. Gott and Metzger decided to fly the flaming aircraft to friendly territory and then attempt to crash land.

Lady Jeanette dropped her bombs. With Gott at the controls, the crippled B-17 proceeded alone to Allied-controlled territory. Once there, Gott had Metzger work his way through the trembling, partially burning aircraft to personally order all crewmembers to bail out. Metzger gave away his parachute plus a spare to men whose chutes had been damaged, thus choosing to remain with Gott to try to land the bomber. With only one normally functioning engine, and with the danger of explosion much greater, the aircraft banked into an open field, and when it was at an altitude of 100 feet it exploded, crashed, exploded again, and then disintegrated. All three crewmembers were instantly killed.

Waist gunner Staff Sgt. William R. Robbins bailed out of the B-17 and landed near Verdun. According to Robbins, the number four engine was knocked off of the aircraft and that the number one engine, as well, was hit by flak and couldn't be feathered. Robbins reported that the gravely wounded Gustafson was the last man out of the bomber. He survived, but Dunlap and tail gunner Staff Sgt. Herman Krimminger, who may have never gotten, or not understood, the order to bail out, perished along with the two pilots.

Gott and Metzger were posthumously awarded the Medal of Honor.

CREW CHANGE

A routine change of duty assignments for one bomber crew on November 6, 1944, was no different from hundreds of changes that took place every day, but it would have consequences for tail gunner Staff Sgt. Frank T. Chrastka, the nineteen-year-old, blond, 185-pound Illinois native who'd been flying with the B-17 Flying Fortress crew of pilot Capt. Ronald E. Bereman.

It had nothing to do with stealing coal. But in a larger sense, perhaps if divine intervention was a factor, Chrastka was being punished.

Chrastka and radio operator Tech. Sgt. Daniel C. "Clint" Pentz were always trying ways to combat the cold in the Quonset hut they occupied. The hut was equipped with an old metal stove that would burn almost anything combustible, but there wasn't much to burn.

"We should grab up some of those boxes the bombs arrive in," said Chrastka.

"That won't work," said Pentz. "Those boxes are made of pressed paper. That won't burn inside the stove."

"Well, then," said Chrastka, "how about we steal some coal?"

"Are you out of your mind?" said Pentz. "Where are we going to find coal?"

The answer was . . . the chaplain.

They found coal on a midnight raid to the chaplain's quarters within walking (or running) distance of their Quonset. Under cover of darkness, Chrastka and Pentz brought a bucket and located a bin where the chaplain had a generous supply. They appropriated some of it, threw the coal into their hut's stove, and for a brief time were as close to being warm as anyone could be at a bomber base in East Anglia.

And then, suddenly, the best friends were no longer billeting together, no longer flying together. Their joint prank-pulling days were over.

Bereman and his men were tapped to become a lead crew of a pathfinder (PFF) aircraft for the 486th Bombardment Group. The PFF planes were the ones that carried the air commanders—Lewis Lyle, Harris E. Rogner, Robert "Rosie" Rosenthal, James A. Smyrl, Marvin D. Lord, and others—on each mission. On a PFF ship carrying a mission leader, the ball turret was replaced with a thimble-like device housing radar. Because the mission leader usually occupied the copilot's seat, on a PFF ship the copilot was relegated to the tail gunner's position, a shift that often created a great deal of disgruntlement and did little to improve a Fortress's defenses from behind. Chrastka thought it was a crazy idea, putting an officer-pilot on his knees, facing to the rear, and making him responsible for a bomber's defense from behind.

"That's how it's done," someone told him.

While Bereman and seven of his nine-man crew remained together, ball turret gunner Staff Sgt. Johnnie L. Jones and Chrastka no longer had a place on the crew. Bereman's crew had completed nineteen combat missions so far and the nine men had a bonding, a cohesion that was torn asunder by this routine change. Pentz felt the crew would never bond the same way again.

Eventually, Chrastka became tail gunner with a different crew led by pilot 1st Lt. Lewis K. Cloud on a plane dubbed *Blue Grass Girl*.

HALPER OVER BERLIN

Pilot 1st Lt. Charles "Chuck" Halper of the 385th Bombardment Group wasn't scheduled to be in the air on December 24, 1944. Once aloft, Halper wondered if he would see the ground again.

"Having been advised that I would stand down the next day, I stayed up reading and writing letters until 3:00 a.m.," Halper wrote in a family memoir.

"Two hours after I had turned out my light, the CQ—charge of quarters—awakened me and said that Operations had changed their mind and I was to fly the number seven position in the lead squadron. After cold water and hot coffee, I was ready for briefing at 6:00 a.m. Brig. Gen. Frederick W. Castle, commander of the 4th Combat Bomb Wing, was to lead the Eighth Air Force in the most gigantic raid ever to hit Germany. Units of the Royal Air Force, the Ninth and Fifteenth Air Forces, and the Soviets would join us."

Halper was right about the magnitude of the mission. That day may have seen the largest aerial formation ever assembled—larger even, than the aerial armada that would travel to Berlin and Magdeburg six weeks later. On that Christmas Eve, the Eighth Air Force dispatched 1,400 B-17s, 646 B-24s, 803 P-51 Mustangs, and 50 P-47 Thunderbolts—a staggering 2,899 warplanes—to more than a dozen military and industrial targets inside the Third Reich.

Castle had been one of the first eight men to create the Eighth Air Force (chapter one). Today, he was flying an unnamed Fortress. Halper wrote:

> Once over the bomb release line, I had the copilot fly the aircraft so that I might observe the action in the sky around us. The bomber named HOT SHOT ABLE called to say enemy fighters approaching our formations from the twelve o'clock position had hit him. What appeared to be flares at about ten thousand feet were actually exploding fighter aircraft. Those striking the ground made an orange flash and then a big black mark in the snow. I saw six ships hit the ground when my attention was drawn to a Focke-Wulf Fw 190 passing from one o'clock high to ten o'clock low with two P-51 Mustangs on his tail.
>
> The Mustang leader left his wingman and on an inside turn cut off the Fw 190. A fairly short burst from the P-51 and the exploding

> Fw 190 threw debris all over the sky. Perhaps another German pilot had seen what happened because with a P-51 on his tail I watched him roll over, jettison his canopy, and bail out of a perfectly good airplane. Almost every attempt by the German fighters to penetrate our escort and get to the bombers was thwarted by our P-51s and P-47s. However, some bomber losses could not be avoided.
>
> From my vantage point, I saw three bombers go down. Two were the result of the ever-present mid-air collision, the other from poor judgment of another sort. I watched as Gen. Castle vacated his lead position and his deputy leader replaced him. Leaving the formation with mechanical problems, he flew well outside the bomber formation and headed back to England without fighter cover. German fighters shot him down before an escort could help him.

Castle struggled with his controls and traveled some distance away from the protection of the bomber force, where he was again attacked. A third attack set both engines on the right wing on fire. Castle ordered the bomber abandoned, but it spun into a dive. The pilots recovered from the dive and seven of the nine crewmen parachuted. The pilot was observed in the nose of the airplane hooking on his parachute, with Castle still at the controls, when the fuel tank in the burning right wing exploded, putting the B-17 into a spin from which it did not recover, crashing near Hods, Belgium. Of the nine crewmen, five survived the crash. Castle did not.

Castle's leadership and heroism are firmly established. His final moments, however, are controversial. Did he or his pilot have a choice about putting their Fortress in a place where it was more vulnerable to swarming German fighters?

"I turned my Fortress over to my co-pilot so I could watch for fighters around us," Halper said in an interview for this book that differed from his written memoir. "I watched German and American fighters. I was directly behind Castle's group. When he was hit, I saw him make the turn out of formation to return to base. There was no radio call from him to alert the fighters to afford him an escort. He was going back all by himself. I remarked to my copilot: 'This is a damn fool thing to do. The Germans have excellent intelligence.' I followed him from nine o'clock around to seven o'clock and the German fighters jumped on him and shot the hell out of him. A green second lieutenant would never have made a turn out of formation like that. He may not have been handling the controls. The pilot may have been. But even if the pilot was doing the flying, Castle could have used the radio."

Castle was posthumously awarded the Medal of Honor. "If he had been First Lieutenant Castle instead of Brigadier General Castle, we would have lamented his loss every bit as much, but he wouldn't have received that award," said Halper.

"That day's mission reminded me once again of how different it was to watch a fighter plane go down compared to a bomber. Fighters were flitting about the sky all the time anyway, so that when it was in an unusual attitude one was not inclined to pay much attention, and the pilot was usually able to bail out of his crippled plane as well. However, the bomber, flying along so majestically straight and level, was an awesome sight when it lost a tail or a wing and slipped into its deadly spin. This was made more so, no doubt, by the realization that there were men inside her fighting to get out."

Halper added: "As we returned to base and circled the field awaiting our turn to land, I saw a great purple cloud in the gathering darkness, which had formed a backdrop for an incoming bomb group. Along with the red and green navigation lights, they had also put on their landing lights. The result produced a spectacle of a giant Christmas tree in the sky.

"It was a beautiful sight that was shortly followed by the sobering thought that the general was gone, hundreds of men had lost their lives on this mission today, and it was Christmas Eve."

CHAPTER ELEVEN

Thirty Seconds over Berlin

Mission to Berlin
February 3, 1945—10:51 a.m. to 11:30 a.m.

THE STREAM OF MORE than a thousand Eighth Air Force bombers, from one end to the other, was 360 miles long. *At 10:51 a.m. British Summer Time on Saturday, February 3, 1945*, when the first wave of Flying Fortresses reached Berlin, the last bomber was over the Zuiderzee in Holland.

At exactly that minute—10:51 a.m.—a bomber dropped out of the bomber stream and turned for home. The aircraft was *Happy Warrior*, piloted by 1st Lt. William Settler of the 838th Bombardment Squadron, 487th Bombardment Group. Although at least one crewmember recalls the sequence of events differently—saying that *Happy Warrior* completed its run over Berlin—official records say that Settler aborted when his number one engine went out and he could not keep up with the formation. By this account, Settler dropped his bombs on a target of opportunity just north of Osnabruck and began the struggle to get home.

The bombers formation continued relentlessly ahead. Colonel Lewis E. Lyle, commanding officer of the 379th Bombardment Group and air commander of the mission, said, "The bomber stream was three to five hundred miles long." Lyle later said that each Fortress crew would spend only between thirty and sixty seconds over the center of Berlin itself, but that "every second would demand vigilance." Lyle was at the front of the bomber stream when the formation, flying at 25,000 feet just north of Osnabruck, turned on the initial point, flying northeast on a heading of sixty-five degrees. *It was 10:52 a.m., British Summer Time.*

The initial point, or IP, was the point beyond which the bombardier of each lead aircraft controlled the flight path, using his Norden bombsight, and the Fortresses were expected to move ahead on an unwavering, straight-line heading, no matter how many flak blasts appeared ahead of them.

Lyle's crew was 100 percent focused on the job of leading and guiding every one of the B-17s in the long lineup.

Lyle, who would be officially credited with sixty-seven combat missions but would claim seventy-two, was universally admired and respected but not always loved. Life aboard a B-17 with Lyle in command was remarkably straightforward, often silent, and sometimes downright sullen. "From the outset, my crew understood that they were not to talk or even eat until we hit the ground after the mission was completed," Lyle later wrote. "If you were talking, your mind was not on the business at hand." Lyle wrote that he became known as a strict disciplinarian who made sure crews "knew that I was the only person operating the aircraft and was the only crewmember that could do something with the airplane for their survival." As commander of the entire Berlin mission, Lyle spent a little less time worrying about throttle, yoke, and rudder and a little more time on navigation, attack, and accuracy.

Lyle often used ten-foot cloth streamers obtained from the base parachute shop and tied to the fins of the lead Fortress's bombs, to increase visibility of the lead airplane's bombs when they were released.

As the first group over Berlin, Lyle's 379th Bombardment Group passed through flak that an intelligence officer called "moderate, black, and accurate." Some clearly felt that "moderate" was not a strong enough descriptor. Six Fortresses in Lyle's 379th group took major damage, a dozen sustained minor damage, and one was lost. The B-17 piloted by 1st Lt. William Webber was hit by flak and lost over the Berlin city center. *It was 11:02 a.m., British Summer Time.*

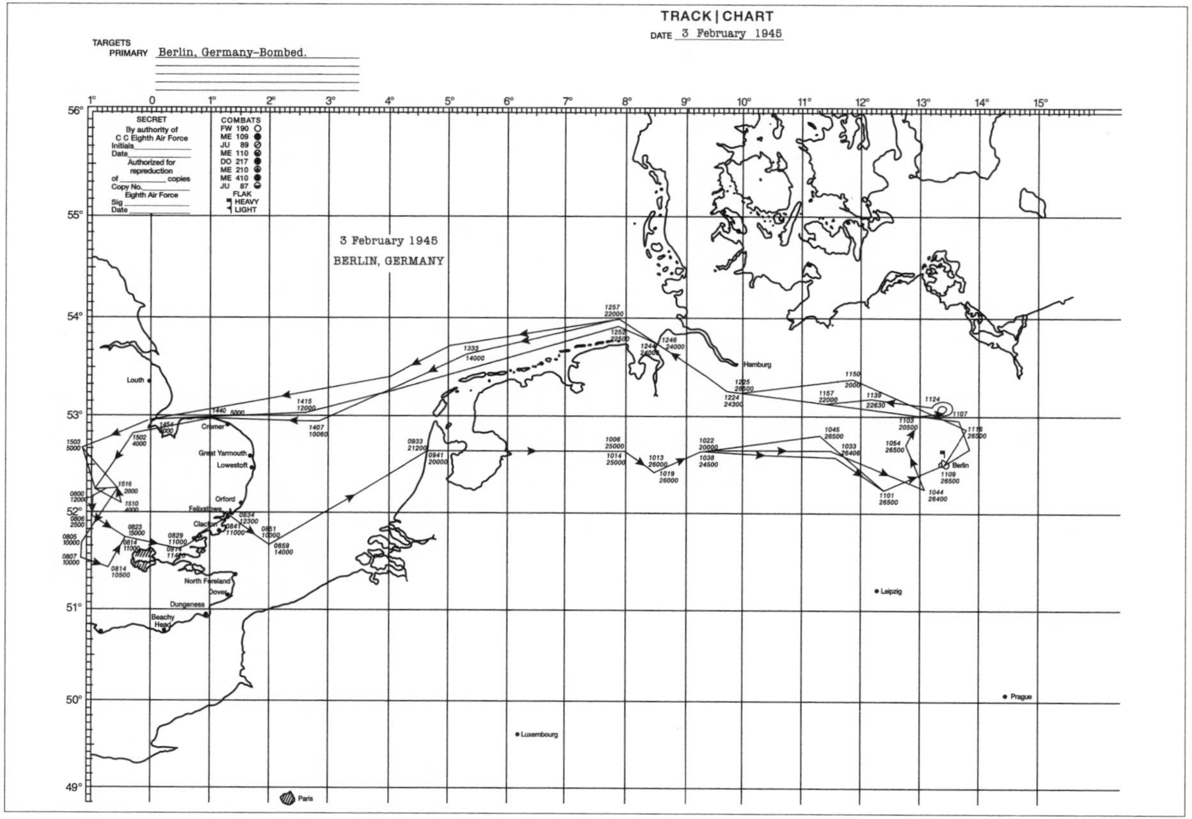

Track chart for Berlin bombing mission of February 3, 1943.

Webber's plane was *The Birmingham Jewel* of the 379th group's 525th Bombardment Squadron. Webber and three others were killed. The Germans captured five crewmembers who survived the war. The dead were Webber, toggleer Staff Sgt. Raymond Weatherbee, radio operator Tech. Sgt. Carl E. McHenry, and ball turret gunner Sgt. William I. Wells. The survivors were copilot 2nd Lt. James T. Kiester, navigator 2nd Lt. Thomas A. Pickett, engineer-gunner Tech. Sgt. Harold F. Francis; waist gunner Staff Sgt. William Scarffe, and tail gunner Sgt. Bennett D. Howell.

Most bomber crewmembers formed few lasting impressions of Berlin itself, a plains city without distinctive terrain features. At the beginning and end of the bomber stream's passage overhead, undercast covered the city's rooftops and avenues. In the middle and end of the long bombing run, smoke churned skyward from bomb explosions. The ball turret gunner and tail gunner of a Flying Fortress—the latter in his uncomfortable, kneeling position facing rearward, had the best view but were busy calling out flak bursts and looking for the Luftwaffe fighters that never came. One member of the 379th group said, simply: "It was a city."

In another bomber of Lyle's 379th group, 1st Lt. Carl L. "Kayo" Cook was minding his bombardier's position in the nose and possibly feeling some temporary relief that his Fortress had not yet been hit. Cook had just written to his wife, the former Helen Kraft, in Pender, Nebraska, cheerfully reporting that he'd be home soon because he had just six missions left to fly. He was the father of two daughters, including one born just three weeks before on January 12, whom he'd never seen. Cook's mother-in-law had recently remarried. The family was planning a big homecoming for him.

A fragment of metal, apparently from a flak explosion, punctured the Fortress's glass nose, continued into the cramped narrow tube of the fuselage, and killed Cook instantly.

No one else in his plane was touched. Cook's crew would make it home without him.

A mighty machine unstoppable in its momentum, unable to slow down or change course, the Fortress formation pressed ahead while flak intensified and undercast and smoke began to shroud rooftops far below. One box of Fortresses after another, the bomber stream passed over the German capital.

STARDUST OVER BERLIN

If the first group over Berlin, Lyle's, lost a crew, things were even worse for the second of the twenty-six groups in the bomber stream—the 384th Bombardment Group.

They were the boys from Grafton Underwood and although a different bomb group (the 100th) often claimed to be the unluckiest and hardest hit, today was a very bad day for the 384th. When it lost an aircraft on its second mission of the war, back in the beginning, a crewmember managed to send a postcard to the group commander from his prison camp in Germany. "Keep the show on the road," Maj. Selden L. McMillin wrote to the 384th group's first commander Col. Budd J. Peaselee. That became the motto of the 384th, and it appeared in documents, painted on the side of a building, and on at least one airplane. Today, keeping the show on the road was difficult.

Stardust, piloted by 2nd Lt. George F. Ruckman, dropped its bombs, pulled off the target, and was struck by a flak blast that severed hydraulic lines and set an engine afire. Trailing gouts of black smoke, *Stardust* departed the formation.

Another engine froze up for lack of oil, but the fire was out in the engine that had started burning. Ruckman remembered the tailwinds that had been behind them all day, concluded he couldn't return to England in this condition, and informed his crew that they were heading for Russian lines. The Americans had conflicting information about what would happen if they fell into Russian hands and as *Stardust* turned to struggle its way eastward, someone was heard to groan on the intercom. The rest of the 384th looked on helplessly as *Stardust* faded into the eastern distance. *It was 11:04 a.m. British Summer Time.*

While *Stardust* was vanishing, the 384th group took another battering when an unnamed Fortress piloted by 2nd Lt. Charles R. Molder was heavily hit by antiaircraft fire. Descriptions of the intensity of German flak over Berlin vary from one bomb group to another, as do descriptions of undercast and smoke over the target (the average crewmember was given about half a minute to look down at the city and form an impression), but no one doubts that Molder's bomber was hit, hard. Molder broke radio silence to report that he had two injured, two engines out, and a fire on his aircraft. "We're going to bail out," Molder said.

Molder's aircraft was later found near the German village of Prenzlau after an apparent, violent forced landing. In fact, the damaged bomber appears to have landed itself. Molder's entire crew took to their parachutes while steering away from the crowded sky over Berlin. Prisoner of war status lay ahead for Molder, copilot 2nd Lt. Hobart W. Treadway, navigator Flight Officer Ernest R. Knowlton, toggleer Sgt. Ralph M. Hayden, engineer-gunner Staff Sgt. Daniel B. Hobkallo, radio operator Staff Sgt. Harold V. Haynes, ball turret gunner Sgt. Damien N. Constantine, waist gunner Sgt. Harris F. Jacobs (who had serious leg injuries), and tail gunner Sgt. Leonard J. Rizzuti. All of Molder's crew survived the war.

The third, final, and worst casualty for the 384th Bombardment Group during its tense seconds over Berlin was *The Challenger*, piloted by 2nd Lt. Robert C. Long. Hit by flak at about the same instant as Ruckman and Molder, Long made what may have been a mistake. He attempted to return to England rather than to cover the shorter distance to Soviet lines.

THE SHOEMAKER CREW

Into the sky over Berlin came the 305th Bombardment Group and the unnamed Fortress piloted by 1st Lt. Daniel G. Shoemaker—one of the many who would not survive this day. Shoemaker's was the fourth bombardment group over Berlin and was "mission lead" for the 40th Combat Group. *It was 11:08 a.m., British Summer Time.*

Shoemaker's was a Fortress that apparently had not been assigned a name.

Shoemaker's copilot 2nd Lt. Roy F. Moullen was handling the Fortress and Shoemaker was checking the instruments. The crew was fighting for survival with Moullen playing the leading role.

Moullen and another crewmember, in a report, later described their situation over target: "All of the men were tense and one could feel the added surge of power," they wrote. "As we left the initial point we did a 360-degree turn between the I.P. and the target and one group slipped in ahead of us. Upon completion of the turn, our lead ship sighted the target. About 11:05 a.m., we began our bomb run. As we approached, flak was bursting around the group ahead of us. As we approached 'bombs away,' ack-ack started to track us with very accurate fire. One burst knocked out the pilot's windshield. Bombs away, and the tail was hit hard."

Shoemaker's tail gunner, Sgt. Gale Snyder cried, "Oh, God, I'm hit!" His leg was shot off at the knee and held on by what appeared to be tendons and skin. The top turret was hit and had a flak hole dead center in the top of the dome. Thirteen to sixteen holes from flak fragments had ventilated the radio room and radio operator Sgt. Raymond Benton had three wounds in his left leg. Crewmembers gave first aid to Snyder while Benton tended to his own wounds.

Benton's oxygen was shot out, as was his radio set. One of the men grabbed morphine, which was frozen, and began warming it—the record does not explain how—for use on Snyder. In the minutes ahead, struggling for balance, working in a temperature of sixty degrees below zero Fahrenheit, their aircraft trembling beneath them, and the sky exploding around them, the members of Shoemaker's crew gave Snyder a quarter-grain of morphine and put a tourniquet around his thigh.

"We also had a hit from below," the Moullen report later said. "It had gone through the wing in front of the filler niche between engines three and four." Badly damaged, debris thrashing about in the rear fuselage, Shoemaker's B-17 departed Berlin while the bomber stream was just beginning to arrive over the German capital. The ordeal for Shoemaker's crew was just beginning, too. *It was 11:10 a.m. British Summer Time.*

The fifth of the twenty-six bombardment groups assaulting Berlin today was the 92nd Bombardment Group from the base in East Anglia known as Podington. This was the group whose air commander for the day, Maj. James A. Smyrl, was in a bomber that had been hit immediately upon arriving over the European continent, continued flying toward the target, and was now coming under fire again. On-scene air commander Smyrl would soon be fighting for the survival of himself and his crew, but for now the job was to get in and get out.

It was counterintuitive—Smyrl, pilot 1st Lt. Russell Bundesen, and navigator 1st Lt. James W. "Bill" Good all knew it—but their job was to remain exactly on course, unswerving, unwavering, taking no evasive action to avoid the bursting flak shells.

Making a visual run, the 92nd group's lead squadron arrived over Berlin on a true heading of ninety-five degrees at a true altitude of 23,900 feet, its high squadron at seventy-seven degrees from 24,400 feet and its low squadron at sixty-two degrees and 23,400 feet. The sky was filled with

Flying Fortresses and falling bombs. Exactly ninety seconds, a minute and a half, elapsed between the time the first and last bombs plummeted from the caverns inside Fortress fuselages of this group and its three squadrons. When the group's last bomb fell, *it was 11:11 a.m., British Summer Time.*

THE UNLUCKY 306TH

Behind Smyrl's 92nd group came the sixth American group over the German capital, the 306th. This was to be an unlucky day for the 306th, one member of which reported "intense, accurate, tracking flak from four minutes before bombs away, lasting eight minutes."

Almost every one of the thirty-five crews in this group had a clear view of what happened to the unnamed Fortress piloted by 1st Lt. George V. Luckett Jr. The bomber "received a direct hit in its left wing at 'bombs away,'" wrote a crewmember from another aircraft. In fact, it appears Luckett's crew may not have had a chance to drop bombs after a direct hit behind the number two engine set the entire trailing edge of the wing aflame. "The wing broke off and the aircraft went down in flames. Two, possible four chutes were reported," wrote the same crewmember. Another wrote: "Down in flames over target. No chutes seen." Yet another wrote that he "could see ribs in the skin where the wing was blown off."

Luckett, copilot 2nd Lt. Gilbert W. Clark, toggleer Sgt. Victor Cunningham Jr., engineer-gunner Sgt. Wayne L. Martin, and waist gunner Sgt. Jack E. Boesel all lost their lives as Luckett's Fortress, one wing torn off, spiraled down like an acorn on the wind, trailing a red plume of fuel-fire. Navigator 2nd Lt. Robert P. Foster, ball turret gunner Sgt. Bernard L. Whitman, waist gunner Anthony L. Spera, and tail gunner Victor M. Spevak are all believed to have gotten out of the Flying Fortress right over the smoke-covered capital, but Whitman and Spera apparently did not reach the ground alive. Foster and Spevak became prisoners and survived the war.

Everything seemed to be happening at once over Berlin now. Buddies watched Luckett's plane fall and watched another, piloted by 2nd Lt. Roland A. Lissner, cut sharply across the formation. It, too, had sustained a hit from an exploding flak shell. Lissner's Fortress, named *The Jones Family*, was clearly in serious trouble.

Not far from Lissner, the Fortress piloted by 1st Lt. Vernon F. Daley Jr., *Rose of York*, was also hit by flak. The plane had been christened in a ceremony by Britain's Princess Elizabeth and was named in her honor. It carried a passenger today, the British Broadcasting Corporation's Guy Byam, at age twenty-six renowned for the youthful enthusiasm of his voice on radio news broadcasts and clearly one of the most intrepid of war correspondents. Several of the crewmembers of *Rose of York* were completing their thirty-fifth and final mission, the benchmark that meant an end to fighting and a ticket home. Because of its distinguished name and its beloved passenger—Byam had been torpedoed at sea and rescued, had parachuted into Normandy with the British 6th Airborne on D-Day, and had jumped again with British paratroopers at Arnhem—this Fortress received considerable attention. The Associated Press reported: "The plane was hit by flak over Berlin. One engine was smashed and a second was leaking gasoline as the big bomber turned for home. It kept lagging behind the main formation. Finally another bomber crew reported hearing . . . distress signals from an area over the Frisian Islands in the North Sea." The exact time of the flak hit appears in none of the stacks of paperwork that survive the war, but it appears Daley's *Rose of York* was hit during an unusually intense and concentrated volley of flak bursts that also claimed the Luckett and Lissner Fortresses. *It was 11:12 a.m., British Summer Time.*

Within a minute, another bomb group, the 457th, "the Fireball Outfit," with the tall West Point alumnus Col. Harris E. "Rog" Rogner as air commander for his group and wing, was passing over a Berlin from which undercast was fast disappearing. The tall, ruffled, athletic Rogner—he was always "Rog" and you were in trouble if you called him Harris—studied rooftops, boulevards, and bomb damage while the bombardier aboard his Fortress enunciated the words, "Bombs away." *It was 11:13 a.m., British Summer Time.*

JOURNEY OF *THE JOKER*

The twelfth of the twenty-six bombardment groups passing over Berlin was the 381st Bombardment Group from Ridgewell. Pilot 2nd Lt. John B. Anderson pressed ahead in his Fortress, which had been named *The Joker* in the recent past, although it's unclear whether the name was still painted on the aircraft. Anderson and his bomber belonged to the group's 532nd Squadron. Anderson stayed on course over the target, resisting the impulse to take evasive action, and dropped bombs amid flak that a witness called "moderate to intense." Anderson was hit.

A witness later wrote: "The plane swerved right off the target, then left, and went into a turning climb and exploded. The plane was under control until the crew bailed out." *It was 11:18 a.m., British Summer Time.*

An official report noted, "The number two engine was on fire and burning for about five minutes. The aircraft was observed to explode after the crew had bailed out." It appears Anderson did not bail out. He may have stayed at his pilot's seat to give his crew its best chance for survival. His remains were later found at Klandorf, Germany, not far from Berlin. All others aboard *The Joker* parachuted to the ground, were captured, and survived the war. They were copilot 2nd Lt. Leonard A. Wall, navigator 2nd Lt. Paul G. Cayori, bombardier Flight Officer James Forres Jr., engineer-gunner Sgt. Carl E. Kemppainen, radio operator Sgt. George R. Nessly, ball turret gunner Staff Sgt. Michael J. Medzie, waist gunner Sgt. Curtis P. Wallace, and Sgt. Robert H. McGreevey.

One of the witnesses, watching from another Fortress, was Staff Sgt. Jeremiah B. Hogan. He suffered a "mild" wound caused by a piece of flak that struck him at the center of the forehead. Hogan was wearing his flak helmet, but the flying metal passed just under the forward brim, without damaging his helmet.

Behind Anderson another member of the 381st Bombardment Group, 2nd Lt. Paul Pucylowski, was piloting a Fortress named *Hitler's Hoe Doe*, also named *Blind Date*, that left formation within two minutes of being over Berlin. "Pucylowski's fate is a mystery," an official report later said. "Nobody noticed anything wrong with his aircraft. It was last seen . . . when it left the formation, made a sharp turn, and slid underneath, disappearing from sight. No chutes were seen." Observers in other aircraft saw no sign of the Fortress being hit by flak—but it must have been. Anderson and copilot Flight Officer Harry M. Yarnes took the aircraft out of formation. Observers in other aircraft did not see the crew bail out—but they did.

Hoe Doe navigator 2nd Lt. John E. Kelleher was killed, although, all these years later, we do not know how. Eight others aboard the Fortress became prisoners and survived the war: Pucylowski, Yarnes, toggleer Sgt.

Herman A. Zichterman, engineer-gunner Tech. Sgt. Clarence E. Way, radio operator Tech. Sgt. Joseph J. Noxon, ball turret gunner Sgt. Stuart R. Mitchell, waist gunner Staff Sgt. Earl E. Green, and tail gunner Sgt. Robert M. Landes.

MARVIN D. LORD

There was more to come. Yes, there was more to come. Of the many bomb groups over Berlin that day, the 91st Bombardment Group from Bassingbourn had it toughest. Having been told there would be no mission, and then that there would, some had taken off for Berlin without little or no sleep. Most had been certain they would not fly today.

Aboard the lead aircraft for the group, with the crew usually led by Maj. Manny Klette—who'd been given a pass to travel to London—Lt. Col. Marvin D. Lord occupied the copilot's seat of 1st Lt. Frank L. Adams' bomber. Well, it was really Klette's bomber as many saw it and it was Klette's crew, but Adams was the pilot and Lord the group air commander.

At the start of the bomb run, Adams' bombardier, Capt. Nando A. "Tony" Cavalieri, engaged his Norden bombsight. Cavalieri had learned that morning of his promotion to captain. Now, the group would bomb on his lead.

First Lieutenant Theodore M. "Mike" Banta watched closely from his Fortress named *Yankee Gal*, not to be confused with another ship named *Yankee Belle* in the same formation. Banta described the tension as bombers passed over the smoke-covered German capital: "As we flew toward the target, each succeeding battery of flak bursts moved closer to us. This is when the sweat begins. Will we reach 'bombs away' before the antiaircraft gunners make the final correction that puts their bursts in the middle of our formation?"

Said Banta: "When bombs are released by the Norden bombsight in the lead ship, one of them will be a smoke marker bomb. As soon as the bombardiers in our other ships see this, they will pull a toggle switch releasing their aircraft's bombs. We bomb as a unit and a tight formation leaves the best diamond-shaped bomb pattern possible."

Cavalieri released. "Immediately after 'bombs away' and before lead pilot Adams could start his evasive turn, the lead ship received a direct hit from an antiaircraft shell right where the trailing edge of the wing meets the fuselage," said Banta. "The lead ship was blown cleanly in half. The nose section went immediately into a dive with engines still under power. The tail section appeared to fly along with the formation for a split second and then drifted out of my sight behind my copilot's window. My copilot told me that it fluttered back over the top of our rear element and was lost from his sight." Another source said the bomber was hit in the waist with a direct burst.

Although an official report places the time as 11:10 a.m., it appears this actually happened several minutes later. What has been in dispute ever since, among all who know about the sudden and total destruction of the Flying Fortress, was a question not about minutes but about seconds. Was it true, as Banta and others wrote later, that Lord's Fortress continued flying straight and level for ten seconds after dropping bombs—an eternity in air combat—making the plane far more vulnerable to flak? Or did someone in the cockpit, Adams or Lord, intend to pull off from the target immediately and fail to do so only because they were hit during the same second they dropped their bombs?

The ever-cheerful, ebullient Marvin D. Lord, a husband and father, a very young lieutenant colonel at twenty-three, a man known for optimism, had his life snuffed out in a blast that not only killed an entire Fortress crew: It also provoked bitterness and hurt that divided supporters of Klette from supporters of Lord. The divisiveness was still alive decades later.

Referring to the man who wasn't aboard the Marvin D. Lord aircraft, another pilot wrote: "Klette took this to heart, not only due to the loss of friends and men he had built into one of the best lead teams in the Eighth, but because he felt that had he been in the aircraft commander's seat and made the usual sharp turn off target, the flak barrage might have been avoided." This was speculation. No evidence exists that Lord did anything differently than Klette would have done.

In an instant, Lord, Adams, and Cavalieri, and all of Klette's crew—one of the most experienced in the Eighth Air Force—were gone. Among the ten who died aboard the Marvin D. Lord Fortress, the radio operator, Tech. Sgt. J. P. Holbrook, had flown 78 missions; the engineer, Tech. Sgt. David C. McCall had done 80; and the waist gunner, Tech. Sgt. George R. Zenz, no fewer than 104.

German authorities retrieved the remains of the ten-man crew. The official report does not provide crew positions for them: Lord, Adams, 1st Lt. Arthur C. Ebarb, 1st Lt. Stanley Sweitzer, 1st Lt. Norman L. Whelan, Cavalieri, 2nd Lt. Donald Shoemaker, McCall, Holbrook, and Zenz.

Aboard a Fortress called *Yankee Belle*, piloted by 1st Lt. George F. Miller, navigator Flight Officer Asay "Ace" Johnson was in his crew position on the left side of his aircraft when the command aircraft carrying Lord and ten others was blown out of the sky in a split second. Johnson did not see the bomber destroyed, but heard someone on the intercom, possibly pilot Miller, exclaiming, "Oh, my God! Look at that!" Just as suddenly, as the other Fortress disappeared to their right, Miller and Johnson were denied any chance to reflect further about the loss of Lord: It was their turn to be hit.

Blast and debris swirled around *Yankee Belle*, piloted by Miller, and another Fortress named *Rhapsody in Red*, piloted by 1st Lt. Elmer O. Johnson. New flak explosions also ripped into the *Belle* and into *Rhapsody*. Both Fortresses plummeted out of formation.

"Everybody stay alert," Miller said on the intercom.

"Our plane was thrown into a spin," said Johnson. "I think the flak hit an ammunition box because I was thrown around inside the plane and was hit by a lot of ammunition. Our toggleer [Sgt. Frank C.] Annis came to my aid."

Miller was a model of calm deliberation as he fought to get his bomber under control. In his official report, Miller later wrote: "All the aircraft control cables were severed except for our elevators and the automatic pilot control cables. This made for a busy time for all as we struggled north, constantly losing altitude. Finally, there was no sky left and our Maker provided a large muddy farm field in which I deposited the *Yankee Belle*."

"The pilot and copilot managed to pull us out of the spin we were in," Johnson said. "We crash-landed into a farmer's field." Luckily, considering the way he had been battered around, Ace Johnson's major injury was a broken collarbone.

Wrote researcher Ray Bowden: "The plane came to earth 20 kilometers [twelve and one-half miles] south of Altentreptow into wooded country and was claimed by the Luftwaffe's 1st Flak Division. German salvage crews inspecting the wreckage later reported *Yankee Belle* as being 40 percent destroyed." Miller and his crew became prisoners of war.

They all survived the war: Miller, copilot 2nd Lt. Walter V. Marxmeyer Jr., Johnson, Annis, engineer-gunner Sgt. John F. Zuvich, radio operator Sgt. Ellsworth H. Stumbo, ball turret gunner Sgt. Clyde J. Garrison, waist gunner Sgt. Julius M. King Jr., and tail gunner Sgt. Denver D. Holton.

Rhapsody in Red, decorated with a knockoff of an Alberto Vargas pinup illustration in the October 1944 issue of *Esquire* magazine, apparently left the formation but did not crash. *Rhapsody* survived the mission and the war.

ENTER THE 34TH GROUP

Altogether, about fifteen thousand bomber crewmembers appeared over Berlin, most remaining over the German capital for only thirty seconds to a minute. One of them was toggleer Ray Fredette aboard *Fancy Nancy* of the 34th Bombardment Group, who wrote in his diary that night:

> It was a fairly long bomb run. I was fully aware of the entire situation—hundreds of bombers bearing down with tons of high explosives to be dropped on Berlin. Berlin! Berlin! The very name of this city pounded on my brains. This was the heart of Naziland. This was the city where Hitler had preached his defiance to the world. This was the city where the throngs had shouted 'Sieg Heil!' but today it was the shriek of falling bombs and the rocking explosions that were heard throughout Berlin.
>
> As we approached flying over Potsdam there were large breaks in the clouds over the ill-fated capital. Large portions of Berlin were visible. Smoke was rising from the bomb hits scored by other bomb groups that had preceded us.
>
> Bomb bay doors were open now and there was flak up ahead. But for the first time I was more intent on the target than the flak. I felt exhilarated. My fingers twitched as I held the toggle [bomb release] switch.
>
> My eyes were glued on the lead ship. Then its bombs dropped along with two white smoke markers that hurtled downward. This was it. I struck the toggle switch and two tons of explosives in *Fancy Nancy*'s bomb bay fell away.

Fredette also wrote of the exhausting journey out of Berlin. Yet like most crewmembers today, he never saw a German fighter, never used his guns. *Purty Chili* copilot Robert Des Lauriers noted in his diary that his crew was in the air for eight hours, thirty minutes, a grueling ordeal with cold, vibrations, and deteriorating hydration for the men aboard the Fortress. Des Lauriers thinks he may have seen German fighters in the distance. He wrote that the German flak was "exceedingly accurate."

GIRL AND *LADY*

Almost an hour had elapsed after the arrival of the first Fortress when, just after noon, the 486th Bombardment Group arrived.

The Fortresses—including *Blue Grass Girl*, piloted by 1st Lt. Lewis K. Cloud, and *Lady V II*, piloted by 1st Lt. Arthur Ogle, dropped their bombs using guidance from H2X radar. As he pulled off the target, Cloud may have felt relieved. Remember, this was the thirty-fifth and last mission for every man aboard his Fortress, *Blue Grass Girl*, including two men who'd been "add ons" to his crew, ball turret gunner Staff Sgt. Johnnie Jones and tail gunner Staff Sgt. Frank T. Chrastka. So far, their bomber was untouched by German defenses.

Perhaps tail gunner Chrastka was disappointed that no Luftwaffe fighters appeared in the air behind him. Perhaps his thoughts were already beginning to turn to the completion of his combat tour and a promising life ahead. But as the spotter who faced to the rear in *Blue Grass Girl*, even without Luftwaffe fighters he had plenty of spotting to do. It was his job to tell the pilot what he saw of bomb damage in the sprawling German capital—handily visible, now that the undercast had cleared. It appears that Cloud pulled the bomber sharply away to the left after releasing bombs.

The "Bloody 100th" was now over Berlin. First Lieutenant Robert Fitzgerald of the 100th Bombardment Group, the bombardier who'd been told the target was a railroad station where panzers were moving toward the eastern front, remembered the hectic moments over Berlin:

"Our navigator was flying with Lieutenant Grant and Major Rosenthal as lead navigator of the 100th Bombardment Group leading the 3rd division behind the 1st division. Our crew was flying as the second deputy lead. We closed in on Berlin about ten minutes behind the last bomb group of the 1st division, giving the antiaircraft gunners plenty of time to get their sights on us.

"The Panzers were also using their 105 and 155mm guns on us," said Fitzgerald. This would be his steadfast, unflinching recollection for years after the war, yet it's preposterous: Not only was the 6th Panzer Army not in Berlin—it was still in Belgium, having never been uprooted for duty on the Eastern Front—it would have been impossible for a tank in the middle of a city to elevate and fire to Fortress altitude. But: "There were lots of white bursts," said Fitzgerald.

Major Robert "Rosie" Rosenthal, the fabled air commander of the 100th Bombardment Group, was in the copilot's seat of the lead aircraft for the 3rd Air Division, an unnamed Fortress. "Rosie" and pilot Capt. John Ernst peered through flak bursts at the flat, densely packed city of Berlin approaching them.

In the book *Flying Fortress*, Edward Jablonski described their arrival over target: "The flak proved to be murderously accurate over Berlin that day—'a beautiful day,' as Rosenthal would later recall it. He was of course referring only to the clear weather. The plane shuddered under the impact of the flak and the air filled with the noises of ripping metal. The number one engine spouted flame, a great white sheet spilling into the air stream behind the wing; the fabric-covered aileron shriveled, exposing the graceful metallic structure."

Pilot Ernst looked at Rosenthal, seeking guidance. "Rosie" gestured to continue, straight ahead. He knew the B-17 would never make it home. He also knew that if his aircraft didn't bomb accurately, the entire 3rd Division might scatter its bombs and needlessly kill civilians.

Also in Rosenthal's 100th Bombardment Group, the Fortress piloted by 2nd Lt. Richard A. Beck was hit by flak on the right wing. A report later said the damage was "thought to have been [caused by] a ground rocket," although the basis of this speculation is unknown and the Germans were not thought to have fielded any surface-to-air missiles. Aboard Beck's aircraft, the starboard engines began to flame and the aircraft nosed over into a steep dive, apparently because the crew was fighting to extinguish the fire.

Seconds later, Beck's aircraft pulled up in a half roll, heading directly toward a brace of 100th bombers, and then did a split "S" and went down.

Two chutes were seen to come from this aircraft as it fell away in a tight spin. When last seen, it was nearly completely engulfed in flames. *It was 11:24 a.m., British Summer Time.*

Navigator Flight Officer Dale B. Snow and bombardier 2nd Lt. Robert D. Carpenter were dangling from those chutes. They became prisoners and survived the war. Killed aboard Beck's Fortress were Beck, copilot 2nd Lt. Walter A. Rosenberger Jr., engineer-gunner Cpl. Pedro A. Martinez, radio operator Cpl. Lavelle E. Giles, ball turret gunner Cpl. Dudley S. Ingraham Jr., waist gunner Cpl. Herald R. Boyd, and tail gunner Cpl. Daniel E. McTaggart.

DIXIE'S DELIGHT

Flying through the same accurate bursts of flak that struck Rosenthal and Beck, 2nd Lt. Waldo J. "Wally" Oldham, pilot of a Fortress named *Dixie's Delight*, took a hit in the right wing and was flung violently to the right. Oldham and copilot 2nd Lt. Carl D. Dunn apparently had little chance to get the Fortress under control. Oldham's Fortress must have been the one 1st Lt. Richard R. "Dick" Ayesh referred to in his diary: "One of our ships in the squadron to the left got hit and was on fire," Ayesh wrote. "It pulled up 500 feet above the formation and peeled off and headed directly for us. We dived to get away from it and it went past us, upside down, just missing us by a few feet."

The crew bailed out. Waist gunner Cpl. Tom E. Ramsey discovered to his delight, while dangling from his parachute, that he had retained his heavy GI boots, which were tied around his neck. Coming down in a heavy forest north of Berlin, some of *Dixie's Delight*'s crew spent days evading capture, but all nine eventually became prisoners of the Germans: Oldham, Dunn, navigator 2nd Lt. Ross F. Purdy, bombardier Flight Officer Howard R. Leach, engineer-gunner Sgt. Patrick J. Tooly, radio operator Sgt. William E. Charlton, ball turret gunner Sgt. Richard G. Chapple, Ramsey, and tail gunner Sgt. Ralph J. Kalberloh.

Ayesh, in low flight, low squadron lead in the nose of his unnamed Fortress, passed through the flak bursts over Berlin without a scratch. Things did not go as well for the unnamed Fortress from the 100th Bombardment Group piloted by 2nd Lt. Orville H. Cotner. The third aircraft to be lost by the "Bloody 100th" in a matter of minutes, Cotner's

Fortress was hit by flak and blown apart in full view of everyone in his squadron. *It was 11:20 a.m., British Summer Time.*

The official report on the loss of the Cotner crew uses only three words to explain what happened: "Exploded in midair." We can assume that the destruction of the Fortress was sudden and the loss of the crew all but instantaneous. In a moment, the 100th group's hard-hit 350th squadron lost Cotner, copilot 2nd Lt. Robert A. Coover, navigator 2nd Lt. Elmer H. Rundy, bombardier 2nd Lt. Stephen G. Monick, engineer-gunner Sgt. Hugh P. Boyd, radio operator Sgt. Reinhardt J. Komloski, ball turret gunner Sgt. John C. Moss, waist gunner Sgt. Harold W. Snyder, and tail gunner Sgt. Donald R. Andres.

Rosenthal's Fortress stayed on a steady course until lead bombardier 1st Lt. Eugene E. Lockhart toggled its bombs, with the other B-17s in the squadron, group, and division following suit.

The 13th Combat Bomb Wing's report on the Fortresses led by Rosenthal told a typical story of accuracy and inaccuracy: "Attacking on a true heading of 52 degrees, the [lead] bombardier was unable to pick up the assigned main point of impact because of smoke from the previous groups' bombs," the report said. "The bombardier selected an alternate aiming point, which had not been hit by any previous bombing. No difficulty was encountered in synchronizing and when the bombs were released synchronization was good. [The C-1 automatic pilot] was used on the bomb run." The report added that the second and third squadrons released off the first squadron's smoke bombs, exactly as intended.

The report added that bombs fell into smoke 3,100 yards east of the assigned main point of impact with some exceptions. It noted there were bomb blasts visible through the smoke "just north of the Corlitzer Railway station, a few of which were seen on the north bank of the river [in the vicinity of another railway station]. . . . There were two to four hits and near misses on the church near the Corlitzer Station."

Rosenthal's Fortress was hit a second time. This time, it was worse. Men in other bombers saw the Fortress lurch upward and then down, as its bomb bay doors closed and then reopened.

Two men were killed instantly. Bombardier Lockhart and navigator 1st Lt. Louis C. Chappel probably never even knew what hit them. The others were enshrouded in choking white smoke that filled the flight deck.

Rosenthal opened his window and peeled off to the right, directing the group's deputy leader to take command. He took the controls from Ernest and headed northeast. A wall of noise roared around him as the aircraft began tearing itself apart while "Rosie" ordered crewmembers to bail out.

If there was time to ring the bailout bell—the signal for the crew to jump—Ernst would have activated it using a switch adjacent to the left-hand seat. Another pilot in the air that day, Robert Des Lauriers, remembered that few Fortress crewmembers had ever heard it. "I heard the bailout bell only once and that was on the ground in an orientation session. It was a high frequency sound over the bass of the engines." Often, in crisis, even though all three men on the flight deck knew the location of the switch, there was no time to use it.

Wrote Jablonski: "Rosenthal, certain that all who were able had leaped from the plane, put it on autopilot and, adjusting his chute harness, left the flight deck. The nearest exit was the forward emergency door just below and in front of the pilot's compartment. Rosenthal squeezed down toward the door, and saw that a man still remained in the ship. He would never know that man's identity, for he had been decapitated."

As the bomber stream continued its long parade over the capital, an official report said more about the results: "Sixteen concentrations of bombs could be seen bursting in the center of the city area south of Under Den Linden and adjacent to the Berlin Tiergarten. [There were] at least eight direct hits on the Air Ministry building. The Potsdam station siding area was heavily hit." The report also spoke to the Friedrichstrasse Railway station being blanketed by bombs.

In the next-to-last of the twenty-six bombardment groups passing in procession over Berlin (the 486th), *Lady V II*, the B-17 piloted by Ogle, with Major John Rex Jr. in the right-hand seat, took engine hits over Berlin.

Ogle began to fall behind the formation at just about the rally point. A third engine started to falter due to overboost and Rex suggested turning east towards Soviet-held territory.

Now, *Lady V II* was losing altitude rapidly. About fifteen miles south of Lake Moritz, Ogle's crew received fighter cover from four P-51s, although the "little friends"—bomber crews' universal appellation for escort fighters—soon had to drop away to the west and head for home.

Ogle's crew destroyed the bombsight and the H2X equipment. They unloaded everything not bolted down. Ogle found a break in the clouds at about 3,000 feet, saw an artillery duel below, and from that recognized the Eastern Front. They put down to the east of the front in a wheels up landing in friendly "recaptured" territory with no injuries to the crew and only slight damage *Lady V II*. It turned out that they were in Poland, and Polish partisans met them and turned them over to Soviet troops.

Ogle's crew thus survived. Cloud's *Blue Grass Girl* crew, with members' thirty-fifth and final trip over the Third Reich behind them, their tour of duty nearly finished, was heading in the opposite direction, bound for the safety of their East Anglia airbase, unscratched by German fighters or flak. In perfect working order, *Blue Grass Girl* had every reason to get through the last phase of the mission—the trip home—and bring Frank T. Chrastka and the others to safety.

It wasn't going to happen.

CHAPTER TWELVE

Squabbling

The B-17 Flying Fortress in the American Air Campaign
January 1, 1945 to February 3, 1945

IN THE MOTION PICTURE *Downfall*, seen in theaters decades after the war, Adolf Hitler tells his staff that that Messerschmitt jet warplanes can still save Nazi Germany from defeat. The celluloid Hitler was a disturbing portrayal by Austrian actor Bruno Ganz, but the movie quotes the Führer accurately. Hitler believed the Third Reich could be saved by Germany's advances in jet aviation and by other so-called "wonder weapons."

Germany's twin-engine Messerschmitt Me 262 (first flight: April 18, 1941) was the world's first jet fighter to enter service. It could have entered service at least a year earlier than it did and might have been available in greater numbers to stalk the B-17 Flying Fortresses and B-24 Liberators of U. S. Eighth Air Force. Total production of Me 262s was about 1,430, but only about 60 were operational at the start of 1945.

Over the years, historians have debated whether Hitler hastened his own defeat by ordering Me 262s converted into "blitz bombers" to strike advancing Allied troops, when the planes were more effective as fighters, intercepting bomber formations.

As described in the biography *Hitler 1936–1945: Nemesis*, by Ian Kershaw, Hitler's concern over the Messerschmitt's fuel consumption led to its top priority for production being lowered.

Hitler changed his mind when the plane was demonstrated to him in December 1943 at Insterburg air base in East Prussia. On January 7, 1944, Kershaw wrote, with "British testing of jet planes almost complete, Hitler demanded production on the Me 262 to be stepped up immediately so that as many jets as possible could be put into service without delay."

In May 1944, following up on remarks he'd made at Insterburg, Hitler ordered the Me 262 fleet converted into bombers. Today, some historians argue that the Luftwaffe essentially ignored the order.

Belatedly, in July 1944, the first Me 262s entered Luftwaffe service. In its first combat on July 25, 1944, an Me 262 attacked a British Mosquito flying a reconnaissance mission over Munich.

Britain's Gloster Meteor, which used more reliable centrifugal-flow turbojet engines, joined the Royal Air Force in 1944. The first practical U.S. jet fighter, the P-80 Shooting Star, reached Europe by May 1945, but saw no combat in World War II.

A typical Me 262 was powered by two 1,984-pound thrust Junkers Jumo-004B axial-flow turbojet engines, was armed with four 30-mm nose cannons, and reached a speed of 540 miles per hour. "By the time the German jets went into production, it was too late and nothing was going to change the outcome of the war," said British aviation writer Jon Lake. Me 262s shot down about one hundred Allied aircraft by war's end, but the Allies also shot down dozens of them. Bomber crewmembers thought about the Me 262 on every mission, heard about it in many briefings, and probably credited it with more than the German jet was really capable of.

"We heard about them around January 1945," said Fortress copilot 1st Lt. Robert Des Lauriers. "We saw them. Man, would they go by fast! On a mission in January, I witnessed an Me 262 flying straight up with a Mustang on his tail, also flying straight up. In briefings, we were told to be alert for them and especially to make note of where they were. We were very much aware that the German jets were very vulnerable when they were taking off and landing. Our intelligence guys wanted to put Mustangs into a position to pick them up off in the airfield pattern." By this time, Mustangs and even portly P-47 Thunderbolts were regularly blasting the German jets out of the sky.

"I saw a few," said *Fancy Nancy* toggleer Tech. Sgt. Ray Fredette. "The jets I saw weren't attacking us. They were observing our bomber stream from quite high up and off to the side. The P-51s took off after them. Just as the P-51s got close, the jets turned on the power and it looked like the P-51s were left standing still."

A German jet was a potent adversary when encountered one-to-one, but the jets had little overall impact. On January 29, 1945, when almost a thousand Fortresses and Liberators were visiting various targets, copilot Des Lauriers jotted in his diary that the weather over Kassel, not the Luftwaffe, was the problem. As they had been doing from day one, bomber crewmembers had to cope with cold, fog, clouds, winds, and the most severe European winter in many years. "You can say it more than once," said Des Lauriers. "We were always cold."

The jets were too late. Their engines were too unreliable. The skilled pilots to man them were too few. Yet even after the men of the American daylight bombing campaign were no longer coming out second best in the air battles over the Third Reich, long after they'd begun to lay waste to targets deep within Germany, and even after they had hobbled the Luftwaffe as an effective fighting force, many did not realize that they were winning the war. Even today, many do not recognize that they'd already won it.

The Allies had defeated Germany by the start of 1945. The war should have ended the previous fall. Even after renegade officers failed to assassinate Adolf Hitler in a plot that led to the conspirators being rounded up and killed, some kind of cease-fire might have been reached before the mission to Berlin described in this narrative. It didn't happen because of the Allied demand for an unconditional surrender—in terms of loss of human life, the costliest ultimatum ever issued in all of human history.

The surviving professionals in the German armed forces knew Germany was defeated, but executed their orders as if they didn't. Because Hitler and many of his lieutenants refused to acknowledge the obvious, the Allies fought the Battle of the Bulge, otherwise called the Ardennes Campaign. Up to 840,000 U.S. troops fought, and the American side suffered up to 80,000 casualties, including 19,000 deaths. It was the largest in which Americans ever fought, larger even than Gettysburg, larger even than Antietam. The Battle of the Bulge was hundreds of times the size of a slugfest soon to be waged on the other side of the world on a chunk of rock called Iwo Jima.

Severely weakened by the loss of a majority of its best pilots, hamstrung by the bombing campaign against oil and synthetic oil facilities, the Luftwaffe launched Operation Bodenplatte, or Baseplate, on January 1, 1945. This was an all-out air effort by 1,035 German warplanes intended to swiftly neutralize the Allied airfields on the continent. It turned out to be a last-ditch effort. At the end of the one-day assault, the Germans had destroyed 495 Allied aircraft, most or all on the ground, but had lost 280 of their own aircraft and had 203 pilots killed or captured. Both sides were continuing to manufacture airplanes, but the Allies had worn down the Luftwaffe by killing so many of its best pilots. On January 1, 1945, Hitler's air arm had a small cadre of keenly skilled pilots who had survived years of constant combat but were exhausted, plus a larger number of pilots with almost no training and very poor skills. This was the Luftwaffe that still existed to defend Berlin, Merseberg, Dresden, and other targets of the bombing campaign, but now could spend entire days or weeks without getting into the air to challenge Flying Fortresses and Liberators. This was the Luftwaffe at the beginning of a new year. In terms of violent loss of life caused by war, 1945 would be the deadliest year in human history.

SHIFTING BOMBER CAMPAIGN

Also on January 1, 1945, Flying Fortresses went to Magdeburg, the site of a synthetic oil facility that was one of crewmembers' least favorite targets. The Eighth Air Force dispatched 428 bombers, but only 11 struck the primary target. Many were diverted elsewhere and unloaded their bombs on secondary targets. About 120 Fortresses and Liberators were dispatched to other targets. The next day, almost as many bombers were dispatched to a variety of targets in Germany. Fortress copilot 1st Lt. Robert Des Lauriers wrote in his diary that he and the crew of *Purty Chili* hauled bombs to a railroad junction at Bad Kreuznach on January 2 and to a marshalling yard at Aschafenburg on January 3.

At his St. Germain-en-Laye, France, headquarters of United States Strategic Air Forces in Europe (USSTAF), which had been moved forward to the Continent from Bushy Park, England, Lt. Gen. Carl "Tooey" Spaatz—soon to pin on his fourth star—greeted 1945 while caught up in a fundamental disagreement about how to conduct the bombing campaign, made worse by the impatience of the bosses in Washington and London who were eager to finish off Nazi Germany and shift resources to the war against Japan. Spaatz drafted a document informing his bosses in Washington that the war was being won. Flak, the antiaircraft gun batteries that defended cities like Berlin, continued to be "too plentiful, too accurate and too deadly," Spaatz wrote, but fighters like the Messerschmitt Bf 109 and Focke-Wulf Fw 190, or even the newer German jets, no longer "can stand in our way with the strength they once mustered." American Flying Fortress and Liberator crews entered 1945 knowing that flak was their enemy, that the cold, high reaches above their targets would be blighted with exploding shells, and that even a single direct hit from an 88mm shell was more than enough to claim the lives of an entire bomber crew. The document Spaatz submitted was all but ignored while an argument about how to bomb the Third Reich grew in intensity.

Spaatz was the perfect field operative for Army Air Forces' commanding general Gen. Henry H. "Hap" Arnold. Arnold was a skilled administrator who knew how to pick the best people, give them leeway to hatch the best plans, and turn them loose. The most senior air officer in American history (he'd been elevated to five-star rank on December 21, 1944, days after the navy's Leahy, King, and Nimitz and the army's Marshall and MacArthur and one day after Eisenhower), Arnold never fired a shot in combat but agonized over the welfare of his bomber crews, constantly searching for ways to reduce their vulnerability. On at least one occasion, learning of high losses among bomber crews on a particular mission, Arnold locked himself into a room and wept.

Spaatz was a seasoned combat veteran of the previous world war with aerial victories to his credit, cared little about administration, but was a superior operator. Both men worried more about bomber crewmembers than about civilians on the ground. Both knew the war was being won, knew it should be happening more quickly, and, unlike Eighth Air Force boss Lt. Gen. James H. Doolittle, wasted little effort pondering moral issues. To historian Randall Hansen, Arnold was "irascible, gruff, and at times crude. He was ruthlessly driven and had no tolerance for those who adopted a more leisurely pace." Another critic deemed him "bloodthirsty." Arnold was a heavy smoker who'd had four heart attacks, suffered other health problems, and was not sure he would live to see Adolf Hitler defeated, let alone to attain his goal of an air force as an independent service branch. He was prepared to do everything necessary to finish up the fight in Europe with minimum casualties to his crew and maximum harm to the foe. Arnold and Spaatz were ready to expand the U. S. bombing campaign to include area bombing of cities and they had plenty of backing from the supreme allied commander, Gen. Dwight D. Eisenhower.

CITY BOMBING

The British willingness to bomb cities vis-à-vis the American insistence on precision daylight bombing of military targets was under debate long before the mission at the center of this narrative. Referring to a city the Americans had not yet bombed, Britain's Royal Air Force Marshal Arthur T. "Bomber" Harris wrote in an internal memorandum: "Dresden, the seventh largest city in Germany and not much smaller than Manchester, is also far the largest unbombed built-up the enemy has got. In the midst of winter with refugees pouring westwards and troops to be rested, roofs are at a premium. The intentions of the attack are to hit the enemy where he will feel it most, behind an already partially collapsed front, to prevent the use of the city in the way of further advance, and incidentally to show the Russians when they arrive what Bomber Command can do."

Harris similarly wanted city bombing—also widely called area bombing—of Berlin. The British had been area-bombing other German cities for years while American missions had focused on specific military objectives. "Berlin is a symbol to the German people," Harris wrote in a separate memorandum that said nothing about any military target. By now, of course, the British and Americans had both made numerous bombing runs over the German capital, but the Americans were still convinced they were carrying out a military mission. "Down at the level where Fortress crews lived and worked, we had no idea there was a controversy," said Fredette.

A sustained bombing effort against Berlin, dubbed Operation Thunderclap, had been discussed months ago. The debate—"squabbling" one assistant to Spaatz called it—had divided the British and Americans into separate camps. As Randall Hansen wrote in *Fire and Fury*, a key member of Spaatz's staff wrote in a memorandum: "It is contrary to [American] ideals to wage war on civilians." Thunderclap was set aside, but the issue of where to place bombs remained a source of disagreement, often argument,

Major Emmanuel "Manny" Klette, center, was one of the most experienced pilots and air commanders in the Eighth Air Force. Some said he was fearless. Some said he had a death wish. On February 3, 1945, when Klette's crew went to Berlin, Lt. Col. Marvin D. Lord took Klette's slot as the 91st Bombardment Group air commander. *U.S. Army*

In a photo posed for publicity, yet indicative of a waist gunner's work, Sgt. Maynard "Snuffy" Smith mans his machine gun. Smith was awarded the Medal of Honor for an action on May 1, 1943. *U.S. Army*

A very young-looking 1st Lt. Dean Hansen was the pilot of Robert Des Lauriers' B-17 named *Purty Chili* during the February 3, 1945, mission to Berlin. *Robert Des Lauriers*

First Lieutenant Robert Des Lauriers was the copilot of *Purty Chili* of the 34th Bombardment Group, on the February 3, 1945, mission to Berlin. *Robert Des Lauriers*

The crew of Vega-built Boeing B-17G-75-VE (44-8629) named *Purty Chili* of the 391st Bombardment Squadron, 34th Bombardment Group, at Mendlesham in East Anglia, just before the Berlin mission of February 3, 1945. Standing, left to right: 1st Lt. Lee F. Sackerman, bombardier; copilot 1st Lt. Robert Des Lauriers; pilot 1st Lt. Dean Hansen; and 1st Lt. Ralph Wathey, navigator. Kneeling, left to right: Sgt. Darryl Young, ball turret gunner; Sgt. Val McClellan, waist gunner; Staff Sgt. John Green, engineer-gunner; Sgt. Harold Griffin, tail gunner; and Sgt. Gerald Shoaf, radio operator. *Robert Des Lauriers*

The crew of Douglas-built Boeing B-17G-15-DL Flying Fortress (44-6465) *Fancy Nancy* of the 7th Bombardment Squadron, 34th Bombardment Group, on the February 3, 1945, mission to Berlin. Back row, left to right: Tech Sgt. Raymond H. Fredette, toggleer/nose gunner; Tech Sgt. Robert E. Sweeney, gunner; 1st Lt. Gordon F. Barbaras, pilot; 1st Lt. Charles W. Ellis, copilot. Front row, left to right: Staff Sgt. Joseph O. Johnson, tail gunner; Tech Sgt. Tay R. Reyes, engineer/top turret gunner; Staff Sgt. Kenneth R. Hagler, ball turret gunner. Not shown: 2nd Lt. Benjamin Eisenberg, navigator. *Raymond H. Fredette*

Technical Sergeant Frank T. Chrastka from Forest Park, Illinois, was the tail gunner on the B-17 Flying Fortress named *Blue Grass Girl*. Chrastka (third from left) is gathered with other enlisted flyers in the Drum Room at the Hotel Savannah in Georgia, in July 1944, before going overseas. *Robert McCall*

First Lieutenant Richard R. “Dick” Ayesh was a bombardier with the 349th Bombardment Squadron of the 100th Bombardment Group, the “Bloody 100th,” on the February 3, 1945, mission to Berlin. *Richard R. Ayesh*

Technical Sergeant Raymond H. “Ray” Fredette was toggleer/nose gunner of the Douglas-built Boeing B-17G-15-DL Flying Fortress (44-6465) *Fancy Nancy* of the 7th Bombardment Squadron, 34th Bombardment Group, on the February 3, 1945, mission to Berlin. *Raymond H. Fredette*

While B-17 Flying Fortresses attacked Berlin on February 3, 1945, B-24s struck the synthetic fuel facility at Magdeburg. One of the bombers was Ford-built B-24H-15-FO Liberator (42-52534) *Witchcraft* of the 790th Bombardment Squadron, 467th Bombardment Group. *Witchcraft* flew 130 combat missions between March 19, 1944, and April 25, 1945. *Vincent Re*

Major Tommy Hayes was one of the P-51 Mustang pilots who appeared over the German capital during the first full-scale mission to Berlin on March 6, 1944. *U.S. Army*

Major Paul A. Conger, commander of the 63rd Fighter Squadron and an ace with ten aerial victories, took the 56th Fighter Group into battle over Berlin on February 3, 1945. *U.S. Army*

Second Lieutenant Grant Turley sits in his P-47 Thunderbolt *Kitty* of the 78th Fighter Group. Sitting in front of the cockpit is crew chief Staff Sgt. Albert Costelnik. On the wing at left is armorer Staff Sgt. James W. Sterner. Also on the wing is assistant crew chief Sgt. Albert J. Turrow. Turley became an air ace and lost his life on a mission to Berlin before his twenty-third birthday. *Turley family*

Colonel Harris E. Rogner, a six-foot-three West Pointer, was air commander for the 457th Bombardment Group and for his wing during the February 3, 1944, assault on Berlin. *Rogner family*

First Lieutenant James W. "Bill" Good of the 92nd Bombardment Group peered from his cramped nose position and watched another aircraft sustain a mortal flak hit over Berlin on February 3, 1945. *James W. Good*

This is a P-51D-5-NT Mustang (44-11622) of the 362nd Fighter Squadron, 357th Fighter Group. The pilot was Maj. Leonard Carson with eighteen aerial victories. The location is AAF Station F-373 in Leiston, England. *Norman Taylor*

A Boeing B-17G Flying Fortress fights its way through puffs of smoke left by exploding German flak shells. *Norman Taylor*

The bombing of German cities left hundreds of square blocks of rubble, ruin, and hollow shells of buildings. This is Magdeburg, but much of Berlin was similar. *Vincent Re*

Visibly weary and afflicted with the "thousand-yard stare" familiar to combat veterans, Maj. James A. Smyrl (left) has just returned from the February 3, 1945, Berlin mission. He is talking to Col. James W. Wilson, 92nd Bombardment Group commander. *James W. Good*

The Smyrl crew just after the February 3, 1945, mission. In the back row are (left to right) navigator 1st Lt. Hershal Crowley, pilot Capt. Russell Bundesen, air commander and copilot Maj. James A. Smyrl, bombardier 1st Lt. Walter Neppel, navigator 1st Lt. James W. "Bill" Good, and radar navigator 1st Lt. Warren Doolittle. The gunners in the front row are unidentified. *James W. Good*

between the two great western allies. Wrote Hansen: "Before 1945, Spaatz tried whenever possible to avoid killing German civilians. Harris killed them deliberately and with equanimity." A study would later show that the British killed 75 percent of the civilians who perished during the bombing of the Third Reich.

British and American officers, including Spaatz and Harris, now revived a version of Thunderclap on a smaller scale. In late January 1945, a senior Royal Air Force officer on Harris's staff proposed a coordinated air attack to help the Soviet offensive in the east and to target German morale. Spaatz discussed the plan with the U.S. commander Gen. Dwight D. Eisenhower. British Prime Minister Winston Churchill raised questions, whereupon Harris's staff recommended bombing missions against Berlin, Dresden, Leipzig, and Chemnitz.

By mid-January, Harris had sent his British night bombers to Nuremberg, Hanau, Munich, and other city centers. On January 16, Harris sent bombers to Magdeburg, which was constantly alternating between number two and number three on the list of key oil targets, and which would soon receive a visit by American Liberators. Magdeburg's military value was enormous, but that did not prevent historian Randall Hansen from pointing out that the city had "churches, narrow streets and [an] elegant city hall, along with fin-de-siecle northern suburbs." Wrote Hansen: "The bodies of women, children and old men were piled up in the gutters."

The American air campaign in the high cold over Europe was being conducted for the most part by staff sergeants and first lieutenants. Most had no idea that the British and Americans, with Spaatz caught in the middle, were arguing whether to bomb people or petroleum. "Spaatz did not come around and ask my opinion," said *Fancy Nancy*'s Fredette. "Later we would be accused of 'terror bombing' and of 'baby killing,' but I was unaware of any shift in our policy until the morning of that massive mission to Berlin."

On January 12, Soviet forces ignored bitter cold weather to launch an all-out offensive that included a goal no less significant than the seizure of Berlin. By that time, the British and Americans were very serious in their fresh examination of Thunderclap, the only plan intended, in effect, to bomb a people into submission. The British, paradoxically, were now arguing that the best way to help the Soviets would be an increased effort against oil targets, but they also wanted a major strike on Berlin, which they said would disrupt the flow of German forces to the Eastern Front. The British were saying that an assault on Berlin should not interfere with the air campaign against petroleum and synthetic fuel. One British officer, recalling the bombing Blitz of London years earlier, questioned the whole idea that bombing city dwellers would cripple the Reich's willingness to resist. "We overlook the fact," this officer said quietly, "that when you bomb people they get mad at you."

While Harris and Britain's planners, widely criticized for killing civilians, were arguing for a campaign against fuel, Spaatz and American officers, seeking a coup that would end the war, were talking up the idea of area bombing of cities. We know today that Doolittle was unhappy about it, but Doolittle was also eager for the acceptance and support of his commanders, none of whom had as much combat experience as he. Although never ambitious in the sense of the traditional West Point military officers with whom he served, nor as restrained in holding back his opinions, the outspoken Doolittle wanted a fourth star and a place at the table when an independent air force was created after the war.

Arnold thought Doolittle needed a rest after years of war and a full year at the helm of the Eighth Air Force. While his autobiography says little about bombing people versus petroleum, or about the moral consequences of the Berlin mission that loomed, or about his voice in the arguments under way, Doolittle wondered if he was measuring up to Arnold's expectations.

"I think he wants to find out if I have mellowed enough to get along with people," Doolittle wrote to a family member. "I feel that I have, although the mellowing is not yet completed. I still have the unfortunate habit of expressing whatever is on my mind, which in many cases, even though it happens to be so, had better not be expressed. This old habit of talking when I should be listening is being gradually corrected. I still slip occasionally, but constant effort is producing results."

Although he personally said little about it later, when plans unfolded for the largest mission ever launched against a single target, Doolittle apparently reverted to form and was unable to keep his mouth shut.

PLANNING FOR BERLIN

On January 14, 1945, the Eighth Air Force dispatched 847 heavy bombers, escorted by 645 fighters, to attack petroleum targets and highway bridges. The Germans shot down seven Fortresses and eight other U.S. aircraft, but American fighter pilots racked up their best one-day record of World War II: They were credited with shooting down a record 174 German fighters. All by itself, the 357th Fighter Group was credited with fifty-six aerial victories, the highest number of kills by a combat group on a single mission. The following day, another 619 Fortresses and Liberators attacked various targets. And on January 16, Liberators went to Magdeburg while Fortresses struck a variety of targets. But while the staff sergeants and first lieutenants were winging their way through the high cold, the weather in Europe was growing dimmer and even colder, while the debate over the bombing campaign was heating up.

Arnold sent a vaguely worded and uncharacteristically indecisive message to Spaatz in late January 1945, making it clear he was under pressure to produce more immediate and more visible results from the bombing campaign, but not telling Spaatz how to achieve this. In retrospect, Arnold's rambling thoughts could be read as a green light for the Eighth Air Force to begin area bombing. It was a bad time to be writing about a change or even about any sort of larger-scale mission because the weather over Europe that month was the worst American crewmembers had ever seen. On a late January mission to oil targets at Neuss, another among a handful of the most heavily defended targets in the Third Reich, *Purty Chili* flew in the lead squadron and was over the target for just thirty-five seconds, long enough for copilot Des Lauriers to note that the weather was deteriorating. Shortly after that mission to Neuss—in which Col. Frank P. Hunter, the widely admired commander of the Fortress-equipped 385th Bombardment Group, lost his life—both the Eighth Air Force in England and the Fifteenth Air Force in Italy canceled several planned missions because of rain, winds, soup, and, as always, the bone-crushing cold that was such a constant companion to bomber crewmembers.

The weather was so bad for several days that no bombers flew at all. It was the longest period of inactivity for the Eighth Air Force, and it was no boon to the crewmembers who never fared well when confronted with idleness. The freezing murk may have given the German side some respite, but by now a few days wasn't going to make much difference. On the European continent, the newly arrived Douglas A-26 Invader was able to fly a few minutes alongside Douglas A-20 Havocs and Martin B-26 Marauders, but the heavy bombers stayed put. The weather kept them still until January 29, 1945, when the Eighth Air Force dispatched 1,001 Fortresses and Liberators to attack rail targets in central Germany and oil and industrial targets at Kassel. *Purty Chili*'s Des Lauriers hated Kassel—"there was simply too much flak there"—but he noted in his diary that the target was a Panzer tank factory. One Liberator and two fighters were lost on the journey.

It is impossible to pin down a date or time when the Americans and British reached some resolution in their squabbling, or when American brass set aside precision bombing for area bombing, or shifted emphasis from petroleum targets to city centers, or singled out the German capital for special attention. Possibly, the ongoing assault on Great Britain by Germany's V-2 ballistic missiles—true "terror weapons" if any ever existed—helped to prod the change in emphasis. According to historian Hansen, U.S. Army Chief of Staff Gen. George C. Marshall passed the word that he wanted a bombing attack on Munich as well as the cities in the Berlin-Leipzig-Dresden corridor. Marshall was said to have the full backing of President Franklin D. Roosevelt. For reasons unclear, Munich never made it to the top of the Eighth Air Force's targeting list, but Berlin did. By late January, working-level intelligence officers at East Anglia's scattered bomb groups were beginning to get hints that something big was coming involving Berlin.

At the end of January, Spaatz flew to England from his USSTAF headquarters in Paris. He met with Air Vice Marshal Norman Bottomley, British deputy chief of air staff, and debated bombing policy. Bottomley was a lesser-known figure than the RAF's Air Marshal Arthur "Bomber" Harris, but even more than Harris, he wanted to step up the pressure on German cities and civilians. After this meeting, Spaatz gave Doolittle verbal orders about when and how to strike various targets, but apparently named Berlin as the only city deep in the east of Germany to be targeted. Both the Americans and the British wanted to make it more difficult for the Germans to reinforce their units on the

Eastern Front. The British thought this could be achieved in part by bombing cities and creating large numbers of refugees. Spaatz appears to have opposed the idea on both practical and humanitarian grounds.

As plans came together for a full-scale assault on Berlin larger than any that had been mounted before, Spaatz insisted that the Fortresses have specific aiming points, such as "industrial plants, administrative headquarters, or possibly railway stations." This was a sign of Spaatz's reluctance to attack civilians, but what was good enough for Spaatz in this regard, as it turned out, was not good enough for the outspoken Doolittle.

Roosevelt, Marshall, and Spaatz didn't visit the Fortress aerodrome at Sudbury to seek out an opinion from Staff Sgt. Frank T. Chrastka of the 832nd Bombardment Squadron, 486th Bombardment Group.

Had they tromped through the cold to Chrastka's Quonset hut and gone inside, they might have discovered that the hut's space heater—the stove—was producing more than an average amount of heat. Had they looked around the base, they might have found that the chaplain's bin of coal was not as full as it was supposed to be. They might have noticed a calendar on Chrastka's wall locker marked up to show that he was approaching his thirty-fifth mission, the number needed to finish a tour of duty and return home. The ex-lifeguard, the prankster, the Polish boy from Milwaukee was already thinking about his future life back home in Wisconsin, but he wasn't thinking about area bombing versus precision bombing. Chrastka liked sports, jokes, and girls, but he apparently spent little time pondering grand strategy. As late as January 30, 1945, and perhaps a day or even two days later, Chrastka may not have known he would be separated from his usual crew headed by Capt. Ronald E. Bereman and from his usual flying mates like best-friend Tech. Sgt. Daniel "Clint" Pentz—or, at least, he did not know which crew he would be on. He apparently had not previously flown with the 1st Lt. Lewis K. Cloud crew on a Fortress named *Blue Grass Girl*.

The other crewmember who'd also been pulled from the Bereman crew, ball turret gunner Staff Sgt. Johnnie L. Jones, had brought a girlfriend down from London and parked her in an inn in Sudbury. Possibly before they knew they would be together on *Blue Grass Girl*, Jones told Chrastka that if anything happened to him (Jones), he wanted Chrastka to visit the inn and give his girlfriend the news. It was not to be.

No president, no prime minister, and no general stopped off at Mendlesham to look for advice from *Purty Chili* 1st Lt. Robert Des Lauriers either. Had they dropped in, they might have found Des Lauriers in a period of self-examination, for he was spending a lot of time reading books about religion and studying Roman Catholicism. On January 30, 1945, Des Lauriers did not know there was a controversy about bombing civilians, but he would reflect upon it later with very mixed feelings. In later years, he commented that if he had known more about "bombing the heart of a city," he might have been more concerned.

"But I wasn't," Des Lauriers wrote. "I was trained to be a pilot, to fly over the enemy and to drop bombs of destruction. Discipline had been drilled into us, that no matter what we thought an order was an order and you carry it out as best you can. That was true of the whole team, the crew, the squadron, and the group. No one even gave it a thought. Or if they did they kept it to themselves."

Added Des Lauriers: "We were fortunate, I guess, because we never saw war as it was fought on the ground or at sea. Yes, we were very aware we were in the enemy's sights on every occasion and they were doing their best to knock us out of the sky. And they did quite well. To see a direct hit on a bomber and see it go down is not so easy to explain or describe in detail." At least some Fortress crewmembers believed that ground troops were better off than they were since, in the end, a Fortress crew was very much on its own up there in the high cold blue.

In "Operation Thunderclap" in Volume 14, Number 1 (March 1991) of the *Journal of Strategic Studies*, Richard G. Davis tracked the developments leading to a moment of truth for Chrastka, Des Lauriers, and others:

> On January 30, Doolittle informed Spaatz of his readiness to undertake Thunderclap but he vehemently objected to the targets in the center of the city that USSTAF had instructed him to hit: "There are no basically important strictly military targets in the designated area." He pointed out that if he was to bomb the center of the city accurately he would have to bomb visually and take his forces over almost all of the three hundred guns defending the city. This would mean heavy casualties for the B-24s, which had a 3,000-foot-lower ceiling than the B-17s. He also questioned the basis of Thunderclap as a morale attack. In

> his opinion the people of Berlin would have plenty of warning to take shelter, and "The chances of terrorizing into submission, by merely an increased concentration of bombing, a people who have been subjected to intense bombing for four years is extremely remote." He appealed to Spaatz. "We will, in what may be one of our last and best remembered operations regardless of its effectiveness, violate the basic American principle of precision bombing of targets of strictly military significance for which our tactics were designed and our crews trained and indoctrinated."

Doolittle recommended that area bombing be left in the hands of the British.

Spaatz replied with just as much ambiguity as had characterized his own recent communication from Arnold. If there was any winner in this back-and-forth, it was the B-17 Flying Fortress. Doolittle would have preferred not to own any B-24 Liberators at all, and although Libs had been to the German capital before, none were being scheduled for the mission now taking shape.

At Mendlesham, in a different billet just a few hundred feet from Des Lauriers, *Fancy Nancy* toggleer Tech. Sgt. Ray Fredette received word that the Eighth Air Force would mount an all-out mission on February 2. He may have been the only enlisted man in the entire Eighth Air Force who was thinking about the same moral issues that Arnold, Spaatz, and Doolittle were dancing around. His diary from the period shows that Fredette felt something fundamental was changing. This was important to him because his job was to release bombs, following the example of a lead bombardier. Fredette had studied the inertia, the force, the blast radius, and the overall impact of the bombs his 34th Bombardment Group was using. He would never regret his duty or his performance, even though questions about bombing everyday human beings in a city center never left his mind.

The working-level details of planning a mission were sorted out at Pinetree, the shorthand term for Eighth Air Force headquarters, which were still located in a mansion in High Wycombe, England, even though Doolittle had moved a command post to the continent. Once told of their target, the Eighth Air Force's intelligence, operations, planning, and supply people began sorting out the details. It was no easy task figuring out how many aircraft would be dispatched, what order they could fly in, what route they would follow, and so on. Long before crewmembers attended a briefing, hundreds of hours had gone into working through the details.

Spaatz's staff was carving out the details of the first American daylight mission to Berlin that would not be directed against a specific military objective. On the morning of February 2, crews all over East Anglia were ready to go. At the 91st Bombardment Group at Bassingbourn, operations officer Lt. Col. Marvin D. Lord helped with the final planning, knowing that he was not scheduled to go on the mission. Major Immanuel L. "Manny" Klette, the very experienced pilot whose crew had endured many dozens of missions already, would be the 91st group's on-scene air commander.

The weather in Europe, which had been a severe foe to the Allies throughout the winter of and especially in the early weeks of 1945, continued to be horrendous. February began. The weather worsened. The continent became socked in. Before they could be briefed, crewmembers in twenty-six bomb groups stood down. They were told in what sounded like authoritative terms that the weather over the Third Reich would be terrible the next day, too. Klette took leave from the 91st group and traveled to London, where it was widely understood he had a girlfriend. It is unclear whether he stayed with a girlfriend or at a familiar haunt like the Columbia Club in Bayswater. It is unclear whether Klette had permission to be absent from the base, but we know today that the entire 91st Bombardment Group—with the possible exception of Lord—was behaving as if nothing was going to happen on February 3.

The mission wasn't happening. Crews were brought to a pitched state of readiness only to stand down. Some in the 91st group remember a party held late into the evening hours of February 2 and spilling over to the morning hours of February 3. Attendees expected to return to their bunks and spend the day sleeping. Apparently, further communications took place between Spaatz and Doolittle.

Unaware of the squabbling, unaware even that there was any issue being debated, Fortress crewmembers like Fredette learned otherwise only when they were briefed for the target on February 3, 1945. Fredette's sudden awakening has already appeared in this narrative (chapter one). At the briefing, as he recalls it, the intelligence officer on stage said, "Your target will be every telephone pole and every square block in the city of Berlin." Fortress copilot Robert Des Lauriers remembers thinking that something had changed "but not yet being fully aware of it." At his briefing, he continued to believe that there was a legitimate military target in Berlin and that Americans would be following their long-held principles.

By the time of the briefings on the morning of February 3, 1945, the brutal British cold and the poor weather over the continent were suddenly far more favorable than anyone had anticipated.

The mission was on.

CHAPTER THIRTEEN

The Way Out

Mission to Berlin
February 3, 1945—11:20 a.m. to 11:47 a.m.

SHORTLY AFTER DROPPING their bombs on Berlin, crewmembers of the 92nd Bombardment Group watched helplessly as flak struck one of their own. Aboard Maj. James A. Smyrl's command aircraft—which had plenty of flak-damage problems of its own—navigator 1st Lt. James W. "Bill" Good peered from his cramped nose position and watched another aircraft sustain a mortal flak hit. *It was 11:20 a.m., British Summer Time, Sunday February 3, 1945.*

The other Fortress was *Demobilizer* of the group's 325th Bombardment Squadron. Its pilot was 2nd Lt. Bernard G. Morrow. "They were just about right over Berlin and suddenly one of their engines was a brilliant torch in the sky," said Good.

In fact, it appears Morrow had pulled off the target and was northeast of Berlin. His aircraft fell behind the formation. The bright flash of flame apparently was temporary, but the number two engine was feathered, on fire, and trailing smoke. The crew began bailing out when five minutes away from Berlin, pilot Morrow when the aircraft was ten minutes away. With no one aboard, the aircraft crashed, within view of Smyrl, Good, and many others in the 92nd.

The loss of this aircraft to German gunfire meant that nine men would become prisoners, although all would survive the war. The men who took to their parachutes were Morrow, copilot 2nd Lt Willis F. Early, navigator 2nd Lt. William J. Wallace Jr., engineer-gunner Staff Sgt. Albert W. Myers, ball turret gunner Sgt. Joseph E. Regan, waist gunner Sgt. Earl H. Cline, tail gunner Sgt. Robert E. Peters, radio operator Tech. Sgt. Charles A. Fyke Jr., and nose gunner Sgt. Wayne E. Ball. Whether Morrow intended to head east toward Poland, hoping to land behind Soviet lines in Poland, is unknown.

Ball turret gunner Regan later wrote: "We bailed out somewhere east of Berlin. I walked five days before being captured. I almost made it to the Russian lines but, thank God, the Germans took me. Many of our fliers were never heard from after being taken by the Russians. The rest of the crew was captured shortly after landing."

While the Americans feared possible cruelty by the Soviets, as did their bosses at Eighth Air Force headquarters, what they weren't hearing was that both the law of war and the rule of law in general were breaking down in Nazi Germany. Prisoner of war camps run by the Germans were now being threatened by the Allied advances on both fronts, and discipline was collapsing. The Geneva Convention on prisoners of war, until now mostly honored by the Germans, was now being honored only on a sporadic and spotty basis. Despite conflicting perceptions of what it might mean to fall into the hands of the Soviets—and there is no evidence that American airmen were "disappeared" by the Russians—this was a bad time to be captured by Germans.

In fact, both German civilians and military men, who would never have done so earlier in the war, now occasionally murdered an Allied flyer who fell into their midst. Regan would survive, but not all did.

Regan's concern about falling into the hands of the Russians may have resulted from a teletype message sent to bombardment groups from Eighth Air Force headquarters. The instruction set these priorities: Battle damaged aircraft should "proceed to home base if possible," "land at friendly bases west of the western front lines if necessary," or "land in Sweden if friendly bases cannot be reached." The fourth choice, landing behind Russian lines, was ordered as a last resort. The teletype message warned of the possibility of "Russian attacks" on American aircraft seeking safe haven. It is unclear how this instruction squares with other correspondence that reflected a bias against diverting to a neutral country (below).

Definitely, no-mistake-about-it, headed for Soviet lines in Poland was the flak-battered *Stardust* of the 384th Bombardment Group, with 2nd Lt. George F. Ruckman doing some fancy piloting and 2nd Lt. John O. Beeby doing even fancier navigating. Ruckman's crew still didn't know whether they would ever walk on solid ground in anybody's territory, but they viewed the diversion to the Soviet area as something to be disgruntled about, not fearful of. And they were preoccupied trying to keep their Fortress in the air.

THE JONES FAMILY

Second Lieutenant Roland A. Lissner, pilot of a Fortress named *The Jones Family*, was in the sixth of the twenty-six bombardment groups passing in an aerial parade over Berlin. It was the Lissner crew's bad luck to be over the German capital during one of the periods in the mission when the German flak gunners were excruciatingly accurate. When a blast shook *The Jones Family*, Lissner knew his crew was in trouble. His Fortress fell behind.

As an official report later indicated:

> At 1121 hours, just after bombs away, #3 engine received a hole from flak and all gas poured out. Left outer wing hit by flak and gas [was] lost in left [main] tank which had been full. #2 turbo inoperative caused by flak hole in exhaust stack and pressure dropped to 18". All oxygen systems except pilot, copilot, engineer, navigator and bombardier [were] knocked out by flak and pressures went to zero immediately. Pilot, navigator and engineer oxygen system [were] also hit, and oxygen pressures went down slowly. #3 engine [was] hit by flak and started to smoke and was windmilling, presumably due to lack of gas. Unable to feather #3 prop.

Amid of all this, and amid the pandemonium that must have reigned aboard *The Jones Family*, others in the 306th Bombardment Group watched Lissner cut across beneath the formation and believed he was making some kind of error. Lissner had already made, or would soon make, the decision to try to nurse his battered aircraft to Sweden (chapter fifteen). How badly Lissner's Fortress was damaged—whether, in fact, the subsequent description of events was accurate—became a topic of debate among crewmembers in other aircraft.

THE SMYRL AIRCRAFT

While *Demobilizer*'s war came to an end and *The Jones Family* scurried away, the rest of the 92nd Bombardment Group, with Maj. James A. Smyrl as the air commander in the Flying Fortress piloted by Capt. Russell Bundesen, dropped its bombs on Berlin.

Previously subjected to minor damage by an uncharted flak battery just after crossing the Dutch coast, the Smyrl Fortress stayed in the air because of a supreme effort of everyone in the crew. It stayed on course—leading not just its group but the 40th Bomb Wing—largely through the efforts of lead navigator 1st Lt. James W. "Bill" Good. As an official citation reported later:

"Good directed the formation to the objective with preeminent skill although the oxygen system was defective and his electrically heated suit was inoperative. In the face of complete cloud coverage he dexterously guided the group to the initial point [about 40 miles from Berlin] where the undercast broke and Good pinpointed the aircraft for the bomb run." The aircraft carrying Bundesen, Smyrl, and Good released its bombs "in a concentrated pattern," read the citation after a visual bomb run with bombardier Capt. Walter Neppel using his Norden bombsight. At the very instant bombs fell away, the Fortress was again hit by flak. *It was 11:25 a.m., British Summer Time.*

Neppel had his flak helmet off and suffered a concussion that blew him into the gunsight of the chin turret. He came to and said: "Oh, I must have hit my head." He was okay.

This time, the flak hit was sudden and serious. The sheer force of the impact caused the Fortress to rise upward ten feet in the air—this, of course, with the German capital passing below, readily visible in the now-clear weather that had opened up and that Good considered a boon to the German flak gunners. Slammed upward, the B-17 now had two engines that were damaged. Still, Bundesen and Smyrl on the flight deck kept the aircraft in the lead position and Good directed the formation in withdrawing from Berlin and making for the coast. Hit two separate times, battered, unbeaten, the Smyrl aircraft was going to struggle toward home.

THE MORRIS CREW

Near the middle of the bomber stream, pilot 2nd Lt. Richard P. Morris of the 334th Bombardment Squadron, 95th Bombardment Group, was at the controls of an unnamed Fortress just after releasing bombs. Flak struck the Fortress. *It was 11:28 a.m., British Summer Time.*

Morris dropped out of formation. A crewmember of another plane later wrote of Morris's bomber that, "a fire started on the wing. Three chutes were seen to leave the aircraft on the eastern edge of Berlin. At the time the aircraft was still on fire but under control. One crew [later] reported hearing the pilot say over the radio that he had a runaway prop but was halfway back to base. No other [radio] contact was made." In fact, the speaker may have been copilot 2nd Lt. Dean M. Ratts. If anyone bailed out over Berlin—and in this case the eyewitness report is questionable—it may have been Morris, about whom conflicting information is available. According to an official report, Morris became a prisoner of war and survived the war. If there was a struggle aboard this Fortress to reach safety, Ratts may have been leading the crew.

Less than five minutes later, a second 95th group Fortress was hit by flak. The pilot was 1st Lt. James D. Taylor. The Fortress had not been assigned a name. A witness said Taylor's Fortress caught fire, pulled out of formation, went into a deep dive, and exploded, with no apparent parachutes being visible.

An official report, filed later, said: "B-17G 43-33899 piloted by 1st Lt. Taylor was hit by flak in the number two engine just after 'bombs away.' The fire spread back to the radio room. The aircraft then peeled off and went down into a steep dive to put out the fire. Just above the clouds at 15,000 feet, the aircraft exploded. Three men were seen to come out but only one chute opened. This was at 1130 hours over Berlin, Germany."

One squadron member recalled incorrectly that Taylor, copilot 1st Lt. Ronald E. Piper, and other members of Taylor's crew diverted to Soviet territory, where Soviet soldiers displayed the usual strong interest in their four-engined bomber. The source of this misunderstanding: On an earlier mission Taylor and his crew landed in Soviet territory before being refueled, taking off, and returning to the 95th group's base at Horham. Another squadron member recalls incorrectly that Taylor and his crew diverted to Switzerland, something no bomber crews were doing at this stage of the war.

In fact, although it did indeed explode in an abrupt flash of fire with little smoke, Taylor's Fortress sprayed nine parachutes into the crowded sky three miles above the smoke-strewn German capital. All of the chutes had crewmembers attached and all snapped open. Most were heavy B8 backpack parachutes with twelve-foot canopies. Taylor's men went floating down into the urban mess where they had just deposited their bombs. After the trauma of being ejected from an exploding bomber, they now descended into the enemy's midst with a spectacular view from above. Like the Fortresses passing above them, their own course altered frequently by the high winds that churned above the city's fires. Taylor's men drifted right down the Unter Den Linden, past the Tiergarten, and on to the government buildings in the center of the city. At this time, throughout portions of the area they were falling into, smoke from bomb damage was rising about 2,000 feet above the city's rooftops. The men descended into this smoke.

Taylor and Piper were flying with, and bailed out with, engineer-gunner Tech. Sgt. Edward Balowski, bombardier 1st Lt. Allan V. Beers, navigator 2nd Lt. William E. Haile, radio operator Sgt. William H. Everett, radio operator Sgt. Ronald E. Piper, ball turret gunner Sgt. Jack A. Bingaman, waist gunner Staff Sgt. Roland N. Ferren, and tail gunner Sgt. John J. Garneier.

Balowski, who became a resident of Stalag Luft 7-A along with his crewmates, grew up in Detroit and was one of seven brothers who all wore the uniform of the U.S. armed forces during World War II. In the decades before the film *Saving Private Ryan*—a story focused on four brothers who served—the Balowski parents never received any form of recognition.

Some of Taylor's crewmembers were gasping and choking when their parachutes settled them down in city streets and in rubble-strewn remains of buildings with smoke everywhere and the sound of antiaircraft guns in the distance. While they were still trying to scramble out of their chute harnesses, German civilians roughed up Bingaman and Ferren. Before the small crowd could get out of control, Germans in uniform—whether soldiers or police, the Americans never knew—fought through the crowd, also choking in the smoke, and rescued the two crewmembers. Bingaman and Ferren became Stalag mates with Balowski. (Bingaman was a first cousin of Imogene Bingaman, of Janesville, Illinois, who taught English in the eighth grade to the author of this narrative and instilled a love of language that endures.)

"ROSIE" ROSENTHAL

Bomber crews in trouble high over Germany now had the option of continuing eastward for a landing behind Soviet lines in Poland. Some made it. Some didn't. Among the nine survivors of the command Flying Fortress carrying Maj. Robert "Rosie" Rosenthal, four men became prisoners of the Germans. They were pilot Capt. John Ernst, copilot 1st Lt. Arthur I. Jacobson, engineer-gunner Tech. Sgt. Dugger C. West, and waist gunner Staff Sgt. Warren Winters. Another crewmember, command navigator 1st Lt. Stewart J. Gillison, came down in German-held territory but evaded capture and eventually reached Russian lines.

Rosenthal parachuted into the midst of Soviet troops, as did radar navigator 1st Lt. Robert H. Stropp, radio operator Tech. Sgt. Charles H. Webber, and tail gunner Staff Sgt. G. A. Windisch.

In the years since, much has been made of Rosenthal's Jewish heritage and he has often been identified incorrectly as the air commander of the entire mission—the job of Col. Lewis Lyle. As noted elsewhere in this narrative, Rosenthal had no family members who were being persecuted by the Nazis and only some idea of the anti-Semitic horrors of Adolf Hitler's regime. Rosenthal considered himself nothing more than an American bomber pilot and officer fighting a war.

The Flying Fortress dubbed "unlucky thirteen" by other bomber crews, with 1st Lt. Arthur H. Ogle and Maj. John "Junior" Rex on board, passed over Russian lines when its fourth and final working engine began to sputter. The pilots attempted to lower the landing gear and found it inoperable because of the flak damage. They sighted an open field and brought the Flying Fortress down in a barely controlled crash landing without injury to any of the crew. Polish guerrillas, who took them to a farmhouse to be met by Russian troops, welcomed the Americans. Ogle and his Fortress crewmembers were later repatriated via Kiev, Tehran, Cairo, Marseilles, and eventually London.

DIVERSION TO SWEDEN

Exactly what happened to pilot 1st Lt. William L. Fry and his crew aboard a Fortress named *Slightly Dangerous* may never be known to Fry's buddies or to history, not because of any error by the Fortress crewmembers but because of the shabbiness of the official report. That document indicates that Fry was right over Berlin—he was two-thirds of the way back in the bomber stream with the rest of the 452nd Bombardment Group—when he "peeled from formation and headed back to Russia or Sweden" with "all props turning." *It was 11:45 a.m., British Summer Time.*

The language in the missing aircrew report, written by a member of another crew, hints at the faint skepticism and resentment with which bomber crewmembers—usually unfairly—watched their fellow flyers steer in the direction of the comforts of Stockholm. Whether it was Lissner's *The Jones Family* or Fry's *Slightly Dangerous*, each time a Fortress headed for Sweden at least some wondered whether its pilot and crew were seeking an easy copout.

Under international law, a neutral country that became host to an American—or German—flyer was expected to "intern" him, taking him out of the fight for the remainder of the war, and this was a fate Fortress pilots Lissner and Fry might reasonably have expected. The myth that some American crewmembers purposely went to Sweden to avoid having to participate in further combat was widely held in Washington by Army Air Forces Commander-in-Chief Gen. Henry H. "Hap" Arnold and by the Sweden desk at the Department of State. In a document citing evidence that didn't exist, months earlier Arnold wrote to Lt. Gen. Carl "Tooey" Spaatz and Lt. Gen. Ira Eaker:

> Evidence has recently been accumulating that an appreciable number of our planes have made landings in neutral countries without indication of serious battle damage or mechanical failure or shortage of fuel. Recently the statements of some interned crew leaders and

> members reported by our consuls [in Sweden and Switzerland] the fact that the landings were intentional evasions of further combat service. An investigation is being conducted to determine the past history of the particular individuals involved in these reports, but it is plainly evident that measures must be taken immediately against such a state of mind among flyers and crews now engaged in extremely active operations.

The order to Spaatz and Eaker called for an investigation to determine whether ideas of escaping cleanly to Sweden and Switzerland "are being fomented" among crews and for action "offsetting this state of mind." In a warning about what would later be called post traumatic stress disorder, or PTSD, Arnold cautioned, "Those individuals or crews who appear to be near the breaking point should . . . be returned [to the United States] for reconditioning."

The author of this volume was American consul in Sweden a quarter century later—when a fictitious Capt. Yossarian was seen escaping to Sweden in the Hollywood's take on Joseph Heller's novel *Catch-22*—and unearthed no record of the reports from consuls cited by Arnold. Most such reports apparently came from Switzerland, even though, ironically, that neutral country treated U.S. crewmembers more harshly. Other reports from consular officials confirmed that U.S. bombers landing in Sweden had suffered severe battle damage. Nevertheless, the idea that crewmembers were trying to escape became deeply rooted. Arnold sent a message to U.S. consular officials in the two neutral countries, with a copy to Spaatz, that concluded: "All United States crewmen should be carefully questioned to determine full details on reasons for forced landings and for general attitude and morale."

Arnold was already in possession of a cable from the U.S. air attache in Sweden who reported to Arnold and Spaatz that he'd completed an investigation of all but two of three dozen U.S. warplanes that had taken refuge in that country. He reported that "all were stragglers and all landed as a result of battle damage except one." He went on to note that most aircraft landed in Sweden with 250 to 400 gallons of fuel remaining (not enough for a return to England), that all aircraft with three exceptions landed with either one or two engines feathered, and that observed battle damage was to engine control and flight control cables, which were shot out. He also reported damage to oxygen, hydraulic, electrical, fuel, and oil systems. A subsequent cable from the U.S. consul in Stockholm spoke of high morale among the American crewmembers interned in Sweden and downplayed the notion that they'd sought to avoid the risks of combat.

A battle-damaged Fortress pulling off the target over Berlin could recover on Swedish soil by flying about 25 percent of the distance back to its home base in England. Information about friendly locations in the parts of Western Europe that had been liberated by the Allies remained muddled and confused after the Battle of the Bulge, which ended a fortnight before the February 3 Berlin mission. For the hundreds of American aircrew members who ended up in Sweden during the war, diverting to that country meant the difference between being a German prisoner of war (at best) or a Swedish internee.

Nevertheless, men like Lissner and Fry would be haunted for the rest of their lives by the stigma that their fellow crewmembers attached to a diversion to Sweden. The bias against those who brought their Fortresses down on Swedish soil was emotional and powerful, and may be reflected in the official report on what happened to Fry and the Fortress named *Slightly Dangerous.*

THE FRY CREW

The report does not say that Fry was hit by flak or that an engine was damaged, although at least one witness was certain both things happened. According to the report, Fry departed the bomber formation in the wrong direction, much as the Lissner and Ogle crews had done. *It was 11:45 a.m., British Summer Time.*

"Those guys were over the city that symbolized the might of the Third Reich, black puffs of flak were erupting all around them, their aircraft had a damaged engine and broken hydraulic lines, and the pilot was fighting to save the lives of nine men," said former Staff Sgt. Michael P. Curphey, who flew with a different crew in Fry's 452nd Bombardment Group and who became familiar with details after the war. "For anyone to imply that these were anything but brave Americans doing their duty, that would be a bunch of crap."

Two minutes after Fry's *Slightly Dangerous* trundled away from the battle area, other Fortress pilots and crewmembers were making difficult snap decisions under pressure.

Trouble came swiftly for an unnamed Fortress piloted by 1st Lt. Irving Spiegel of the 486th Bombardment Group. Apparently untouched by flak, Spiegel and his crew encountered a mechanical malfunction. Men in other bombers overheard Spiegel break radio silence to talk to a ground station operated by the 3rd Air Division. Spiegel said that an engine had quit and he was diverting to Poland, where the Soviets were. He reported "my crew is okay," but he was low on fuel. The ground station appeared to give its blessing to a diversion to Soviet territory but cautioned Spiegel after landing to "guard the aircraft." "Could not see any sign of trouble," an official report said later. "Aircraft headed east toward Poland."

THE ROTHSTEIN CREW

The 487th Bombardment Group at Lavenham enjoyed an uneventful thirty seconds over the center of Berlin, pulled off the target, and headed home. One of its bombers, an unnamed Fortress, was exposed to flak, but the crew never really knew whether exploding shells grazed their bomber. The pilot was 1st Lt. Alvin S. "Buddy" Rothstein. A brief note in a group history says simply that the aircraft developed engine trouble after bombing and was escorted back by fighters.

The situation was more serious aboard another 487th group bomber, *Happy Warrior*, piloted by 1st Lt. William Settler of the 838th Bombardment Squadron. Apparently, Settler did not really abort at 10:51 a.m. as claimed in records (chapter eleven). Hanging beneath the Fortress in his ball turret position, Staff Sgt. Curtis E. Roper saw the flak exploding nearby as Berlin passed below. He felt vibrations. It may have been an illusion, given that he was heavily bundled up, but he also thought he could hear the thump-thump of exploding flak shells. After *Happy Warrior*'s bombs were away, Settler came on the intercom to say that the number one engine was badly damaged and that he was feathering a propeller.

"It changes the rhythm of the whole airplane," said Roper. Pilot Settler's voice came on the intercom again and this time he was talking to the navigator. "Well, Dave, it's your turn," Settler said. "You've got to take us home."

Almost unnoticed by some of the nine men on board, *Happy Warrior* was now pointed in the direction of home base at Lavenham but was falling out of formation—a straggler. Roper scanned the skies and did not immediately see any sign of German fighters, but he knew they were in trouble. Even if Settler could keep the bomber aloft, being lower and slower than everybody else was an invitation to be picked off.

But ball turret gunner Roper had one experience the others lacked: Back in training, before shipping over, he had been forced to bail out of a crippled bomber in a midair mishap over Gulfport, Mississippi. Maybe parachuting from an airplane was like riding a bicycle. Maybe it was something you never forgot how to do.

Whether the abort happened before or after Berlin, whether the Fortress bombed Osnabruck or Berlin, *Happy Warrior* was now in serious trouble, fighting its way home, out of tune, out of rhythm, not particularly happy, but still in the air and still struggling.

ROSE OF YORK

We shall never know when, exactly, the Fortress named *Rose of York*—the bomber that Princess Elizabeth had christened and that had once been named *Princess Elizabeth*—ended the last of her sixty-two combat missions, the first and last of which took her to Berlin. We can only speculate that pilot 1st Lt. Vernon F. Daley, copilot 2nd Lt. Joseph J. Carbine, and engineer-gunner Tech. Sgt. Reisel R. Horn struggled desperately to save their bomber, perhaps with the intrepid war correspondent Guy Byam, who'd survived so many previous battles, peering intently over their shoulders. We can envision radio operator Tech. Sgt. Porfirio J. Marquez sending out high frequency distress signals.

There are those who suggest that *Rose of York* is still out there today, still fighting her way across the English Channel, caught in a time warp in another dimension, undefeated and unwilling to go down. It is a fanciful thought—a ghost of a Flying Fortress, timeless now, forever continuing its flight and its fight to survive.

The reality is less romantic. After being torpedoed, after airdrops at Normandy and Arnhem, correspondent Byam's luck had run out.

No trace has ever been found of *Rose of York*, Daley, Carbine, navigator 1st Lt. Paul A. Becker, nose gunner Staff Sgt. Robert E. Crede, Horn,

Marquez, ball turret gunner Staff Sgt. George W. Petrillo, waist gunner Staff Sgt. Silvio P. DeZolt, tail gunner Sgt. Okey R. Coplin, and Byam. It appears no air-sea search effort was ever mounted to try to find the plane or the men. The official report concludes: "Pilot of aircraft reported over radio that one engine was shot out and another losing gasoline." There is nothing further.

THE SHOEMAKER CREW (II)

The Flying Fortress of 1st Lt. Daniel G. Shoemaker limped away from Berlin with a shattered windshield, a wounded pilot, a tail gunner's leg blown off, and a radio operator bleeding profusely on the floorboards. The copilot of Shoemaker's unnamed Fortress, 2nd Lt. Roy F. Moullen, who was pivotal in the crew's fight for survival, later described the horror. "The squadron followed the bomber columns on course over the coast to the North Sea and started S.O.P. [standard operating procedure] letdown from 24,000 feet," he wrote. "After leveling off, we hit prop wash and went into a violent turn. Then we left the squadron and started to drop to the lower squadron on our right. Before we were able to join the squadron, our left rudder cable snapped at station 6." Moullen called engineer Sgt. Ira Roisman into the pilot's seat—Shoemaker nursed serious wounds on the flight deck, then stood between the two pilot seats —to hold pressure on the right pedal to try to regain control. The interphone, which had been working intermittently, now stopped working and crewmembers could not talk to each other.

Moullen and Roisman detected smoke in the cockpit. They could not find the source. On further examination, they discovered a fire in the right wing, coming out of a flak hole on the top surface.

Wrote Roisman: "Somebody yelled, 'Bail out' and I reached behind the pilot's seat to get my chute and handed the co-pilot his. Shoemaker had his and started for the nose. I jettisoned the navigator's escape hatch. The navigator and the toggleer were in the nose and they did not know what was going on. The fire was getting more intense and the heat was starting to curl the skin."

Distracted by the flames, Shoemaker may not have initially realized that they'd just crossed the Dutch coast and were descending toward the North Sea. It was commonly said among crewmembers that a man immersed in the frigid North Sea could live for only three to six minutes before succumbing to the cold. Again, as always, the cold and the thought of more of it was a constant companion. "When I looked down, all I could see was water," wrote Roisman.

CHAPTER FOURTEEN

Mission to Magdeburg

The B-24 Liberator and the Mission to Magdeburg
February 3, 1945

WHILE FLYING FORTRESSES attacked Berlin on Saturday, February 3, 1945, the Eighth Air Force's 2nd Air Division dispatched 434 B-24 Liberators to bomb Magdeburg.

No one was perfect at navigation or formation flying so the two types of bombers, which should have been at different altitudes and out of eyesight of one another, sometimes came close to being in contact. At one point while approaching Berlin, Fortress crews saw a huge gaggle of Liberators passing at an angle beneath them. That's where Liberators usually were: Although faster and farther-reaching with a heavier bombload, the Liberator could not routinely fly as high as a Fortress.

Because of some confusion in the formation and unexpected weather issues, only 116 Liberators reached the primary target, while 246 hit a secondary target, the marshalling yard at Magdeburg. Dozens of Liberators attacked other targets of opportunity nearby.

This was the day when many would accuse the Eighth Air Force of resorting to area bombing (that is, indiscriminate bombing of civilians, called "baby killing" by some, as the British were doing on their nocturnal missions). Those accusations would be leveled against the mission to Berlin, not the simultaneous assault on Magdeburg. When he wanted to justify the bombing campaign to critics, Eighth Air Force commander Gen. James H. "Jimmy" Doolittle—who opposed area bombing—often cited Magdeburg as an example of a target of prime military importance.

Magdeburg and the B-24 Liberator might have been made for each other.

The European War's "other" bomber was being hurled against the Third Reich's "other" target.

Magdeburg, on the Elbe River, once one of the most important medieval centers of Old Europe, was in 1945 one of the Reich's principal manufacturers of synthetic fuel. Located just seventy-seven miles west of Berlin, it was one of the most heavily defended targets in history. Germany needed synthetic fuel so badly that Albert Speer sent five separate pleas to Adolf Hitler to find ways to enhance production. American bomber crewmembers, in turn, did their best to inhibit production. Except for "Merciless Merseberg," Berlin and Magdeburg became the targets crewmembers feared most.

Today's mission was part of a series later be called the "siege of Magdeburg," a sustained effort to deny the Germans the use of their synthetic fuel facilities. The siege would bring B-24 Liberators over the city half a dozen times.

The B-24 Liberator was the plane that never seemed to get enough recognition. Detractors called it "the box the B-17 came in." Former 1st Lt. James Van Ginkel, who piloted the B-24, said that it "didn't get any attention. In much the same manner, Magdeburg was the 'other' target. The B-17 got more publicity. Berlin got more publicity. But we would not have been able to wage war in the heavens above the European continent without the Consolidated B-24 Liberator."

One of the men taking off for Magdeburg on February 3, 1945, was engineer gunner Sgt. Vincent Re, who felt charged up but also uncomfortable about where he was asked to sit on takeoff. Re belonged to the 467th Bombardment Group, the "Rackheath Aggies," maybe the most underrated group of the war led by the most underrecognized commander, Col. Albert Shower. The author of this volume spent considerable time with

Re, Shower, and other "Rackheath Aggies" and came to view their story as a symbol for all who flew the Liberator—a plane that no one ever called pretty but an essential part of every aspect of the war, the air campaign, and the siege of Magdeburg.

"It was tough up there," said Re. "It was cold. It was hectic. They were shooting at us. I would not have wanted to climb aboard any four-engined heavy bomber that did not have the term 'B-24' stenciled on it."

LIBERATOR DESIGN

The Liberator owed its design to a unique wing sold to Consolidated Aircraft Company in prewar years by a near-destitute inventor, David R. Davis. Though Reuben H. Fleet, the founder and boss at Consolidated, had doubts, wind tunnel tests demonstrated that Davis's slender wing with its sharp camber provided superior lift.

The prototype XB-24 made its initial flight at San Diego on December 28, 1939. In March 1939 the U.S. Army ordered seven YB-24 service-test bombers with turbo superchargers for high-altitude flight. Next came nine B-24C models, none of which saw combat, and the B-24D, which fought everywhere. The turret-equipped B-24H model appeared on June 30, 1943, followed by the B-24H, J, L, and M, which had full gun armament—including a nose turret. The force that attacked Magdeburg consisted of these last four versions. Van Ginkel's Liberator was an "H" model named *Ol' Witch*.

Ten thousand American bombers fell in battle during World War II. A mighty chunk of that total consisted of B-24s of the Eighth Air Force. In looking back to those days, when the sky was pungent with exhaust, black with exploding shellfire, and swarming with Messerschmitts and Focke-Wulfs, some men wondered simply how they had done it. One described seeing a Liberator with eleven crewmembers on board—a larger crew than usual—disappear in an abrupt, high-octane fireball. When Liberators took part in the first bombing mission to Berlin (chapter six), the number of Germans killed on the ground by American bombs was about the same as the number of B-24 crewmembers who died high overhead.

"Conditions were the worst you could imagine," said Lt. Col. Frank Tribulent, a Liberator navigator with the 392nd Bombardment Group.

"You wondered if you would get off the ground in the English fog with all those bombs on board. You wondered if you might collide with a buddy after you did. You worried that you'd drop a glove, or have a sleeve torn away, and get frostbite. And when German fighters were swarming around you, the adrenaline churned like crazy." And the cold? "Yes," said Tribulent. "We were always cold."

The interior of a B-24 was especially uncomfortable when you were bundled up against the elements. First Lieutenant Lyman Delameter, a bombardier with the 461st Bombardment Group, said, "The B-24 was not pressurized like the B-29 Superfortress and the aircraft that we fly today. We had to wear oxygen masks above a certain altitude [10,000 feet]. I remember talking to one 'veteran' aircrew member who advised me to wrap a towel around my neck like a scarf to collect the moisture that would accumulate under my chin from the oxygen mask. Of course when we got to a higher altitude, this moisture would freeze into a little ball of ice and that would have to be cleared away from time to time.

"The B-24 was not exactly airtight," Delameter said. "The nose turret had to rotate from side to side and the wind used to leak through the area where the nose turret joined the aircraft. The standard temperature lapse rate is two degrees colder per one thousand feet. So if the temperature on the ground was forty degrees, the temperature at 20,000 feet [6,096 meters] would be forty degrees colder. To compute bombing altitude, we had to know the temperature at our bombing altitude."

B-24s rolled out of American assembly plants not only in greater numbers than any other bomber, but in greater numbers than any U.S. aircraft, ever. No fewer than 19,276 Liberators were built, compared to 7,366 British Lancasters and 12,731 American Flying Fortresses. The B-24 figure exceeds production totals for Dakotas, Mustangs, Thunderbolts, Mitchells, and Marauders. Liberators rolled off production lines operated by Consolidated (in San Diego, California, and Fort Worth, Texas), Douglas (at Tulsa, Oklahoma), Ford (at Willow Run, Michigan) and North American (at Dallas, Texas).

At one base in the American Southwest during the war, Liberators were parked wingtip-to-wingtip as far as the eye could see, stretching off the end of the airfield and out into the desert. "We were building them faster than we could muster pilots to fly them overseas," a veteran said. "You could look out, and there was no end to the sight of Liberators heading toward the horizon."

When Doolittle replaced Lt. Gen. Ira Eaker as commander of the Eighth Air Force, it was a distressful moment for B-24 crews. Eaker wanted to stay, or wanted his subordinate, Maj. Gen. Idwal H. Edwards, to get the job.

Doolittle was an aviation pioneer and hero who skyrocketed to the top of the ranks. Following his April 18, 1942, attack on Japan with B-25 Mitchells launched from the aircraft carrier *Hornet*, Doolittle had gone from lieutenant colonel to brigadier general without ever wearing the silver eagles of a colonel and had received the Medal of Honor to boot.

But to heavy bomber crews, Doolittle was the leader who despised the B-24 Liberator.

To the end of their lives, Eaker and Doolittle, intimately acquainted since the 1920s, addressed each other as, "General," rather than by first names. The tautness between them was exacerbated by their differences over heavy bombers. Doolittle believed that in its developmental process the B-24 had become too heavy to operate at the high altitudes needed to dodge flak over Germany. The B-17 could fly higher. But Doolittle was overlooking other considerations that were matters of life and death: B-24 could carry more, fly faster, and travel farther.

The Liberator's designer Mac Laddon chose the Pratt & Whitney R-1830 radial engine over the contemporary Wright R-1820 Cyclone of the Flying Fortress because of the smaller frontal area, and reduced penalty in aerodynamic drag, of the twin-row P&W design. The mechanically supercharged R-1830-33 installed on the first Liberators, however, did not have the high-altitude performance of the turbo-supercharged R-1830-41 that came later. Even later, definitive B-24H/J models made use of four 1,200-horsepower R-1830-65 models, but even then the Liberator with its service ceiling of 28,000 feet could not reach the same heights as its competitor. There was almost a 40 percent difference in the 35,800-foot service ceiling reached by the B-17G with four 1,200-horsepower R-1830-97s.

The Flying Fortress's wingspan of 103 feet, 9 inches defined a slightly smaller aircraft than the Liberator, whose high-aspect Davis wing spanned 110 feet. But the main landing gear track of the Liberator was slightly narrower, making it marginally easier to move around on a crowded ramp.

A B-17 fuselage was slightly longer at 74 feet, 4 inches than the fuselage of a B-24 at 67 feet, 2 inches, but both had comparable interior volume. A fully loaded B-17G tipped the scales at 65,500 pounds while a B-24H/J, true to Doolittle's concern, weighed fully 71,200 pounds.

The basics are beyond dispute. The B-17 was better looking, flew higher, and was regarded by many as more survivable. The B-24 was faster, carried more bombs, and went farther. Depending on temperature and altitude, a Liberator operating on three engines could overtake and pass a Flying Fortress churning along on all four.

A persistent myth is that the Flying Fortress predominated the European war in terms of sheer numbers. That was true in the Eighth Air Force, of course—although by a smaller margin than is generally understood—but the balance changes if the Italy-based Fifteenth Air Force, also a factor in Europe, is taken into account. The Flying Fortress equipped twenty-three combat groups in England, the Liberator nineteen. But the Fifteenth Air Force had four Fortress and fifteen Liberator groups, so the total was twenty-seven B-17 groups exceeded by thirty-four Liberator groups.

To some, the B-24 also didn't feel right. In the words of 1st Lt. Bud Markel, who flew the aircraft in the Mediterranean, "The B-24 was a cantankerous, lumbering, drafty, unforgiving son of a bitch, heavy on the controls, overgrossed, and difficult to fly in formation, with an ancient boiler gauge-style fuel quantity system that was almost useless. The heaters never worked when you needed them and were removed by many combat groups as being too dangerous to operate because of the fuel lines on the flight deck necessary to feed them."

MISSION TO MAGDEBURG

Taking off in his "Rackheath Aggies" Liberator, engineer-gunner Sgt. Vincent Re was poignantly aware that he was seated in the least safe location during the most dangerous phase of the flight—symbolic of everything that happened in Col. Albert Shower's 467th Bombardment Group.

Just before he arrived in England to begin his crewmember duty, Re learned that far-reaching, twin-engined Messerschmitt Me 410s had followed his bomb group home from a mission, attacked the Liberators as they approached Rackheath airfield near Norwich, and shot down two of the bombers, killing seventeen crewmembers. It was a bold strike by the

Luftwaffe, and the miracle was that Adolf Hitler's airmen didn't try it more often, since the Eighth Air Force was especially vulnerable around its own airfields and in the airfield pattern. To the very end of the war, the Luftwaffe had a limited capability to attack exhausted bomber crewmembers when they were struggling to land after a long mission, often with mechanical problems and battle damage; we may never know why the German side never seized what appears, in retrospect, a golden opportunity.

Perhaps taking his cue from 467th commander Shower, Re's pilot Capt. Alfred P. Wheelock decreed a solution against any such future attack. "From now on you ride in the turret on takeoff and landing."

"Huh?" said Re. Like many bomber crewmembers, he wanted to be in the safest location during the critical moments of climb-out and formation assembly.

"They come after us, you're going to shoot them," Wheelock said.

"But," said Re, referring to being in his gun position at takeoff, "that's against regulations." Crewmembers, except the two pilots and the engineer, were supposed to be strapped down firmly in the Liberator's waist position in case of a mishap during the chaos of takeoff, climb, and assembly. Manning guns during takeoff was not merely foolhardy. It was dangerous. Moreover, the Me 410 attack on Rackheath had happened months ago, when the Luftwaffe was stronger and more proactive. "Anyway," Re said later, "on Wheelock's crew, that is how we did it."

Said Re: "Our job was to crawl into an aluminum tube with wings—a cantankerous craft with an impossibly thin wing, crammed full of gasoline and bombs." Like their brethren in Flying Fortresses, in order to bomb the Third Reich, the men in Liberators flew at altitudes where they would die without oxygen and freeze without electrical heat. "All our lives, our best friend would be the B-24 Liberator," Re said.

The unique spot in history occupied by Re's group commander, Shower, is told by these numbers: Among 243 combat groups in the Army Air Forces, including 125 bomb groups of which 72 were "heavy" groups, only *one* was established, formed, trained, taken into battle, led to victory, and brought home by a single commander. Every other outfit had more than one commander during the war.

Said Shower: "I had a lot of things going for me. I picked up an excellent maintenance officer from another group. We worked hard on bombing accuracy and on defeating German fighters." A ramrod-stiff West Point alumnus (1932), Shower clamped iron discipline on his men—and they hated him.

COMBAT LEADER

"We hated his guts," said pilot 1st Lt. Ralph Davis. "He was always on our backs. When you were not flying combat missions, he would have you out flying practice missions. When weather was bad, he would have you in a Link trainer. We trained and trained and trained." When a general visited and observed the spit and polish at Rackheath, the general commented, "I wear out my goddamned arm saluting whenever I come to this base."

Lieutenant Colonel James J. Mahoney, a less strident figure, was brought in as number two to "mellow out" Shower's impact. Mahoney said, "Discipline and training were essentials to our mission. Shower provided us with a full and continuing diet of both." Other bomb groups dispensed with formality. The Rackheath Aggies held inspections, dress parades—and relentless flying rehearsals.

But were Re, Shower, the Rackheath Aggies, and eleven other bombardment groups going to the right target on February 3? Given the priority it placed on the German capital, why did the Eighth Air Force not send them to Berlin, as it had done during previous, less sizeable attacks on the capital? Just as there were quirks in the B-24 itself, there were peculiarities about the job assigned to B-24. In the past, Flying Fortresses and Liberators had often struck the same target on the same day. So with the Forts going to the German capital, did the Eighth Air Force really intend from the beginning to send the Liberators to Magdeburg? Accounts from crewmembers and official records seem to suggest that Magdeburg was the primary target for the B-24 force, but some sources indicate that it was a secondary target and that the planning and execution of the mission went poorly.

Whatever the case, Liberators were over Magdeburg at twenty minutes before noon. The 303rd Bombardment Group, one of the combat groups in the Magdeburg formation, had dispatched thirty-nine Liberators and a pilot of one later reported that flak was "moderate at most." The fighters of the Luftwaffe did not engage the Liberators. The word "moderate" would recur in an assessment of how much damage the Liberators inflicted on the synthetic oil plant at Magdeburg. Liberators would visit the city four times during the month. Each time, weather, formation flying glitches, flak, and the fog of war prevented them from inflicting more than moderate devastation.

BONNAR B-24 CREW

"Moderate" would have been a word that provided little comfort at 11:49 a.m. when the war became very personal for 1st Lt. Robert W. Bonnar, pilot of a Liberator named *Delectable Doris* of the 566th Bombardment Squadron, 389th Bombardment Group. Flying in and out of undercast near Hanover at 14,000 feet, a flak blast made a direct hit on *Delectable Doris*, near the center of its fuselage.

The stricken Liberator rolled out of cloudy cover with a trail of black smoke washing back into its exhaust. Pilot Bonnar was unconscious and severely wounded. The aircraft came apart in pieces. "The ship disintegrated," wrote copilot 1st Lt. John W. Merrill in a postwar casualty questionnaire. Merrill was blown out of the aircraft and sent flying in space. "I saw pieces pass me in the air when I was in my chute." Engineer-gunner Staff Sgt. Billy E. Wiedman also got out of the Liberator and got a good parachute canopy.

Wiedman landed in a tree and was immediately captured by Germans angry because British Spitfire fighters had been strafing them earlier. The Germans showed Wiedman two bodies, one of which he recognized as Bonnar's, with both legs blown off. The other body was too badly burned to be recognizable. Altogether, seven men perished aboard *Delectable Doris*: Bonnar, navigator 1st Lt. Rene Van De Voorde, engineer Tech. Sgt. Edward C. Rosengren, radio operator Tech. Sgt. Charles F. Runchey Jr., nose gunner Staff Sgt. John H. Springer, waist gunner Staff Sgt. Carl E. Brewer, and tail gunner Staff Sgt. Arthur M. Magellan.

RACKHEATH AGGIES

Col. Albert Shower's "Rackheath Aggies," the 467th Bombardment Group, was scattered and ended up hitting several targets, but at least some of Shower's Liberators were over the main synthetic oil plant at Magdeburg. Mahoney, Shower's deputy, said: "Many crews recall [and not kindly at the time] Al Shower circling the group in flak-filled skies over the cloud-shrouded primary target, hoping for a visual drop after other groups had opted for secondaries or targets of opportunity. No one ever accused the colonel of asking more, or even as much, of his men as he demanded from himself." By this juncture in the war, Shower's pilots and crewmembers were beginning to understand that they had one of the lowest casualty rates in the Eighth Air Force and one of the best records for bombing accuracy and effectiveness.

"Colonel Shower forced us pilots to handle a B-24 with the nimbleness of a fighter," said 467th pilot Davis. "Everyone who hated the son of a bitch from day one had discovered by now that training, training, training and discipline, discipline, and discipline made us one of the best combat groups of the war. Everyone who complained about the spit-shines and the practice flights and the hand salutes had realized by now what Colonel Shower had really done for us. When other bombers fell in battle and ours didn't, we realized you owed your life to this great man."

There was plenty of flak over Magdeburg and a handful of German fighters were viewed off in the far distance. As was the situation at Berlin not far away, the Luftwaffe engaged Mustangs but never attempted to disrupt the bomber stream. The Luftwaffe's antiaircraft batteries were another story. An after-action report by another bomb group called it a "difficult" mission "with moderate"—that word again—"flak noticed before and after the bomb run." Albert Shower's Rackheath Aggies bombed Magdeburg, came home, and filled out individual crew reports that made frequent use of the word "routine." One of the Liberators in the group, named *Witchcraft*, bombed Magdeburg routinely and eventually flew no fewer than 130 sorties without an abort, due in part to hard work by crew chief Sgt. Joe Ramirez. Like Shower, Ramirez was on the job from the beginning of his group's role in the war until its end.

WANN B-24 CREW

Like the Flying Fortresses working their way home from Berlin, the B-24 Liberators that had struck Magdeburg struggled to find the way home. For many, it really was routine. By this juncture in the war, statistics for combat flying over the Third Reich showed that most bomber crews had an excellent chance of completing their assigned thirty-five missions. Indeed, in February 1945 many were doing so without ever being fired upon by a

German fighter. It was still cold, it was still uncomfortable, and the scale of the air campaign was larger than ever, but there was significantly less chance of being killed or captured.

That didn't mean it was routine, at least not for everyone.

Although it was no comfort to the crewmembers affected, losses at Magdeburg on February 3 were extraordinarily light. Just two B-24s were lost, including the ill-fated *Delectable Doris*. One more was damaged beyond repair and fifty-eight more damaged in varying degrees.

During the bomb run over the synthetic oil plant, a flak explosion ripped the number one engine of a B-24 belonging to the 446th Bombardment Group, the "Bungay Buckaroos." (Bungay, alias Station 125, was in Suffolk in East Anglia). The Liberator was *L'il Snooks* of the group's 707th Bombardment Squadron, with pilot 2nd Lt. Richard L. Wann and instructor copilot 1st Lt. William S. Hanna at the controls. The aircraft was named for a well-known radio comic personality, Baby Snooks; in postwar years Wann insisted it was a B-24J model, but numerous records show it to be an H. It was Wann's second mission and for the rest of the crew, with the exception of the experienced Hanna, their first.

The bomber was separated from the formation and struggled for many miles trading altitude for distance.

After traveling possibly one hundred miles from Magdeburg on the way home, the Liberator was hit by flak a second time. Apparently, shards of flying shrapnel ripped into the fuselage and the number four engine. *L'il Snooks*'s radio went out and Wann's crew lost voice communication with the outside world.

As Wann's engineer-gunner Cpl. James R. "Ray" Barber noticed immediately, the Liberator was not only mushing along on two and a half engines, it was leaking fuel at a furious rate. Barber reported that fuel was being siphoned out through flak holes in the wing. Wann came on the intercom to say that he would try to get the bomber to the Allied side of the front lines and make an emergency landing.

Beneath him, Wann saw a heavy undercast that made it impossible to search visually for a potential landing spot. As the senior officer on board, Hanna decided that the crew should parachute from the Liberator rather than attempt to ride it down. He became the last of the ten men to bail out.

"We tried to trade altitude for distance," said Wann. "We couldn't. The B-24 Liberator had the gliding qualities of a brick. We were down to 8,500 feet in clouds, knowing there were 8,000-foot mountain peaks nearby. We had one engine that was feathered. We had one engine that was running away, unable to control. Yet another engine was in and out of fuel with the fuel lines broken, so we effectively had the use of just one engine. It was just enough to hold the bomber level long enough for us to bail out."

They were near between Zweibrucken, Germany, and Strasbourg, France, right over the front lines when they hit the silk. Observers on the ground saw the B-24 make a wide circle. The last crewmembers to depart the bomber were over German-held territory.

Five of *L'il Snooks* crewmembers made easy, comfortable parachute landing in the middle of American soldiers of the 45th Infantry Division. A sixth, tail gunner Cpl. George L. Shanks, also came down in territory held by the division's 693rd Field Artillery Battalion, but became entangled in a tree. He dangled helplessly for more than an hour before GIs were able to free him.

Four more men descending earthward in parachutes landed in German-held territory. Left waist gunner Cpl. Douglas J. Ryan climbed out of his parachute harness, walked a short distance, and came face-to-face with a German soldier. The German apparently couldn't make sense of what he was seeing and took no action while Ryan nodded, walked past the German, and trekked for more than an hour to a creek bed where the American and German armies faced each other.

Ryan was making his way down on a steep bank to a meadow when he found himself looking into a dugout occupied by two German soldiers. They saw him at the same time he saw them. Ryan walked away and the Germans made no attempt to stop him. After these eyeball-to-eyeball encounters with the enemy, Ryan decided that boldness was the best course of action so he crossed an open meadow and waded across the creek a few yards downstream from the German dugout and in full view of both German and American infantrymen. "Why he was not fired upon is difficult to explain," the 45th division's Maj. Claude H. Studebaker reported later in the day. "Probably his boldness bewildered the enemy and they were undecided what to do. Their instructions from their leader probably did not include directions for the proper handling of aviators approaching from the rear."—Studebaker may have had tongue in cheek here. "He made his way up the American side of the valley to be pleasantly surprised at being challenged in English."

With help from U.S. infantrymen, Hanna and engineer-gunner Barber were rescued behind German lines. The American side thus recovered every crewmember except *L'il Snooks*' pilot, Wann.

"After the bomber almost collided with me in midair, I landed in the top of a big evergreen tree right on the top of a mountain," said Wann. His immediate, clutching fear was that *L'il Snooks*—now with no one on board—and still circling overhead might now decide to crash on top of him. After the bomber crashed, Wann initially felt relief. But he was in fog and haze, behind German lines, and was injured. Ahead of Wann lay a seven-day period of escape and evasion—and capture by the Germans, followed by exceedingly harsh treatment.

Numerous other Liberators and Liberators brought their crews to safety but at enormous cost. Typical of these was a Fortress piloted by 1st Lt. Craig P. Greason of 457th Bombardment Group. Greason's was one of about a dozen bombers during the war years to be named *Lady B Good*. Just as *L'il Snooks* was depositing its crew into thin air, Greason guided *Lady B Good* to a shaky crash landing near Ypres, Belgium, which had been liberated from the Germans. There was no injury to the bomber's crew.

DEFENDING THE MISSION

In his autobiography, *I Could Never Be So Lucky Again*, written with Carroll V. Glines, Doolittle never mentioned that he'd objected to his boss Lt. Gen. Carl "Tooey" Spaatz about area bombing that made the city center of Berlin—hence, civilians—the aiming point for Fortress bombardiers on February 3, 1945. Doolittle's supporters insisted that he harbored deep moral concerns about the way bombing was employed. If Doolittle had any detractors, they might have wondered if he was bitter on missing out on the show. At least twice, Doolittle had requested Spaatz to allow him to fly on a mission to Berlin. Spaatz had actually agreed at one point, but reversed himself. Doolittle wanted to be the only American bomber pilot to visit all three Axis capitals—he'd previously bombed Tokyo and Rome—but it was not to be.

In life, Doolittle wore his morality on his shoulder. In his autobiography, however, he seems to some extent an apologist for British nighttime area bombing, despite his abhorrence of civilian casualties. When it came time to choose a familiar target to make his arguments, Doolittle chose not Berlin but Magdeburg. He argued not that the bombing campaign was killing innocents, but that it was hampering the German war effort.

Fuel was the Achilles' heel of the Reich. While they continued to manufacture weapons, engines, and airplanes, Germany never had enough fuel. Magdeburg was one of a half-dozen oil centers that were bombed often, usually by Liberators, whose greater bomb capacity was ideally suited for petroleum targets. In the immediate aftermath of at least one such mission, Italian forced laborers added to the destruction by pouring fuel on the flames.

At Magdeburg, the Eighth Air Force struck the top-priority synthetic gasoline plant at Rothensee, Doolittle wrote. The attack included a strike on the Krupp plant at Buchau, which made tanks, shells, and guns; the ordnance depot at Fredrichstadt, where weapons were collected for distribution to German units in combat on the Western and Eastern fronts; and the Junkers factory, turning out the newest engine powering the Fw 190.

Britain's Royal Air Force, Doolittle wrote, "followed this [at night] by the destruction of the urban area. The final phase not only destroyed the houses of the factory workers and interrupted vital military industrial transport, but also destroyed a very large part of the remaining factories in this highly developed industrial center. In an armament city of this kind, most of the industries were interdependent, using common sources of power, raw materials, and transport, with many smaller plants making parts for final assembly of war materiel in the larger ones." No American crewmember who took the high risks associated with a bomb run over Magdeburg is known to have ever had any difficulty sleeping at night.

CHAPTER FIFTEEN

The Way Home

Mission to Berlin
February 3, 1945—11:47 a.m. to 3:00 p.m.

FLYING FORTRESSES HAD PLOWED over Berlin, dropped bombs, and begun their struggle to reach safety before most P-51 Mustang pilots were ever given reason do more than watch. When German radio announced at exactly noon that American bombers were over Hitler's capital, the news flash was about an hour behind the actual event. The radio announcement said nothing about P-51s, which, according to lore German leader Hermann Göring had boasted would never appear over the Reich. Never mind that Göring's quote is one of the most misquoted and misunderstood of the war. In reality, the rotund and unpleasant Göring had said that Hitler's realm "will not be subjected to a single bomb . . . or you can call me Meier!" Interpreted as an anti-Semitic slur, the unfortunate quote was actually something else entirely. Because Meier in its several spellings is the second most common German surname, the expression was a common German idiom to express that something is impossible. Göring is also reported to have said that no Allied warplane would reach Berlin within a thousand years.

Having done exactly that and not for the first time, most of the Fortresses were turning toward England or headed toward ditching in the North Sea. Several were diverting to Soviet lines in Poland and two were headed toward Sweden.

Only after the last bomb had fallen on Berlin, P-51s became caught up in a spree of actions to the west and northwest of the German capital.

Most Fortress bomber crewmembers never saw the Mustangs that protected them by ranging far ahead, to the side, and behind, the Fortresses. Except for one or two sightings in the far distance, no one aboard a Fortress spotted any German aircraft at all. The air-to-ground and air-to-air fighting by Mustangs took place miles away from the bomber stream. P-51 pilots eventually found targets for their six .50-caliber Browning M2 machine guns but not in the middle of, or even very close to, the parade of Fortresses.

Mustang pilots were fulfilling Lt. Gen. James H. Doolittle's doctrine, which gave them latitude to roam.

THE OGLE CREW

Although he later said that P-51 Mustang fighter escort was "excellent" on February 3, 1945, Fortress pilot 1st Lt. Arthur H. Ogle ran into trouble the fighters couldn't help him with.

One of the last aircraft over Berlin was a 486th Bombardment Group Fortress named *Lady V II*, piloted by Ogle and carrying Maj. John "Junior" Rex as mission leader for the group. The Fortress was destined for trouble if anyone wanted to read the tea leaves: Its crew was listed on the daily operations report as crew number thirteen. The aircraft had the digits 13 in its plane number. It flew in the number thirteen slot in the formation.

The bomber was finishing one of the final bomb runs over a smoke-covered Berlin when a burst of flak knocked out one of its engines. With a feathered propeller, it continued on the bomb run and released its bombs. As the last bombs left the Flying Fortress, another flak explosion shook the aircraft and damaged two of the remaining three engines.

Ogle and the others on the flight deck found themselves fighting to control a Fortress that didn't want to be controlled and couldn't keep up with the formation. A hasty conversation inside the noisy flight deck reached the inevitable conclusion: *Lady V II* had no way to fly back to England. Moreover, Ogle realized, as the bomber's speed and stability began to deteriorate, the Fortress crew would become meat on the table for any German fighters that happened to be wandering around. Ogle and Rex were in agreement: They were in a jam. Losing altitude rapidly, Rex radioed that *Lady V II* would head east to try to land behind Soviet lines in Poland. *It was 12:05 p.m., British Summer Time.*

THE WYMAN CREW

Getting rid of your bombload, starting for home, and beginning to feel relief after the quick run over the target could produce a false sense of comfort. First Lieutenant Linwood S. Wyman, pilot of *Sitting Pretty* of the 96th Bombardment Group, was pulling away from Berlin at 26,500 feet when a flak shell exploded within arm's length of his Fortress. Wyman knew immediately that the damage to his B-17 was mortal.

"I was unable to tell the crew to bail out as the interphone and alarm system were out of order due to battle damage," Wyman later wrote in an official report. "I told the copilot [Flight Officer George L. Lewis] and engineer [Tech. Sgt. John W. Jones] to bail out and they both went forward to the nose escape hatch. I remained at the controls holding the ship level for at least a minute. When I left the controls, the ship went into a spiral, I assume because number one and number two engines were out and props were windmilling. I was thrown back through the bomb bay."

Wyman saw Lewis, nose gunner Staff Sgt. Rolando Sias, radio operator Tech. Sgt. Harold W. Doran, and tail gunner Staff Sgt. Burl A. Glendening bail out of *Sitting Pretty*. Thrown from his plane, Wyman parachuted into the midst of a battalion of the Werhmacht, or German army. *It was 12:20 p.m., British Summer Time.*

After being taken prisoner, Wyman wrote, navigator Flight Officer Walter J. Moore Jr., ball turret gunner Staff Sgt. Newton W. Blough, and waist gunner Charles G. Baird Jr. "were missing." Wyman felt their loss personally: Like all Fortress pilots he was the commander of his crew and they were his family. But Blough and Baird never got out of *Sitting Pretty*. Wyman wrote that nose gunner Sias told him that navigator Moore "did not appear to be wounded but was dazed and made no attempt to put his chute on. However, the navigator did motion for Sias to bail out. Sias saw the copilot bail out and followed him."

Wyman wrote that radio operator Doran "saw the fire in the wing and ran back through the waist and tried to open the escape door. Baird and Blough (both missing) were in the waist section and Doran said they appeared not to be wounded. It was Baird who opened the door for Doran to bail out."

Wyman continued: "The tail gunner [Glendening] came forward to his escape hatch as soon as we were hit and saw Blough and Baird unwounded in the waist. When he saw Doran come back and bail out, he went out his own escape hatch.

"I didn't see the ship blow up," Wyman wrote, "but it must have, for I saw a wing falling by itself."

In a final paragraph that was testimony to how order had deteriorated in the Third Reich, Wyman wrote: "If the missing members of my crew did get out of the ship alive, it is highly possible they may have been killed on the way down. I could hear the Germans shooting at us with rifles as we floated down in our parachutes."

Ultimately, it was determined that three members of the *Sitting Pretty* crew were killed (Baird, Blough, and Moore) and six became prisoners. All of the prisoners survived the war.

55TH ON THE ATTACK

Over Boizenburg, Germany, near Hamburg and considerably to the northwest of Berlin, Lt. Col. Elwyn Guido Righetti of the 55th Fighter Group, today using the call sign Tudor Leader, peered ahead from his P-51D Mustang and thought he saw odd-looking Luftwaffe aircraft approaching him. Righetti was in the lead of a formation of Mustangs prowling deep into Luftwaffe territory, intending to prevent German fighters from interfering with bombers that had already passed over Berlin but were still in hostile skies. He was a supremely accomplished fighter pilot who had been a competitive horseman before the war. His Mustangs were strung out all over the sky in close-knit formations of four, their silvery wings flashing in the sun, and they were moving inexorably toward the depths of the Reich. *It was 12:30 p.m. British Summer Time on Saturday, February 3, 1945.*

Righetti, an "old" fighter pilot at twenty-nine, nicknamed "Eager El" by buddies not for being reckless but for being friendly, commanded his group's 338th Fighter Squadron and was de facto commander of the entire group. He was piloting a P-51D Mustang named *Katydid* after his wife Katherine. He enjoyed by now a reputation as one of the most aggressive pilots and leaders in the Eighth Air Force. "Eager El" was especially renowned for his low-level attacks on German railway locomotives—a task for which the Mustang was less well suited than its partner the P-47 Thunderbolt. Not for nothing, Righetti was called "the king of the strafers" by his crew chief. Aggressive, experienced, dynamic, Righetti had seen it all, but he had never, ever, seen an aircraft as strange as those he was about to engage.

One of the 904 men piloting P-51 Mustangs over the Third Reich was 1st Lt. Brooks J. Liles, later to be nicknamed "Pappy," of the 343rd Fighter Squadron, 55th Fighter Group. Liles's plane, named *Sweet Marie II*, was a P-51K model, identical to the better-known, bubble-canopy P-51D but with a different propeller (an Aeroproducts, four-bladed hollow steel propeller instead of the more familiar Hamilton Standard version). Already credited with an air-to-air victory over a Focke-Wulf Fw 190, Liles was itching for more air-to-air action. Yet he saw no fighters. He saw no flak. Nothing remarkable was happening in the northwestern Germany that passed beneath his wings.

It appears Liles's was one of the early Mustang actions of the day, but that it took place long after the Fortresses had done their duty. At Stade, a hamlet 180 miles northwest of Berlin near the North Sea coast facing Sweden, Liles came upon a Luftwaffe airfield that didn't seem especially busy but had several Heinkel He 111 twin-engined bombers lined up on the taxiway. Like de facto 55th group commander Righetti, Liles could deservedly have been called the king of the strafers, or at least the prince. He took *Sweet Marie II* down to treetop level and started shooting.

"I saw the bursts from my guns bracketing them and then striking them," Liles said later. Liles was credited with one Heinkel destroyed and one damaged. Flying with him, 1st Lt. Victor P. Krambo was credited with damaging one He 111.

Krambo's Mustang was named *Lucky Wabbit II* in homage to the Looney Tunes character Elmer Fudd, the nemesis of Bugs Bunny. Krambo appears not to have had an opportunity for air-to-air shooting on this day. Squadron mates and family members later said that in battles that came before and after February 3, Krambo racked up aerial victories against German aircraft that he didn't claim because recognition wasn't important to him. In an air force of very young men, Krambo was in his thirties and seemed downright avuncular. Like most U.S. airmen in the fight high over Europe, Krambo seems to have had some sense that prisoner of war conditions on the ground were deteriorating and he vowed never to be shot down and captured. It was a promise that would be put to the challenge, but not today.

Liles's squadron mate, 1st Lt. Bernard H. Howes, in a Mustang named *L'il Honey* was in the air on this mission and was about to encounter action of his own. The record is unclear on this point, but Howes may have helped Liles to shoot up Stade airfield. Now, Liles, Howes and the 55th Fighter Group continued toward Hamburg, still 160 miles west of Berlin.

Liles and Howes had known each other since beginning military duty, had service numbers that were only ten digits apart, and had agreed that if one were ever shot down, the other would attempt a rescue (something they grapple with later in the war).

BATTLING THE MISTELS

"Eager El," could not believe his eyes.

Coming straight at him were several aircraft that Lt. Col. Righetti would later call "Fw 190-bomber combos, flying a sloppy 'V' formation at about 600 feet." Another pilot in the group would later call them "a Junkers Ju 88 married to a Focke-Wulf Fw 190 and appearing to be on their wedding night." The Germans called this aircraft the Mistel (Mistletoe) or the "Vater und Sohn" (Father and Son) after a popular German strip cartoon: Each was a Junkers 88 that had been transformed to a huge missile by replacing its cockpit with a four-ton warhead, placing a mount on its back for carrying a mounted fighter aircraft—an Fw 190—and connecting the unmanned bomber's flight controls to the fighter, so that the fighter's pilot could fly the dual aircraft all the way to the target. What looked like a Ju 88 carrying an Fw 190 on its back was exactly the opposite, an Fw 190 hauling a Ju 88. The Germans intended the word Mistel only for the lower component of the two-aircraft combo, but the term was often used to refer to the whole package. This was an air-to-ground weapon, an early and crude kind of cruise missile, and it was not what Righetti and the Mustang pilots were looking for. But they had found it and they would fight it.

First Lieutenant Bernard H. Howes—pilot of *L'il Honey* and fellow Mustang flyer Liles's best friend—reported on the action that followed.

"I was flying White 3 [his radio call sign] on the mission of February 3," Howes wrote in his after-action report. "At about 12:30 p.m., we dropped to the deck to strafe. On pulling up from the first pass on a locomotive, I sighted a formation of three pick-a-backs, Fw 190s on Ju 88s, in string formation at about 400 feet. I turned into the second combo with my wingman, Lt. Moore [2nd Lt. Patrick L. Moore], behind me."

Howes continued: "I fired a short burst from 90 degrees at about 350 yards, observing a few strikes on the 190. As I fired on this, the 190 in the third unit was released. [Apparently, Howes did not understand that the Fw 190 was the carrier aircraft of the "combo," while the Ju 88 was being carried]. The prop was windmilling and on release the 190 seemed to nose up for a minute and then, apparently out of control, the nose went down and it headed for the ground. I claim this Fw 190 as destroyed."

"As soon as the 190 was released, the 88 turned sharply left," Howes continued. "I followed, firing a short burst, but observed no strikes. I fell outside of the turn and lost sight of the 88 momentarily. My wingman behind me was in position and shot the 88 down. [The Ju 88, effectively a cruise missile, probably had no one on board but the Americans did not know that.] When I looked back, I saw it crash into the ground. On pulling up I saw the first unit I had fired at about 300 yards in front of me. There were flames coming out of the 190, so I went after it again. I started firing and the combo turned into me, dropping to the deck. As I fired, another large burst of flame came from the 190. On making a second pass, the right engine of the 88 burst into flame and I saw them both crash into the ground." Noting that he had expended 1,440 rounds of .50-caliber ammunition while fighting at 1,500 feet in overcast with scattered holes, Howes claimed and was officially credited with three aerial victories that were added to one he'd scored on an earlier mission.

For the Mustang with its seemingly limitless supply of gas, its powerful, 1,420-horsepower, two-staged V-1650 Rolls Royce liquid-cooled engine and its ability to turn on a dime, a Mistel wasn't exactly a first-line challenge. The pilot's handbook credited the Mustang with a maximum speed of 437 miles per hour, but pilots said it could go faster. The U.S. Congress's Truman Senate War Investigating Committee—no friend of the U.S. aircraft industry—labeled the Mustang "the most aerodynamically perfect pursuit plane in existence." By this stage in the war, American Mustang pilots were far more experienced that all but the hardest core of the Germans they faced, and—as cannot be said too often—they were defeating the Luftwaffe by killing its pilots. Eventually, American Mustang would be credited with destroying 4,950 enemy aircraft in Europe to make them the highest scoring U.S. fighter in the theater.

Today, however, as the strange battle with the Mistels unfolded, the biggest danger to the Mustangs was from uncharted flak batteries in the area. The Americans' best chance of success lay in staying too close to the German aircraft to attract fire from the ground.

GIBBS VERSUS MISTELS

Second Lieutenant Richard G. Gibbs, also of the 55th Fighter Group under Righetti, filed a report that was almost a carbon copy of Howes's but referred to a different trio of Mistels:

> I was flying TUDOR White 2 [his radio call sign] on the mission of February 3, 1945. We were on the deck and about to strafe a loco in the vicinity of Boizenberg, when Tudor Leader Lt. Col. Righetti called in a gaggle of three Fw 190–bomber combos, flying a sloppy 'V' formation at about 600 feet. We attacked from a level turn port stern.
>
> Lt. Col. Righetti took the middle combo of the three, and I took the 3rd and last one of this gaggle. I started firing on the Ju 88 at about 45 degrees from about 800 yards, closing to about 300 yards with a 2-second burst. I observed many strikes on the left wing root of the Ju 88, where it began to burn. After a short dive the FW 190 was released. The 190 appeared to be rather unstable in the air, but it managed to get in violent evasive action during the ensuing combat. I fired a short burst from astern beginning at about 200 yards and closing to zero yards. I saw many strikes all over the aircraft and observed parts of the cowling and the canopy fly off. There was also fire in or around the cockpit. I then overran the enemy aircraft and skidded out to the right. As I looked back I saw where the 190 had crashed into the ground.

With an economical 720 rounds of ammunition, Gibbs had claimed one Ju 88 and one Fw 190 destroyed.

Captain William M. Lewis of the 55th Fighter Group was also in the fight against the Mistel "combos." Lewis was well known for air-to-ground strafing and for air-to-air prowess. He'd once downed a Messerschmitt Bf 109 without firing a shot, by outmaneuvering his Luftwaffe adversary. They were in a near vertical dive when the Bf 109 lost a wing and crashed, enabling Lewis to claim not only an aerial victory but "ammunition austerity." Today, Lewis was in the fray alongside Gibbs and shot down one of the Ju 88s.

Righetti was credited with no fewer than three aerial victories in the fight with the "combos." One of these was his fifth kill, making him an air ace.

The bizarre Mistel "combo" was not the only unusual aircraft spotted by roving Mustang pilots while the Fortresses headed away from Berlin. At the controls of a Mustang named *Mah Ideel* of the 55th Fighter Group near Germany's Templin airfield, 1st Lt. Dudley M. "Dixie" Amoss happened upon a pair of Focke-Wulf Fw 58 Weihe ("Harrier") twin-engined transports, which the Luftwaffe used to train multiengine pilots, gunners, and radio operators. The Fw 58 was also sometimes used as a utility transport and could have been carrying someone important, but that seems not to have been the case this time.

It was almost too easy for Amoss, who had tallied up flying experience with the Royal Air Force before joining Righetti's 55th group and who would later become the first member of the group to shoot down a Messerschmitt Me 262 jet fighter. The Fw 58s were partly fabric-covered, easy to see, armed with only two machine guns, and very slow. Amoss teamed up with another pilot, pulled *Mah Ideel* in tight behind the Focke-Wulfs, and blasted away. He was credited with 1.5 aerial victories, sharing an Fw 58 kill with the other Mustang pilot, 1st Lt. Lester F. Spiecker. During the same action, 1st Lt. Keith R. McGinnis was credited with destroying a Fieseler Fi 156 Storch (Stork) liaison airplane on the ground. The Storch was a lightweight, two-seat, high-wing aircraft well known for its ability to land and take off in very short distances.

The postmission report said that six Mustangs were lost, three to antiaircraft fire, one to engine failure (1st Lt. Frederick Powell) and two to unknown causes. Six more Mustangs stationed in England landed at bases on the continent rather than travel all the way home.

THE GIBBS CREW

The final Fortress crew to give up any chance of getting home belonged to 2nd Lt. Henry H. Sherman of the 863rd Bombardment Squadron, 493rd Bombardment Group, which had passed over Berlin, dropped bombs, and exited the target unscathed. Heading away from the target, Sherman and copilot 2nd Lt. Al Janulis were far from German flak blasts when something went wrong with their aircraft. According to the official report:

> At 1230 hours, approximately forty-five minutes after attacking the primary target, aircraft number 242, which was leading the No. 2 element at the time, called to the formation leader that he lost a propeller governor, which threw off the propeller of the number one engine.
>
> The leader told Sherman to stay in the bomber stream if possible and fire green-green flares and call for escort fighters. Sherman replied with 'Roger' and was last seen lagging behind the formation in the bomber stream at 24,000 feet, under control but losing altitude steadily on a heading of 270 degrees, at this point, no crewmember had been seen to bail out.

It is unclear whether any "little friends," the ubiquitous P-51 Mustangs, showed up to nurse Sherman's crew. In any event, the crew did bail out; all became prisoners and survived the war: Sherman, Janulis, navigator 2nd Lt. Paul E. O'Connell, engineer-gunner Sgt. Raymond D. Fisher, toggleer Sgt. Walter A. Flahertty, radio operator Staff Sgt. Harry A. Koerner, ball turret gunner Sgt. Carl W. Hultman, waist gunner Sgt. Robert G. Smead, and tail gunner Sgt. Douglas O. Adnest. Koerner had been pulled from duty for medical reasons after being wounded on a Fortress mission a year earlier and had insisted on flying again.

THE LISSNER CREW

While two P-51 Mustangs escorted it to the German coast and then peeled off, the Flying Fortress known as *The Jones Family* piloted by 2nd Lt. Roland

A. Lissner of the 306th Bombardment Group struggled toward the Baltic. In an official report, Lissner later wrote:

> The following factors entered into my decision to come to Sweden: (1) I figured that with the loss of gas we could remain aloft for only one and one-half hours; (2) I figured that by using walk-around oxygen bottles filled from the co-pilot's system we could remain at altitude for 45 minutes; (3) our number two engine was smoking and running low manifold pressure; (4) number one and number four engine cylinder head temperatures were at 240 degrees due to high power settings when we were attempting to remain in the bomber stream; (5) the number three prop which was windmilling began vibrating and the engine began to throw oil.

After leaving the Mustangs behind, Lissner began losing altitude until reaching the Swedish coast. He later reported with some relief that he encountered no Swedish antiaircraft fire or fighters, although Swedish Seversky J9 fighters (the neutral country's version of the U.S. P-35A) fighters were en route with orders to escort him to safety. After circling the Swedish west coast city of Malmo twice, peering through undercast in search of an airfield, Lissner was approached by two J9s. He lowered and raised his landing gear in the international signal of surrender and followed the fighters down through clouds to Bulltofta Airport, home of the Royal Swedish Air Force unit known as F10 Wing. When Lissner's wheels touched pavement, the radar unit known as a PFF ball (for pathfinder) was torn apart, but the rest of his Flying Fortress was undamaged. Apart from tail gunner Sgt. George W. Beck—who'd been nursing an injury in his left wrist caused by flak shrapnel and was quickly hospitalized—no one in Lissner's crew was seriously hurt. *It was 12:45 p.m., British Summer Time.*

A surviving newspaper clip shows stern-looking Swedish police officers escorting Lissner and the officers of his crew to a limousine that will take them to a hotel.

No written report could be found on the other Fortress that went to Sweden that day. First Lieutenant William L. Fry's *Slightly Dangerous* of the 452nd Bombardment Group landed in Rinkaby, Sweden, an active fighter base.

About 267 American aircrews with a total of 1,400 men were interned in Sweden, which was officially neutral but tended to lean toward the side that was winning. Late in the war, the United States gave Sweden permission to keep nine intact B-17s in exchange for repatriating about half of the interned crewmembers.

It appears that repatriation was prompt for *The Jones Family*'s Lissner, copilot 2nd Lt. Chester J. Britton, navigator 2nd Lt. Finley G. Robbins, radar navigator Flight Officer James O. White, bombardier 2nd Lt. Donald C. Haagenson, engineer-gunner Sgt. Lloyd W. Miller, radio operator Sgt. Jere L. Fennerty, waist gunner Sgt. Harold R. Bometz, and the wounded Beck. Like all who diverted to neutral territory during the bombing campaign, they filled out extensive reports on return to U.S. control and went on with their lives.

Similar treatment was accorded to *Slightly Dangerous*'s Fry (who had been on his twenty-third combat mission), copilot 2nd Lt. John Kurrack (who had been on his first and only combat mission), navigator 2nd Lt. Christian Tack, toggleer Tech. Sgt. Eugene Dreyfus, radio operator Tech. Sgt. George Clark, right waist gunner Staff Sgt. David Lowery, engineer-gunner Tech. Sgt. Russell Pyle Jr., and left waist gunner Staff Sgt. Marvin Beolkens. This crew, too, suffered only one casualty: Clark had an injured back, apparently from the Fortress being hit by flak.

THE SHOEMAKER CREW (III)

All Ira Roisman could see was water.

Cold, cold water.

The Flying Fortress of 1st Lt. Daniel G. Shoemaker, Boeing-built B-17G-55-BO Flying Fortress (42-102555/KY-F), was off the European continent now, the North Sea remarkably brown in appearance, the aircraft failing, the crew battered.

Engineer Sergeant Roisman was not happy. He later described the situation an official report:

> I started back away from the hatch [awed by the sight of so much open water] and Lt. Shoemaker hollered, "Let's ditch the damned thing!" The navigator had his chute on and the co-pilot returned to his seat. Then I began firing green-green and red-red flares. After I had

> fired eight or ten, I started to the radio room. The radioman and the Sperry gunner [ball turret gunner] were at the waist door. The door was missing. The waist gunner had bailed out. The co-pilot started to slip the plane down, but pieces of the wing began to fall off. He then feathered the number two and three engines to prevent the props from falling off. Shoemaker was still standing in the well between the pilot's and co-pilot's seat.

Shoemaker's B-17 began its run-in for a ditching, skimming the North Sea just above the surface at 200 miles per hour. *It was 2:30 p.m., British Summer Time, Saturday, February 3, 1945.*

Shoemaker got into his seat, facing a windshield that had been destroyed and a furious rush of cold air. "We do not know whether he fastened his safety belt," Roisman wrote. "The co-pilot let down half flaps at 140 miles per hour and turned sideways in his seat. The plane stalled at approximately 90 miles per hour. In the radio room, the Sperry ballman and the radio operator were in their proper ditching positions. The top hatch stuck and the radioman and I had to break it out.

"I was standing when we hit. There were two impacts—not too hard. The ship filled up with water very quickly due to the two hatches being gone.

"I started to climb out of the top hatch. The right dinghy was in the water right side up, only half inflated with nothing in it. The left dinghy never did get out. The pilot was about half out of his window and the co-pilot was on top of the plane. The Sperry ballman hollered, 'Get away from the ship!' and jumped over the dinghy into the water. He went down and never did come up. The navigator was swimming away from the ship to the 10 o'clock position of the ship.

"The pilot's harness got caught and the co-pilot helped him out onto the left wing. Then I hollered to Lt. Shoemaker to get into the dinghy but he just looked over me into space. Blood was running down his face. The tail gunner never got out and the toggleer went crazy and refused to move.

"I pulled the dinghy nearer to the pilot but he refused to move. Lt. Moullen, the co-pilot, was trying to release the other dinghy but he could not.

"The plane started to go down and the tail section hit me on the head, pushing the dinghy and me under water. I still had my parachute on and I was groggy and scared. The ship went down nose first. When I hit the surface the ship was gone and there was a lot of stuff in the water. Lt. Moullen was on top of the ship when it started down; he saw the tail hit me and looked for the pilot but was unable to find him. He then jumped into the water trying to get the dinghy, which had wrapped itself around the tail section. (The dinghy, covered with oil, was hard to recognize from the air). Lt. Moullen broke the static cord holding the dinghy to the ship and turned it over, as it was wrong side up. Then he climbed into the dinghy by slowly twisting his body from right to left as he started to stiffen up. I then saw both the dinghy and Lt. Moullen and shouted for help. He began to paddle towards me using his hands. It seemed like a million years. He finally got to me and helped me to the side of the dinghy and gave me a string to hold. Then he paddled toward the radio operator.

"He tried to get Staff Sgt. Benton into the dinghy, but Staff Sgt. Benton was in a bad way. His face was cut open (left cheek) and was purple, as were his lips. His eyes were glassy and he made noises. He made no effort to help Lt. Moullen, who got him to the side of the dinghy and part way in. He floated away on his back, looking toward the sky. He looked dead, eyes wide open."

Copilot Moullen scanned the area where the B-17 had been and saw another body, face down, showing no sign of movement or life. Another B-17 now appeared overhead and began to circle, but it was not clear that the bomber's crew had pinpointed the ditching or the men afloat on the surface.

Moullen and engineer Roisman, now the only survivors of the Shoemaker crew, struggled to help each other in the dinghy, Moullen using freezing hands to help remove the parachute from Roisman's harness. His purpose was to create a parachute canopy that would help rescuers to pick out the dinghy in the cold brown North Sea. But to operate the quick-release, Moullen had to turn a cap clockwise through 90 degrees, pull a safety clip, and strike the cap a sharp blow with his hand. This was an almost insurmountable challenge in the frigid temperatures, but somehow Moullen popped the chute. The sixteen-foot canopy emerged, and the two men struggled to spread it on the water to make themselves more visible.

A Royal Air Force Wellington bomber, part of air-sea rescue forces, appeared overhead and began dropping smoke markers and flares. The men saw a red-nosed P-47 Thunderbolt, also part of air-sea rescue, circling them at low level. A second Wellington dropped a lifeboat, suspended by two parachutes.

"The boat drifted downwind," Roisman wrote. "Its chutes did not collapse. The boat began to drift away. One of the lines was about fifteen yards away." The men were twenty-five yards from the airdropped lifeboat when a British rescue boat appeared. The boat crew's first attempts to throw a lifeline failed, but they tried again and were able to take Moullen and Roisman on board. They removed the men's frozen clothing, wrapped them in blankets, administered first aid, and gave them rum. They also gave the badly injured Roisman morphine. *It was 3:00 p.m., British Summer Time.*

Those never recovered from the North Sea were Shoemaker, navigator 1st Lt. Ermal Pinkley, tail gunner Sgt. Gale Snyder, radio operator Staff Sgt. Raymond Benton, toggleer Sgt. Armando Cantu, waist gunner Sgt. Bob K. Buckley, and ball turret gunner Staff Sgt. Q. A. Bastani.

Moullen was awarded the Distinguished Service Cross, the nation's second highest award for valor.

CHAPTER SIXTEEN

Wheels Down

Mission to Berlin
February 3, 1945—3:00 p.m. to 12:00 midnight

THE BOMBERS CAME HOME.

Most did, anyway.

In formations that reflected the flight discipline of the entire day, many crossed the coastline of the British Isles and made orderly letdowns to their East Anglia airfields. At one East Anglia airfield after another, ground crews watched in anticipation and felt relief, most of them, as their bombers dropped landing gear and settled down on pavement. Here and there, a Fortress popped flares to signal trouble, made a shaky landing, and groundlooped before the crew walked away, exhausted.

But many of the Fortress crewmembers who attacked Berlin on Saturday, February 3, 1945, were not yet finished with their travails.

And they were not yet finished dying.

There was a happy ending, at least, for *Happy Warrior*: With its number one engine feathered and its airspeed down, 1st Lt. William Settler's crew approached Lavenham alone—a straggler that had eluded German fighters and flown back with battle damage. Ball turret gunner Staff Sgt. Curtis E. Roper—like the rest of the crew, a member of the 838th Bombardment Squadron, 487th Bombardment Group—remembers that the few comments made on the intercom were made by men who were unruffled, and who could handle returning in a Fortress with three engines. Roper's strongest hope was that he would not have to repeat his experience, back during stateside training, of parachuting from a stricken aircraft. He did not like the idea of jumping from an aircraft with a parachute. It never came naturally.

In keeping with procedure for landing, Roper climbed up from his ball turret and settled in the radio room. The intercom and the view outside the Fortress told him that Settler was going to attempt a normal landing. There was a distinctive bump that told him *Happy Warrior*'s landing gear was down and locked. This crew had been in the air almost exactly eight hours. *It was 3:00 p.m. British Summer Time, Saturday, February 3, 1945.*

Happy Warrior touched pavement, Roper heard the engines throttle back, and the Fortress began to slow and to run out of runway room. In plenty of time, Settler turned off on a taxiway, followed instructions, and took the Fortress back to its parking slot. Some of the crewmembers were so weary they did not move, initially, when the Fortress came to a halt. Even after Settler cut the throttles, it took the men some time to get themselves together and get out of the aircraft.

As other Fortresses taxied in, there was noise and bustle. Pilots went through their postlanding checklists. Crewmembers checked their gear. They were the lucky ones. They were soon parked with engines shut down.

But many Fortress crewmembers were not yet even close to home. The day was far from over.

BLUE GRASS GIRL

The journey into the jaws of Berlin's defenses was eventless for the crew aboard 1st Lt. Lewis K. Cloud's Flying Fortress, *Blue Grass Girl*, of the 486th Bombardment Group stationed at Sudbury in East Anglia. One crewmember believed he saw a German fighter in the distance. All saw flak, a lot of it. Those black, puffy bursts of smoke at times appeared quite close, but not so much as a piece of shrapnel seems to have grazed the Fortress. In fact, German defenses failed to touch *Blue Grass Girl*. There was not a nick, not a scratch, on the natural metal skin of the Fortress. *Blue Grass Girl*'s four 1,200-horsepower Wright R-1820-97 Cyclone nine-cylinder, air-cooled radial engines were performing as expected. The aircraft undoubtedly had a very smooth and clean look, unvarnished, unblemished, but we shall never know for certain because no photograph of it has survived. At the pilot's controls, Cloud was very much in control, and everything was purring nicely.

When *Blue Grass Girl*'s crewmembers looked down at the German capital, they witnessed destruction between gaps in the clouds that had begun to appear over the city about midway through the passage of the bomber stream, after the first bombers encountered clear weather. From his cramped perch in the Cheyenne turret at the very rear of the fuselage with large windows in three directions, Staff Sgt. Frank T. Chrastka peered down from 26,500 feet at a sprawling city-scape of devastation and chaos.

A crewmember in another Fortress, looking down at the destruction, smoke, and debris and thinking of the very real human beings in Berlin, whispered aloud to himself: "God help them . . . "

Blue Grass Girl was manned by a "put-together" crew, as one veteran later described it—nine men who did not usually fly together but who shared one important reality today: This was the thirty-fifth and last mission for all of them. This was not their first mission together, but several of them had begun with other crews and may have felt mixed loyalties. Two of the men, ball turret gunner, Staff Sgt. Johnnie L. Jones—who had a girlfriend awaiting him in a Sudbury hotel—and tail gunner Chrastka had until recently flown with a different crew headed by Capt. Ronald E. Bereman.

"Jones was like a father to me," said 1st Lt. Robert McCall, the navigator of Bereman's Fortress. Like so many, McCall felt deferential toward Jones being almost a decade older; his exact age is not on record, his early thirties apparently. However, he was by far the oldest aboard *Blue Grass Girl*.

"Jones was ball turret gunner and we lost him when we started flying a radar-equipped aircraft [the radar antenna was in place of the ball turret]," said pilot Bereman, "and we lost Frank because we became lead crew, because in my right seat would be an air leader [the 486th group's mission leader] in charge of the forming, timing, decisions on weather, and selecting another target, etc." Today, Bereman was at the controls of a different Flying Fortress, but he still felt, because of the bonds they'd forged flying together, that Jones and Chrastka belonged to him.

Aboard *Blue Grass Girl*, there appears to have been a sudden jubilation when enemy territory fell behind and the Fortress churned out over the North Sea with no battle damage, no mechanical issues. Jones had been especially nervous about going to heavily defended Berlin today and may have felt greater relief than anyone else. Each man in *Blue Grass Girl*'s crew had survived worse than they'd faced today, worse in terms of German fighters, worse in terms of flak, and they'd overcome every challenge in their path and had finished their war. Today, they'd earned the "Lucky Bastard Club" certificate that was given to every crewmember that completed his missions. For them, the war was over.

They wanted to celebrate. The four men in the rear fuselage—plus the engineer, Tech. Sgt. Richard H. Warlick—gathered in the radio compartment forward of the ball turret. *Blue Grass Girl* descended over the North Sea and made landfall. Pilot Cloud set course to travel southwest across East Anglia toward a landing at Sudbury. *It was 3:05 p.m., British Summer Time.*

Someone who wasn't there at all, Tech. Sgt. Daniel C. "Clint" Pentz of the Bereman crew and Chrastka's best friend, would later spend plenty of time thinking about how Chrastka left his tail gun position and made his way forward through the cramped fuselage to the radio room. "I guess he would have left his parachute in the tail," said Pentz. "Or, more likely, he started forward and left his parachute in the waist gunner's position." That would have placed the chute between eight and twelve feet behind Chrastka. Others may have left their chutes back there, as well.

A brief transmission from the radio room hinted that some kind of celebration was taking place. And why not? It was, after all, a big deal to survive a tour of duty and to be ready to go home.

Those who know about *Blue Grass Girl* will argue forever about what happened next. No one will ever be able to say with certainty.

No one really knows how the fire got started.

FLAMES RAGING FURIOUSLY

In later years, men would hold different recollections. Those differences would rise to the level of controversy and would evoke high emotion. The men best equipped to know what happened were not part of the strong-willed discussions that came later. They were not around to explain or defend themselves.

Copilot 1st Lt. John Uzdrowski of the Bereman crew observed *Blue Grass Girl* flying normally. He had also witnessed the Cloud crew drop its bombs normally before turning for home. He often used the word "normal" in describing what he witnessed—right up to the instant when nothing was normal any more.

"I had seen bombers hit by flak," said Uzdrowski. "I had seen bombers suffer damage. But I never saw anything quite like this. Usually, when there's a fire, there's smoke. But I did not see any smoke. One minute, everything was the way it was supposed to be. The next minute, there were red-orange flames lashing out of the rear of the fuselage."

Crewmembers aboard at least half a dozen bombers—including Bereman's crew—saw flames lapping upward and increasing in intensity at the *Blue Grass Girl*'s waist windows. In the air, nothing was more terrifying than a fire, and this was a big one with long tongues of flame pouring back from the waist gun position. Within a minute, most of the fuselage of Cloud's bomber was engulfed in flames. White-hot fire washed back into the bomber's slipstream. Initially, there was little or no smoke. But soon, black gouts of smoke were leaving a distinctive trail behind the Fortress.

Aboard *Blue Grass Girl*, Engineer Warlick was first to become aware of the fire, which seems to have begun directly behind the ball turret. Warlick worked his way forward to tell pilot Cloud. He grabbed a fire extinguisher. Apparently at Cloud's direction, he returned to the radio room and handed the extinguisher to Jones. Warlick said he didn't think it would do any good to try to put the fire out. It was, Warlick said, now completely out of control. The wooden floorboards of the B-17 were ablaze for quite some distance back. Even the metal interior of the fuselage was burning.

The celebration was over. Cloud put the aircraft into a gradual bank and turned out of the squadron formation. "I'll take a look," he said. He handed the controls to copilot 1st Lt. Frederick T. Stehle, stood, and went some distance back in the fuselage to get a look at the extent of the fire. At this point, it was no longer possible to continue backward through the bomb bay to the radio room. The fire was too intense, the heat too great. Except for ball turret gunner Jones, who was separated from the others by the location of his crew position—he apparently had not gone to the radio room to celebrate—it is likely that by now all of the men in the rear of the Fortress were gone, consumed within a storm of raw heat.

Warlick notified navigator 2nd Lt. Charles N. Scott and bombardier Capt. James J. McDermott of the fire and of the need to abandon ship. As he recounted it later, McDermott went back and looked at the fire, possibly looking over Cloud's shoulder. He apparently saw a solid wall of flame and was nearly overcome by the heat. McDermott turned to go forward, and now, with first-hand knowledge of the extent of the fire, Cloud returned to the pilot's seat and told copilot Stehle: "Get out of the aircraft!" Those were the last five words of Cloud's life.

Later, legend held that Cloud gave his parachute to another crew-member. That is not known for certain, and Stehle, who might have been able to confirm it, never did. The only certainty is that Cloud, who was of course in charge, never bailed out. Warlick, the only witness to events in the rear fuselage of *Blue Grass Girl*, was first to leave the aircraft, followed by Scott, McDermott, and Stehle. Ball turret gunner Jones also wriggled his way out of *Blue Grass Girl*, but by then the bomber was too close to the ground and Jones' parachute did not open. Among those who did not escape from *Blue Grass Girl* were Cloud, radio operator Staff Sgt. Arnold R. "Ray" Welch, waist gunner Staff Sgt. Gus T. Hodge, and Chrastka.

Bombardier McDermott, a "strapping young man with a 'devil may care' attitude, cocky and full of life," later described his bailout to his son, John M. McDermott. "They were on the return leg of the mission, crossing the Channel, when news came from the rear of the aircraft that there was a fire," the younger McDermott said. "My father told me that when he looked back—I think he said through the doors—-the whole back end was raging.

"My father was deathly afraid of the water. He couldn't swim at all and was deeply concerned about the aircraft making it back over land before they had to bail out. By the time my father exited the aircraft, they were over England. He was falling and his chute didn't immediately open. He told me he was looking down and he saw a marshy area below. He told himself, 'Jimmy, you're going to land in that marsh and it's going to be soft and you're gonna get up and walk right out of it.'

"About that time, his chute deployed and slowed his descent. He did, in fact, land in the marshy area. A local gentleman helped him out ['an old man with a bike'] and let my father borrow the bike to ride to the place the plane itself had crashed. He got there as fast as he could and was trying to get to the plane, but the locals stopped and held him back, insisting he couldn't do anyone any good."

DESTROYED AND DEBATED

There was no way anyone was going to be rescued inside that burning wreckage. McDermott watched the aircraft consumed in flames, knowing that those still aboard had already perished. He was able to see Cloud's remains as the Fortress burned.

The official report was damning. Investigators made it clear they were accepting engineer Warlick's account only begrudgingly and only because "he is the only person that escaped that saw the fire close enough to have knowledge of the exact location and possible cause thereof."

Once begun, the fire may have been fed by a broken oxygen connection, the report concluded. "The fire burned with such an intensity that the control cables evidently were severed and caused the aircraft to go out of control," it stated. The report continued:

"Crew discipline aboard the plane was very poor just before the fire was discovered. Part of the crew being in the radio room with no men in the waist or tail section is definitely against S.O.P. [standard operating procedure]. Had there been member or members of the crew in the waist, the fire could have been noticed sooner and could possibly have been put out. At least enough warning could have been given to allow all the occupants to escape. Also, it is believed that at least two members of the crew [left] their parachutes in the waist section and could not get to them because of the fire." Those two crewmembers would have been waist gunner Hodge and tail gunner Chrastka.

The official finding was that the cause of the loss of *Blue Grass Girl* was "50% material failure and 50% personnel failure on the part of the crewmembers who were not at their proper stations," the report said, placing most of the responsibility on the pilot, Cloud.

Left out of all of the official documents was what many crewmembers in nearby Fortresses thought they knew: *Blue Grass Girl*'s crew had been celebrating by firing flares out the waist window using a Very pistol. Bereman said he observed this. Others aboard Bereman's plane also said they observed it. Bereman wrote:

> We were returning on a mission to Berlin and had crossed over the English coastline at an altitude of around two thousand feet. We did not know at the time that it was *Blue Grass Girl* nor who was flying

> it. We found out at debriefing that two of our gunners [Jones and Chrastka], due to return to the mainland the next day, were on the plane and killed in the crash. When we first noticed the plane, [it was] firing Very Pistol flares out the waist windows, but shortly [it] stopped firing and smoke was pouring out the rear of the plane. For a few seconds we saw the smoke stop and then start again. Then we observed four chutes followed by the plane pitching over and straight down and exploding when it hit the ground.
>
> It is mine and [my] crewmember opinions that a Very Pistol flare somehow got shot inside the plane and set it on fire. The pilot can certainly be commended for staying with the aircraft in an attempt to somehow make a belly landing to save the crew, but it was not to be. He paid the price and is a hero in my eyes and deserves the highest praise.

But were *Blue Grass Girl*'s crewmembers playing around with a Very pistol and shooting flares into the air to mark the completion of their tour of duty? Other crews had done this from time to time, but it was a breach of safety rules and perhaps of common sense. Bereman's copilot Uzdrowski later said it was possible, but he simply wasn't sure he ever saw any flares come flying out of the aircraft. Of course, no one would have seen a flare that detonated inside the plane.

One member of Bereman's crew, radio operator Tech. Sgt. Daniel C. "Clint" Pentz who once stole coal from the chaplain along with Chrastka, isn't buying the story that Cloud's crew was "fooling around" with flares. Pentz was Chrastka's best friend, going back to shared experiences when they trained together stateside. "The idea that they were fooling with flares makes no sense to me," said Pentz. "The flare pistol was up front, forward of the bomb bay, in the flight engineer's [Warlick's] position. How would it have gotten to the radio operator's [Welch's] room? I do not believe flares had anything to do with it." The problem with Pentz's conclusion: We already know that engineer Warlick traveled back to the radio room and Warlick was the custodian of the Very pistol.

Said Pentz, opening a familiar wound among some crewmembers: "The pilot, 1st Lt. Lewis Cloud, gave his life trying to save his crew. On December 24, 1944, Brig. Gen. Frederick W. Castle did the same thing and he was given the Medal of Honor. Cloud received nothing. I guess rank counts."

British Police Superintendent William Franks saw *Blue Grass Girl* on fire and the crew bailing out while he bicycled through the village of Wrentham near the larger town of Reydon just a few miles from the Sudbury airfield. *It was 3:10 p.m., British Summer Time.*

Blue Grass Girl was engulfed in flames and, yet, for a moment, seemed still to be under control. And then, the bomber veered downward. According to the official report, "The aircraft was seen to go into a steep turn and crash to the ground, explode, and burn." An observer on the ground said it crashed with a heavy thumping sound at Church Farm, Reydon, near Southwold, Suffolk, and was consumed by flames. *It was 3:14 p.m., British Summer Time.*

The loss of Cloud's crew was a devastating blow to the morale of the 486th Bombardment Group. It didn't seem fair. The men had finished their war. They had survived a final mission to the heavily defended German capital. And then, fire had intervened after they were supposed to be safe. Some bomber crewmembers were superstitious. To them, this was something that just couldn't happen.

So far as it was possible to learn when reviewing this incident decades later, no Fortress crewmember went to the inn in Sudbury to tell Jones' girlfriend that he had been lost in a terribly sad and tragic aircraft mishap. When and how she learned is not known.

HOMEWARD BOUND

Hundreds of other Fortresses made the journey to Berlin, released their lethal cargoes, and headed for home without being touched by German antiaircraft defenses. Accounts of the severity of flak barrages were markedly different from one bomb group to another.

The 401st Bombardment Group had all of its Fortresses back on the ground by late afternoon with two exceptions. A Fortress piloted by 1st Lt. Myron L. King (below) diverted to Soviet territory. The situation was more serious aboard 1st Lt. Carl P. Djernes of the group's 615th Bombardment Squadron. The Fortress was named *The Farmer's Daughter*. Djernes' Fortress took a severe flak hit that shook the aircraft from one end to the other and knocked some of the crew around like sardines in a can.

One engine sputtered to a halt. But Djernes' Fortress, although wobbly, remained in the air.

Like so many of the crewmembers fighting in the high cold, Djernes, from Hamilton, Nebraska, at age twenty-seven was an oldster for a Fortress pilot and a citizen-soldier with no military tradition. Before finding himself in the pilot's seat of a Fortress, Djernes has been a mail carrier in Omaha and had made saddles for the Shrine Mounted Patrol. He'd chosen the auspicious date of December 6, 1941, to marry Margaret Farmer, with whom he had no children. Djernes was thus an ordinary man from Nebraska, struggling, now, to keep his bomber aloft while shifting through the choices: Crash land? Divert to Sweden? Divert to Soviet territory? Djernes had lost one engine and his Fortress was shaking like a washing machine out of control, but he believed he could do better.

With a crew that included copilot 2nd Lt. Raymond H. Spiva, navigator 2nd Lt. John F. Canale, toggleer Staff Sgt. Gordon Reiher, engineer-gunner Tech. Sgt. Donald Chiu, radio operator Staff Sgt. Lucene La Crosse, waist gunner Staff Sgt. A. E. Wagner, and tail gunner Staff Sgt. Ora Akins—two of whom were wounded, although the record does not say which two—Djernes managed to keep his Fortress airworthy. He was able to pick up a pair of P-51 Mustangs to keep him company for almost an hour while he came out of Germany, cut across a corner of the Netherlands, and headed out to the North Sea. His report of conditions aboard the battered Fortress appears not to have survived, so we can only imagine crewmembers providing first aid, monitoring the engine, and helping the pilot. When the Fortress drew within eyesight of the British Isles, there must have been jubilation aboard.

Djernes remained in charge. With home base out of reach and with his radio operator declaring an emergency, Djernes landed instead at Woodbridge, an airfield in East Anglia closer to the coast, with low fuel, brakes out, and the two wounded crewmembers. Remarkably, Djernes brought his Fortress to a halt with an ambulance approaching, cut power, and felt the aircraft come to a standstill. This particular Fortress returned to the war a few days later.

HAPPY HOMECOMING

Purty Chili prepared to come home after a flight time of no less than eight hours, thirty minutes. *It was 3:45 p.m., British Summer Time.* Flying well ahead of their squadron as part of a six-ship, chaff-drop formation, pilot 1st Lt. Dean Hansen and copilot 1st. Lt Robert Des Lauriers looked long and hard to make certain they were in the right slot to land in their assigned order and to avoid a collision. They were cold. They were always cold. But the thought of suddenly finding another Fortress right in front of you was enough to keep you wide awake and fully alert, Des Lauriers said.

Plenty of other aircraft filled the sky around the Flying Fortress. In part because of battle damage, in part because of sheer exhaustion, the Fortresses of the 34th Bombardment Group were as orderly coming home as they'd been when heading out. At least one Fortress appeared to be weaving drunkenly over the English countryside, although it eventually got down intact. "If you dropped the ball while you were preparing to land, you could get in trouble," said Des Lauriers. "You needed to maintain flight discipline continuously all the way down, all the way until you turned off your motors in the parking slot."

The gunners in the back (radioman, waist, ball, and tail gunners) who had gathered in the radio room for takeoff remained—wearily—at their duty station for landing. The Germans never fully exploited the opportunity to follow Fortresses home and pick them off during their vulnerable final approach and landing.

Had the Luftwaffe known how exhausted American crews were near the end of a mission, they might have tried it despite their limited resources. It happened rarely but because of the prospect, men in the rear fuselage stayed at their guns. "The Jerrys followed us home sometimes and attacked on landing," said 34th Bombardment Group toggleer Tech. Sgt. Ray Fredette.

The exigencies of war did not exempt *Purty Chili* pilot Hansen and copilot Des Lauriers from the requirement to take each other through a before-landing checklist. This included verifying that the altimeter was set and confirming that members of the crew were in their assigned positions for landing, an item on the checklist that *Blue Grass Girl*'s pilots never reached.

Scrutinized by an unforgiving engineer-gunner Staff Sgt. John Green, Hansen and Des Lauriers together verified that the autopilot was off, booster pumps were on, fuel mixture controls were set at "auto rich," and carburetor filters were open. The checklist also included verifying that wing de-icers were off, but this requirement had become something of a laughing stock and had been scrapped. "We removed the de-icers from the planes the moment they arrived in the British Isles from the United States," said Des Lauriers, referring to the cumbersome, rubber-covered hydraulic heaters mounted in the leading edge of the Flying Fortress's 103-foot, 10-inch wing. "We did get formations of ice on the wing. We could get an inch, or an inch and a quarter. We had to maneuver the aircraft to shake off the ice. The de-icers were useless because even a minor flak hit would rupture the rubber that coated them."

Purty Chili continued letting down over the wet, green—and cold—farmland near Mendlesham. Green stood between Hansen and Des Lauriers, monitoring instruments. Entering the airfield pattern, Hansen flew downwind, or parallel to the runway and made a ninety-degree turn to the base leg. That was when pilot and copilot put down the main landing gear on the base leg and did a visual check to confirm that the wheels were down and locked. "You're sitting up on top of the world in a B-17," said Des Lauriers, "so you have no difficulty seeing that the wheels are in position. All Flying Fortresses were equipped with a retractable tailwheel: The pilots lowered and locked it as well. Just before final approach, they completed the 'before landing' checklist."

Hansen: "Hydraulic pressure?"

Des Lauriers: "Okay. Valve closed."

Hansen: "RPM at 2,100."

Des Lauriers: "Set."

Hansen: "Turbos?"

Des Lauriers: "Set."

Hanson: "Flaps."

Gripping the crank that moved the large flight surfaces on the trailing edge of the wing, Des Lauriers responded, "Flaps one-third down."

On final approach, Hansen signaled to move the flaps to one-half down and to raise RPM to 2,200. Once assured that he was lined up on final approach, Hansen turned to Des Lauriers and called for full flaps.

Hansen landed the Fortress in the normal manner, which was to try for a three-point landing with the tailwheel touching ground at the same time as, or even ahead of, the main wheels under the wings.

Purty Chili's wheels touched pavement at Mendlesham. *It was 4:00 p.m., British Summer Time.*

But it was not time for celebrating. Now, the two pilots began a new routine with an "after landing" checklist that included reviewing hydraulic pressure, opening and locking cowl flaps, and switching off booster pumps. As soon as the Fortress began to settle in its landing roll, they raised wing flaps, unlocked the tailwheel, and shut off generators. "We wanted to quiet the plane down and make sure everything was in order," said Des Lauriers. "I saw it happen too often that after a mission, one plane would taxi into another on the ground. There were so many aircraft moving about, you could easily run your plane into somebody else's plane."

Another bomber crewmember made the point that everyone had a responsibility. "The only responsibility an air crew gunner had on the ground was to be sure there were no bullets in the chamber of the gun after landing. It was a court martial offense to leave a shell in the chamber when returning your gun to the ground armorers. My tail gunner left a round in the chamber when we were back in training in Pocatello, Idaho, and in the armor shop it fired and went through several offices and a soldier's leg. My tail gunner went through court martial proceedings but was given a second chance because they needed crews so bad at the time."

"The time for celebrating was after you climbed out of the aircraft and dropped to the ground," said Des Lauriers. "A lot of the guys bent down and kissed the ground. At that time, you're completely worn out and you just want some relief. It had been a tough mission." Only after debriefing, *Purty Chili*'s crew headed for the showers and the mess hall.

Purty Chili on this day had been in the hands of pilot Hansen, copilot Des Lauriers, navigator 1st Lt. Ralph "Iron Balls" Wathey, bombardier 1st Lt. Lee Sackerman; engineer-gunner Green, radio operator Sgt. Gerald Shoaf; ball turret gunner Sgt. Darryl Young, waist gunner Sgt. Val McClellan; and tail gunner Sgt. Harold Griffin. None was harmed during the mission. All survived the war.

THE MORRIS CREW

Not everyone was so lucky. The unnamed Fortress of the 95th Bombardment Group with 2nd Lt. Richard P. Morris as pilot and 2nd Lt. Dean M. Ratts traveled a considerable distance toward safety, apparently with most of the crew struggling every inch of the way. The struggle lasted fully four and a half hours after being hit by flak over Berlin. They apparently were not in radio contact with anyone in the bomber stream or with escort fighters that could have kept them company during their struggle for survival. It is possible Morris was no longer on board when the rest of the crewmembers fought to keep the Fortress in the air. The plane's marathon struggle ended west of the island of Texel in Holland. No longer able to stay aloft, the Fortress dipped, plunged nose down, crashed, and burned. *It was 4:00 p.m., British Summer Time.*

Killed aboard this B-17 were Ratts, navigator Flight Officer Kenneth G. Wood, Bombardier Flight Officer Leonard A. Pospisil, engineer-gunner Sgt. Leroy R. Hansen, radio operator Sgt. Kenneth L. Peterson, ball turret gunner Sgt. Marion L. Bell, waist gunner Sgt. Milton S. Onie, and tail gunner Sgt. William T. Watt. As indicated earlier (chapter thirteen), the record is unclear on what happened to Morris. He appears to have become a prisoner of war and survived the war.

ROBERT ROSENTHAL CREW

The long journey westward toward America's bomber bases in England, or eastward for those diverting elsewhere, wasn't easy for anyone, but in one important respect things were better than they'd been earlier in the war. Fortress pilots now had options they hadn't had when the air campaign began. Bomber crews caught up in crisis over Germany now had the choice of diverting to Sweden or continuing eastward for a landing behind Soviet lines. Eight B-17 Flying Fortresses landed in Soviet-held territory, while additional American crewmembers parachuted into the midst of Soviet troops.

One who arrived by parachute was Maj. Robert "Rosie" Rosenthal. The Russians were friendly to him from the moment he met his first Red Army soldier. Unfortunately, the Germans captured Rosenthal's pilot, Capt. John Ernst. When Ernst bailed out, his leg struck the jagged edge of his Fortress's bomb bay door, inflicting a serious gash. Ernst's German captors were forced to amputate the leg shortly before he was liberated by friendly troops—prompting Rosenthal, who was also wounded, to quip in later years that Ernst was "one of the most skillful, courageous and dedicated men I ever severed with."

In addition to Ernst, Rosenthal's crew included three more who became German prisoners of war: copilot 1st Lt. Arthur I. Jacobson; engineer-gunner Tech. Sgt. Dugger C. West; and waist gunner Staff Sgt. Warren Winters. Command navigator 1st Lt. Stewart J. Gillison came down in German territory but evaded capture. Those who landed behind Russian lines were Rosenthal, radar navigator 1st Lt. Robert H. Stropp; and tail gunner Staff Sgt. G. A. Windisch. Navigator 1st Lt. Louis C. Chappel and bombardier 1st Lt. Eugene E. Lockhart were killed.

MYRON L. KING CREW

Among the Fortresses that diverted to Soviet territory in Poland in the afternoon of February 3, 1945, was *Maiden USA* of the 614th Bombardment Squadron, 401st Bombardment Group. The pilot was 1st Lt. Myron L. King. "Sustained flak damage and landed in the Soviet Union," read an official report, although the location appears to have been a Soviet airfield in Poland.

King's crew experienced nothing unusual at the hands of their Soviet allies. The Russians did, however, muster an enormous number of men to climb all over *Maiden USA*, scrutinize through its interior, and pillage it for parts. At least one historical source indicates that the Fortress was returned to the 401st group—as was the crew, which did not fly again—but *Maiden USA* does not show up on inventory lists for the post-Berlin period, suggesting strongly that the Soviets kept it.

King's crew included copilot W. A. Sweeney III, engineer-gunner D. M. Killian, navigator 2nd Lt. R. I. Lowe, radio operator Sgt. P. A. De Vito, toggleer Staff Sgt. R. E. Pyne (not Payne as cited on an official report), waist gunner Speelman, ball turret gunner Sgt. P. A. Reincehl and tail gunner Sgt. K. H. Atkinson. This was the twenty-first and last mission for King's crew.

Stardust of the 384th piloted by 1st Lt. George F. Ruckman, was still struggling to stay in the air when navigator 2nd Lt. John O. Beeby spotted an airfield and Ruckman decided they had a good chance to get their Fortress on the ground. A few Soviet fighters were parked in the middle of the field and there were bomb craters, but Rucker found a spot, dropped his landing gear, and brought *Stardust* down, blowing a tire in the process. Skidding on snow and ice, *Stardust* came to a halt in Torun, Poland.

Stardust's crew was lucky. All survived the war, including Ruckman, copilot 2nd Lt. Fiorino Cinquanta, Beeby, bombardier Flight Officer Jack W. Rivall, engineer-gunner Sgt. Johnnie E. Young, radio operator Sgt. Jack G. Garstak, ball turret gunner Staff Sgt. Albert S. Horan, waist gunner Sgt. Alonzo R. Rice, and tail gunner Tech. Sgt. Frederick Sorenson.

Also down behind Soviet lines in Poland: the unnamed Fortress piloted by 1st Lt. Irving Siegel of the 490th Bombardment Group that had suffered a malfunction and was leaking fuel. Joining other Americans in Soviet hands at Plock, Poland, were the crew of Spiegel, co-pilot 1st Lt. William J. Bole (whose surname is not really legible on the official report), navigator 2nd Lt. Raymond Patulski, toggleer Staff Sgt. Charles V. Sandusky, engineer-gunner Cpl. John J. Caffrey, radio operator Tech. Sgt. Maurice D. Carpenter, ball turret gunner Staff Sgt. Salvator M. Novarra, waist gunner Staff Sgt. Frank Stockton, and tail gunner Staff Sgt. Dale C. Tyler.

1ST LT. ARTHUR H. OGLE CREW

The Flying Fortress dubbed *Lady V II*, with 1st Lt. Arthur H. Ogle and Maj. John L. "Junior" Rex Jr. on board, passed over Russian lines when its fourth and final working engine began to sputter. Losing height and speed fast, Rex notified the squadron that he was flying east toward Soviet-liberated Poland. Dipping the Fort's wings in a farewell sign to the group, the crew headed for sanctuary in the east. The Fortress was down below 8,000 feet when *Lady V II*'s crew observed sprawling battle lines and an artillery duel under way. They flew on until their fourth and last engine quit. By one account they spotted an open field. By another, they came upon Rogozno airfield, thirty miles north of Poznan in Soviet-held Poland. They attempted to land the Fortress, but the landing gear had been hit and would not come into position. The bomber made a loud, mashing belly landing, in which none of the crew was injured.

The survivors of *Lady V II* included Ogle, Rex, copilot 2nd Lt. Albert Holman, navigator 1st Lt. Richard Higgins, navigator 1st Lt. John Yep, navigator 1st Lt. Abraham Gornstein, bombardier 2nd Lt. James Nolte, flight mechanic Tech. Sgt. George Taylor, radio operator Tech. Sgt. Wayne Lewis, and tail gunner Sgt. Ben Gale.

Before the men could get out of the *Lady V II*, a small party of armed Polish Maquis surrounded them. Not sure of each other's identity, the Ogle

B-17 crew and the civilian militia cautiously investigated one another. Once the resistance fighters were certain that Ogle and his crew were Americans, and the Americans ascertained that the Poles were friendly, the Maquis placed a guard on the plane and led its crew to a deserted farmhouse. A guard patrolled the grounds while the exhausted men gathered inside, shed much of their gear, and collapsed. The Poles provided water and some bread. Most of the Fortress's crewmembers were too weary to care much about eating.

"By midnight," said Rex, "we had all dozed off." That was when a contingent of Soviet soldiers stormed into the house. "Boy," said Rex, "were we scared!" *It was 12:00 midnight, British Summer Time, Saturday, February 3, 1945.* The day had ended for the mission to Berlin.

CHAPTER SEVENTEEN

Wrap-Up

Bombers and Fighters in the final months
February 4, 1945 to May 8, 1945

THEY DID NOT get Hitler.

Twenty-four hours after the assault of Saturday, February 3, 1945, Berlin lay in chaos, dead and wounded were everywhere, and bands of thugs prowled the rubble, day and night. Ralph Hewins, a correspondent for the *Daily Mail*, filed a story from Stockholm—where very limited telephone contact with Berlin existed—partly entitled "Terrified Crowd Told, 'You Must Stay.' " Wrote Hewins: "Gauleiter Goebbels tonight issued a standstill order to the millions of refugees in Berlin, forbidding them to leave the city. After suffering terrible casualties in yesterday's great air attack, the homeless masses are now trapped in this still burning capital and must share whatever disaster may befall it."

Propaganda Minister Joseph Goebbels (the term "gauleiter" meant regional party leader) did his best to put a lid on information getting out of Berlin, but most of the world now knew that the city had reeled beneath a mighty wave of bombers. Most of the world also knew the Red Army was closing in.

Estimates of the number of people killed in the February 3 mission run as high as thirty thousand. One of the fatalities was Berlin's "hanging judge," Roland Freisler. Already responsible for thousands of deaths, Freisler was conducting a trial of anti-Hitler conspirators. A warning siren prompted Freisler to adjourn court and sent people in Freisler's courtroom scrambling for nearby bomb shelter, but "Raving Roland" returned to retrieve important papers, including documents about Adjutant Fabian von Schlabrendorff, who was on trial that day and was facing execution for his role in the previous year's assassination plot against Hitler. A falling beam collapsed on Freisler. A doctor brought in from the street diagnosed Freisler's injuries as fatal. The day before, Freisler had sentenced the doctor's brother to death.

Tens of thousands were killed, maimed, or left homeless. A significant number of the American bombs had one-, two- and six-hour delay fuses, intended to wreak havoc amidst rescue and recovery efforts.

Two days after the American air armada assaulted Berlin, *Svenska Dagbladet*, a newspaper in neutral Sweden, reported:

"Berlin today is a city of confusion and disruption, of hunger and wild rumors, a city of flames and smoke and mounting fear. German censorship has suddenly clamped down with a complete blackout on news. Casualties . . . were very high. The bombs caused a massacre among refugees crowded in and around the railway stations. As the attack was intended to hamper German troop movements to the Eastern Front, railway stations were targets."

London's *Daily Express* reported:

"Photographs show that Berlin's 'Whitehall' [a term for the center of government] was heavily battered. The German Air Ministry received eight direct hits and eighteen concentrations of high explosives blanketed the area occupied by the War Office, the Chancery, Ministry of Propaganda, Gestapo headquarters, Ministry of Agriculture and other important buildings near the Air Ministry. There is fire and smoke over an area two miles long by one mile wide. A huge column of smoke billowed up to a height of more than two miles as the Forts headed for home."

The *Daily Express* noted that Col. Lewis E. Lyle led the first formation. The newspaper also reported: "1st Lt. Joe Conroy remembers the mission vividly. Flying with his 306th Bombardment Group, the number four and number three engines on the right wing of his B-17 were knocked out by flak over the target and his aircraft fell out of formation. His aircraft and crew limped home after number two engine was also hit by fire."

Of the 1,003 Flying Fortresses launched against Berlin, 965 were "effective," meaning that they reached the target or bombed an alternate target, such as Bromsche or Gatow. Of the 434 Liberators sent to Magdeburg, 405 were effective, including 16 that bombed Wesermunde. Of 948 fighters dispatched, 885 reached their objectives.

As nearly as can be measured, the attack force carried 6.9 million pounds of bombs, nearly all of which were dropped. The bombers carried 7.1 million .50-caliber cartridges, almost none of which were fired in anger because aerial gunners had no Luftwaffe fighters to shoot at. The fighters brought an additional 885,000 rounds of ammunition into the battle and pumped a significant number of them into Luftwaffe planes and pilots.

On February 3, 1945, Franklin D. Roosevelt and Winston Churchill met on the island of Malta in preparation for their strategy conference to begin the next day at Yalta on the Crimean Peninsula. British and American air senior officers, including U.S. Army Chief of Staff Gen. George C. Marshall and Maj. Gen. Laurence Kuter (representing Army Air Forces' chief Gen. Henry H. "Hap" Arnold, who was too ill to travel) had spent several days at Montgomery House on Malta discussing strategy, including the ongoing debate over area bombing versus precision bombing that recur as a constant theme in this narrative. Adolf Hitler was not in Berlin on February 3 but at the Berghof, his residence in the Bavarian Alps near Berchtesgaden. Ironically, Hitler presented awards for valor, including a Knight's Cross to Egon Agtha, a Feuerwerker (a German Army firefighter), who was well known for disarming unexploded bombs in Berlin during previous bombings near the city. Also on February 3, 1945, Hitler wrote a note to Martin Bormann, reiterating his hatred for what he called "the Jewish race."

Bormann, who was in the Führer's bunker in Berlin that day, was also writing a letter, to his wife in Obersalzberg: "The Reich Chancellery garden is an amazing sight—deep craters, fallen trees, and the paths obliterated by a mass of rubble and rubbish. The Fuehrer's residence [in Berlin] was badly hit several times; all that is left of the winter gardens and the banquet hall are fragments of the walls; and the entrance hall on the Wilhelmstrasse, where the Wehrmacht guard was usually mustered, has been completely destroyed." If Bormann sensed impending defeat, he did not reveal this to his spouse. "In spite of it all," Bormann wrote, "we have to go on working diligently, for the war continues on all fronts!"

IS BERLIN BURNING?

Berlin remained a place of paradox. Lawless gangs controlled dozens of square blocks of partial rubble. Many city streets were impassable. For most Berliners, food was scarce and disease rampant. Yet many in the Nazi leadership seemed to be in denial about the war closing in on them. Soon after the bombing mission that makes up the core of this narrative, however, the Führer was spending his time in the ravaged capital, much of it in his bunker beneath the New Reich Chancellery, shielded by about fifty feet of concrete and untouched by bombing.

If bombing Berlin was supposed to drive a nail into the Third Reich coffin, atrocious weather in East Anglia and on the continent stymied several more missions that were scheduled in the days that followed. On February 13, 1945, bad weather cancelled a planned mission to Dresden that took place the following day. On February 15, 1945, B-24 Liberators returned to Magdeburg while B-17 Flying Fortresses again attacked Dresden. It would always be Dresden that was associated in the public mind with the bombing of cities, rather than military or industrial targets; with the suffering of civilians rather than military adversaries; and with allegations by some that the Allied bombing effort was a war crime.

In fact, all of those issues had been confronted when attacking Berlin at the beginning of the month. As Lt. Gen. James H. "Jimmy" Doolittle's concern about the Berlin mission demonstrated, it was Berlin, not Dresden, where the controversy began. It was Berlin, not Dresden, where Americans first bombed a city center rather than military or industrial targets. It was Berlin, not Dresden, where the notion of pickle-barrel precision bombing was set aside and area bombing of cities became part of American strategy. To be sure, there were very few such American missions flown in the final months of the war, but it was Berlin, not Dresden, that set the precedent.

The controversy over bombing civilians has never been as important in the United States as in Great Britain, where the Royal Air Force conducted night bombing throughout the war. "This was a gratifying mission to have participated in because the target was the German capital," said Sgt. Val McClellan, waist gunner of *Purty Chili*. "The Germans may have called us the 'North American killers,' but we certainly did not lose any sleep over the destruction of these places." Like so many Americans, McClellan saw himself performing a legitimate military mission.

The aftermath of the mission to Berlin brought better news for some than others. The nine-man crew of the unnamed Fortress piloted by 1st Lt. Irving Spiegel of the 490th Bombardment Group that landed near Plock, Poland, all returned to duty without incident. After falling into the arms of the Russians, the crew of 1st Lt. Arthur H. Ogle's bomber *Lady V II*, Maj. John L. "Junior" Rex Jr. included, might have been frightened when Soviet troops first appeared, but as it turned out they received what one crewmember called "royal treatment." They did not yet know that a few dozen miles away in Torun, Poland, also surrounded by Soviet troops, the crew of 2nd Lt. George F. Ruckman's *Stardust* ate Russian food, drank vodka, and sang ballads with their Soviet hosts.

"The Russians praised American hardware and toasted everything American during a party," said Robin Smith, a relative of a crewmember. "When they ran out of things to toast, they went back down the list. The crew noted that there were a lot of American goods on display. The Russians even enjoyed Spam. They must have been really hungry!" The Ogle crew was flown back to base through Kiev in the Ukraine, which was the nearest transportation hub, repatriated via Kiev, Tehran, Cairo, and Marseilles, to London, receiving good treatment at every juncture. The crew chief who had bestowed the names *Lady V* and *Lady V II* on a pair of successive Fortresses never saw Ogle's crew or bomber again—apparently the Soviets repaired and kept the aircraft—but he did remain on duty until war's end, one of the thousands of unsung heroes who kept America's warplanes in the air. As fate would have it, however, there was never to be a *Lady V III*. The fiancée who had been the inspiration for the name sent a "Dear John" letter to the lovelorn crew chief and promptly married someone else. Given another opportunity to name a plane, the crew chief called his third ship *The Lonesome Polecat*. Absent certain knowledge, we can only hope that the crew chief did not remain lonesome ever after and that he, too, eventually married someone else.

While the crew of *Lady V II* survived (even if the crew chief's engagement did not), the handling of American bombers that landed in the middle of Soviet forces in Poland became an issue.

FIGHTER PILOTS

On February 19, 1945, P-51 Mustang pilot 1st Lt. Bernard H. Howes of the 55th Fighter Group was credited with his fifth aerial victory, making him an air ace. Howes' best friend and constant flying partner 1st Lt. Brooks J. Liles was destined to end the war with just one kill to his credit; Liles added four MiGs in Korea to become an ace seven years after Howes did.

On February 27, 1951, Mustang pilot 1st Lt. Victor P. Krambo lost his bid to avoid becoming a prisoner. "He spoke later about encountering a large armada of German aircraft just before he went down that were manned by inexperienced pilots that were thrown into the air as a last ditch effort by the Germans. He said most dove for the ground when fired upon and didn't put up much of a fight." One of them, apparently, put up enough of a fight to riddle Krambo's Mustang named *Lucky Wabbit II* with gunfire and force him to hit the silk. It was a time when order was breaking down everywhere in Germany and an American flyer who reached the ground alive had no guarantee of staying that way. Krambo was one of the fortunate ones. He became a prisoner and survived the war.

On March 1, 1945, Mr. and Mrs. F. Chrastka—as they signed their names—of Forest Park, Illinois, sent a letter handwritten with a fountain pen to Fortress navigator 1st Lt. Robert "Mac" McCall. McCall received the letter at his home in Fairmont, Minnesota, where he returned after flying thirty missions with the Capt. Ronald E. Bereman crew. The Chrastka couple clearly seemed hesitant about intruding on him.

"Perhaps we are taking too much for granted thinking that you may be home or will be soon, but could you give us any information as to how our son, Staff Sergeant Frank Chrastka, met his death?" the couple wrote. "Was he ever transferred to another crew? We would appreciate any information you could give us."

In all the years since the war, McCall has regretted not replying.

The pact between Mustang pilots Howes and Liles, each of whom had vowed to rescue the other if the need should arise, finally faced the test on March 3, 1945. Liles was on a strafing run when flying steel ripped into his Mustang named *Sweet Marie II.* A third Mustang pilot, 1st Lt. Marvin Satenstein, described what happened next in an official report that was reiterated in the book *Double Nickel–Double Trouble* by Robert M. Littlefield—its title being a reference to the number assigned to the 55th Fighter Group.

Wrote Satenstein: "At about 1300 hours on 3 March, 1945, while cruising around at about 2,000 feet in the Prague [Czechoslovakia] area looking for targets of opportunity, Prague/Letnany airdrome was observed full of parked aircraft. My flight, RED flight, and the remainder of YELLOW flight decided to attack it. We did so, making our passes individually.

"On Liles's pass from north to south he was hit on the right side of his engine by light flak from the guns at the southwest end of the field. I observed flame coming from the engine. Liles said that he had been hit. I was directly above and behind him and could see that he had the aircraft under control but could not get much power. He flew the aircraft for about three or four miles south of the airdrome where he bellied it in successfully on an open field. I saw Lt. Liles get out of the aircraft, just after that it caught fire.

Continued Satenstein: "The remaining six A/C circled the spot, and Lt. Howes, TUDOR YELLOW 3, called over the [radio] that he was going to land to try to pick up Liles. After one try, Howes made a successful landing in the same field. After discarding their parachutes, both Howes and Liles were able to get into [Howes'] aircraft. It appeared as if it was hard to get the plane started rolling from its parked position. As they started to roll, Howes called, 'Gang, keep your fingers crossed and we'll make it.' The aircraft rose into the air once, but apparently didn't have enough flying speed because it settled to the ground again. Then it bounced into the air, dropped off on its left wing in a stalled attitude, and cartwheeled to the left, eventually flattening out. The aircraft caught fire, but when I buzzed the wreck I saw both Howes and Liles walking away in an easterly direction towards a large highway. Both pilots looked all right and they waved to me as I passed over them."

Howes confirmed later that they discarded their parachutes so they could squeeze into the single seat of his tiny cockpit. Howes may have been emboldened by the knowledge that several such rescue pickups had been achieved earlier in the war, although none so far from home. But now, Howes explained, they started taking intense small arms fire from near the airfield. Howes made a good takeoff roll but just prior to liftoff there was a moment of hesitation and their plane struck a ditch, bounced into the air, and cartwheeled to a stop, as Satenstein witnessed. A single bullet had hit the throttle quadrant, which reduced power at a critical instant. Liles suffered a broken nose and other minor injuries. Howes received a severe blow on the forehead, which resulted in a temporary blindness that lasted for two days. The two pilots headed for cover with Liles leading the blinded Howes by the hand. The Germans captured them within hours. They were taken to Prague, interrogated, and received medical treatment in a local hospital. After several moves, the two Mustang pilots ended up in the prisoner of war camp known as Stalag VII A at Moosburg. A nineteen-day forced march to Moosburg, plus a diet of bread and barley soup, reduced Howes's weight from 160 pounds to 126 pounds in the two months that he was imprisoned. But Liles and Howes survived the war.

MISSION TO TOKYO

While the British and the Americans continued their debate about "area bombing" versus "precision bombing" in Europe—to say nothing of the Americans squabbling about it among themselves—the distinction vanished in the Pacific.

On the night of March 9, 1945, U.S. strategy in the war against Japan took a new turn when Maj. Gen. Curtis E. LeMay—once the creator of tactics employed in Europe and now in charge of the air campaign against the Japanese home islands—launched a huge bombing mission against Tokyo. LeMay was now commander of XXI Bomber Command located on Guam, having followed in the footsteps of two earlier generals whose performances did not satisfy Gen. Henry H. "Hap" Arnold, the Army Air Forces' commanding general. In the Pacific, LeMay was even more beholden to Arnold than were Lt. Gen. Carl "Tooey" Spaatz and Lt. James H. "Jimmy" Doolittle in Europe: LeMay's command was part of Twentieth Air Force, commanded directly by Arnold from his office in the newly constructed Pentagon building. It was an unusual command arrangement indeed, and no one disliked it more than the Allied commander in the Pacific, Gen. Douglas MacArthur, who had become barely a footnote in the final fight over the Japanese archipelago.

The B-29, the "super bomber" of its era, was designed with a pressurized cabin for daylight bombing from very high altitude, a luxury that would have been unthinkable to oxygen mask-wearing Fortress crews in Europe. Perhaps even better than pressurization, the B-29 had an internal heating system, something Fortress crews would have begged for. Powered by four 2,200-horsepower Wright R-3350-23/23A turbo-supercharged radial engines, the B-29 was bristled with guns to protect itself from fighters. It was the perfect bomber for war at high altitude and against the wishes of his crewmembers LeMay wanted to take it down low. LeMay made the difficult decision to attack at low level, at night with all guns aboard the B-29s, except for tail guns, left behind.

Not only did LeMay completely alter U.S. bombing strategy in the way he decided to use the B-29, but he also made a change in what the Superfortress carried. LeMay's bombers struck Japan's capital not with explosives but with fire.

The U.S. military had pondered the idea of using firebombs against Japan—a nation of buildings made from wood and paper—since the earliest days of the war. Curiously, although many cities in Europe would have been vulnerable, incendiaries were never used on a broad scale there. Some in Washington wanted to focus on Japanese industry while others wanted to attack urban centers. Ultimately, experts decided on what historian E. Bartlett Kerr called "a dual strategy for attacking Japan—bomb the factories, then burn the cities."

The AAF developed thermite and napalm incendiary bombs. Bombers dropped them in tests on a mock Japanese city built at Dugway Proving Ground, Utah. The tests showed that the enemy's infrastructure was uniquely vulnerable to firebombing. The growing B-29 force obtained good results in small-scale incendiary raids—still at high altitude and in daylight—before the March 9 mission.

But LeMay's change in tactics rankled some. B-29 crews liked the safety of height and the protection afforded by guns.

LeMay wanted to catch the foe by surprise. Moreover, a low-level raid would use less fuel, enabling the B-29s to carry more bombs. Attacking at low altitude would also spare bomber crews the need to struggle with the powerful winds at high altitude that had thusfar impeded flights over Japan.

That night, LeMay launched 346 Superfortresses from ten bomb groups belonging to three bomb wings. Each plane had an eleven-man crew. Because he had been briefed on a future secret weapon still under development in the United States, LeMay could not fly the mission and run the risk of capture. Brigadier General Thomas Power, a LeMay disciple, had had a key role in planning the incendiary raid from the beginning. Of the bombers that took off, 279 actually dropped bombs on Tokyo, led by special pathfinder crews who marked a central aiming point.

For two hours, the roar of Superfortresses filled the night sky over the Japanese capital. The raid leveled sixteen square miles of the city. Approximately eighty-four thousand people died. A million were made homeless. John Pimlott of Britain's Royal Military Academy at Sandhurst, author of a book on the B-29, called the raid a "bludgeon." U.S. literature released a few months after the assault on Tokyo (and with knowledge of the subsequent atomic bombings of Hiroshima and Nagasaki) claimed that Tokyo incendiary mission ignited the hottest fires ever to burn on the Earth.

As LeMay had hoped, the Japanese did not have an effective force of night fighters. Antiaircraft gunfire damaged forty-two bombers and was responsible for the total loss of fourteen B-29s.

It seemed a small price. The Tokyo raid was regarded as an enormous success. Over the weeks that followed, several other firebomb missions were mixed in with other bombing missions that used conventional weapons. More than five hundred Superfortresses flew one subsequent raid. By this juncture in the war, Arnold and LeMay were looking to expand the air campaign against Japan, in anticipation of the Allied invasion that would soon come, and were already thinking about positioning the Eighth Air Force in the western Pacific. Although they could spare no B-29s to fight in Europe, they were eager to bring the European war to a close because they knew every last American resource would be needed for the final fight against Japan. Spaatz and LeMay among others—although apparently not Doolittle—were among the very few who knew about a secret weapon then being developed that would alter the calculus of the war.

RECALITRANT RUSSIAN ALLIES

On March 22, 1945, Maj. Gen. John R. Deane Jr., head of the U.S. military mission in Moscow, sent a "top secret" report to U.S. Army Air Forces commanding general Gen. Henry H. "Hap" Arnold and other leaders "for your information," but with the assurance that "every effort is being made to solve the problem here." Deane began with the fate of a B-24 Liberator that had force landed near Mielec, Poland, months earlier:

"When our repair crews visited the site for the purpose of effecting necessary minor repairs to make the plane flyable," Deane wrote, "they found that it had been chopped up in small pieces and that two of the engines had been hauled away by the Soviets. Strong protest was made over this incident, and Marshal [Sergei] Khudyakov [the chief of staff of the Soviet air force] informed me that he had issued instructions to place guards on all force landed aircraft to preclude the possibility of a recurrence."

Turning to 1st Lt. Arthur H. Ogle's *Lady V II*, Deane continued: "In spite of this, information had just been received that B-17 # 448130 [44-8130], which landed at Rogozno Airfield, Poland [30 miles north of Poznan], was similarly destroyed by the Soviets." Deane also cited another Flying Fortress from the same mission that the Soviets "stripped of all parts." "In the latter case, local Soviet authorities reported to our representatives that the parts were being used in their B-25s," Deane's reference to the North American B-25 Mitchell medium bomber, which, unlike the B-17 or B-24, was used in squadron strength by Soviet forces. He indicated he was taking strong action, but it is questionable whether Deane had much clout in the situation.

A separate report, apparently from a Deane subordinate, told of the belly landing near Jarocin, Poland, of a Fortress of the 338th Bombardment Squadron, 96th Bombardment Group, piloted by 2nd Lt. Leonard G. Kramer (mistakenly called Kremer in the report). The crew was unhurt and apparently was repatriated without difficulty. The report said the Fortress was "salvageable," but there is no record of the aircraft being returned to U.S. control.

Another American who fell into the clutches of the Russians was Maj. Robert "Rosie" Rosenthal, the group air commander who'd had two crew-members killed and four captured by the Germans. Later to receive the Distinguished Service Cross, the second highest award for valor, for his struggle to save his fellow airmen, "Rosie" was transported to Moscow, given a guided tour, and taken to a party even more lavish than anything Ogle attended. He eventually was repatriated and flew one more mission—a humanitarian supply drop—bringing his wartime total to fifty-three.

Spaatz received a temporary promotion to the rank of general on March 11, 1945.

"With a cold and cruel winter behind us, it was a beautiful spring day," said Fortress pilot 1st Lt. Charles W. Halper of the 385th Bombardment Group's 548th Bombardment Squadron, who had been given a brief respite from the war. He was referring to April 12, 1945. "I had just left my London hotel and was crossing a park on my way to the Red Cross Club. A British major walking towards me returned my salute and then stopped to address me.

"He said, 'Lieutenant, we have suffered a great loss this day.'

"I replied, 'What in the world has happened, sir? I thought we were winning this war.' He told me the news. 'Your great president and England's great friend has died this day. I am so sorry for both of us.' It was then that I heard the catch in his voice. With a quick salute, he was on his way.

"As I continued my walk to the club, I was approached by one person, and then another, extending their condolences. Many had tears in their eyes.

"Their heartfelt expressions of sympathy touched me deeply. They acted as though President Franklin D. Roosevelt was one of their own people." Halper soon discovered that Britons and Americans alike knew very little about the man who had abruptly become the 33rd president of the United States, Harry S Truman.

RACKHEATH AGGIES

On April 15, 1945, Col. Albert Shower's indomitable "Rackheath Aggies" of the 467th Bombardment Group took their Liberators to Point de Grave and set a record for bombing accuracy, with twenty-four Liberators dropping 2,000-pounders squarely on a German installation from 21,000 feet. This was one of the group's last missions of the war: In all, the group flew 212 missions, logged 5,538 sorties, and lost 235 airmen and 46 Liberators. The Liberator named *Witchcraft* remained the group's best-known bomber with 130 sorties. By this time, with Germany tottering close to defeat, many bomber crewmembers were flying humanitarian missions, dropping food to prison and concentration camps. Bombers were also being used increasingly to ferry fuel needed by Gen. George S. Patton's Third Army and other Allied ground troops. The 467th was among many Eighth Air Force groups tapped for these new duties, which everyone understood meant that the end of fighting was at hand.

THE FINAL HOURS

On April 16, 1945, as the Red Army began the Battle of Berlin by attacking German front line positions along the rivers Oder and Neisse, Adolf Hitler encamped in his bunker.

One of the pilots who survived the journey to Berlin—but not the war—was P-51 Mustang air ace Lt. Col. Elwyn Guido Righetti. He had been de facto commander of the 55th Fighter Group and took on the job for real on February 22. Widely credited with restoring morale and spirit to a weary unit, Righetti continued to rack up victories over German warplanes and strengthened his reputation as "king of the strafers" when attacking German railway locomotives. "Eager El" was one of the best-liked fighter pilots of the war, a distinction several other group commanders could not claim, and although significantly older than the men who flew with him, he was respected.

On his thirtieth birthday on April 17, 1945, Righetti was striking an airfield near Dresden. He came over the airfield from east to west, encountered a Focke-Wulf Fw 190, and shot it down. He strafed aircraft on the ground and destroyed nine of them. But moments later, antiaircraft fire tore into his P-51. There must have been a horrendous noise and a lot of debris whipping around him as Righetti attempted to regain control of the Mustang. Temporarily out of the eyesight of his wingman, 1st Lt. Carroll D. Henry, Righetti brought his Mustang down to a shaky belly landing deep inside the Reich and not far from people he'd been strafing.

"I was at about 3,000 feet and over-ran him due to excess speed gained while letting down," Henry later wrote. "He was at six o'clock to me and I rolled out on 270 degrees. I chopped my throttle and when I looked back I couldn't locate him. About 30 seconds later he called in."

In his earphones came what seems, now, a mournful message from the group commander. "I broke my nose, but I am okay," Righetti radioed from the cockpit of his downed P-51."Tell my family I am okay," he said, referring to his wife and young daughter. "It has been a hell of a lot of fun working with you, gang. Be seeing you." While Henry made a circle, helpless, unable to spot his downed commander, Righetti ended his transmission and was never again seen or heard from. Veterans of the 55th Fighter Group say he was killed by a mob of furious German civilians, a fate that befell many airmen in the war's closing weeks. Righetti was posthumously given the Distinguished Service Cross, the second highest award for valor.

Apparently on the same day in another part of Germany, guards uprooted a group of American prisoners of war and prodded them on a forced march to another location. Among the prisoners were the wounded Sgt. Joseph D. "Dave" Bancroft and an uninjured Staff Sgt. William G. Logan, who'd bailed out of two Fortresses after a midair collision. Bancroft had been the only survivor of his unnamed Fortress, Logan one of only two crewmembers to parachute from *Maude an' Maria*. Seemingly having little difficulty coping with a traumatic bailout, captivity, and now forced relocation, Logan always did his best to help nurse Bancroft's injuries. Today, despite it all, Logan had a smile on his face.

Allied warplanes strafed them.

Bancroft watched helplessly as Allied machine gun bullets chewed into the dirt and foliage around them—and into Logan, who was killed instantly.

Three days later, April 20, 1945, on his fifty-sixth birthday, Hitler made his last trip to the surface above his bunker to pin Iron Crosses on boy soldiers of the Hitler Youth who were manning flak batteries. It was surreal, an old man far past his actual years decorating children thrust into a grownup conflict. Many writings of these final weeks make it clear Hitler was out of touch, did not understand the military situation, and still harbored illusions that the war was not yet over.

The final major combat mission by the Eighth Air Force took place on April 21, 1945, when 111 Fortresses went to railyards in Munich, 186 Liberators traveled to Salzburg but were unable to bomb because the city was socked in and 212 Fortresses visited other targets. After that date, Fortress bomber crews flew humanitarian relief missions, took ground crew members on tours of targets past, and hauled freight and supplies. Fortress pilot 1st Lt. Jesse Jacobs recalls a food drop to the Netherlands: "The Dutch were so grateful as they were so starved that they had actually been eating tulip bulbs. We saw tulips in bloom in huge beds. They had spelled out "THANK YOU" in English, for our benefit when we flew over. I assume they did this by cutting swaths in the beds to spell the words. The war hadn't officially ended at this point, but when I flew over German antiaircraft positions, I saw the flak gunners standing ramrod straight at attention—and doing nothing."

Some Fortress crews ended up carrying men home to the United States. The Eighth Air Force had triumphed in the high cold reaches above Europe, but the situation on the ground was still disturbingly unsettled.

PRISONER OF WAR

The fate of thousands of American bomber crewmembers who fell into German hands is beyond the scope of this narrative. One, however, 2nd Lt. Richard L. Wann, pilot of the B-24 Liberator *L'il Snooks*—the only member of his crew to be captured after bailing out—was especially gruesome. It will be used here to symbolize all of the times and places when severe treatment was meted out to prisoners.

When he leaped from his Liberator, Wann lost his flying boots. Injured, with part of his right foot split open, amid temperatures that were below freezing, Wann struggled to avoid capture.

"By the fourth or fifth day of exposure, both of my feet were frozen," Wann said. "I had no food and only the water I could get from eating snow. I was hiding in an area of intense American artillery fire, which continued twenty-four hours each day. After seven days of the foregoing, I was in very bad physical and mental condition, considering the events before bailing out and the subsequent injury to my ankle, extreme cold, frozen feet, and exposure. All of this was aggravated by my being subjected to nearly continuous American and German small arms and artillery fire and several days without food.

"On the seventh day in the middle of the afternoon, an eight-man German patrol saw my parachute hanging from the top of the tree I had landed in. The Germans were collecting firewood and decided to cut down the tree holding my chute.

"The tree was in such a position that had I remained in my original hiding place, the tree would have fallen on top of me. At that time, artillery fire commenced, which fell directly in our area."

They apprehended Wann. An SS officer slapped him around. Yet another SS officer stuffed Wann into a motorcycle sidecar, transported him to a lakefront, and placed a pistol on Wann's forehead. They didn't shoot Wann, but they beat him badly before he eventually ended up, with a badly injured leg and ankle, at what he later called the "horror hospital" at the prisoner of war camp in Heppenheim, Germany. In his history of the 446th Bombardment Group, Harold E. Jansen wrote:

"Of the 309 Americans [at Heppenheim], fifty-three had died of starvation, infection, and lack of medical care. The remainder were tearful, walking skeletons with matchstick arms and legs which they could barely lift. A large number of the prisoners were members of the 106th Division, cut off at the Ardennes. The prisoners' wounds had not been cared for during the two weeks prior to their liberation [by arriving Allied forces] on March 27, 1945. The prisoners told newspaper reporters that the German major in charge threatened to cut off what bandages they wore for German use."

Wann, whose weight had dropped from 164 pounds to 130 while in captivity, eventually recovered from his injuries. He later credited his survival to German Field Marshal Wilhelm Keitel, the OKW commander who, Wann was told, refused to carry out an order to execute American prisoners of war. "I hated to see him get executed after the Nuremburg war trials," Wann later said. As the situation in German crumbled, not all American prisoners escaped execution at the hands of their captors.

FINAL TALLY

On April 30, 1945, at just after three o'clock in the afternoon, Adolf Hitler shot himself in the right temple inside his private study in the Führerbunker. Advancing Russian infantrymen were only about a thousand feet away.

German forces in the West surrendered on May 7, 1945. The Russians received a second surrender on their front the following day, with hostilities ending on May 9, 1945. Victory in Europe Day, or V. E. Day, is celebrated on May 8.

At war's end Eighth Air Force fighters had been credited with shooting down 5,280 enemy aircraft and destroying 4,100 more on the ground.

Losses were 2,113 in total. No fewer than 260 VIII Fighter Command pilots became air aces. The best known were Lt. Col. Francis S. Gabreski and Capt. Robert S. Johnson of the 56th Fighter Group with 28 aerial victories each, plus Maj. George E. Preddy (26.83 kills) and Lt. Col. John C. Meyer (24) of the 352nd. Gabreski was shot down and captured in July 1944 and Preddy was killed in December. Gabreski was far from the only fighter pilot who—like so many crewmembers of the heavy bombers—survived captivity to be released and returned to the United States. Another was Thunderbolt pilot Flight Officer Robert Magel. When his brother David was killed on the mission to Berlin of February 3, 1945, fellow pilots in the 56th Fighter Group believed they'd lost both brothers within a span of a few months. Long declared dead, Robert Magel came home alive.

From modest beginnings came the greatest strategic striking force ever created. The Eighth Air Force eventually numbered 375,000 men and forty-two combat groups. The Eighth waged a three-year campaign and dropped 640,036 U.S. tons of bombs on German targets and destroyed 18,512 German aircraft but lost 43,742 American airmen (more combat deaths than the U.S. Marine Corps experienced in World War II) and lost 4,456 bombers in combat. Of the 210,000 flight crewmembers who flew out of East Anglia, 26,000 were killed, a fatality rate of 12.38 percent. An additional 21,000 Eighth Air Force crewmembers became prisoners of war.

The war in the high cold over the Third Reich was especially difficult in its early phase. As historian Rob Morris has pointed out, in the early months of the American daylight bombing campaign, the chances of a crewmember completing the requisite twenty-five missions were almost nonexistent. Wrote Morris: "Of those who flew the original twenty-five mission bomber tour in 1942–43, just 35 percent survived. Assuming a loss rate of 4 percent per mission, no aircrews would survive to complete their tours. Even at a loss rate of only 2 percent per mission, a man had only a fifty-fifty chance of survival." The situation improved dramatically as the war progressed but being a crewmember on a B-17 Flying Fortress or B-24 Liberator never ceased being one of the most dangerous duties of the war.

In the face of determined opposition and at grievous human cost, this force eventually took command of the air and contributed substantially to the outcome of the war.

On May 8, ball turret gunner Staff Sgt. John T. "Jack" Durkin of the 390th Bombardment Group enjoyed a respite from flying and found an opportunity to drink a couple of warm 3.2 beers with fellow Fortress crewmembers. They were not giddy, not somber, not happy, and not sad. They were simply awaiting whatever would come next as a routine part of military life. As Durkin commented so often, being in the military meant a lot of "hurry up and wait." At the moment there was no hurry about anything. The beer was coincidental. There was no celebration going on. Most Fortress crewmembers do not remember any particular celebration taking place on V-E Day.

"You know," said one of the Fortress gunners. "The Germans have surrendered. It's over, here in Europe."

"Yup," said another crewmember in the rear of the group as if tacking on a comment about the weather. He was looking up at low-hanging clouds. Even in May it was cold. It was always cold. "I think it might rain this evening."

And then as an afterthought: "Yup," said Durkin's buddy for a second time. "We won."

Acknowledgments

These first-person accounts of pilots and crews in combat are the result of 182 interviews completed in 2009 and 2010. This book would have been impossible without the help of many.

The following Berlin air combat veterans were interviewed for this book:

Richard A. Ayesh, Theodore M. Banta, James Ray Barber, Charles R. Bennett, Loren Bennett, Caesar J. Benigno, John Bozek, William A. Buckley, Arnold Burton, Michael P. Curphey, Ralph Davis, Robert Des Lauriers, John T. Durkin Sr., Raymond H. Fredette, Robert H. Friedman, James W. "Bill" Good, Charles W. Halper, Jesse P. Jacobs Jr., Asay "Ace" Johnson, George H. Keating, Russ Kyler, Conrad Lohoefer, Joseph Long, Don Maier, Robert McCall, Guy McCardle, Hap Nicholas, Daniel C. Pentz, John Pesch, Dean Portz, Robert "Punchy" Powell, Vincent Re, George Roberts, William L. Roche, Curtis E. Roper, Robert Shoens, Albert Shower, Charles N. Stevens, Roland Stewart, Robert Sweeney, William E. Uphoff, and Chester Van Etten.

Thanks also to family members of veterans and scholars of the war, including:

Gordon Alton, Russ Askey, F. Clifton Berry, Thomas O. Boggs, Ray Bowden, Jerry Boyd, Walter J. Boyne, Bob Brunn, Don Byers, Bob Collis, Sherry Crail, Valarie Dinkel, John Doughty, Michael Faley, Marlyn Flauter, Robert Forsyth, Ralph Franklin, Lowell Getz, Lucy Greguska, Robert A. Hadley, Richard Hallion, Eric Hammel, Paula Hintz, Sam Hurry, David Lord, Barbara Isaacs, Don Jay, Bill Jones, Sharon Vance

Kiernan, Sam Korth, Victor Krambo, Brooks Liles, Conrad Lohoefer, John M. McDermott, Luann McCain, Dwight S. Mears, Gary L. Moncur, Michal Mucha, Fridolin Nachtigal, Barbara Neal, Donald Nijboer, Joe Noah, Stan Piet, Fred Preller, Gary Price, Wayne Reece, Brett Reistad, Edward Rogner, Mary Nell Roos, Patty St. Onge, Joseph Secrist, Edward Sion, Robin Smith, Doug Sterner, Jenny Green Taylor, Barrett Tillman, Rebecca Tisdale, Cedric Welch, Ian White, and Vernon L. Williams.

Carolyn Beaubien of the 390th Memorial Museum shared wartime information on the size and sequence of the bomber formation. Joe Ferris gave permission to quote from *Raid on Berlin*, a family memoir by L. W. "Mac" McFarland. Suzanne Hahn of the Indiana Historical Society provided Richard L. Wann interviews from the Douglas E. Clanin collection. Dr. Vernon L. Williams provided a wealth of documents from the East Anglia Air War Project at Abilene Christian University in Texas. Edward Scion provided the map of U.S. bomber bases in East Anglia. Natalya McKinney translated terms from Russian into English.

I have a special debt to those who make books: Brian Trandem, Richard Kane, Scott Pearson; and to those who sell books: Joyce Burns, Bill Dawson, Natalya McKinney, and Steve Daubenspeck.

I followed usage generally accepted in the aviation community. Every Messerschmitt 109 ever built was designated Bf 109 and I have used that term (even changing quotes), even though Americans called it the Me 109, or Me-109, or ME-109. During World War II, units were officially called bombardment squadrons, groups, and wings. Crewmen often shortened "bombardment" to "bomb" in everyday conversation.

Some topics important to the air campaign, including the prisoner of war experience, the role of the Fifteenth Air Force, and the German side in this battle, are outside the scope of this narrative. Mistakes are inevitable in a story this complex. Any mistakes appearing here are the sole fault of the author.

Robert F. Dorr
Oakton, Virginia

APPENDIX ONE

Some Aircraft on the Mission to Berlin, February 3, 1945

9:45 a.m. Lost in collision over Holland
[Unnamed]
Boeing B-17G-90-BO Flying Fortress (43-38697/N7-M)
603rd BS, 398th BG
Pilot: 1st Lt. Perry E. Powell

9:45 a.m. Lost in collision over Holland
Maude an' Maria
Boeing B-17G-45-BO Flying Fortress (42-97387/K8-H)
602nd BS, 398th BG
Pilot: 1st Lt. John McCormick

9:45 a.m. Continued toward Germany and Berlin
Miss Prudy
Vega-built B-17G-70-VE Flying Fortress (44-8556)
4th BS, 34th BG
Pilot: 1st Lt. Charles B. "Chuck" Alling

10:51 a.m. Dropped out of formation en route to Berlin
Happy Warrior
Boeing B-17G-80-BO Flying Fortress (43-38254)
838th BS, 487th BG
Pilot: 1st Lt. William Settler

11:00 a.m. Hit by flak, later ditched; two rescued; seven killed
[Unnamed]
Boeing-built B-17G-55-BO Flying Fortress (42-102555/KY-F)
422nd BS, 305th BG
Pilot: 1st Lt. Daniel G. Shoemaker

11:02 a.m. Downed by flak over Berlin; four killed; five prisoners
The Birmingham Jewel
Vega-built B-17G-25-VE Flying Fortress (42-97678/LF-J)
525th BS, 379th BG
Pilot: 1st Lt. William Webber

11:04 a.m. Hit by flak; diverted to Soviet territory; nine returned to duty
Stardust
Douglas-built B-17G-55-DL Flying Fortress (44-6592/SO-S)
547th BS, 384th BG
Pilot: 2nd Lt. George F. Ruckman

11:04 a.m. Hit by flak; crew bailed out; all survived
[Unnamed]
Vega-built B-17G-40-VE Flying Fortress (42-97960/SO-M)
547th BS, 384th BG
Pilot: 2nd Lt. Charles R. Molder

11:04 a.m. Hit by flak; ditched in North Sea; three killed, six rescued
[Unnamed]
Boeing B-17G-50-BO Flying Fortress (42-102501/BK-H)
546th BS, 384th BG
Pilot: 2nd Lt. Robert C. Long

11:12 a.m. Downed by flak over Berlin; seven killed; two prisoners
[Unnamed]
Boeing B-17G-85-BO Flying Fortress (43-38407/GY-P)
367th BS, 306th BG
Pilot: 2nd Lt. George V. Luckett Jr.

11:12 a.m. Hit by flak over Berlin; ten killed
Rose of York
Boeing B-17G-60-BO Flying Fortress (42-102547/GY-F)
367th BS, 306th BG
Pilot: 1st Lt. Vernon F. Daley Jr.

11:18 a.m. Hit by flak over Berlin; one killed; eight prisoners
The Joker
Boeing B-17G-60-BO Flying Fortress (42-102873/VE-H)
532nd BS, 381st BG
Pilot: 1st Lt. John B. Anderson

11:19 a.m. Hit by flak over Berlin; one killed; eight prisoners
Hitler's Hoe Doe
Boeing B-17G-100-BO Flying Fortress (43-38898/GD-G)
534th BS, 381st BG
Pilot: 2nd Lt. Paul Pucylowski

11:20 a.m. Downed by flak northeast of Berlin; crew bailed out, became prisoners
Demobilizer
Boeing B-17G-85-BO Flying Fortress (43-38364/NV-L)
325th BS, 92nd BG
Pilot: 2nd Lt. Bernard G. Morrow

11:24 a.m. Hit by flak over Berlin, seven killed, two prisoners
[Unnamed]
Boeing B-17G-60-BO Flying Fortress (42-102958/LN-Z)
2459th BS, 100th BG
Pilot: 2nd Lt. Richard A. Beck

11:26 a.m. Hit by flak over Berlin, nine killed
[Unnamed]
Douglas-built B-17G-40-DL Flying Fortress (44-6500/LN-U)
350th BS, 100th BG
Pilot: 2nd Lt. Orville H. Cotner

11:28 a.m. Hit by flak over Berlin; crashed in Holland, one prisoner, eight killed
[Unnamed]
Boeing B-17G-60-BO Flying Fortress (42-102951/BG-Q)
334th BS, 95th BG
Pilot: 2nd Lt. Richard P. Morris

11:30 a.m. Hit by flak; nine prisoners
Dixie's Delight
Douglas-built B-17G-40-DL Flying Fortress (44-6092/LN-F)
350th BS, 100th BG
Pilot: 2nd Lt. Waldo J. Oldham

11:45 a.m. Departed formation over Berlin, diverted to Sweden
Slightly Dangerous
Boeing B-17G-85-BO Flying Fortress (43-38358)
730th BS, 452nd BG
Pilot: 1st Lt. William L. Fry

11:47 a.m. Encountered mechanical malfunction, diverted to Soviet lines in Poland; nine returned to duty
[Unnamed]
Douglas-built B-17G-30-DL Flying Fortress (43-38150)
849th BS, 490th BG
Pilot: 1st Lt. Irving Spiegel

12:05 p.m. Hit by flak over Berlin, diverted to Soviet lines in Poland; nine returned to duty
Lady V II
Vega-built B-17G-45-VE Flying Fortress (44-8130/4N-B)
486th BG
Pilot: 1st Lt. Arthur Ogle

12:20 p.m. Downed by flak, three killed; six taken prisoner
Sitting Pretty
Douglas-built B-17G-50-DL Flying Fortress (44-6170/MZ-M)
337th BS, 96th BG
Pilot: 1st Lt. Linwood S. Wyman

12:30 p.m. Encountered mechanical malfunction; crew bailed out; nine prisoners
[Unnamed]
Boeing B-17G-80-BO Flying Fortress (4338242)
863rd BS, 493rd BG
Pilots 2nd Lt. Henry H. Sherman

12:45 p.m. Hit by flak over Berlin, landed at Bulltofta, Sweden
The Jones Family
Vega-built B-17G-25-VE Flying Fortress (42-97658/XK-T)
367th BS, 306th BG
Pilot: 2nd Lt. Roland A. Lissner

3:05 p.m. Landed at a forward location near Langemark, Belgium
Lady B Good
Boeing B-17G-90-BO Flying Fortress (43-38594)
749th BS, 457th BG
Pilot: 1st Lt. Craig P. Greason

3:14 p.m. Bereman crew observed Cloud aircraft
[Unknown]
Vega-built B-17G-45-VE Flying Fortress (44-8025)
832nd BS, 486th BG
Pilot: Capt. Ronald E. Bereman

3:14 p.m. Tail gunner Staff Sgt. Frank T. Chrastka aircraft; went into a steep turn and crashed, exploded, and burned
Blue Grass Girl
Boeing B-17G-75-BO Flying Fortress (43-38031/3R-V)
832nd BS, 486th BG
Pilot: 1st Lt. Lewis K. Cloud

3:30 p.m. Landed safely after a struggle to get home
The Farmer's Daughter
Boeing B-17G-50-BO Flying Fortress (42-10468/IY-C)
615th BS, 401st BG
Pilot: 1st Lt. Carl P. Djernes

3:41 p.m. Myron L. King and crew diverted to Soviet lines in Poland; nine returned to duty
Maiden USA
Douglas-built B-17G-55-DL Flying Fortress (44-6508/IW-A)
614th BS, 401st BG
Pilot: 1st Lt. Myron. L. King

1st Lt. Robert Des Lauriers aircraft
Purty Chili
Vega-built B-17G-75-VE Flying Fortress (44-8629/D)
391st BS, 34th BG
Pilot: 1st Lt. Dean Hansen

Tech. Sgt. Ray Fredette aircraft
Fancy Nancy
Douglas-built Boeing B-17G-50-DL Flying Fortress (44-6465)
7th BS, 34th BG
Pilot: 1st Lt. Gordon F. Barbaras

F/O Asay "Ace" Johnson aircraft
Yankee Belle
Boeing B-17G-35-BO Flying Fortress (42-32085/DF-H)
324th BS, 91st BG
Pilot: 1st Lt. George F. Miller

1st Lt. Richard R. "Dick" Ayesh aircraft
[Unnamed]
Vega-built B-17G-60-VE Flying Fortress (44-8334/XR-B)
349th BS, 100th BG
Pilot: 1st Lt. Gene Jensen

Col. Lewis E. Lyle command aircraft
[Unnamed]
Vega-built B-17G-75-VE Flying Fortress (44-8669/WA-H)
379th BG
Pilot: 1st Lt. George Miller

Maj. James A. Smyrl command aircraft
[Unnamed]
Vega-built B-17G-25-VE Flying Fortress (42-97660/JW-X)
Boeing B-17G Flying Fortress
327th BS, 92nd BG
Pilot: Capt. Russell J. Bundesen

Lt. Col. Marvin D. Lord command aircraft
[Unnamed]
Vega-built B-17G-20-VE Flying Fortress (42-97632/DF-R)
324th BS, 91st BG
Pilot: 1st Lt Frank L. Adams

Col. Harris E. Rogner command aircraft
[Unnamed]
Vega-built B-17G-50-VE Flying Fortress (44-8157)
750th BS, 457th BG
Pilot: Capt. Edmund G. Coomes

Maj. Robert "Rosie" Rosenthal command aircraft; landed in Soviet territory
[Unnamed]
Vega-built B-17G-60-VE (44-8379/EP-J)
418th BS, 100th BG
Pilot: Capt. John Ernst

Van Ginkel Liberator on the Magdeburg mission; unharmed
Ol' Witch
Ford-built B-24H-25-FO Liberator (42-95194/6L-J)
Pilot: 1st Lt. James Van Ginkel

Bonnar Liberator crew hit by flak on Magdeburg mission
Delectable Doris
Ford-built B-24J-1-FO Liberator (42-50551/RR-R+)
566th BS, 389TH BG
Pilot: 1st Lt. Robert W. Bonnar

Wann Liberator crew on Magdeburg mission; bailed out near friendly lines
L'il Snooks
Ford B-24H-20-FO Liberator (42-94936)
707th BS, 446th BG
Pilot: 2nd Lt. Richard L. Wann

Fighter pilot who destroyed German aircraft
Katydid
North American P-51D-10-NA Mustang (44-14223/CL-M)
338th FS, 55th FG
Pilot: Lt. Col. Elwyn Guido Righetti

Fighter pilot who destroyed German aircraft
Sweet Marie II
North American P-51K-10-NT Mustang (44-14175/CY-Q)
343rd FS, 55th FG
Pilot: 1st Lt. Brooks J. Liles

Fighter pilot who strafed German aircraft
Lucky Wabbit II
North American P-51D-15-NA Mustang (44-15406/CY-U)
343rd FS, 55th FG
Pilot: 1st Lt. Victor P. Krambo

Fighter pilot killed in air-to-air combat
[Unnamed]
Republic P-47D-28-RE Thunderbolt (44-19777/UN-M)
63rd FS, 56th FG
Pilot: 1st Lt. David M. Magel

Fighter pilot who shot down German aircraft
[Unknown]
Republic P-47D-28-RE Thunderbolt (44-19937/UN-B)
63rd FS, 56th FG
Pilot: Capt. Cameron M. Hart

Fighter pilot who shot down German aircraft
[Unnamed]
Republic P-47D-30-RE Thunderbolt (44-20455/UN-Y)
63rd FS, 56th FG
Pilot: Maj. Paul A. Conger

APPENDIX TWO

Some Aircraft of the Air Campaign, December 7, 1941, to May 8, 1945

August 17, 1942: early Eighth Air Force mission
Butcher Shop
Boeing B-17E Flying Fortress (41-2578)
97th Bombardment Group
Pilot: Maj. Paul W. Tibbets

August 17, 1942: early Eighth Air Force mission; carried Maj. Gen. Ira Eaker
Yankee Doodle
Boeing B-17E Flying Fortress (41-9023)
414th BS, 97th BG
Pilot: 1st Lt. John Dowswell

August 17, 1942: credited with first shootdown of a German fighter
Birmingham Blitzkrieg
Boeing B-17E Flying Fortress (41-9100)
414th BS, 97th BG
Pilot: 1st Lt. Thomas H. Border

October 9, 1942: first B-24 mission
Teggie Ann
Consolidated B-24D-5-CO Liberator (41-23754)
409th BS, 93rd BG
Pilot: Col. Edward J. "Ted" Timberlake

October 9, 1942: first air-to-air victory
Ball of Fire
Consolidated B-24D-1-CO Liberator (41-23667)
330th BS, 93rd BG
Pilot: Capt. Joseph Tate

January 3, 1943: St. Nazaire; Sgt. Arnold Burton and 2nd Lt. James W. Hensley aboard
Heavy Weight Annihilators
Boeing B-17F-10-BO Flying Fortress (41-24482)
322nd BS, 91st BG
Pilot: 2nd Lt. Don C. Bader

March 18, 1943: 1st Lt. Jack Warren Mathis Medal of Honor mission
The Duchess
Boeing B-17F-25-BO Flying Fortress (41-24561/BN-T)
359th BS, 303rd BG
Pilot: Capt. Harold L. Stouse

March 23, 1944: Struggle for survival returning from Brunswick
Four Freedoms
Douglas-built B-17G-30-DL Flying Fortress (42-38157)
731st BS, 452nd BG
Pilot: Capt. John Pesch

May 1, 1943: Sgt. Maynard "Snuffy" Smith
Medal of Honor mission
[Unnamed]
Boeing B-17F-80-BO Flying Fortress (42-29649)
423rd BS, 306th BG
Pilot: 2nd Lt. Lewis P. Johnson

July 28, 1943: F/O John "Red" Morgan Medal of Honor mission
Ruthie II
Boeing B-17F-70-BO Flying Fortress (42-29802/JW-C)
326th BS, 92nd BG
Pilot: Capt. Robert L. Campbell

December 20, 1943: Tech. Sgt. Forrest Lee "Woody" Vosler Medal of Honor mission
Jersey Bounce Jr.
Boeing B-17F-65-BO Flying Fortress (42-29664/VK-C)
358th BS, 303rd BG
Pilot: 1st Lt. John Lemmon

December 20, 1943: Capt. Marvin D. Lord Silver Star mission
Big Time Operator II
Boeing B-17F-60-BO Flying Fortress (42-29570/VE-D)
532nd BS, 381st BG
Pilot: Capt. Marvin D. Lord

February 20, 1944: Truemper/Mathies Medal of Honor Mission
Ten Horsepower
Boeing B-17G-35-BO Flying Fortress (43-31763/TU-A)
510th BS, 351st BG
Pilot: 2nd Lt. Clarence R. "Dick" Nelson

February 20, 1944: Used in successful Azon bomb drop
Lorelei
Consolidated B-24H-10-CF Liberator (41-29300)
753rd BS, 458th BG
Pilot: Lt. Col. Robert W. Vincent

March 6, 1944: Among bombers shot down on first Berlin mission
[Unnamed]
Vega-built B-17G-15-VE (42-97483/LG-L)
322nd BS, 91st BG
Pilot: 2nd Lt. Brent Evertson

March 6, 1944: Escorted bombers to Berlin
Frenesi
North American P-51D-5-NA Mustang (44-13318/C5-N)
364th FS, 357th FG
Pilot: Maj. Tommy Hayes

April 11, 1944: 1st Lt. Edward S. Michael Medal of Honor Mission
Bertie Lee
Douglas-built B-17G-30-DL Flying Fortress (42-38131/WF-D)
364th BS, 305th BG
Pilot: 1st Lt. Edward S. Michael

June 5, 1944: Lt. Col. Leon Vance assigned aircraft
Sharon D.
Ford-built B-24H-15-FO Liberator (42-94759/T4-N)
489th BG
Pilot: Lt. Col. Leon Vance

June 5, 1944: Lt. Col. Leon Vance Medal of Honor mission
Missouri Belle
Douglas B-24H-10-DT Liberator (41-28690/QK-I+)
66th BS, 44th BG
Pilot: Capt. Louis Mazure

June 12, 1944: First heavy bomber to land in Liberated Europe
Normandy Queen
Ford-built B-24H-25-FO Liberator (42-95237)
790th BS, 467th BG
Pilot: 1st Lt. Charles Grace

November 2, 1944: 2nd Lt Robert E. Femoyer Medal of Honor mission
Hotshot Green
Douglas-built B-17G-25-DL Flying Fortress (42-38052)
711th BS, 447th BG
Pilot: 2nd Lt. Jerome Rosenblum

November 9, 1944: 1st Lt. Daniel J. Gott and William E. Metzger Medal of Honor mission
Lady Jeanette
Vega-built B-17G-35-VE Flying Fortress (42-97904/R)
729th BS, 452nd BG
Pilot: 1st Lt. Daniel J. Gott

December 24, 1944: Brig. Gen. Frederick W. Castle Medal of Honor mission
[Unnamed]
Vega-built B-17G-65-VE Flying Fortress (44-8444/H8-C)
487th BG
Pilot: 1st Lt. Robert W. Harriman

APPENDIX THREE

The Bomber Stream

This is the sequence in which B-17 Flying Fortresses proceeded to, and over, Berlin on February 3, 1945. The force consisted of 1,003 aircraft dispatched in two air divisions, with eight combat wings containing twenty-six combat groups, each with three or four squadrons.

Mission air commander: Col. Lewis E. Lyle

1st Air Division

The 1st Air Division consisted of 12 groups (36 squadrons of 12 aircraft each, 27 squadrons with 500-pound general-purpose bombs, plus 9 squadrons with a mixed load of 500-pound general-purpose bombs and Mk117 incendiaries.) The division preceded the 3rd Air Division over Berlin. The division had 60 aircraft that sustained major battle damage and 124 that sustained minor battle damage.

Interval between groups: one minute

41ST COMBAT WING (CBW)

1st over Berlin: (10:59 to 11:03 a.m.)

A: 379th Bombardment Group (Triangle-K), Kimbolton; mission, division, wing, and group air commander: Col. Lewis E. Lyle

Flak "moderate black and accurate."

One aircraft lost:

- 1st Lt. William Webber, others, in *The Birmingham Jewel*; three killed, five captured; bombardier 1st Lt. Carl Cook killed aboard another aircraft

2nd over Berlin: (11:03 to 11:04 a.m.)

B: 384th Bombardment Group (Triangle-P), Grafton Underwood; group air commander: Lt. Col. Theodore R. Milton

One aircraft diverted to Soviet territory:

- 2nd Lt. George F. Ruckman, others, in *Stardust*; nine returned to duty

Two aircraft lost:

- 2nd Lt. Charles R. Molder, others, in an unnamed aircraft; all survived
- 2nd Lt. Robert C. Long, others, in *The Challenger* ditched; three killed, six rescued

3rd over Berlin: (11:04 a.m.)

C: 303rd Bombardment Group (Triangle-C), Molesworth; group air commander: Capt. Robert J. Hullar

40TH CBW

Wing air commander Col. Anthony Q. Mustoe

4th over Berlin: (11:05 a.m.)

A: 305th Bombardment Group (Triangle-G), Chelveston; group air commander: Maj. O. W. Shelton

- 1st Lt. Daniel G. Shoemaker, others, in an unnamed aircraft, hit, ditched; two rescued, seven killed

5th over Berlin (11:06 to 11:08 a.m.):

B: 92nd Bombardment Group (Triangle-B), Podington; group air commander: Maj. James Smyrl

6th over Berlin: (11:08 to 11:12 a.m.)

C: 306th Bombardment Group (Triangle-H), Thurleigh; group air commander: Lt. Col. Eugene C. LeVier

"Intense, accurate, tracking flak from four minutes before bombs away lasting eight minutes."

Lost three aircraft:

• 2nd Lt. Roland A. Lissner, others in *The Jones Family* diverted to Sweden

• 2nd Lt. George V. Luckett, others, in an unnamed aircraft; hit by flak; five killed

• 1st Lt. Vernon F. Daley Jr., others, in *Rose of York*, hit by flak; ten killed

94TH CBW

Wing and group mission leader: Col. Harris E. Rogner

7th over Berlin: (11:12 to 11:13 a.m.)

A: 457th Bombardment Group (Triangle-U), Glatton; group air commander: Col. Harris E. Rogner

8th over Berlin: (11:13 a.m.)

B: 401st Bombardment Group (Triangle-S), Deenethorpe; group air commander: Capt. J. R. Locher

• 1st M. L. King, others in *Maiden USA* diverted to Soviet territory

9th over Berlin: (11:15 a.m.)

C: 351st Bombardment Group (Triangle-J), Polebrook; group mission leader Major Roper)

1ST CBW

10th over Berlin: (11:16 a.m.)

A: 398th Bombardment Group (Triangle-W), Nuthampstead; group air commander Lieutenant Colonel Ensign

• 1st Lt. Perry E. Powell, others, in an unnamed aircraft and 1st Lt. John McCormick, others, in *Maude an' Maria*, lost in a midair collision; fifteen killed, three became prisoners of war

11th over Berlin: (11:17 a.m.)

B: 91st Bombardment Group (Triangle-A), Bassingbourn; group air commander Lt. Col. Marvin D. Lord

- Lord, others, in an unnamed aircraft hit by flak; ten killed
- 1st Lt. George F. Miller, others, in *Yankee Belle*, hit by flak; ten prisoners

12th over Berlin (11:18 a.m.)

C: 381st Bombardment Group (Triangle-L), Ridgewell; group air commander: Capt. Edward M. MacNeill

The group dispatched 37 aircraft. "Flying weather was good, and, although the formation found a solid undercast from the European coast almost to Berlin, the clouds broke at the target and it was wide open over Berlin. Ours was the twelfth Group to bomb and strike photos show our explosives landing to the right and on the assigned [target]." Two aircraft were lost:

- 2nd Lt. John B. Anderson, others, in *The Joker*, shot down by flak; one killed, eight prisoners
- 2nd Lt. Paul Pucylowski, others, in *Hitler's Hoe Doe*, departed formation; one killed, eight prisoners

3rd Air Division

The 3rd Air Division consisted of 14 groups (42 squadrons of 12 to 13 aircraft each, 12 squadrons with 500-pound general-purpose bombs, 18 squadrons with 1,000-pound general-purpose bombs, and 12 squadrons with a mixed load of 500-pound general-purpose bombs and Mk117 incendiaries). The division had 33 aircraft that sustained major battle damage and 122 aircraft that sustained minor battle damage, plus two Category E losses (meaning damaged beyond repair).

13TH COMBAT WING (CBW)

13th over Berlin: (11:26 to 11:28 a.m.)

A: 100th Bombardment Group (Square-D), Thorpe Abbotts; division, wing, and group air commander: Maj. Robert "Rosie" Rosenthal

Lost four aircraft:

- Rosenthal, others, in an unnamed aircraft hit by flak; four prisoners, five reached Soviet territory
- 2nd Lt. Waldo J. Oldham, others in *Dixie's Delight*; nine prisoners
- 2nd Lt. Richard A. Beck, others, in an unnamed aircraft; seven killed, two prisoners
- 2nd Lt. Orville H. Cotner, others, in an unnamed aircraft; nine killed

14th over Berlin: (11:28 a.m.)

B: 390th Bombardment Group (Square-J), Framlingham; group air commander: McHenry

15th over Berlin: (11:28 a.m.)

C: 95th Bombardment Group (Square-B), Horham; group air commander: Maj. James O. Frankowsky

Lost two aircraft:

- 2nd Lt. Richard P. Morris, others, in an unnamed aircraft hit by flak, one prisoner, eight killed
- 1st Lt. James D. Taylor, others, hit by flak; nine prisoners

45TH CBW

16th over Berlin: (11:30 a.m.)

A: 388th Bombardment Group (Square-H), Knettishall; group air commander: Maj. John Goodman

17th over Berlin: (11:31 a.m. to 11:34 a.m.)

B: 452nd Bombardment Group (Square-L), Deopham Green; group air commander: Maj. Arthur L. Barnes

"Target area was well smoked-up from groups in front. We bombed the primary target in squadron formation, making a visual run with PFF [pathfinder aircraft] assist due to haze and smoke restricting the visibility at the target. Flak over the target was meager but accurate."

18th over Berlin: (11:34 a.m.)

C: 96th Bombardment Group (Square-C), Snetterton Heath; group air commander: Maj. Clarence Godecke

One aircraft lost:

• 1st Lt. Linwood S. Wyman, others, in *Sitting Pretty* hit by flak, three killed; six taken prisoner

93RD CBW

19th over Berlin: (11:35 a.m.)

A: 34th Bombardment Group (Square-S), Mendlesham; group air commander: Capt. Roy E. Tavasti

"A complete cloud cover slipped in below us. This 10/10 cover persisted until we reached the target. None of Germany was visible to us on our course in."

No aircraft lost.

• 1st Lt. Robert Des Lauriers, others, in *Purty Chili*

• Tech. Sgt. Ray Fredette, others, in *Fancy Nancy*

20th over Berlin: (11:38 a.m.)

B: 493d Bombardment Group (Square-S), Little Walden; group air commander: Maj. John Phillips

Lost one aircraft:

• 2nd Lt. Henry H. Sherman, others, in an unnamed aircraft; suffered mechanical malfunction; nine prisoners

21st over Berlin (11:38 a.m.)

C: 490th Bombardment Group (Square-T), Eye

• 1st Lt. Irving Spiegel, others, in unnamed aircraft, had a mechanical failure and diverted Poland; nine returned to duty

4TH CBW

22nd over Berlin: (11:39 a.m.)

A: 94th Bombardment Group (Square-A), Bury St. Edmunds; group air commander: Maj. John Stewart

23rd over Berlin: (11:40 a.m.)

B: 487th Bombardment Group (Square-P), Lavenham

• 1st Lt. William Settler, others, in *Happy Warrior*, dropped out of formation

24th over Berlin: (11:42 a.m.)

C: 447th Bombardment Group (Square-K), Rattlesden; group air commander: Lt. Col. Edward McRae

25th over Berlin: (11:45 a.m.)

D: 486th Bombardment Group (Square-O/W), Sudbury; group air commander: Lt. Col. Harold W. Norton

- Frank T. Chrastka, Lewis K. Cloud, others, in *Blue Grass Girl*

26th over Berlin: (11:50 a.m.)

E: 385th Bombardment Group (Square-G), Great Ashfield; group air commander: Maj. Charles A. Reid

APPENDIX FOUR

What Happened to Them?

Henry R. "Hap" Arnold (June 25, 1886–January 15, 1950), who agonized over the safety of his bomber crewmembers on the February 3, 1945, mission to Berlin, lived to see the U.S. Air Force become an independent service branch on September 18, 1947. He had been a pioneer of air power tactics and strategy in the prewar era and is credited with an excellent job of steering America's air arm through history's greatest war. The last American officer to reach five-star rank with the sole exception of Omar Bradley, Arnold was promoted to general of the army on December 21, 1944. The name of his rank was changed on May 7, 1949, to general of the air force, making him the only person to hold this grade. His health too poor to permit a leadership role in the postwar era, Arnold published an autobiography, *Global Mission*, in 1949. All three of Arnold's surviving sons served as colonels in the air force.

Arnold Burton, the engineer-gunner on *Heavy Weight Annihilators* on the January 3, 1943, mission to St. Nazaire, left the army as a technical sergeant in 1945. Born February 25, 1921, after flying in Europe he was briefly an aviation cadet before the end of the war put his goal of becoming a P-47 Thunderbolt fighter pilot out of reach. Burton acquired a civilian license and owned, successively, an Interstate L-6 and a Fairchild PT-19 Cornell. Thrice married with three children, he worked as a pressman in the printing facility for *Popular Mechanics* magazine until 1958 when he launched a marketing and printing business. He retired in 1999. At age eighty in 2001, Burton began seven prolonged stays of several months each in Kazakhstan with his third wife, a Russian. When this volume went to press, Burton was preparing for his ninetieth birthday and resided in Geneva, Illinois, with his daughter, Leslie Ann Burton.

Frank Chrastka (March 3, 1925–February 3, 1945) is interred at Woodlawn Cemetery in Forest Park, Illinois. He never married. He had a brother and three sisters. It is believed that he has no surviving family members today.

Robert Des Lauriers, the copilot of *Purty Chili*, spent most of his life as an architect in San Diego, California. Born February 29, 1924, he married Shirley Marie McHenry (1925–2009) on V-J Day, August 15, 1945, in Sioux City, Iowa. He graduated from the University of Colorado in 1949 with a bachelor of science degree in architectural engineering and moved to San Diego, where he has lived since. Working for architectural firms, he designed the first moving sidewalk for a local hotel. He opened his own architectural studio in 1958. He designed sixty-five churches of all denominations. He also designed two mosques and about a dozen medical offices. Des Lauriers and his wife are the parents of two children. His wife, Shirley, died on January 17, 2009. Des Lauriers still lives in San Diego.

James H. "Jimmy" Doolittle (December 14, 1896–September 27, 1993), the aviation pioneer and Medal of Honor recipient for the April 18, 1942, attack on Japan, commanded the Eighth Air Force on February 3, 1945, and until war's end. Doolittle married Josephine E. "Joe" Daniels on December 24, 1917; they had two sons. Doolittle never found the job he hoped for in the postwar air force. He reverted to inactive status at three-star rank on May 10, 1946, having been the highest-ranking reserve officer in modern history, and retired from the air force on February 28, 1959. In 1946, he helped create, and became the first president of, the Air Force Association. In 1985, he was advanced to four-star rank while in retirement. Daniels died in 1998. Doolittle wrote an autobiography, *I Could Never Be So Lucky Again*, with Carroll V. Glines. The book makes no mention of his objections to the February 3, 1945, mission to Berlin. (Curiously, many Eighth Air Force crewmembers do not remember the name of their commander from January 6, 1944, to July 19, 1945). He will be remembered best as the architect and leader of what history will always call the Doolittle Raid on Japan.

Ray Fredette, the toggleer of *Fancy Nancy*, retired from the air force in 1970 as a lieutenant colonel. Born April 26, 1924, he married Pamela Dorsey in 1946 and graduated Tufts University in 1949 with a degree in history. He received a master's degree in international relations at Tufts' Fletcher School of Law and Diplomacy in 1950. A reservist, he was recalled to active duty in 1951 and had assignments in Morocco, South Dakota, and Colorado Springs. He was a Russian linguist and an intelligence officer. He was associated with the Office of Air Force History for many years and is an authority on military aviation during the Great War of 1914–1918. He is author of *The Sky On Fire: The First Battle of Britain, 1917–1918* (New York: HarperCollins, 1991). Fredette maintained a correspondence with Charles A. Lindbergh and Lindbergh's family for many years. Fredette and his wife are the parents of a son who is a student counselor in Taipei. His wife, Pamela, died in 2010. He lives in Mount Vernon, Virginia.

Cameron M. Hart (October 8, 1919–February 16, 1946), the P-47D Thunderbolt pilot who became an air ace on February 3, 1945, was killed barely than a year later when his P-47N Thunderbolt crashed at Craig Army Air Field, Alabama.

James W. "Jim" Hensley (April 12, 1920–June 21, 2000), the bombardier on *Heavy Weight Annihilators* on the January 3, 1943, mission to St. Nazaire, was married in 1937 to Mary Jeanne Parks. They had one child together and divorced while he recovered from war wounds in 1945. He was remarried later that year to Marguerite "Smitty" Johnson. They also had one child together, Cindy Lou Hensley. She inherited his business and in 1980 became the second wife of Sen. John McCain R-Arizona, a presidential candidate in 2000 and 2008. Hensley and his daughter were considered among the wealthiest people in Arizona.

Curtis E. LeMay (November 15, 1906–October 1, 1990), who had a pivotal role in shaping tactics used in the air campaign in Europe, later commanded the XX Bomber Command during the firebombing of Tokyo and the atomic bombing of Hiroshima and Nagasaki. LeMay took over the Strategic Air Command in 1948, pinned on his fourth star in 1951, and shaped America's long-range bomber and tanker force during the Cold War. He was air force vice chief of staff from 1957 to 1961 and chief of staff from 1961 to1965. He clashed with Washington policymakers during the Vietnam era, spoke of the United States having the capability to "bomb them to the stone age" in Vietnam, and for years afterward disclaimed suggesting any such thing. With MacKinlay Kantor, he wrote an autobiography, *Mission With LeMay*. He will be remembered by history as the archetypical "bomber general," who shaped the air force of the Cold War era.

Brooks J. Liles (June 3, 1923–May 28, 2008), the P-51 Mustang pilot who strafed a German airfield on February 3, 1945, entered Duke University after the war, missed flying, quit school, and became a light aircraft instructor in Beaufort, North Carolina, where he met his future wife, Betty Ruth Hussey. In December 1947, he re-entered the Air Force. He held various fighter assignments before joining the 336th Fighter-Interceptor Squadron. He flew one hundred missions in the F-86 Sabre and scored four more kills on top of his single aerial victory from World War II to become an ace. Squadronmates nicknamed him "Pappy" at the age of twenty-eight. He held many other fighter assignments before retiring from the air force in 1965. He lived in Goldsboro and Raleigh, North Carolina, until his next retirement in 1990. He and his wife had four children.

Marvin D. Lord (March 30, 1921–February 3, 1945) is interred at Woodlawn Cemetery in Milwaukee, Wisconsin. His wife, Evelyn, known as Evey, died in 2010. His daughter, Marlyn Flauter, lives in Chesterfield, Missouri; his brother, David Lord, in Neillsville, Wisconsin.

Lewis E. Lyle (June 22, 1916–April 6, 2008), the commander of the February 3, 1945, mission to Berlin and of the 379th Bombardment Group, had a long and successful career in the air force. He completed sixty-nine combat missions and served in bomber, missile, and reconnaissance units. His awards included the Distinguished Service Cross, the second highest award for valor. He retired as a major general in 1967. Lew Lyle and his wife, Betty, had a son, John, and a daughter, Lynda. Lyle was deeply involved in the establishment and expansion of the Eighth Air Force Museum in Savanna, Georgia.

John Pesch (July 20, 1921–January 10, 2010) married his wife, Gloria, in 1945. They had two sons and two daughters. Pesch left the military in 1946. He joined the Maine Air National Guard while attending the University of Maine. He was recalled to active duty in 1950, was assigned to Germany, and remained in uniform thereafter. Pesch led the Air National Guard from 1974 to 1977, when he retired from the military at the rank of major general. His son, John Pesch Jr., an F-105 Thunderchief pilot, died in an aircraft accident in 1978. The author interviewed Pesch at the Falcons Landing retirement home in Virginia.

Harris E. "Rog" Rogner (August 15, 1914–December 18, 1951), the air commander for the 457th Bombardment Group on February 3, 1945, was a West Pointer who stayed in uniform, reached the rank of colonel, married, and had four children. He went on to fight in Korea. On August 25, 1951, Rogner, vice commander of Far East Air Forces Bomber Command, led thirty-five B-29 Superfortresses of the 19th, 98th, and 307th Bombardment Groups against the North Korean target city of Rashin, which had previously been taboo because of its proximity to the Soviet Union. The bombers received a partial escort from F2H-2 Banshees and F9F Panthers from the aircraft carrier USS *Essex* (CV 9). "We clobbered them," Rogner later said. Rogner died December 19, 1951, in a B-29 crash near Barksdale Air Force Base, Louisiana, at age thirty-seven.

Robert "Rosie" Rosenthal (June 11, 1917–April 29, 2007), the pilot-lawyer and 3rd Air Division air commander on February 3, 1945, was awarded the Distinguished Service Cross, the second highest U.S. award for valor, for completing the bomb run that day and for struggling to save his crew. He completed fifty-three combat missions. He reached the rank of lieutenant colonel before leaving the military shortly after the war. Rosenthal, already an attorney while flying as a pilot, became a prosecutor in the Nuremberg war crimes trials and interrogated Hermann Göring. He married Phillis Heller, another lawyer, at Nuremberg. It appears he spent the remainder of his life practicing law and raising a family. When Rosenthal died in White Plains, New York, on April 20, the *New York Times* quoted him on the Nuremberg war trials: "Seeing these strutting conquerors after they were sentenced, powerless, pathetic and preparing for the hangman was the closure I needed."

Carl A. "Tooey" Spaatz (June 28, 1891–July 14, 1974), who commanded U.S. bomber forces during the February 3, 1945, mission to Berlin, had been an airpower pioneer before the war and became the first chief of staff of the air force, serving from September 26, 1947, to April 24, 1950. He had been born with the name Spatz but added the extra "a" at the request of his wife and daughters, hoping in vain that others would pronounce his surname correctly (to rhyme with hots). He was a champion of air-to-air refueling, the heavy bomber, attacks on German oil, and of the U.S. Air Force Academy, which graduated its first class in 1959. He is interred on the academy's grounds in Colorado Springs, Colorado.

Richard L. Wann (1920–2005), the only crewmember of the B-24 Liberator *L'il Snooks* to fall into German hands, received a bachelor's degree in agriculture from Mississippi State University in 1950 and a master's degree from Purdue soon afterward. He married Ruth Procter. Their home was in Elwood, Indiana. He joined the Firestone Corporation in 1952 and "finished my career in charge of tires all over the world" in October 1982. He showed no bitterness toward his captors and was cheerful when describing his horrific treatment as a prisoner during interviews with historian Douglas E. Clanin long after the war.

Notes

Chapter One

Said an airman who flew with Chrastka: Author interviews with Joseph Long and Daniel "Clint" Pentz.

Lord taking lead: Banta interviews; e-mail message from Sam Halpert.

Lord as singer and dancer: Interview by author Dorr of his sister, Phyllis Carpenter.

Pace, said that some men prayed B-24 Liberators accompany them: *Happy Landing*, by Joseph D. Pace.

LeMay quote on "raids:" LeMay, by Barrett Tillman, p.37.

McFarland quotes: McFarland memoir, published with permission.

Merseburg: website for the 389th Bomb Group Memorial Association: http://www.398th.org/History/Articles/Remembrances/Ostrom_Merseburg.html.

Fitzgerald quote: December 15, 2000, letter from Fitzgerald to the author Dorr, also published in the December 2000 Eighth Air Force News.

Berlin was in ruins: The Fall of Berlin 1945, by Anthony Beevor.

Doolittle and Spaatz quotes: Fire and Fury, by Randall Hansen.

Hitler quote: October 9, 2009, e-mail message from Des Lauriers.

Chapter Two

Michael Curphey, an RAF intelligence analyst: Author interview with Curphey, 1987.

Also in the group was Capt. Frederick W. Castle: *Mighty Eighth War Diary*, by Roger Freeman, p. 404; *Above and Beyond*, by Barrett Tillman, p. 129.

the dark, cold early hours of August 17, 1942: Castles in the Air, by Martin Bowman, p. 14.

Mathis was bent over his Norden bombsight: from *Above and Beyond,* by Barrett Tillman, p. 61.

Chapter Three

Lord quote about the Silver Star: September 1, 1943 letter written by Lord.

" . . . fear . . . " Missing Planes of the 452nd Bomb Group, by Edward Hinrichs.

"The night before you removed your guns from the plane:" Author interview.

Freeman quote: letter to the author.

Chapter Four

a moderately pompous little fellow: *My War*, by Andy Rooney.

"Attention was paid to increasing the Thunderbolt's radius of action: Mighty Eighth War Diary, by Roger Freeman, p. 40.

Shelhamer quote: *Half a Wing, Three Engines, and a Prayer*, by Brian D. O'Neill.

unknown to the Americans the Regensburg portion: *The Jet Race and the Second World War*, Michael Sterling Pavelec.

Kozak quote on the first Schweinfurt mission: *LeMay*, by Barrett Tillman.

Hammel quote on "Monk" Hunter's fighter tactic: *The Road to Big Week*, by Eric Hammel.

acting as squadron commander for about 10 days: Letter by Marvin D. Lord to his parents on October 2, 1943.

the Eighth Air Force dispatched 546 bombers: *Mighty Eighth War Diary*, by Roger Freeman, pp. 151-152.

The Luftwaffe was up in strength: *Above and Beyond*, by Barrett Tillman, p. 91.

Chapter Five

McKinley quote: His letter in the *Eighth Air Force News*, December 2000, p. 47.

Quote from Lyle about conditions over target: His mission report dated February 3, 1945.

Jones as ball turret gunner: Author interview.

Copilot role: *B-17 Combat Missions*, by Martin Bowman.

Ralph Wathey: Family documents; author interviews with Des Lauriers.

Harold M. Mauldin: A personal memoir provided courtesy of the 401st Bomb Group (H) Association.

a pilot accusing Rogner of taking unnecessary risks: *The Young Ones: American Airmen in World War II*, by Erik Dyreborg.

Chapter Six

Howard low-key, pleasant and focused: Author interview with Barrett Tillman.

Howard the greatest fighter pilot of World War II: *My War*, by Andy Rooney.

Michel quote: "The P-51 Mustang: The Most Important Aircraft in History?" in *Air Power History*.

Craven and Cate on Big Week: *Europe: Argument to V-E Day, January 1944 to May 1945*, by Wesley Frank Craven and James Lea Cate.

"We tried twice to get to Berlin, the 3rd and the 4th of March, and were recalled:" Author interview with former Capt. Charles R. Bennett, July 1, 2010.

Ethell and Price quote about the significance of the March 6, 1944 mission: *Target Berlin: Mission 250: 6 March 1944*, by Jeffrey L. Ethell and Alfred Price.

Chapter Seven

Charles Alling German fighter quote: *A Mighty Fortress*, by Charles Alling, p. 79; author interview with Alling; in later years, Alling insisted that he witnessed the German fighter come apart in midair. The author could find no record of anyone else in the bomber stream witnessing this. Other aspects of Alling's account raise the question whether—as happened so often—he was remembering a different mission. In postwar years, Alling held key responsibilities with the air force office of history, so his account must be taken seriously.

Chapter Eight

". . . Capt. John Pesch heard the two words uttered by bombardier . . .": Author interviews with Pesch September 6, 2004; September 14, 2004; and June 12, 2009.

". . . a military document summarized his contribution as a B-17 Flying Fortress pilot" : Pesch family document provided to author, 2009.

German fighters singled out Bertie Lee and attacked the bomber recklessly: Medal of Honor citation for 1st Lt. Edward Stanley Michael.

Both pilots were startled: *Above and Beyond*, by Barrett Tillman, p. 103.

Chapter Nine

"Hart later wrote . . .": From an after-action report by Hart, February 1945.

According to Robert Forsyth: Interview with Forsyth via e-mail March 22, 2010.

Val McClellan quote: An unpublished family manuscript by McClellan.

The control stick handle on most WWII fighters was like gripping a big umbrella handle: Interview with P-51 Mustang pilot Robert "Punchy" Powell, who is not related to Frederick Powell.

"I tried repeatedly to restart the engine . . . " Interview of Frederick Powell conducted by John R. Doughty Jr. and used with permission.

Chapter Ten

"I had flown with McPartlin": Author interview with George A. Parrish, August 30, 2010.

"Now he is trying to decide whether to put in for a 30-day leave: "Doyle Gathers 7 State Fliers," by Robert J. Doyle, *Milwaukee Journal*, August 13, 1944.

"There are more boys over there who would rather come home to see their babies than for any other reason you can name": Author interview with David Lord, June 5, 2010.

Lord and baby: "To the World He's Lt. Col. at 23, to One That Counts He's 'Dad,' " Journal Staff, *Milwaukee Journal*, October 22, 1944.

"the Eighth Air Force sent 1,174 bombers and 968 fighters": *Mighty Eighth War Diary*, by Roger Freeman, p. 375.

Femoyer's "conspicuous gallantry and intrepidity": Medal of Honor citation for 2nd Lt. Robert Edward Femoyer.

"The aircraft was hit by flak": U.S. Army Missing Air Crew Report (MACR) covering the loss of the Gott/Metzger Medal of Honor aircraft.

"Three of the aircraft's engines were damaged beyond control and on fire": Gott Medal of Honor citation.

Halper of the 487th Bombardment Group wasn't scheduled to be in the air on December 24, 1944: Halper family documents provided to author, 2009; author interview with Charles Halper.

Halper quote: family memoir courtesy of Louise Halper Pitman; a slightly different version appeared in *Eighth Air Force News*, December 2004, p. 14.

The largest aerial formation ever assembled: *Mighty Eighth War Diary*, by Roger Freeman, pp. 398–400.

Chapter Eleven

Settler crew's experience: The History of the 487th Bomb Group (H), by Ivo De Jong.

Lyle quote: *B-17 Combat Missions*, by Martin Bowman.

Webber aircraft loss: A family website maintained by Betty Hathaway (http://carlhathaway.com/berlinraid3.htm).

Shoemaker crew's story: Official Survivors Report by 2nd Lt. Roy F. Moullen and Sgt. Ira Roisman, which also appears in *John Burn One-Zero-Five*, by William Donald.

92nd Bombardment Group over Berlin: The group's February 4, 1945, report on planning and execution of the mission; author interview with James W. "Bill" Good.

Luckett crew: 305th BG documents.

Lissner crew: Pilot's Mission Report, U.S. Legation, Stockholm, Sweden, February 9, 1945; 306th BG documents.

Miller quote: *Plane Names & Fancy Noses*, by Ray Bowden (London: Design Oracle, 1993).

Miller and Johnson aboard Yankee Belle: Author interview with Asay "Ace" Johnson, July 3, 2010.

Fitzgerald quote: Letter from Fitzgerald to the author, December 15, 2000, which was also published in the December 2000 *Eighth Air Force News.*

Bailout bell description: e-mail message from Des Lauriers, June 26, 2009.

Chapter Twelve

Irascible, gruff, and at times crude: *Fire and Fury*, by Randall Hansen, p. 33.

Contrary to [American] ideals: *Fire and Fury*, by Randall Hansen, p. 33.

Before 1945, Spaatz tried . . . to avoid killing German civilians: *Fire and Fury*, by Randall Hansen, p. 282.

British attack on Magdeburg: *Fire and Fury*, by Randall Hansen, p. 244.

Doolittle and mellowness: A letter written by Doolittle, quoted in *I Could Never Be So Lucky Again*, Doolittle with Glines, p. 399.

Doolittle on Thunderclap: *Operation Thunderclap*, by Richard G. Davis.

Doolittle quote: *Fire and Fury*, by Randall Hansen, p. 252.

Chapter Thirteen

Morrow crew: author interview with James W. "Bill" Good, Missing Air Crew Report (MACR) 12031; interview with Wayne Reece. The author was unable to resolve minor discrepancies in the time and location of Morrow's B-17 being hit and the crew bailing out. The time given for the Morrow aircraft loss is from the MACR.

Joe Regan wrote: Letter of September 24, 199,3 from Joe Regan in *92nd Bombardment Group News*, date unknown.

U.S. internment in Sweden: Arnold cable to Spaatz and Eaker, WARX 71515 July 27, 1944; Arnold telegram to consular officials, W65309, June 15, 1944; U.S. air attache in Stockholm cable to Arnold and Spaatz; U.S. air attache Stockholm cable to Arnold and Spaatz, June 24, 1944.

Good directed the formation: Citation for the award of the Distinguished Flying Cross to Good.

"sheer force of the impact caused the Fortress to rise": Interview with Good.

Fry crew: Author interview with Michael P. Curphey.

Shoemaker crew: Official Survivors Report by 2nd Lt. Roy F. Moullen and Sgt. Ira Roisman, which also appears in *John Burn One-Zero-Five* by William Donald.

Chapter Fourteen

4667th BG, Vincent Re, Albert Shower: Author interviews.

The experiences of Cpl. Ryan: From a February 3, 1945 written report by Maj. Claude H. Studebaker of the 45th Infantry Division.

Doolittle and Magdeburg: *I Could Never Be So Lucky Again*, Doolittle with Glines, p. 402.

Chapter Fifteen

Lissner crew: *Pilot's Mission Report*, U.S. Legation, Stockholm, Sweden, February 9, 1945; 306th BG documents.

Chapter Sixteen

Some details on Blue Grass Girl: Author interviews with former Tech. Sgt. Daniel "Clint" Pentz.

McDermott bailout: Author interview with John M. McDermott.

The 3:14 p.m. time and most details on Blue Grass Girl: E-mail exchanges with, and official documents provided by, researcher Bob Collis of Suffolk, England. A description *The Mighty Eighth War Diary* by Freeman is believed to contain errors, including the spelling of Lewis K. Cloud's name.

The 3:45 p.m. landing time for the 34th Bombardment Group: Fredette's diary. Fredette may be as much as a half hour early in his record of the time.

The 4:00 p.m. landing time for Purty Chili: Des Lauriers's diary.

Purty Chili approach and landing: B-17 Flying Fortress pilot's manual; author interview with Des Lauriers, June 29, 2010.

"The only responsibility an air crew gunner had on the ground": Letter from John Harold Robinson, a waist gunner with the 445th BG *Eighth Air Force Journal*, June 2005.

Chapter Seventeen

"Gauleiter Goebbels tonight issued a standstill order": "Terrified Crowd Told, 'You Must Stay,' " by Ralph Hewins, *Daily Mail*, February 5, 1945.

965 were effective: *Mighty Eighth War Diary*, by Roger Freeman, p. 432

6.9 million pounds of bombs: Author interview with, and research by, Joseph Secrist.

Val McClellan quote: An unpublished family manuscript by McClellan.

Victor Krambo: Author interview with (son) Victor Krambo.

Liles, Howes rescue attempt: Pilots Personal Encounter Report by Satenstein, repeated in *Double Nickel-Double Trouble*, by Robert M. Littlefield.

Maj. Gen. John R. Deane complaint: Deane report to U.S. officers dated March 22, 1945; interview with researcher Michal Mucha.

British on Roosevelt's death: Author interview with Charles W. Halper.

Richard L. Wann quotes: Wann interviews in the Douglas E. Clanin collection, Indiana Historical Society, courtesy of Suzanne Hahn.

Jansen quote: *The History of the 446th Bombardment Group*. The Netherlands: Private Printing.

Morris quote: *Untold Valor*, by Rob Morris.

Appendix Three

384th BG location: 303rd BG document.

303rd BG location: 303rd BG document; Calenberg diary.

40th CBW and 92nd BG location: The group's February 4, 1945, report on planning and execution of the mission; author interview with James W. "Bill" Good; author interview with Wayne Reece; memoir by John Sloan.

381st BG location: 381st BG website.

452nd BG location: The group navigator's report; interview with Patricia St. Onge.

Target area was well smoked-up: The group navigator's report.

Bibliography

Allen, Thomas B, "The Wings of War," *National Geographic*, March 1994.

Alling, Charles. *A Mighty Fortress: Lead Bomber Over Europe*. Havertown, Pa.: Casemate Publishing, 2002.

Beevor, Anthony. *The Fall of Berlin 1945*. New York: Penguin, 2002.

Bowden, Ray. *Plane Names & Fancy Noses*. London: Design Oracle, 1993.

Bowman, Martin. *B-17 Combat Missions*. London: Metro Books, 2008.

———. *Castles in the Air: The Story of the B-17 Flying Fortress Crews of the U.S. 8th Air Force*. Wellingborough: Patrick Stephens, 1984.

———. *P-47 Thunderbolt vs. Bf 109G/KEurope 1943–45*. New York; Osprey, 2009.

Craven, Wesley Frank and James Lea Cate. *Europe: Argument to V-E Day*. Washington: Office of Air Force History, 1983.

Daso, Dik Alan. *Doolittle: Aerospace Visionary*. Dulles, Va.: Potomac Books, 2003.

Davis, Richard G., "Operation Thunderclap: The U.S. Army Air Force and the Bombing of Berlin," *The Journal of Strategic Studies*, Vol. 14, No. 1, March 1991.

De Jong, Ivo. *The History of the 487th Bomb Group (H)*. Nashville: Turner Publishing Co., 2004.

Donald, William. *John Burn One-Zero-Five: The Story of Chelveston Airfield and the 305th Bomb Group in Pictures*. Peterborough, UK: GMS Enterprises, 2005.

Doolittle, Gen. James H. with Carroll V. Glines. *I Could Never Be So Lucky Again*. New York: Bantam, 1991.

Dorr, Robert F. and Fred L. Borch, "Airmen received Purple Hearts for frostbite," *Air Force Times*, February 11, 2008.

Doyle, Robert J., "Doyle Gathers 7 State Fliers," *Milwaukee Journal*, August 13, 1944.

Dyreborg, Erik. *The Young Ones: American Airmen in World War II*. New York: iUniverse, 2007.

Ethell, Jeffrey L. and Alfred Price. *Target Berlin: Mission 250: 6 March 1944*. London: Janes, 1981.

Freeman, Roger A. *The Mighty Eighth War Manual*. Osceola, Wisc.: Motorbooks International, 1990.

———. *The Mighty Eighth War Manual*, Osceola, Wisconsin: Motorbooks International, 1993.

Hammel, Eric. *Air War Europa*. Pacifica, Calif.: Pacifica Press, 1994.

———. *The Road to Big Week*. Pacifica, Calif.: Pacifica Press, 2009.

Hansen, Randall. *Fire and Fury: The Allied Bombing of Germany, 1942–1945*. New York: Penguin, 2008.

Hess, William N. and Thomas G. Ivie. *Fighters of the Mighty Eighth*. Osceola, Wisc.: Motorbooks International, 1990.

Hewins, Ralph,"Terrified Crowd Told, 'You Must Stay,' " *Daily Mail*, February 5, 1945.

Hinrichs, Edward. *Missing Planes of the 452nd Bomb Group*. Self-published. Forest Lake, Minn.: 1994.

Howitzer, the yearbook of the U.S. Military Academy, 1937.

Jablonski, Edward. *Flying Fortress*. New York: Doubleday, 1965.

Jansen, Harold E. *The History of the 446th Bombardment Group*. Private printing: The Netherlands.

Journal Staff, "To the World He's Lt. Col. at 23, to One That Counts He's 'Dad,' " *Milwaukee Journal*, October 22, 1944.

Kozak, Warren. *LeMay: The Life and Wars of General Curtis LeMay*. Washington: Regnery Publishing, 2009.

Lead Navigator's Narrative for the Mission of 3 February 1945. 452nd Bombardment Group, February 3, 1945.

Littlefield, Robert M. *Double Nickel-Double Trouble*. Carmel, Calif.: Littlefield, 1993.

McClellan, Val. An unpublished family manuscript about bombing Berlin.

McFarland, L. W. "Mac." *Raid on Berlin: Some Remembrances*. Family memoir provided by Joe Ferris.

Michel, Marshall L., "The P-51 Mustang: The Most Important Aircraft in History?," *Air Power History*, Vol. 55 No. 4, Winter 2008.

Morris, Rob. *Untold Valor: Forgotten Stories of American Bomber Crews Over Europe in World War II*. Washington: Potomac Books, 2006.

O'Neill, Brian D. *Half a Wing, Three Engines, and a Prayer*. New York: McGraw Hill, 1999.

Pace, Joseph D. *Happy Landing*. New York: iUniverse, Inc.: 2009.

Pavelec, Sterling Michael. *The Jet Race and the Second World War*. Annapolis: Naval Institute Press, 2007.

Pilot's Mission Report. U.S. Legation, Stockholm, Sweden, February 9, 1945.

Report on Planning and Execution of Operational Mission, 3 February 1945, "Target: Berlin, Germany," 92nd Bombardment Group, February 4, 1945.

Rooney, Andy. *My War*. New York: Random House, 1992.

Scutts, Jerry. *P-47 Thunderbolt Aves of the Eighth Air Force*. Botley, Oxford: Osprey Publishing Ltd, 1998.

Sion, Edward M. *Through Blue Skies to Hell: America's 'Bloody 100th' in the Air War Over Germany*. Drexel Hill, Pa.: Casemate, 2008.

Streitfeld, Leonard. *Hell from Heaven: Memoirs of a World War II B-17 Bombardier*. Egg Harbor City, N.J.: Laureate Press, 1994.

Tillman, Barrett. *Above and Beyond: The Aviation Medals of Honor*. Washington: Smithsonian Institution Press, 2002.

———. *LeMay*. New York: Palgrave Macmillan, 2007.

Index

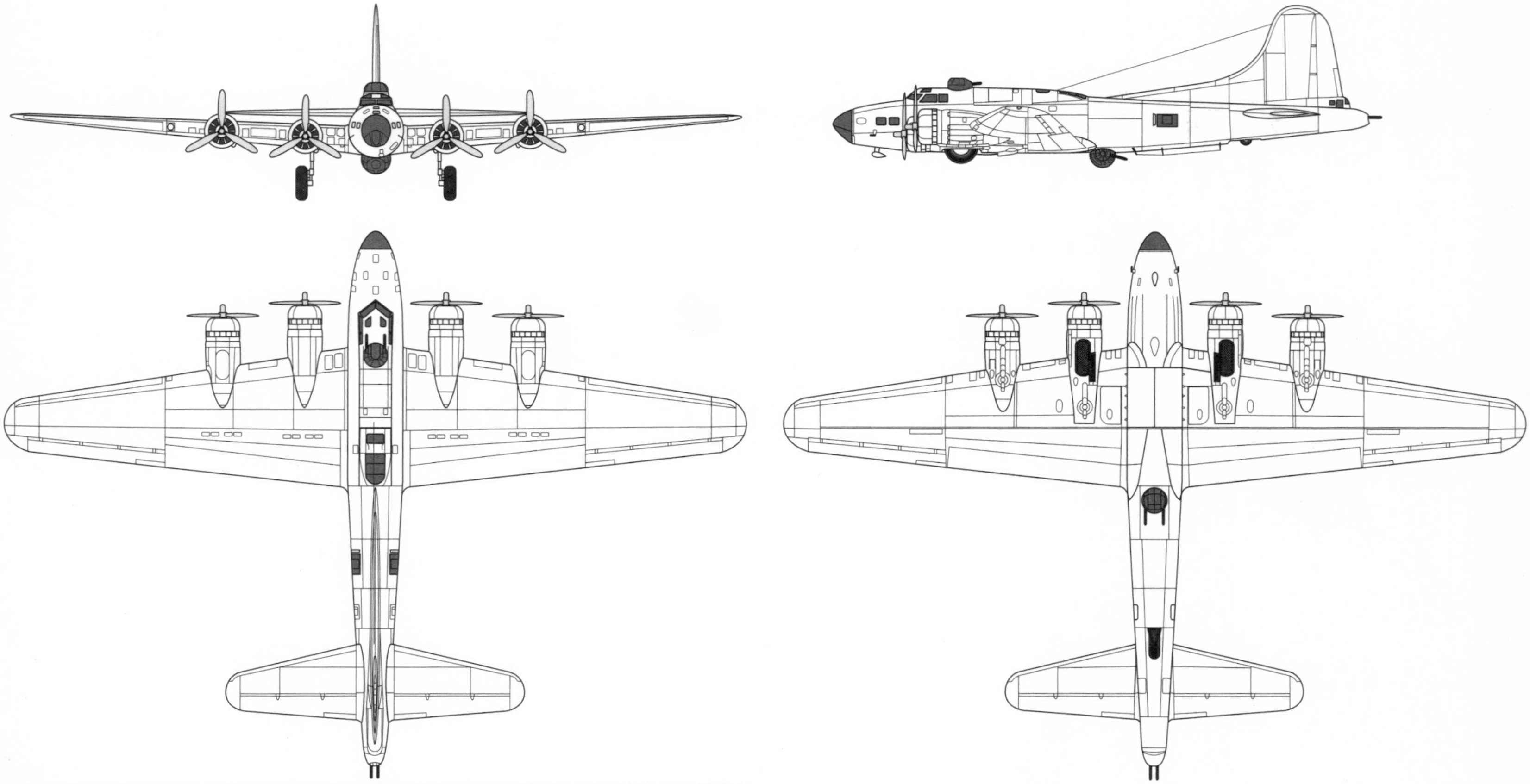

B-17F